THE CONTROVERSIAL CONVERSION OF CHARLES CHINIQUY

TEXTS AND STUDIES IN PROTESTANT HISTORY AND THOUGHT IN QUEBEC

Editorial Board

Richard Lougheed, *Institut de formation théologique de Montréal* and president, *Société d'histoire du protestantisme franco-québécois*

Marie-Claude Rocher, *Institut sur le patrimoine culturel*, Université Laval, Quebec City, Quebec

A. Donald MacLeod, *Tyndale Theological Seminary*, Toronto, Ontario

Richard Vaudry, *The King's University College*, Edmonton, Alberta

Rob Clements, *Clements Academic*, Toronto, Ontario

Jean-Louis Lalonde, *Société d'histoire du protestantisme franco-québécois*

Jason Zuidema, *McGill University* and *Farel Reformed Theological Seminary*, Montreal, Quebec

Vol. 1 – *The Controversial Conversion of Charles Chiniquy*, Richard Lougheed, 2008.

Vol. 2 – *The Life and Thought of David Craig (1937-2001) Canadian Presbyterian Missionary*, Jason Zuidema, 2008.

THE CONTROVERSIAL CONVERSION OF CHARLES CHINIQUY

RICHARD LOUGHEED

CLEMENTS ACADEMIC
Toronto

THE CONTROVERSIAL CONVERSION OF CHARLES CHINIQUY
Copyright © 2008 Richard Lougheed

Published 2008 by
CLEMENTS PUBLISHING
6021 Yonge St., Box 213
Toronto, Ontario M2M 3W2 Canada
www.clementspublishing.com

All rights reserved. No part of this publication may be reproduced, stored in a retrieval system, or transmitted, in any form or by any means, electronic, mechanical, photocopying, recording or otherwise, without the prior permission of the publisher or the Copyright Licensing Agency.

Library and Archives Canada Cataloguing in Publication

Lougheed, Richard, 1953–
The Controversial Conversion of Charles Chiniquy /
Richard Lougheed
(Texts and Studies in Protestant History and Thought in Quebec)

Includes bibliographical references.

ISBN: 978-1-894667-93-7

1. Chiniquy, Charles, 1809–1899. 2. Catholic ex-priests—Québec (Province)—Biography. 3. Catholic ex-priests—United States—Biography. 4. Protestant converts—Québec (Province)—Biography. 5. Presbyterian Church in Canada—Clergy—Biography. I. Title.

BX9225.C43L68 2008   285'.271092   C2008-906597-2

TABLE OF CONTENTS

ABBREVIATIONS ix
TABLES OF FIGURES AND IMAGES xi
DEDICATION xiii
PREFACE xv
PROLOGUE 1
   A Brief Biography 1
   This new contribution 6
INTRODUCTION
QUEBEC RELIGIOUS AND SOCIAL CONTEXTS 1833-1899 9
   Lower Canada before 1840 10
   Anti-clericals 10
   Protestant evangelism 12
   Alcohol 19
   Ultramontane Quebec 21
   Conclusion 27

1. A RISING STAR IN QUEBEC 29
    His Youth (1809-32) 29
    The Young Priest (1833-46) 34
    The Apostle of Temperance (1846-51) 43
2. PIONEER IN ILLINOIS (1851-55) 57
    Kankakee County 57
    The Catholic Diocese of Chicago 61
    Summary of the Illinois context 64
    Colonizing priest 64
3. REBEL PRIEST (1856-58) 73
    The Spink Trials 73
    Bishop Anthony O'Regan (1854-1858) 74
    Property disputes 75
    Suspension and Excommunication 80
    External support 86
        Politicized publicity for the schism 88
        Clerical support 93
    Reconciliation attempts 97
    Catholic anti-Chiniquy missions 100
4. FRANCO-AMERICAN PROTESTANT (1858-87) 107
    Catholic Christian (1858-59) 107
    American Presbyterian (1860-62) 117
    Pastor of St. Anne (1862-87) 121
5. ANTI-CATHOLICISM 129
    An evangelical version 129
    Anti-Protestant provocations in Ultramontane Quebec 135
    A polemical age 138

Clergy conversions and apostasies 141
Anti-Catholic literature 147
Cooperation with anti-clericalism 149
Conclusion 154

6. A PROTESTANT CHAMPION 155
Sentinel 155
   Evangelist and polemicist in Montreal (1870, 1875-78) ... 155
   On the road 163
Anti-Catholic friends and contacts 165
Grand Old Man (1888-98) 172
His last days (1898-99) 177

7. WHAT KIND OF CONVERSION? 179
Opposing myths about Chiniquy 179
   Catholic interpretation 180
   Evangelical Protestant interpretation 184
The evangelical model of conversion 193
Ex-priests 197
Psychology of conversion 198
Total submission to the Church 208

8. THE RELIGIOUS CONVERSION OF CHINIQUY 213
Chronology of the conversion 213
   Antecedents 213
   Convergence of events and influences 216
Subsequent interpretations 225
   Refined conversion accounts 230
Fruits 233
Transformations and continuity 235

9. THE SOCIAL CONVERSION OF CHINIQUY 245
    Sociology of conversion and of apostasy 245
    His anti-Catholicism 248
    His nationalism 256
    His method of confronting opponents 260
    His social relations and his language 268
    Transformations and continuity 270

10. THE LEGACY OF CHINIQUY 273
    Among French Protestants 273
    Among Catholics in Quebec 282
    Among evangelicals outside Quebec 289
    A diverse legacy 296

CONCLUSION 299

APPENDIX 1 Historiography of Chiniquy 307
    Writings by Chiniquy 307
    Writing about Chiniquy 310
    This book's historical approach 316
        Objective and primary sources 316
        Methodology 318

APPENDIX 2 Correspondence of Chiniquy 321
APPENDIX 3 Equivalencies of Chiniquy autobiographies 339
APPENDIX 4 Chronology of Chiniquy 341
APPENDIX 5 Supporters of Chiniquy 343
BIBLIOGRAPHY 347
INDEX 359

ABBREVIATIONS

Archives
AAQ: Archives de l'archidiocèse de Québec (Quebec City)
ACAM: Archives de la chancellerie de l'archidiocèse de Montréal
AP: Allan Pequegnat collection of Chiniquy family papers (Elliot Lake)
ASQ: Archives du seminaire de Québec (Quebec City)
CBA: Canadian Baptist Archives (Hamilton)
CIHM: Canadian Institute for Historical Microreproductions
LAC: Library and Archives Canada (Ottawa)
RLB: Register of letters of Bishop Bourget (in ACAM)
SL: Samuel Lefebvre papers (McGill Rare Books, Montreal and now in AP)
UCM: United Church Conference Archives (Montreal; now housed in Archives nationales du Québec)
UCT: United Church National Archives (Toronto)
UND: Archives of the University of Notre Dame (South Bend IN)

Newspapers and journals
A: *l'Aurore* (Montreal)
Av: *l'Avenir* (Montreal)
CC: *Converted Catholic* (New York)
CCHA: *Canadian Catholic Historical Association Study Session*
CCHS: *Canadian Catholic Historical Studies*
CFA: *Citoyen franco-américain* (Springfield MA)
CHAR: *Canadian Historical Association Report*
CHR: *Canadian Historical Review*
Cour: *Courrier du Canada* (Quebec City)
CT: *Chicago Tribune*

G: *The Gazette* (Montreal)
JI: *Journal d'Illinois* (Kankakee IL, then Chicago)
KG: *Kankakee Gazette* (Kankakee)
KD: *Kankakee Democrat*
MW: *Montreal Witness*
Presby: *The Presbyterian* (mostly Montreal but when indicated another paper in Philadelphia)
RHAF: *Revue d'histoire de l'Amérique française*
RHPhR: *Revue d'histoire et de philosophie religieuses*
SC: *Semeur canadien* (Napierville QC, then Montreal)
SCH: Studies in Church History
SCHEC: *Société canadienne d'histoire de l'Église catholique*

Reference works:
DCA: *Dictionary of Christianity in America*
DCB: *Dictionary of Canadian Biography*
MEM: *Mandements des évêques de Montréal*
MEQ: *Mandements des évêques de Québec*

Chiniquy writings:
50 Years: *Fifty Years in the Church of Rome*
40 Years: *Forty Years in the Church of Christ*
LQO: *Chiniquy: L'homme qui osa défier le puissant empire de Rome*

Organizations:
APA: American Protective Association
CPC: Canada Presbyterian Church (1861-74)
FCMS: French Canadian Missionary Society
FTÉ: Faculté de Théologie Évangélique (Montreal)
GL: Grande Ligne Mission
PCC: Presbyterian Church in Canada (1875-1925)
UQAM: Université du Québec à Montréal

FIGURES

Cover   Chiniquy photo, 1889   **AP** 04-003
Frontispiece   Woodcut from *50 Years*, 1886 ed.
1   Opposing traditional perspectives (diagram).. 4
2   Brief chronology of Chiniquy.. 8
3   Narcisse Cyr 17
4   The Drunkard's Progress, 1846 20
5   Bishop Ignace Bourget, 1862 25
6   Chiniquy genealogy 30
7   **Map** of major locations mentioned in this book 31
8   Nicolet Seminary 33
9   Bishop Joseph Signay, 1836 34
10   Sucking pig cartoon 35
11   Dying priest cartoon 37
12   Beauport monument 38
13   *Manual of Temperance* 43
14   Chiniquy temperance tours, 1849 46
15   Lithograph of Hamel painting 47
16   Temperance cross 48
17   **Map** of Kankakee County, 1874 58
18   First St. Anne church 59
19   Pioneer cabin 59
20   First St. Anne school 59
21   Bishop Van de Velde 61
22   Young Lincoln 74
23   Bishop Anthony O'Regan 75
24   Chiniquy letter, October 1856 76
25   Bishop O'Regan letter, August 1856 81

26	Chiniquy, c1859	83
27	Moise Brassard	94
28	Bishop Duggan	105
29	*Montreal Witness*, Sept. 4, 1858	108
30	Chiniquy family photo, c1889	126
31	*American Advocate*, Feb. 1899	137
32	Chiniquy's Anti-Protestant pamphlet	139
33	Protestant response to Chiniquy's pamphlet	140
34	American Protective Association tribute	148
35	*Primitive Catholic* cartoon	150
36	House in St. Anne, Illinois	153
37	**Map** of Montreal, 1891	156
38	Abjurations, 1877	159
39	Heavy schedule in England, 1896	171
40	French Protestant picnic	174
41	The elderly Chiniquy at his Elgin Rd cottage	175
42	*New York Times* obituary	177
43	Traditional myths (diagram)	191
44	Chiniquy photo, c1864	200
45	Move from Catholicism to Protestantism (diagram)	241
46	At his St. Anne office prior to 1892	242
47	Subjects of Chiniquy lectures	250
48	*Converted Catholic* issue	255
49	Shrine of Reparations	283
50	*La Croix* newspaper case, 1912	284
51	Cannons in Hobart	291
52	Poster with supporting denominations, 1897	292
53	Tombstone on Mount Royal	298
54	*Times* of London obituary	306

Images

1	Plamondon portrait, 1842	28
2	**Map** of Illinois, 1855	56
3	Temperance Medallion, 1849	72
4	Chiniquy pamphlet, 1869	128
5	Letter to Kate Lighthall, 1886	244
6	Wife and daughters, Kankakee, c1877	338

DEDICATION

To those Chiniquy admirers who gathered materials and kept the story alive, in particular Joseph Provost (Congregationalist), John Spreeman (Plymouth Brethren), Jacques Smith (Anglican), Violette Lefebvre (United Church), Nelson Thomson (Convention Baptist), Lois Meier (Presbyterian), Serge Thériault (Catholic Christian), Allan Pequegnat (Fellowship Baptist), Jason Zuidema (Reformed) and Jean Simard.

THE CONTROVERSIAL CONVERSION OF CHARLES CHINIQUY

PREFACE

As an evangelical Protestant, familiar with the peculiar difficulties of French Protestantism, and as one who has left his own denomination after theological conflict, I have experienced two important situations which are crucial to an understanding of Chiniquy.

As a post-Vatican II Christian who has lived for two years in somewhat traditional Roman Catholic l'Arche communities, who has spent three years in a Catholic theological faculty and who is now involved in a radical new consortium with a Catholic seminary, I have developed a sympathy for much in Catholicism, and a greater understanding of those other practices and beliefs which I still do not share. As a Mennonite I seek to promote reconciliation among the followers of Jesus.

From this background I long for greater understanding and co-operation between French evangelicals and Roman Catholics in the extremely secular Quebec culture. French Protestants have too often become obnoxious and bitter with their anti-Catholicism. In much of Quebec, evangelicals are still classified as 'cult' members and face an ingrained hostility against their attempts to rend the religious uniformity in Quebec. Roman Catholics and evangelicals fight each other instead of enlightening the darkness outside any church. A re-examination of Chiniquy's conversion may be a surprisingly helpful method of reassessing past attitudes and facilitating future dialogue. In addition, I pursue a historical goal of granting due credit to a character in Quebec history who has long been either defamed or intentionally not mentioned.

I am indebted to invaluable collaborators: Nelson Thomson encouraged me to pursue this as a thesis topic and then led me to the most valuable sources; the late Jacques Smith and the late Sam Lefebvre provided me with matchless information and insight; Alan Pequegnat managed to acquire, preserve and provide public access to all the Lefebvre documents in his priceless Chiniquy Collection. He also provided wonderful photos.

Min Bedard, Lois Meier and Richard Strout all contributed valuable material that they had gathered. Among the many libraries, I received exceptional help at ASQ, ACAM, UCM, Andover-Harvard, and through Hylda Thomson at the Faculté de Théologie Évangélique.

For insight and contacts, I revelled in attending the sessions of the 1992 Wheaton conference on Evangelicalism in Trans-Atlantic Perspective and the 1995 Queen's conference on Evangelicalism in Canada (both sponsored by the Institute for the Study of American Evangelicals). All the members of the executive of the Société d'histoire du protestantisme franco-québécois have driven me deeper and farther into the subject.

Fellow Lougheeeds Jack (my father) and Barb (my sister) as well as Jason Zuidema offered helpful corrections. The staff and students at my former college (FTÉ) provided enthusiasm and suggestions. My thesis director, Gilles Chaussé, always encouraged me and provided an essential Catholic counter-balance. Margaret, my wife, made research possible in many ways by providing me the necessary time. She also spent many hours of her time on a final edit. My parents were the greatest enthusiasts and provided financing for the book. My children have taken continued interest and obliged me to explain the present-day relevance of the study.

Years of lectures and articles on Charles Chiniquy have not lessened my enthusiasm for the subject nor has the interest of others disappeared. Clearly it is the French evangelical community in Quebec that has been the most interested in their hero. English speaking interest is more diffuse so this English version has been late in arriving. Encouraged finally by Jason Zuidema I address this scattered group and also newcomers to provide them with a more balanced account. May you enjoy the stories and legends and vibrant characters as much as I have.

Thanks are due to Nathan Donaldson for extensive formatting, and especially Clements Academic and Farel Reformed Theological Seminary for the vision and organization of this new series.

This is a corrected, updated and illustrated edition of my PhD thesis in English, in parallel with my upcoming second French edition.

In referring throughout to "evangelical" I am using this as a short form for Protestant evangelical while "Catholic" is referring to Roman Catholic. Also the male form "he" is used generically in order to lighten the text.

PROLOGUE

A BRIEF BIOGRAPHY

Who was Chiniquy?

Fifty years after the British Conquest of Quebec, in 1809, Charles Chiniquy junior was born. This first son of a French Canadian notary and his well-connected wife began life in the small town of Kamouraska. He spent eleven years in the Nicolet College in elementary and secondary education and then theological studies, before being ordained a Roman Catholic priest in the cathedral of Quebec City in 1833.

The young priest's work remained inconspicuous until 1839 in Beauport when he began the first French Catholic temperance society. The disastrous social and economic costs of uncontrolled cheap alcohol were publicized primarily through the efforts of Chiniquy. A new popular cause aimed to free the nation from the curse of alcohol. Chiniquy wrote his first book, a manual for temperance societies, which soon became a best-seller. Numerous requests for temperance campaigns around the province soon began to impinge on his parish work.

THE CONTROVERSIAL CONVERSION OF CHARLES CHINIQUY

Chiniquy joined the Oblate Order but only completed his novice year. He left to become the specialist in temperance missions for Montreal Diocese. The climax of Chiniquy's popularity in Lower Canada came between 1847 and 1850. Perhaps half of French Canada abandoned alcohol in those years, with Chiniquy as the primary stimulus. He was called the Apostle of Temperance by Bishop Bourget and was honoured and even funded by the Canadian Parliament. The highest honour came in the form of a blessing and a crucifix from Pope Pius IX. Chiniquy's energetic campaigns led to great excitement and hero-worship.

In 1851 an accusation of sexual misdemeanours was brought against the Apostle of Temperance. It was discreetly handled in order that the famous priest be given a second chance. He became the priest responsible for a group of French Canadian emigrants south of Chicago, at St. Anne, Illinois. Several letters that he wrote to Quebec papers, lauding the settlement opportunities in Illinois, were severely attacked by the clerical press and by bishops' letters. Conflict soon followed with his local Irish bishops in Chicago. Various disputes culminated in an episcopal order to move to a distant English-speaking parish. Chiniquy refused and was excommunicated in 1856.

Chiniquy continued, however, to function as a Catholic priest with the support of virtually his whole parish. He protested that the supension was unjust and therefore null and void. Just after the excommunication Abraham Lincoln, an aspiring Presidential candidate, successfully represented the rebel priest in his legal defence against a parishioner.

For two years there were various reconciliation attempts originating with the Quebec bishops or with Chiniquy himself. Several of these were effective to some extent but in the end all failed. The bishop of Chicago visited St. Anne in 1858 to announce the final excommunication of Chiniquy and all his followers.

The dissident priest then created the Catholic Christian Church. His followers continued on in the same building, still claiming to be loyal Catholics protesting against one unjust bishop. Several months later Chiniquy returned to Lower Canada (Quebec) to explain his startling rebellion. This tour proved to be decisive: the Quebec Catholic bishops

PROLOGUE

successfully moved to isolate the Apostle of Temperance from his previous following and to oblige Chiniquy to openly side with Protestantism. Violent attacks and death threats against the ex-priest surfaced for the first time. Cut off from all his acquaintances (his parents had died already while his brothers lived in Illinois) he faced his many hardships with firm determination.

In 1860 Chiniquy joined the Chicago Presbytery of the Old School Presbyterian Church. Not long after, Chiniquy became embroiled in conflict with various local Presbyterian pastors. When Chicago Presbytery suspended him he joined the Canadian Presbyterians in 1862. Internal church matters then settled down with the ex-priest serving as Presbyterian pastor in St. Anne for most of the rest of his life. In 1864, at the age of fifty-five, he married.

Following a promising evangelization campaign in Montreal in 1870, Chiniquy returned there for three years beginning in 1875 - his most successful Protestant campaign. Thousands in Montreal signed abjurations, new churches were overflowing and hope was stirred for a Protestant breakthrough. But Chiniquy wore himself out. He was obliged to take an extended holiday of two years. This involved touring Australia and New Zealand to explain the dangers of Catholicism. There were invitations also to Great Britain to counter 'ritualism' and Catholic political rights. Even his retirement in Montreal did not stop the octogenarian from frequent lecture tours in New England, Quebec, Ontario and Europe.

Besides his tours, Chiniquy communicated through his immensely popular autobiographies and his many pamphlets. Most efforts at French evangelization and many anti-Catholic movements around the world relied on this inspiring French Canadian ex-priest. As the grand old man of Protestantism, he continued to plough into any controversy and to rally the forces. Stones were still hurled at him in his late eighties. When he died not long before his ninetieth birthday, there was a huge funeral in Montreal reported prominently even in the *New York Times* and *The Times* of London.

THE CONTROVERSIAL CONVERSION OF CHARLES CHINIQUY

But who was the real Chiniquy?

To understand the changes in Chiniquy's life one must know who his friends were, what happened to him, his quirks, his biography. In this case that is not enough since there have been such opposite one-sided interpretations. On comparing the standard biography of Charles Chiniquy by Marcel Trudel[1] with his autobiographies, one is surprised

TRADITIONAL CATHOLIC PERSPECTIVES	TRADITIONAL EVANGELICAL PERSPECTIVES
Expelled from the Church due to his immorality	After his conversion, he quit the Catholics.
This temperance hero fell into pride and then error. Other temperance leaders were just as important to the cause.	The Apostle of temperance became the hero of French Protestants
Constantly involved in sexual scandals.	Victim, after he became a Protestant, of defamation, as are all ex-Catholics.
He broke his solemn vows and 'married' his young cleaning lady.	He married at age 55, six years after leaving the Catholics. Marriage is normal for clergy.
Rebellious and in difficulty with all authorities (Catholic and Protestant)	Independent, but always submitted to the Bible. He commanded great respect of Protestant leaders.
Compulsive liar (e.g. that he was a close friend of Lincoln)	Always sincere, he revealed the Jesuit plot to assassinate Lincoln
A traitor to French Canada	A patriot isolated from his people by jealous bishops
A demagogue spreading obscene hate speech	One of the great orators and a champion of truth who exposed evil
A hack writer of sensationalist hate literature and pornography	The most published French Canadian writer edifying many.
A braggart who exaggerated all his actions to satisfy his pride	Humble, he visited any small churches when asked
He provoked riots by his blasphemies	Victim of many attempted assassinations and attempts to block freedom of speech and religion
His tours were designed for his financial gain.	Generous to a fault and living simply, he died with little money for his heirs.
He proselytized without any success	An evangelist who led thousands of Catholics to new spiritual life
The great apostate	**The Luther of Canada**

Figure 1

---

1. Marcel Trudel, *Chiniquy* (Trois-Rivières, 1955). Henceforth referred to simply as 'Trudel'. Virtually all historians since have followed his analysis of non-theological issues. Ironically he now opposes traditional Catholicism but this does not change his portrayal much in his "Chiniquy. L'homme et sa légende" (Montreal, 2004). Cf. Appendix I.

PROLOGUE

to find that two diametrically opposed myths developed around the ex-priest.[2] Whether the starting point is traditional Catholicism (e.g. Trudel) or evangelical anti-Catholicism (those who continue to publish the works of Chiniquy), the same events can provide opportunity for opposite interpretations.

Whom should one believe?

These two interpretations of history each presuppose that the other side habitually distorts the truth. There are two detailed autobiographies by Chiniquy and one could suppose that he knew what actually happened.[3] The autobiographies are exciting and provide helpful details to understand the period and the man's personality. They seem very accurate when a letter is quoted. It seems that Chiniquy kept a copy of every letter. His accounts show the extent of opposition against him and his evangelical beliefs but their polemical or propagandist spirit insulting the Catholic Church at every point, leaves many readers to be offended and very sceptical. Even when believed, Chiniquy's books leave out many important events in his life.[4]

The respected Quebec historian Marcel Trudel has produced an academic book full of research and an attempt at critical analysis. Despite his historical rigour in some respects the bias that Trudel shows prevent a balanced evaluation. He credits all Catholic accounts as reliable with even bizarre anti-Chiniquy legends as worth consideration. His starting point, or at least his advice to us is "as long as one forgets that Chiniquy

---

2. See Figure I.

3. Trudel used *Fifty Years in the Church of Rome* (Chicago, 1886, 832 p). We will quote this accessible and most complete version (henceforth *50 Years*). The original version in French is occasionally quoted as *50 Ans*. The second volume, *Forty Years in the Church of Rome*, 498 p. (henceforth *40 Years*) was published posthumously in 1900. Two condensed editions of these works have been produced in French: *Mes Combats* (Montreal, 1946) and *L'homme qui osa* (Beauport, 1976). See Appendix 3.

4. In fact, Trudel describes the Temperance successes of Chiniquy more than the Apostle of Temperance did himself.

lied systematically, one will be forced to accept his fantastic autobiography". The fact that this book precedes Vatican II means that he could produce nothing else but a strong denunciation of the 'apostate'. Finally in 2004 Trudel provided background to his research, explaining that he had been pressured at all points, that he had to be very careful and that he barely even managed to get the book published.[5] Meanwhile evangelicals avoid the "Catholic propaganda" of Trudel and reprint the autobiographies. Since Trudel wrote the only serious history it remains the only source for Catholics and academics. Chiniquy demonized the Catholic Church and Trudel demonized Chiniquy. Where can we find the truth?

THIS NEW CONTRIBUTION

The first half of my book[6] is primarily biographical, with the odd digression to fill out related contexts that illuminate Chiniquy's situation. The most crucial period for his conversion - between 1848 and 1862- will occupy most of my attention. Chiniquy's writings have been commented on in detail by Marcel Trudel, mostly in order to attack them. This means that to provide another historical perspective, I will carry on a running dialogue with Trudel in the footnotes of these chapters.

For my part, I have based my writing on the hypothesis, often confirmed in my research, that all versions of the events need to be read and evaluated to understand the events but that one should give the benefit of the doubt to Chiniquy's version, except where there is compelling proof otherwise.

Of course every author has his\her own perspective and consciously or not shapes the facts. I assume then that the Catholic authorities and Chiniquy himself recount the events subjectively according to their vision

---

5. Trudel, "Chiniquy. L'homme et la légende", p. 131-133. A 2001 summary in 62 pages with Lidec Press drops the polemic but includes no decisive shift or change of mind. Neither his 1955 nor 2001 books was ever translated or updated into English despite attempts by historian Paul Laverdure. Trudel comments in "Chiniquy, L'homme et la légende", p. 133 that Lidec and this article allowed him the freedom to be more calm. Yet the initial conclusions persist.

6. See Appendix I for more detail on this section.

and reports that they have heard. This means that in a context of controversy and polemics, each was concealing certain facts and misinterpreting others while insisting too much or exaggerating other aspects.

I wish here to reject the propaganda from both sides by using new sources from the Chiniquy family archives[7] and Protestant newspapers. These neglected sources give a quite different picture of the man. In addition, a much more complete collection of his correspondence permits us to concentrate on the period around his conversion. On the subject of conversion I will study the question from as many angles as possible (psychology, theology, sociology, language, personality types, changes in behaviour). Many details become clear by placing Chiniquy in his context: a French speaking Protestant in a hostile milieu, one of the ex-priests viewed as the worst of apostates, a fallen hero, part of a worldwide Protestantism which was unabashedly anti-Catholic.

This book will portray a situation and a character much more complex but much more human than in previous treatments. Let us demystify this unique character - neither angel nor demon but certainly an exceptional person.

---

7. The Sam Lefebvre collection at McGill listed henceforth as **SL** and the even more extensive part of the family collection that has been housed since 1999 in the private archives of Allan Pequegnat (**AP**). Pequegnat's Chiniquy Collection is now available for sale directly on CD ROM or by consultation in the libraries of Farel Seminary in Montreal or Queen's University, Kingston.

THE CONTROVERSIAL CONVERSION OF CHARLES CHINIQUY

A BRIEF CHRONOLOGY

1809 Born in Kamouraska, Quebec to a Roman Catholic notary of Basque ancestry
1821 Death of his father leading to eventual studies at Nicolet Seminary **12 years old**
1833 Ordained Roman Catholic priest in Quebec City **24 years**
    Served as priest in charge at St. Roch, Beauport and then Kamouraska
1839 Began a temperance society **30 years**
1844 Publication of 1st edition of his *Manuel de tempérance*
1846 Moved to Montreal and concentrated on Temperance missions
1847 Received a blessing and a crucifix from the Pope
1850 Great success in Canadian Parliament for his temperance efforts.
    Called the Apostle of Temperance by Bishop Bourget **40 years**
1851 Became colonizing priest in Illinois (St. Anne, Bourbonnais)
1853-6 Disputes between Chiniquy and his Irish Bishops in Chicago
  1856 Suspended for insubordination and violent language **47 years**
  1856 Ignored the order and continued on in his church and with his pastorate.
      Abraham Lincoln was his lawyer against Catholic opponents
  1856-8 Repeated attempts at reconciliation
  1858 Definitively excommunicated. Founded Catholic Christian Church
  1859 Speaking tour of Quebec. Catholic bishops banned all
      communication with him. Attacks against him began **50 years**
1860 He and his congregation joined the Presbyterians of Chicago
    Took a 6 month speaking tour around England and the Continent
1862 Suspended by Chicago Presbytery over various misunderstandings
    Cleared by Canadian Presbyterians to whom his congregation transferred
    Pastor in St. Anne until 1888 except for 6 scattered years
1864 Married to Euphémie Allard. They had 3 children **55 years**
1870 Invited to Montreal by the French Canadian Mission Society for six months
1875-8 Back to Montreal as Presbyterian missioner and then pastor of
    Canning St or St. Sauveur Church **66 years**
    Wrote his first major Protestant book: *The Priest, The Woman and the Confessional*
1878-80 A lecture and rest tour around Australia and New Zealand
1880-88 Pastor back in St. Anne IL   at return **71 years**
1885 Publication of his most famous book: *Fifty Years in the Church of Rome*
1888 Official retirement **79 years**
1893 Received Doctor of Divinity at Presbyterian College, Montreal
1896-7 Last major lecture tour (3 months) of England and the Continent **87-8 years**
1899 Healthy until 2 weeks before his January 16 death in Montreal.
    Huge funeral and procession to Mount Royal Cemetery **90th year**

Figure 2 Note indented years indicate his non-Catholic, non-Protestant years

INTRODUCTION

THE QUEBEC SETTING: RELIGIOUS AND SOCIAL CONTEXTS 1833-1899

When Charles Chiniquy was ordained to the priesthood in 1833, the Roman Catholic Church in Lower Canada (the future Quebec) was on the verge of a crisis. The Montreal bishops, Lartigue and his successor, Bourget, identified three major perils: an anti-clerical group, proselytism by Swiss Protestants and the ravages of alcohol.[1] Battle was successfully waged with all three adversaries, leaving a dominant ultramontanism[2] by the end of the nineteenth century. Chiniquy was intimately involved with resistance to all three perils and with the rise of ultramontanism. Let us now examine the general context before 1840 and then the battle with these three enemies of ultramontane Catholicism. After that we shall survey the aspects of Quebec ultramontanism most relevant for understanding Chiniquy.

---

1. One might add the menace of non-Catholic schools but these were primarily dangerous as one of the means of anti-clericalism or proselytism.

2. From the French context where some Catholics looked to the French king for direction (Gallicans) while more orthodox Catholics looked over the Alps or mountains (ultramontane) to Rome. Fierce loyalty to the Pope's direction resulted. See the end of this chapter for more.

LOWER CANADA BEFORE 1840

The British conquest of Quebec in 1759 had established the Church of England as the official state church of the entirely French-speaking colony. This obliged the Roman Catholic bishops of Quebec to walk a fine line between cooperation and protest. The Catholic Church was weakened by a critical shortage of priests; of the 196 priests in 1759, 22 returned to France, while new emigrants from France were refused. By 1790, there were only 107 priests left.[3] The dearth of clergy prevented service to isolated areas and tended to result in inadequately trained priests being rushed into parish responsibilities. At the same time, church finances, Catholic education and political rights for Catholics were precarious. While the Catholic Church was tolerated, it was also suspect. Nevertheless concessions emerged as realistic governors of Canada pointed out to the British government that there existed a dangerous alternative in French Canadian collaboration with the Americans.

ANTI-CLERICALS

Certain members of the educated French middle-class of Lower Canada chafed against British political-economic control, and social control by the Catholic Church. Of these, a few openly contested both authorities. Even when the French group acquired the majority in Parliament this proved ineffective for fundamental change. By 1837, many French Canadians came to the point of outright revolt. The general popularity of the nationalist bourgeoisie's opposition to Britain was probably not matched by support for their republican and anti-clerical objectives. Voltaire[4] and Lamennais in France, with their criticism of Catholic authorities, were inspirations for only a few of the French Canadian elite.

As leader of this group, Louis-Joseph Papineau was a compelling figure, willing to take on bishop or governor. His valour was not matched by his realism in combating both authorities at the same time. The failure of the

---

3. L. Lemieux, *Les années difficiles* (Montreal, 1989), pp. 101-2.
4. Trudel, *L'influence de Voltaire au Canada* (Montreal, 1945), 2 volumes.

INTRODUCTION

1837-1838 rebellions encouraged some short-term anti-clerical feeling over the "collaboration" of the bishops.[5] This anti-clericalism was greatly diminished by the flight of anti-clerical leaders and the adoption of a more pragmatic attitude by those, such as Louis Lafontaine, who remained.[6]

The *Institut canadien*[7] of Montreal, at its inception in 1844, enjoyed clerical favour[8] for its intellectual stimulation by means of lectures and a library. Its members initially admired Pope Pius IX as a reformer. Anti-nationalist statements by this same pope in 1849 led to a parting of the ways between republicans or *rouges*, and Catholic loyalists. This more radical group deemed essential the separation of Church and State, in order to reduce priestly domination of society.[9] While they did not oppose Catholic belief or worship, they did oppose control by the clergy and the Pope's interference in politics.

Although the *Institut canadien* was feared by its foes, it proved to be too radical and too intellectual to pose a significant threat. In particular its sophisticated nationalism was ready even to support annexation to the United States. The more straightforward, traditional, rural nationalism proposed by the Catholic Church won out. Then the organization of political parties after the 1840 union obliged *rouge* politicians to prioritize either their political or their religious views. As was the case for the 1837 rebels, it was too difficult to fight on two fronts. *Institut* members matured or were pressured with ecclesiastical threats, until most of them had to insist on their own Catholic orthodoxy. After 1850 anti-clerical support declined substantially, as ultramontanist loyalty to the pope strengthened.

---

5. Chaussé, *Jean-Jacques Lartigue* (Montreal, 1980), chapter 6.

6. Brunet, "L'Église catholique du Bas-Canada et le partage du pouvoir à l'heure d'une nouvelle donne" (*CHA Papers*, 1969), pp. 38-9.

7. A literary circle and library designed to permit and encourage discussion of all subjects. See Bernard and Eid below.

8. Sylvain and Voisine, *Réveil et consolidation* (Montreal, 1991), p. 110.

9. J. P. Bernard, *Les rouges* (Montreal, 1971). This remains the classic for detail on the 1848-1867 period.

The small group of impenitent anti-clericals failed to persuade the populace to abandon church authority. Instead they continued to offer an alternative for freethinking individuals who could meet, discuss and produce newspapers, in order to keep their issues in the public forum. This group delighted in publicizing any embarrassing items about the Catholic Church. Such an approach proved counter-productive. The anti-clericals were marginalized after 1858, through church discipline of those who participated in anti-clerical events, or even of those who read the *rouge* newspapers.

In 1869 when the *Institut canadien* yearbook was put on the "Index" of forbidden books by Rome, their cause was lost. The *rouges* had also been decisively defeated at the polls. From that point, in effect, one could not stand against clerical control of society without standing against the Catholic Church. The Joseph Guibord burial case[10] ended in 1875, reinforcing the perception of a British alliance with anti-clericals against nationalist French Canadians and their faith. Despite their status as heroes in the rebellions of 1837-8, the anti-clericals had become stigmatized, in public at least, as enemies of the Church and nation. In 1877, with the *rouge* newspaper *Le Pays* dead and the *Institut canadien* about to close, Laurier disassociated his Liberal party from any religious radicalism of the *rouge* forerunners.

PROTESTANT EVANGELISM

After the Conquest there was limited cooperation between Roman Catholics and Anglicans. However, the projects of Bishop Jacob Mountain of Quebec to assert the established status of the Church of England naturally produced mutual suspicion. Relations between Roman Catholics and other Protestant groups, viewed as "sects", were much worse. All Protestants were deemed "heretics" in private correspondence of Catholic

---

10. See DCB, v. 9, pp. 342-3. An *Institut* member was refused Catholic burial. His widow took it to court and finally won.

INTRODUCTION

bishops.[11] In 1851, pressure from Catholics and other Protestants resulted in abolition of the legal privileges of the Anglican Church. Even so, Catholics continued to regard the threat of protestantization under Governor Craig and Bishop Mountain as a typical case of true Protestant intentions.[12]

There were frequent mid-century conversions to Catholicism in overwhelmingly Catholic rural areas particularly as prerequisites of mixed marriages. Clerical authors have denied active recruitment[13] but the reports by Chiniquy are convincing about Catholic proselytization in hospitals and schools, aiming particularly for High-Church Anglicans.[14] Catholic leaders (even Bourget) were reluctant to publicize conversions lest they encourage anti-Catholic sentiment among British officials.

Conversions to Protestantism were rare. Anglican attempts at French mission after the Conquest were a poorly organized failure. The few other evangelistic missions prior to 1834 foundered because of the lack of French evangelists. However the aftermath of the Rebellions of 1837-8 was propitious for Protestant evangelistic initiatives in French Canada. With the defeat of the radicals combined with a popular resentment towards the collaboration of the Catholic hierarchy, new avenues opened up.

Swiss missionaries from Lausanne had already come in 1834 to begin a promising mission effort in the Grande Ligne village near l'Acadie. They were aided by the influential land-owner (*Seigneur*) William Plenderleath Christie.[15] An ex-priest, Léon Normandeau, and a former rebel leader, Dr. Côte, were converted to the cause and joined this small group. Eventually this Grande Ligne mission (GL) was affiliated with the Baptist denomina-

---

11. Bp. Bourget letter to Father Dequoy, 28 December 1850 (**ACAM** RLB 6:285-6).
12. Lougheed, "A Historiography of French Protestantism" (unpublished, 1991), 55 p.
13. Lemieux, *Les années difficiles* (Montreal, 1989), p. 338; Maheux, "Le problème protestant" (*RCSHC*, 1940), p. 50.
14. *50 Years*, chapter 29.
15. Black, "A Crippled Crusade: Anglican Missions to French Canadian Roman Catholics", (U. of Toronto, 1989), ch. 2 and Françoise Noel, *The Christie Seigneuries* (Montreal, 1992).

tion. Meanwhile, in 1839, a group of evangelical members of the Montreal English elite[16] organized the French Canadian Missionary Society (FCMS).[17] This aimed to expand the French mission on an interdenominational basis. With financial resources greater than those of the GL, the FCMS soon employed many workers throughout Quebec and eastern Ontario.

The FCMS and GL co-operated in part and used the same strategy: importing Swiss missionaries to be colporteurs,[18] to pastor French converts, and to establish French Protestant schools. They had a difficult time in established parishes where the local priest was all-powerful. Colporteurs were denied lodging while converts were often harassed or their businesses were boycotted.[19] Grande Ligne and several other outposts succeeded in new or isolated settlements which possessed no resident priest or school. Within twenty years, most of the workers for both mission groups were French-Canadian converts, trained in the French Protestant schools.

The various Canadian Presbyterian[20] denominations united fully in 1875. Among the products of this union was a powerful new player in French mission. The Presbyterian Board of French Evangelization[21] soon so dominated French Protestantism that the FCMS disbanded and gave most of its assets to the Presbyterians. These included the important Pointe aux Trembles Institute.[22] A very influential French section of the Presbyterian

---

16. This group included John Dougall, John Redpath, Rev. Henry Wilkes, James Ferrier, James Court, Dr. Holmes, and military leaders E. P. Wilgress, Capt. Young and John Maitland.

17. Scorgie, "The Early Years of the French Canadian Missionary Society" (Regent College, 1982). Jean-Louis Lalonde, *Des loups dans la bergerie: Les protestants de langue française au Québec 1534-2000* (Montreal, 2002) is an excellent survey history for all this section.

18. Travelling evangelists with Bibles or pamphlets to distribute.

19. *MW*, 15 November 1877, p. 2.

20. For the Presbyterian history, William Gregg, *Short History of the Presbyterian Church in the Dominion of Canada* (Toronto, 1892); J. Moir, *Enduring Witness: A History of the Presbyterian Church in Canada* (Don Mills, 1974).

21. Strout, "The Latter Years of the Board of French Evangelization of the Presbyterian Church in Canada" (Bishop's U., 1986).

22. A residential school on Montreal Island which lasted till the 1960s. See J. R. Cooper, *The Story of Pointe aux Trembles* (Montreal, 1940), 40 p.

INTRODUCTION

College in Montreal was developed, providing the only Protestant theological training in French in North America.[23]

The threat of assimilation had been constant since the days of New France for the powerless French Protestant minority. In the beginning they were excluded from living in New France unless they renounced their faith. Following the Conquest, a new choice was available to French Protestants: either assimilating to the French Catholic group or to the English Protestants. There was no third possibility for long-term survival. The mid-19th century evangelism at last provided a few possibilities for French Protestant education and worship. A convert had to be very determined though in order to withstand the social pressure to conform to the majority French Catholic outlook.

Virtually all the first converts lived in rural areas close to Montreal. The French mission stations that survived were usually those established near anglophone churches, which could provide encouragement and protection. In addition to the threats and the more rare physical attacks, converts faced exclusion from, or strong pressure in, Catholic institutions. In the late 19th century, clerically controlled institutions became all-encompassing in Quebec, embracing schools and hospitals, social clubs, and, later, unions. Jobs and educational possibilities were limited to loyal Catholics. Ostracism and boycotts were used effectively.[24] Freedom of speech about religion was also restricted for the French press and for lecturers, through episcopal excommunications or mob attacks.[25] Some converts were taken to court for making anti-Catholic statements or for non-payment of tithes. Even English Protestant support was not always available. Sometimes rural French Protestant members were left alone

---

23. The Baptists did briefly have a French program at Andover-Newton Seminary in the U.S. at the end of the 19th century.

24. E.g. Baptist churches in Maskinongé and Sorel. See Lafleur, *A Semi-Centennial Historical Sketch of the Grande Ligne Mission* (Montreal, 1885), pp. 82-83.

25. Villard, *Up to the Light* (Toronto, 1928), pp. 110-118; Lougheed, "La marginalisation des franco-protestants" (Montreal, 2006).

when, due to financial shortfalls, evangelists came no more or churches closed.

Since the early days of the mission societies, many Quebecers had emigrated to the U.S. or to other parts of Canada. Most of these sought greater economic opportunity but, for a minority, religious freedom was the primary goal. Emigration drew away the large majority, and many of the most enterprising, of the converts. Up to 80% of French Protestants left Quebec or other French communities of Canada prior to 1925.[26] A few French Protestants chose to move to new areas of Quebec with stronger French Protestant communities (e.g. Namur). While this improved the chances of survival of faith it was a costly choice. The security of heading for English communities held a greater appeal. Since the social pressures were greater in small rural parishes, gradually French Protestants became more urban. French congregations were larger and more stable in the city. In the city they benefited from English Protestant presence and greater access to schools, jobs and a social life outside of Catholic control. Chiniquy's converts were even offered English lessons in order to survive economically in Quebec.[27]

Growing Catholic confidence towards the latter part of the 19th century permitted enormous pressure to be exerted on dissidents through isolation, rather than through overt persecution. A barrier was established to protect French Catholics from outside contamination. By the turn of the 20th century some Protestants were rejoicing in the improved climate as a sign of the end of hostility. This was shortsighted. In fact the new course proved to be just as effective in containing French Protestants, while being less provocative than the confrontational approach of Bishop Bourget's era.

French Protestants were inevitably less nationalistic than their compatriots. The converts owed their reception of the gospel, at least indirectly, to either a Swiss or an English-Canadian mission. In a hostile environment,

---

26. Dominique Vogt-Raguy, a researcher from France in a letter to me in April 1991. She later wrote "Les communautés protestantes francophones au Québec: 1834-1925" (U. de Bordeaux III, 1996), 1024 p.

27. *MW*, 17 January 1876, p. 1.

INTRODUCTION

small churches naturally remained very dependent on anglophone money and political protection, as well as on European educators. Even though most loved their race and language, French Protestants found it hard to sever the linkage of French nationalism and Catholic faith. As the European dominance decreased, Presbyterians such as R. P. Duclos and Baptists such as Narcisse Cyr were among those who promoted a different nationalist stance. This involved working to protect the French language, to improve French non-Catholic education and to free Quebec from "papal domination". There is no record of anglophone attempts to hinder those goals. Nationalism would have been stronger among French Protestants if there had been French theological training in Quebec for all groups (it stopped completely in 1925). It also would have been considerably stronger if the experimental united French Reformed Church of the FCMS had survived.[28] Instead, each major anglophone denomination ended up with a small French minority. Inevitably, French needs were marginalized in each church.

Figure 3 Narcisse Cyr
(Duclos, v. 1, p. 210)

The *Institut canadien* attracted French Protestants who were sympathetic to its anti-clericalism and to its efforts to separate Church and State. Freedom of the press, non-confessional schools and rejection of the tithe were among the shared concerns. "The *Avenir* is absolutely essential for the cause of liberalism and reform",[29] wrote the French Protestant editor, Narcisse Cyr. Though the *Institut* and French Protestants helped each other on occasion, the two small groups were easier to attack for their mutual association. Soon both were overwhelmed by the Catholic tide.

It appears from indications in the *Semeur canadien* (1851-61) and the *Aurore* (1866-1983) that 19th-century French Protestants tended to

---

28. It lasted from 1858-80. See *FCMS Annual Report* 1881, pp. 45-6.
29. *SC*, Napierville, 13 March 1851, p. 15 (my translation).

vote *rouge* or Liberal. These two important Protestant newspapers did not hesitate to give political opinions. Both were very sympathetic to the *Institut canadien* and several of the newspaper writers were members, although they contested any anti-religious statements. Likewise, their newspapers defended the Freemasons as harmless, even though few French Protestants joined the society. French Protestant leaders adopted these controversial positions because liberty and reduction of Catholic control and propaganda were prerequisites for their prosperity. The Protestant newspapers naturally delighted in printing abjurations[30] and pointing out alleged cases of Catholic persecution, undue political influence and use of the Index. Despite this they did not resemble the rabidly anti-Catholic tone of certain Ontario papers.

Catholics noted, correctly, that enormous sums were expended on French evangelization. Yet it is clear that the missions were chronically short of funds. The combination of French Protestant emigration and assimilation into the English milieu prevented financial self-sufficiency for the French congregations. French Protestant schools could always attract students since so few schools were available but they incurred considerable expenses to maintain so many subsidized students.

It was often claimed in French Protestant literature that most Catholics were coerced into attendance at mass and were, in effect, unbelievers. Nominal or indifferent Catholics were considered very fair game for evangelism. There is no question though that French Protestants, in common with virtually all evangelicals, believed that even active Roman Catholics needed salvation by grace, through faith and conversion. Voices such as Anglican Bishop Fulford[31] and the few 19th century Protestant liberals were in a minority among committed Canadian Protestants in opposing evangelism in Quebec.

Evangelicals sought progress and liberty for their fellow French Canadians through evangelism and education. Statements by French Protestants and

---

30. Publicly renouncing their former faith. This however, legally, had to be published to avoid paying the Catholic "tithe" and other levies: *A*, September, 1964, p. 4.
31. Black, "A Crippled Crusade", ch. 5.

INTRODUCTION

their evangelists never opposed the French language or race. On the other hand, they were strongly anti-Catholic. French Protestants tended to agree with the English about the dangers of papal authoritarianism, the Index, separate schools and undue clerical influence in politics. At times they did provide mild criticism of provocative anti-Catholicism, as expressed by some Ontario Protestants. This critique was ignored by both Catholic and Protestant journals, which were more interested in a polarized propaganda.

Notable French Protestants included short-term Quebec Premier Henri-Gustave Joly, Médéric Lanctot, Senator Jacob Nicol and J.P.Boucher-Belleville. But in order for them to remain prominent, their beliefs or origins had to be hushed, while any co-operation with Catholic clergy was emphasized. Unlike Catholics, political aspirations required French Protestants to minimize their religious affiliation. The dynamism of the evangelism, which had touched so many families and regions, began to dwindle around the time of Chiniquy's death. French Protestantism was crippled by emigration, assimilation and the absence of one united French Protestant denomination. In the 20th century, actual decline in Quebec membership and numbers of French Protestant congregations began.

ALCOHOL

In the early 19th century, Protestant evangelicals in the British Commonwealth and in the United States began to vigorously attack the problems stemming from alcoholism. Temperance (usually meaning total abstinence) societies were established all over North America and Britain to persuade individuals to abandon alcohol and to persuade governments to at least restrict alcohol sales.[32] They first organized in Montreal in 1828. Involvement in these Protestant organizations was problematic for Catholics. By the 1830s, however, Father Theobald Mathew[33] was pioneering Catholic Temperance societies in Ireland.

---

32. See Jan Noel, *Canada Dry* (Toronto, 1994), especially her chapters 11 and 12 on Chiniquy.
33. A Capuchin priest (1790-1856). Price, "Aux origines" (*RHAF*, 1959), p. 523.

THE CONTROVERSIAL CONVERSION OF CHARLES CHINIQUY

Figure 4   The Drunkard's Progress, 1846 (Wikimedia Commons)

From 1839 on, east of Quebec City, Chiniquy and several other priests began Catholic Temperance societies. At first these required pledges of moderation but soon Chiniquy switched to pledges of total abstinence. Besides the inspiration of Father Mathew, another very important foreign influence was Bishop Charles de Forbin-Janson of France who visited Lower Canada from 1840 to 1841.[34] As a secondary feature of his immensely popular Lower Canadian retreats, Forbin-Janson promoted the temperance pledge and the formation of temperance societies.

The tremendous cost to their society of heavy alcohol consumption managed to create an unlikely union of clergy[35] and anti-clericals for this crusade. While cooperation for other subjects such as colonization or the St. Jean Baptiste Society was short-lived, cooperation for temperance work continued on. The liberal *Avenir* and the Catholic *Mélanges religieux* both praised Chiniquy's temperance crusades. Liberal judge Charles Mondelet

---

34. C. Galarneau, "Mgr de Forbin-Janson au Québec en 1840-1841" IN *Les ultramontains canadiens-français* , J. Hamelin and N. Voisine eds. (Montreal, 1985), pp. 121-142.

35. Bp. Bourget in his circular letter of 31 May 1848 (*MEM*, vol. 1, p. 473), calls drunkenness, "the most dangerous and the most terrible enemy that we have to fight."

and the ultramontane Chiniquy exchanged compliments.[36] Temperance as a national cause became the catalyst for the popularization and triumph of ultramontanism,[37] and the religious revival of the late 1840s.[38]

The practical effects of temperance were more short-lived, such as a crisis for alcohol producers and the cooperation, on a moral issue, between Protestants and Catholics. This cooperation was, nevertheless, noteworthy for Chiniquy. He had received encouragement from Protestants[39] and, either through mediated Catholic sources, or directly, he adopted a pattern of biblical quotations[40] and altar calls that closely resembled Protestant missions.

ULTRAMONTANE QUEBEC

Ultramontanism has been studied often, including its Quebec form.[41] My interest lies not in its political ramifications, but in examining the principles of Quebec ultramontanism, which provided the basis for social and religious interaction.

One fundamental principle held by most societies prior to the 20th century was that there should be a single national Church that would jointly decide matters with the civil leaders. Among the rare opponents of this unity-of-Church-and-State principle were the 16th century Anabaptists, 17th century Baptists (in England and America) and 18th century revolutionaries in France and the United States. A British colony such as

---

36. *Manuel des sociétés de tempérance* (Montreal, ³1849), pp. 137-40; *Av*, 18 April 1849, pp. 1-2.

37. Noel, "Dry Patriotism" (*CHR*, 1990), pp. 189-207.

38. Ares, "Les campagnes de tempérance" (UQAM, 1990).

39. *50 Years*, pp. 368-70 for John Dougall. Also Trudel, *Chiniquy*, pp. 18-20 on Dr. James Douglas.

40. One could easily take his *Manual of Temperance*, despite the *Imprimatur*, for a Protestant book, lacking reference to Mary (except in the devotional exercises of the appendix) while appealing frequently to Scripture.

41. On its ideology: Eid, *Le clergé et le pouvoir politique au Québec* (Montreal, 1976). For a wider view: Hamelin and Voisine, eds., *Les ultramontains canadiens-français* (Montreal, 1985).

Canada posed a problem for advocates of one official church. The French Catholic populace refused to become Anglican and yet they lacked the political power to control their own destiny.

Following the British Conquest, it became evident to Catholic leaders that unity of French-speaking Canadians was essential for their social and political survival in the new English colony. In order to foster this unity, language and religion would have to be protected from any attempt to split them. This episcopally supervised French-Canadian unity was damaged by the Rebellions of 1837 and 1838. Historians Eid, Bernard and Monière reduce the clergy reaction at that time to a simple power struggle. An alternative interpretation that respects theology would attribute consistency to the Catholic bishops.[42] While bishops often encouraged nationalism, neither armed revolution nor anti-clerical measures were ever options for them. Most Protestants at the time would have agreed, based on biblical texts such as Romans 13:1-2.

The Rebellions were an eye-opener for Lartigue and others. While their own leadership was in peril, so was the unity of French Canada. Henceforth, the goal must be uniformity of belief rather than just French-Canadian unity. This growing awareness prevailed first in the Diocese of Montreal and later in St. Hyacinthe (Bishop Prince) and Trois Rivières (Bishop Laflèche) before reaching Quebec City. While the United States had abandoned such a concept of uniformity and 19th century Britain was moving towards greater individualism, most strongly Catholic nations, until recently, have retained a dominant corporate sense. In North America there had to be innovations since a Catholic monarch did not control the political process. The only solid basis for uniformity available was the infallible Roman definition of faith and society. Anything else might be legitimately contested. If French Canada and its Catholic Church were to survive it was imperative that ultramontanism be promoted. To achieve uniformity in this situation required close monitoring of any deviance, along with enforcement by socio-religious means.

---

42. Chaussé, *Lartigue* (Montreal, 1980), pp. 229-230.

INTRODUCTION

Uniformity required submission, either voluntarily because "they know better than I", or by constraint. One effective strategy accused the deviant of breaking the essential unity in Catholic Canada. The accused person thus became the enemy of God, the Church, the French language and the race for questioning one central aspect of the ultramontane dogma. While this is hard for modern interpreters to understand, it is important to grasp the logic of uniformity for survival, and the perceived need for a reliable authority. Any organization needs allegiance to some principles, along with disciplinary procedures to preserve unity of purpose. Pressure for homogeneity exists in all societies. At that time these means were not so difficult and not so repugnant as moderns presume.

It has been noted that ultramontanes did not discuss or explain, but pronounced.[43] While many interpreters see this as a sign of intellectual weakness, they are ignoring the ultramontane principles. If there truly is an infallible authority then there is no need to justify. Instead publication and application are needed. Evidence so far indicates general acceptance of this among Catholics in Quebec.

As for dissidents, arguing would not convince them anyway. They had apparently accepted the principle of private interpretation or free thought. The Church only had two options left for them: correction or isolation. Thus democracy, debate and compromise were not legitimate alternatives for Catholic leaders. While reconciliation with dissidents was sought, it had to be accomplished on the Church's terms. Otherwise the whole ultramontane belief in its hierarchy was brought into question.

Exiled priests from republican France helped to define the deviance. Everything republican was considered anti-Catholic. So emigration to the US, annexation of Quebec to the US, democracy and all the liberties Americans promoted were to be avoided. Only clerical control of education, the press and (indirectly) of political parties would preserve ultramontane principles. Rome interpreted 'freedom of religion' to mean

---

43. See e.g. Eid, *Le clergé* (Montreal, 1976), p. 117.

only the freedom **for Catholics** to practise and promote their religion.[44] While no violence was to be done to Protestants, French Protestants and especially apostates had to be marginalized using all social and economic means.

The priests constituted the focus of village life. They were the mediators with the government (though the liberal members of Parliament eventually threatened this privileged position), the guardians of the race with its language, culture and traditions, and the guardians of the faith with its sacred mysteries. It became increasingly difficult to survive in a rural or small town parish, if one disagreed with the priest. The French civil code permitted civil enforcement of church decrees (e.g. the tithe, contributions for parish schools and new church buildings), which stifled dissenters. As English government interference subsided, clerical control became absolute at the parish level. Punishment for not paying the tithe included excommunication and court action. Abjuration was the only legal option for a dissenter to avoid a court case. If the dissenter pursued this, usually the parish ostracized him.

By the 1840s, the triumphalism of ultramontanism was sweeping the province. Rectories were built to impress and religious festivals became more elaborate. Specific Catholic practices such as indulgences and devotion to the saints were heavily promoted by the clergy. The early Chiniquy participated in and avidly promoted all these practices. In an effort to counter the indifference and even anti-clericalism of many laity, a more rigorous approach to morals was strongly encouraged. Both Catholic and Protestant sources note the lack of Catholic religious fervour prior to 1840. However as the number of priests increased, this reversed.

Catholic leaders considered all attempts to "evangelize" Catholics as preposterous; in reality, these had to be veiled attempts to anglicize. Such "evangelism" only encouraged reaffirmation of the perceived need of French Catholics for homogeneity of language and faith. All who dis-

---

44. Siméon Pagnuelo, *Études historiques et légales sur la liberté religieuse au Canada* (Montreal, 1872), 409 p. He was a counsellor of Bp. Bourget.

INTRODUCTION

sentered either in their language or in their faith were deemed traitors to this homogeneity in all its parts. Thus the small French Protestant groups had an importance far beyond their small numbers, in constituting a peril for the national solidarity. French Canadian apostates, particularly priests, received much greater venom. Lionel Groulx blamed Roubaud as the cause of many of the anti-Catholic projects after the Conquest. The former rebel Dr. Côte and Chiniquy were seen as both apostates and then as traitors who joined the English Protestant side. The French Protestants were branded as Swiss Methodists and therefore both foreigners and sectarians. As for the FCMS with its English name and money, it was an easy target for nationalist criticism.

Figure 5 Bp. Ignace Bourget, 1862 (© McCord Museum)

One further cause of conflict was the distribution of Protestant bibles. Bishop Plessis deplored and forbade these "heretical" versions and tried to produce a Catholic version in French. However, the practical effect of his action was to remove and burn the bibles in circulation, and to punish their readers, while leaving no French Catholic alternative available for thirty years.[45] Chiniquy, as priest, was at the forefront of Catholic attempts to encourage Bible study, but bishops were very wary of the negative effects of independent Bible study by laity.

Around 1840, a Catholic reaction[46] began to aggressively counter Protestant proselytization. On the negative side were heavy-handed use of episcopal directives and the Index for books, Protestant materials and the press. More positively, a Catholic newspaper, *Mélanges religieux* was

---

45. Lemieux, *Les années difficiles* (Montreal, 1989), pp. 341-2. The Baillargeon version was published in 1846.

46. This is a positive term for Léon Pouliot in his book *La réaction catholique* (Montreal, 1942).

begun to provide authoritative interpretation of events. Religious revival[47] followed the province-wide retreats of Bishop de Forbin-Janson. Catholic historian Pouliot credits Protestant proselytism for provoking all of these.[48] Motivated by some Protestant successes, Bishop Bourget spent a summer in Europe to recruit clergy for the short-staffed Quebec church. An amazing transformation came about from the fragile Catholic Church after the 1837 and 1838 Rebellions to the triumphant church of the mid 1840s. As Bourget's recruits arrived and French Canadian candidates increased, the Catholic Church was able to branch out.[49] In Bourget's ultramontane philosophy it was vital to get priests, nuns or brothers to staff education, social services and colonization, as well as to supply all the outlying parishes.

The Quebec Catholic homogeneity, though often threatened, actually increased over time. Dissident French liberals and Protestants eventually had no room to exist, let alone grow. The variety that had prevailed in the pre-rebellion period of politically flexible Plessis, pro-France Quiblier, anti-clerical Papineau and ultramontane Lartigue, disappeared. Dissidence was ever more effectively squelched. The bourgeoisie with its anti-clerical and democratic tendencies could have been a possible ally for the Protestants, but it chose, almost unanimously, to acquiesce in the episcopal vision of homogeneity.

Both Catholic and Protestant religious leaders had moved quickly to profit from the vacuum following the political failure of the 1837 Rebellion. Both had pointed to a better means of fulfilment through religious faith. French Catholic advantage in numbers, the status quo and nationalism easily matched potential English political clout, Protestant money, and an appeal to anti-clericalism.

---

47. Louis Rousseau and Frank Remiggi, *Atlas historique des pratiques religieuses: Le Sud-Ouest du Québec au XIXe siècle,* (Ottawa, 1998), 235 p.

48. Pouliot, pp. 7-10.

49. There were 5 new male religious communities and 10 female between 1837 and 1850 according to Bernard Denault, "Sociographie générale des communautés religieuses au Québec 1837-1970" IN *Éléments pour une sociologie des communautés religieuses au Québec*, Denault and Lévesque eds. (Montreal, 1975), p. 72.

INTRODUCTION
CONCLUSION

Just as evangelical Protestants were beginning missions among the French-Canadian population, the Catholic Church managed to fight from extreme vulnerability to acquire all the necessary powers (French civil code with the tithe, education and more diocesan bishops) to guard its flock. As political and religious liberty for the Catholic Church increased, social and religious liberty in the broader French society and in the parish decreased.

Chiniquy was a major Catholic leader in his attacks on all three of the perils to the Catholic Church: the anti-clerical party, proselytism by Swiss Protestants and the ravages of alcohol. Then he metamorphosed to join the second and to ally himself with the first. As one example of the radical changes he underwent, we find that Chiniquy agreed to give a lecture at the 'liberal' *Institut canadien* in 1848. The lecture never took place because of his new anti-liberal crusade against the *Avenir*. Ten years later in the *Avenir*, certain 'liberals' promoted Chiniquy's rebellion. Later again funds were sought from him to finance the Guibord appeals.[50] While Chiniquy lived for 36 years in Illinois, his actions and words were constantly tied to the context of Quebec society.

---

50. Letter Joseph Doutre to Chiniquy, 8 May [1874] (**UCT**, Charles Chiniquy Personal Papers).

Image 1 Father Chiniquy by Antoine Plamondon 1842 © **AP**

1

A RISING STAR IN QUEBEC

HIS YOUTH (1809-32)

The Chiniquy family was of Basque origin. The paternal ancestors of Charles emigrated from Bayonne, France to Quebec City in 1740, not long before the British Conquest. Chiniquy mentions his grandfather's naval skills and the reception of a French government land grant.[1] Catholic accounts are more interested in this same ancestor's 'treason' at the Conquest,[2] and also in an apostate priest uncle, Father Martin Chiniquy (born Joseph).[3]

After 1760, Chiniquy's grandfather became chief naval pilot in Quebec City. Two of his sons studied for the priesthood at the Seminary of Quebec. Chiniquy's father, Charles Thélesfor, followed his brother Joseph (see above) and pursued his theology to the point of receiving the clerical tonsure and the clerical robes. This stage necessitated no vows beyond a commitment to pursue further theological studies. Subsequently he left the clerical state to study law. Reine Perrault, Chiniquy's mother, was the daughter of a schoolteacher from Cap St. Ignace, down-river

---

1. *40 Years*, p. 27.
2. P-G. Roy, "Les traîtres de 1759" (*Cahier des Dix*, 1936), pp. 48-51.
3. Trudel, p. 4.

Descendants of Martin Echenneque

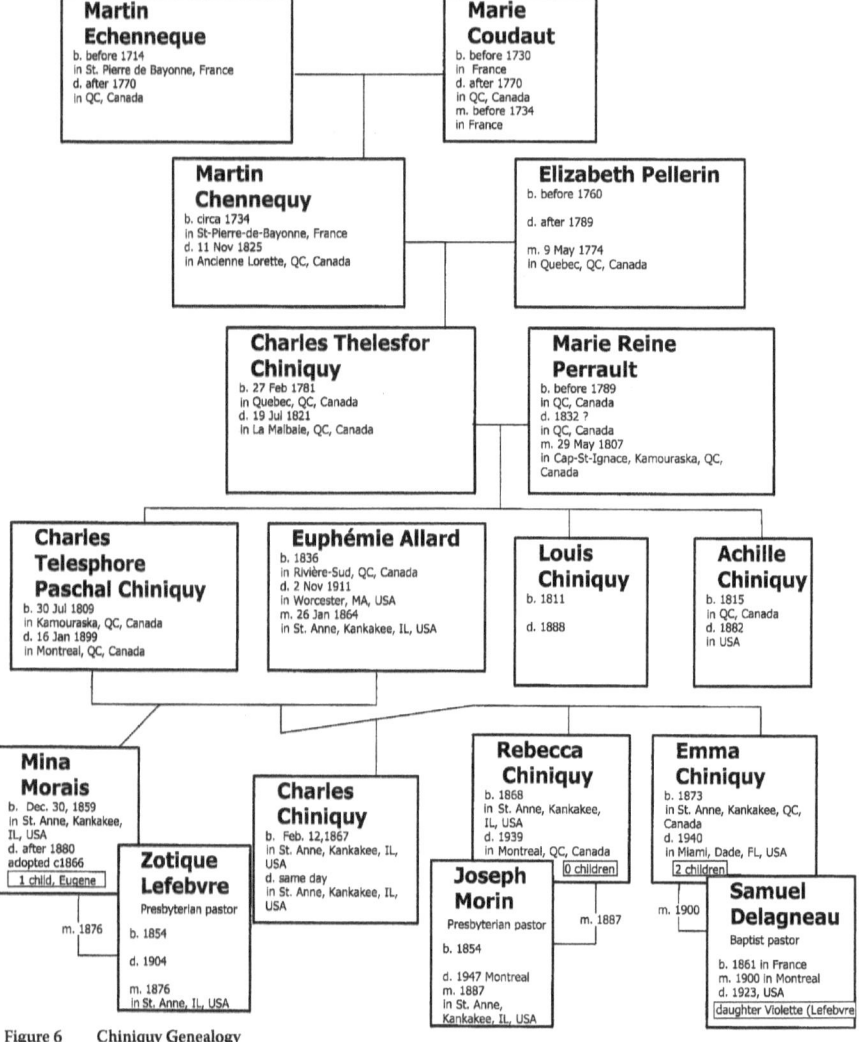

Figure 6   Chiniquy Genealogy

from Quebec City. Her sister had married into the prominent Dionne and Chapais families who became *seigneurs* or landed gentry controlling most of the South shore of the St. Lawrence River below Quebec.

Soon after his marriage, Chiniquy's father received his credentials as a notary. Instead of settling down, he moved his family from Kamouraska to

1. A RISING STAR IN QUEBEC

Figure 7 Map of major locations mentioned in this book

Portneuf and later to Malbaie. Charles was born in Kamouraska with all the nobility of the region at his baptism.[4] While the father earned a good wage, he apparently spent even more.[5] There is no hard evidence for a problem of alcoholism[6] but it would fit with his debts, his premature death and his wife's deathbed insistence that her son promise to be a moderate drinker. It also might explain much of Charles Chiniquy Jr.'s passion for temperance. However Chiniquy never blamed or criticized his father either in print or in sermon. His autobiography, *50 Years*, begins with the words "my father" and recalls a basically happy childhood.

What could have been the psychological effect on 12 year old Charles when his father died without warning? This loss was accentuated since he was the eldest of three boys, for whom the father had left no money. Premature responsibility was thrust on him as his mother mourned. Their home was repossessed and the family split apart. Charles ended up with his aunt in Kamouraska. Although he was among his extended family, his close relationships with his dead father and his separated

---

4. Trudel, "Chiniquy. L'homme et sa légende" (Montreal, 2004), p. 133.
5. *50 Years*, p. 44.
6. Against Pierre Berton in *My Country* (Toronto, 1976) who on p. 143 draws the typically hasty and sensational conclusion that the father was a drunkard.

mother both disappeared within weeks of each other. We know nothing more about his mother except that she died in 1830.

Charles Jr. was a good student, beginning under an English Protestant teacher in St. Thomas de Montmagny. Early on, his public speaking talents were commented on. He was also very serious about religious matters.[7] In Kamouraska, Chiniquy expressed an early desire to become a priest. His uncle Amable Dionne[8] obliged by financing an education in Nicolet, across from Trois Rivières.

From 1822 to 1833 Chiniquy studied at the relatively new Nicolet College and Seminary. A few years after arriving he managed to anger his uncle so much that financial aid was cut off. The early evidence mentions a dispute over money and "the rest" which is not explained in the only letter still extant.[9] A Chiniquy relative, Bishop Têtu, is another source followed by Catholic accounts.[10] These claim that Chiniquy molested his own female cousin. This suggestion clashes with a letter in which the director himself took up the financing of this good prospect, after what he seems to consider a minor fault, duly confessed.[11] This hypothesis is less likely given the existence of a continuing relationship between Chiniquy, his aunt and other Dionne relatives.

At this early date Chiniquy had started to earn the reputation at school of being a ringleader or troublemaker. His autobiography is believable in recounting numerous occasions in which he verbalized objections to stated beliefs or practices. Each time he was deterred from pursuing his questions by his superiors' reminders that the young novice was in danger of heresy.

---

7. He recounts incidents about the Bible, confession, clerical imperfections and scandalous anti-clericalism. It should be remembered that the autobiography had a polemical religious rather than a biographical purpose. This obviously influenced the choice of incidents narrated.

8. 1781-1852. See *DCB*, 8: 222-4.

9. Letter from Joseph-Onésime Leprohon, Nicolet College director, to Bp. Plessis, 13 October 1825 (**AAQ**, 515 CD, Sem de Nicolet, vol. B:101).

10. S. Smith, *Pastor Chiniquy* (London, 1908), p. 17 followed by Price, Trudel and most others.

11. Leprohon to Bp. Plessis, above.

1. A RISING STAR IN QUEBEC

At the same time, Chiniquy took piety seriously enough to be hailed by classmates,[12] and many others, as another St. Louis de Gonzague.[13]

Chiniquy's Protestant autobiography still expressed respect for his professors though he deplored the syllabus.

Figure 8   The old Nicolet Seminary (Album-Souvenir, 1953, p. 71)

The works of Alphonse de Liguori, Dens,[14] Bailly and Thomas Aquinas were favoured theological reading material at the seminary. More argumentative books such as those of Lamennais were only allowed to students as long as doubts were not voiced.[15] Chiniquy excelled particularly at rhetoric, Latin and mathematics.[16]

How intriguing is the fact that Chiniquy's Latin teachers between 1823 and 1825 were two future apostate priests: Louis Fluet and Hubert Tétreau, while he himself later taught Latin there. Nicolet Seminary Latin classes were thus taught in the mid-19th century by three of the four most famous future Quebec ex-priests.[17]

Other professors included the future Bishop Prince and historian J.B.A. Ferland. Professor Moise Brassard was first his benefactor and then

---

12.   J.G. Barthe, *Aurore des Canadas*, 28 March 1844, p. 3.

13.   A pious saint. This is repeated in the effusive eulogy by Hector Langevin in Chiniquy's *Manuel de Tempérance*, 1849, later copied as a preface for *Mes combats* (1946) and *LQO* (1976). His exemplary piety was also attested later by Brassard to Bp. Bourget, 26 January 1851 (**AAQ**, 7 CM, E.U., VII:200, p. 13).

14.   Laverdure, "Religious Invective" (McGill, 1984), p. 37, observes that these are Chiniquy's two favourite Catholic sources in his *The Priest, The Woman and the Confessional*.

15.   *50 Years*, p. 161.

16.   Price (*RHAF*, 1959), p. 520; *A*, 31 July 1897, p. 6.

17.   Louis Normandeau of Quebec Seminary was the other.

became his closest and most supportive friend.[18] Classmates[19] Charles Félix Cazeau (future Vicar General of Quebec Diocese), Isaac Desaulniers (future Vicar General of St. Hyacinthe),[20] Jean Charles Chapais (future MP and relative) and Étienne Baillargeon (priest in Quebec Diocese) remained comrades of Chiniquy until his apostasy.

THE YOUNG PRIEST (1833-46)

Figure 9 Bishop Joseph Signay 1836 (Plamondon, Wikimedia Commons)

In 1833 Chiniquy was ordained in Quebec City by Bishop Signay without further conflict.[21] After eleven years far from family and laity, he now went back down the river to begin the priesthood in parishes around Quebec City. Chiniquy was named vicar for a short while in St. Charles de Bellechasse (Rivière Boyer)[22] and then briefly at Charlesbourg. Here he faced the 1834 cholera epidemic.

St. Roch (1834-8)

Shortly after the epidemic Chiniquy became one of the vicars (along with Louis Parent and Étienne Baillargeon) at the huge St. Roch parish

---

18. *50 Years*, p. 738. See Michel Pratt, *Dictionnaire historique de Longueuil, de Jacques-Cartier et de Montréal-S*ud (Longueuil, 1995), p. 52 for a biography.

19. See for lists of professors and students: Douville, *Histoire du Collège-Séminaire de Nicolet* (Montreal, 1903), vol. 2. Trudel, (Montreal, 2004), p. 134 reverses himself, now denigrating the education received because the senior students acted as tutors for the younger and partially blaming Chiniquy's future on this.

20. *50 Years*, p. 738; *Av*, 26 May 1849, p. 1.

21. Trudel, pp. 14-5, however gives some credence to a legend about his superiors having doubts about ordaining him.

22. A "Notebook of all kinds of things" of Chiniquy's, begun 10 May 1834 at Rivière Boyer has recently become available in the **AP** collection. This hand-written treasure chest of 105 pages contains copies of advice from Bp. Plessis, rules for parish Council meetings, part of a book by Lamennais, a résumé of all the Ecumenical Councils, biblical statistics, a complaint about the Sulpician order and even a recipe for ginger beer. **AP** 02-001

1. A RISING STAR IN QUEBEC

in Quebec City. This consisted mostly of poor labourers' and their families. By lot, Chiniquy was assigned charge of the Northeast section of the parish, including the Quebec Marine Hospital.

At this hospital, Chiniquy converted to practising abstinence from alcohol. The main cause of this transformation was the multi-talented Protestant physician Dr. James Douglas.[23] Added to the demonstrations and statistics of Douglas came the previous deathbed plea of Chiniquy's mother and the further plea of an alcoholic woman who, in a drunken stupor, had killed her daughter.[24]

Figure 10   Sucking pig image (Christian Herald, London, April 8, 1897) **AP** 15 C1-F022-05

Meanwhile, the young vicar was beginning a long series of clashes with his bishops. Apparently[25] he was the inspiration behind the organization of a One-Mass Society to prevent "simony" by Bishop Signay.[26] Archival evidence confirms the existence of this Society although the name of the instigator was not mentioned. Certainly the bishop was worried about a dissident group of 67 priests who were going to organize their own One Mass Society.[27]

When Father Leprohon, the Nicolet director, requested Chiniquy as his assistant at the College in 1835, the Bishop Signay refused:

> This young priest, too haughty due to the praise he has received, has acted with such indiscretion and so indelicately in

---

23. *DCB*, 11: 271-2; Douglas, *Journal and Reminiscences* (NY, 1910), (pp. 239-45 on Chiniquy); Chiniquy, *Manuel*, pp. 90-91.
24. *50 Years*, ch. 28.
25. *50 Years*, ch. 25-26.
26. Circular letter to priests from Quebec Diocese, 18 March 1836 (*MEQ*, vol. 3, pp. 340-341).
27. Signay to Lartigue, 8 February and 10 March 1836 (**AAQ**, Reg. 17:296, 317).

> this situation, by setting conditions for his bishop and by certain remarks against the procedure of the corporation that it would be impossible ... to close our eyes to the undesirable consequences which would inevitably occur in a Seminary if a person was sent there who was full of bad attitudes, pretentiousness, love of reform, etc.[28]

It appears that the contesting of the Three-Mass Society was the reason for this refusal and for the subsequent refusal to send Chiniquy out for Western missions in 1836.[29]

Chiniquy received his first public notice for successful representations to Governor General Gosford to reprieve the notorious Chambers gang from the death penalty.[30] While at St. Roch, one often repeated Chiniquy pattern began: long-term overwork producing a very serious illness, followed by an unexpected recovery. In this case, Chiniquy gave credit to the miraculous intervention of St. Philomena and St. Anne. His love for dramatic gestures and ceremonies induced Chiniquy to commission the up and coming artist Antoine Plamondon[31] to paint the miraculous scene for the St. Anne de Beaupré church.[32] Eventually, in 1858, this painting was burned in response to Chiniquy's apostasy.[33] So early on Chiniquy had offended his bishop and managed to receive public recognition twice.

In 1837, a political confrontation of immense importance swirled around Lower Canada. The "Rebellions" were less marked around Quebec City but Chiniquy claimed to have been involved in suppressing them. He

---

28. Douville, vol. I, p. 248ff (my translation).
29. Bp. Provencher to Bp. Signay, 23 November 1836 (**AAQ**, 330 CD, R.R., I:80).
30. Louis Fréchette, *Mémoires intimes* (Montreal, ^{2}1977) pp. 105-6; also John Hare, *Histoire de la Ville de Québec* (Ottawa, 1987), p. 20 8. Trudel, p. 260, claims that this was a Chiniquy lie.
31. *50 Years*, p. 327. He also painted Chiniquy in 1842 (Trudel, p. 44). This second portrait, seen on the cover of *LQO* was longtime in the family collection but has recently been acquired by the Canadian National Gallery. See it on our p. 28.
32. Trudel, p. 23 calls this an 'invention' when at most the public response is exaggerated.
33. *50 Years*, p. 332.

1. A RISING STAR IN QUEBEC

affirmed reporting to Governor Gosford a rebel plot to attack Quebec City. The governor then took steps to prevent it.³⁴ If such an incident occurred, it would fit with the Catholic bishops position to protect the French Canadians from their own folly in rebelling.³⁵

Figure 11   Dying priest image (*Christian Herald*, London, April 8, 1897) **AP** 15 C1-F022-05

Beauport (1838-42)

Chiniquy consistently argued with his bishops' decisions to reassign him to new parishes. Many other priests must have objected to their lack of involvement in these decisions.³⁶ Probably Chiniquy had been quite interested in the two previous offers (professor at the Nicolet college or missionary out West), which had been refused by his bishop. Whether the new appointment to Beauport was an unwanted burden³⁷ or an honour,³⁸ the rampant alcoholism there repulsed the young priest.

After four years in the Quebec suburbs, he now moved a few kilometres east, to the notorious village of Beauport. In his autobiography, the reception is described as being very cool, especially when he mentioned the concept of temperance. Nevertheless, Chiniquy's drive, vision and eloquence were compelling. Eventually he turned the majority of the parish around, first to moderate use of alcohol³⁹ and then to an abstinence position. Inspired by both Father Mathew and Dr. Douglas,

---

34. *40 Years*, pp. 31-2. Trudel is sceptical (p. 24).

35. See Chaussé, *Jean-Jacques Lartigue* (Montreal, 1980). Also note the pro-government rally held at Chiniquy's St. Roch Church on 29 November 1837 (Julienne Barnard, *Mémoires Chapais* (Montreal, 1961), vol.1, p. 147).

36. Lemieux, *Les années difficiles* (Montreal, 1989), pp. 139-140 describes the procedure.

37. *50 Years*, p. 336. This corresponds to Signay's previously quoted comments.

38. Trudel, p. 31.

39. Chiniquy's autobiography does not mention this phase.

Figure 12 Beauport monument **AP** 12-098

Chiniquy officially founded a local Temperance Society in March 1839.[40]

It is hard to evaluate how much Chiniquy pioneered in wider temperance work at this period, given the revisionist attempt to minimize his role in Quebec history. From 1839 on, he was cooperating with Father Beaumont to preach temperance retreats. Chiniquy covered the area north of the St. Lawrence River. Soon he became extremely busy with local parish work plus temperance retreats in other parishes.

Protestant biographies put a heavy emphasis on Chiniquy's concern from an early age for knowing and distributing the Bible. In 1841, this desire led to a petition among clergy to persuade Bishop Signay to approve popular distribution of the Bible with Catholic commentaries. Chiniquy was, according to his autobiography, successful in enlisting virtually all the priests, including the future Bishop Baillargeon. Bishop Signay approved the project.[41] Chiniquy's influence in this area is demonstrated in the published address of his Beauport parish to him: it contains four quotes from the Latin Bible.[42]

Although Chiniquy may have exaggerated their intimacy, certainly he and the famed Bishop de Forbin-Janson from France shared many causes. Both were strong ultramontanes who used a similar rhetorical style and retreat method to promote spiritual renewal and temperance. Chiniquy claimed

---

40. Others refer to a document which claims 1840 (Trudel, p. 32) but the third anniversary was celebrated on 29 March 1842 (**LAC**, Charles Chiniquy collection, MG 24,J20).

41. *40 Years*, chapter 3. Baillargeon to Bp. Signay, 24 January 1842 (AAQ, DQ, 1:146), talks of a prohibition from Rome for such editions but it was published in 1846 (see p. ix of Charles Baillargeon, *Le Nouveau Testament*, Quebec, 1865).

42. **LAC**, Charles Chiniquy collection (MG 24,J20).

1. A RISING STAR IN QUEBEC

that they also shared a willingness to distribute Catholic Scriptures.[43] The Beauport priest managed to enlist the French bishop to dedicate his local temperance monument, a spectacular event that attracted 10,000 people. No doubt the success of the Forbin-Janson retreats encouraged Chiniquy to adopt a similar strategy. However, all the elements were embryonic in Chiniquy before the arrival of the bishop of Nancy.

Chiniquy recounted that in 1841 the visiting bishop publicly supported him against Bishop Signay on the question of total abstinence.[44] While unsubstantiated the account is credible. Signay certainly opposed total abstinence as a requirement for all Christians,[45] although he promoted reduced consumption. Chiniquy, along with most temperance preachers, became adamant about the necessity of a total abstinence position. He viewed those who opposed this as being opposed to temperance; hence his later charges of clerical and episcopal opposition to temperance. He viewed as "hypocritical" priests those who signed a temperance pledge but still drank. This stance provoked clerical opposition to his "extremism".[46]

Still, temperance became a very popular progressive cause. Bishop Bourget and his *Mélanges religieux* began promoting Chiniquy. The young priest was invited to preach at the cathedral in Montreal in October 1841 and then sent Bishop Bourget 80 pages documenting his views (especially total abstinence), his methods and successes. Included in these pages were details of a visit by Dr. Douglas to Beauport in order to demonstrate the physical effects of alcohol. Prior to receiving these letters Bourget had already talked to the Pope and received his blessing

---

43. *40 Years*, p. 57.
44. *50 Years*, p. 357-8.
45. *MEQ*, vol. 3, p. 416. This circular letter in support of Temperance societies comes only after their successes and after a Bp. Bourget circular letter. It was designed, in part, to provide for episcopal control of temperance missions. See also Bp. Signay to Chiniquy, 5 December 1841 (**AAQ**, Reg. 19:608) where the bishop prefers the sobriety emphasis of Mailloux.
46. See a contemptuous response in *50 Years*, p. 345.

for a temperance campaign. However the Montreal bishop's waited till January 1842, immediately after Chiniquy's documentation,[47] to produce his first Pastoral letter on the subject.

After convincing Beauport, Chiniquy managed to inspire 2,000 temperance signatures in his former parish of St. Roch. The wave of success, marked by extravagant praise for Chiniquy, had started. Many French Catholics already regarded him as a messianic figure.[48]

Temperance was not the only reform associated with Chiniquy in his Beauport years. Catholic schools were opened in Beauport, partly as a result of temperance economies and new vision. Education remained a consistent priority for Chiniquy, as it was for many other clergy. Another early sign of things to come was a public debate in 1842 between Chiniquy and the French Protestant missionaries, Henri Morel and Claude Prévost in Quebec City.[49]

Kamouraska (1842-46)

Once again, after being told by the bishop to move, the popular priest of Beauport did not go quietly. Since it was useless to confront the bishop directly, Chiniquy merely mentioned it to the parish who quickly took up the cause. He also sent a sly note to the Diocese secretary to apply more pressure. Nothing succeeded so he duly left in September 1842.[50]

Chiniquy thus returned to the parish where he had been born and where he had spent several years of his youth. His mother was buried there and

---

47. *MEM*, vol. 1, pp. 154-5.
48. See the hagiographic introduction to his *Manual of Temperance*.
49. Letter from C. Prévost to Joseph Provost, July 1899 in "Prévost Journal", p. 14 (**UCM**, French Protestant Collection).
50. Trudel, p. 49 reports a rumour about Chiniquy having been ousted due to a sexual scandal. My experience has found that modern Quebecers presume sexual activity on the part of any clergy and spread such rumours. *MW*, 23 March 1875, p. 3, reports a letter from Beauport with charges against Chiniquy but discounts this as propaganda. Trudel's rumour is similarly unsubstantiated and suspect when not mentioned till after apostasy has come.

1. A RISING STAR IN QUEBEC

his Dionne relatives lived there still. The priest in charge had served Kamouraska since Chiniquy was a boy. Although the new assistant priest had a hard time at first, again he won the parish over to temperance and was idolized. There were two exceptions to this adulation who constantly worked to get rid of him: Chiniquy's uncle Amable Dionne and an influential ally, Jean Baptiste Taché.[51] Not all Dionne family members were hostile. Several visited Chiniquy later in Illinois, while Chiniquy regularly sent back greetings to his dear aunt.[52]

Perhaps mission work was even more welcome with these local tensions. Chiniquy, at any rate, always loved travelling, preaching and having new crowds to convince. The invitations to preach missions multiplied and he accepted most of them. To meet a perceived need for organization in the temperance movement he wrote a book, which was published in March 1844.[53] Along with the influence of Father Mathew's letters, Chiniquy's efforts pre-empted partial temperance with the new standard of total abstinence.[54] While Bourget and Signay privately cautioned against extremism, Chiniquy's message won many hearts.

After having triumphed in the Quebec City area, his next conquest was the Lower Saint Lawrence. He travelled as far afield as New Brunswick in June 1844. The future writer Louis Fréchette was overwhelmed for years after over his childhood experience of the eloquence and power of a Chiniquy sermon.[55] As the priest's popularity mounted J.B. Meilleur, superintendent of education in Lower Canada, tried to enlist Chiniquy's help in

---

51. Trudel, p. 128.
52. Chiniquy letter to Jean-Charles Chapais, 29 March 1856, cited in Barnard, *Mémoires*, vol. 2, pp. 129-31.
53. For an analysis of its editions, its structure and its effects see Ares "Les campagnes de tempérance de Charles Chiniquy: Un des principaux moteurs du réveil religieux montréalais de 1840" (MA thesis, U. de Québec à Montréal, 1990), 347 p.
54. Trudel, p. 59.
55. Fréchette, *Mémoires intimes*, pp. 108-110. This was published originally in the *Monde illustré* of 4 and 11 July 1900.

promoting the creation of schools.[56] When Chiniquy finally became the priest in charge of Kamouraska his workload increased again.

In the summer of 1846 Chiniquy allegedly propositioned a young woman in the confessional, during a temperance retreat in St. Pascal. The account claims that he was caught when he arrived at the planned meeting place. No investigation was made and no letters from that period that remain in the files recount anything about such an incident. A résumé of accusations dating from 1884,[57] 38 years after, is the first document to provide any details about this incident.

I have not found any evidence that this incident was used in Quebec Archdiocese condemnations of Chiniquy's apostasy.[58] According to Trudel this incident was supposed to have resulted in Chiniquy's banishment from the Diocese. Yet he still maintained cordial relations with Secretary Louis Cazeau and, apparently, with Bishops Baillargeon and Turgeon. If this sexual scandal happened, then it must have been very discreetly suppressed at the time.[59] In addition, it was rarely publicized after Chiniquy's apostasy, even when it could have destroyed his reputation.

What one believes about St. Pascal becomes crucial to interpret Chiniquy's departure from Kamouraska (and from the diocese). He left his parish shortly after the date of the alleged incident, in September 1846. Was the departure due to overwork and an invitation from the Oblates[60] or was he exiled in disgrace, then shamelessly exploited it?[61] In any event Chiniquy managed to attend the annual diocesan clergy retreat just before

---

56. Meilleur letter to Chiniquy, 14 October 1853, cited in *Cahiers des Dix*, 38 (1973), p. 73.

57. Letter from Jesuit Father Resther of Montreal to a researcher in Britain, 1884, 7 p (**ACAM** 402.102, 884-1). This is the 'anonymous' manuscript mentioned by Trudel, p. 67.

58. Nevertheless, S. Smith and Trudel rely on Resther, and then Price, Berton, Roby and Noel rely on Trudel, stating that this is certain. Only Brettell and Laverdure leave any room for doubt.

59. It is not an uncommon occurrence in denominations even today to quietly move the offender and thus provide a second chance.

60. *50 Years*, p. 403.

61. S. Smith and most others following him.

1. A RISING STAR IN QUEBEC

leaving. There he outdid all but one priest in his financial contribution to the construction of the bishop's new residence.[62]

THE APOSTLE OF TEMPERANCE (1846-51)

Oblate novice (1846-7)

Chiniquy next travelled up-river to the booming city of Montreal. In October 1846, he became one of the first Canadian novices of the Oblate order. This order specialized in organizing and preaching at retreats or missions, with temperance as one of the common preaching themes. Here was a chance to concentrate on temperance preaching, without the extra burden of parish work. Prior to receiving that opportunity, Chiniquy had to prove himself in their yearlong noviciate, separated from the outside world and following a disciplined regimen of devotions.

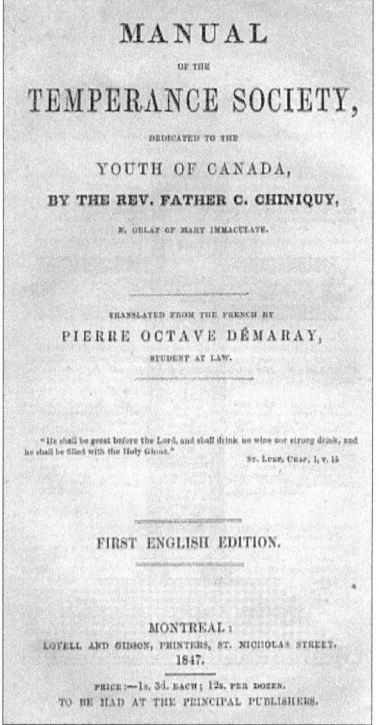

Figure 13   English book AP 01-61

While the new novice expressed joy to some correspondents about his restful spiritual state,[63] his critical tendency led him, once again, into conflict with his superiors. Chiniquy's autobiography, written much later, raises issues of Oblate sexual scandals. Originally, it appears that Chiniquy and Father Brassard were concerned that Oblate director Guigues had illegally opened Brassard's letters[64] and that his authority

---

62. *MEQ*, v. 3, p. 490.
63. Chiniquy to Cazeau, 24 November 1847 (formerly **AAQ**, Kam 11:15 but now in St. Anne-de-la-Pocatière Diocese Archives).
64. *50 Years*, p. 452, claims that Guigues apologized before becoming Bishop.

was harming the simple lifestyle of the Oblates.[65] Chiniquy's accusations even managed temporarily to block Guigues' elevation to the bishopric of Ottawa.[66] After leaving the monastery, Chiniquy continued to quarrel with the Oblates over a convent in Longueuil.[67]

As usual, there are two accounts of Chiniquy's departure. Did he quit because of Oblate immorality or did he get out just before he was dismissed as a troublemaker? In this case the two stories can be reconciled. The Oblate superiors disliked Chiniquy's insubordinate temperament, and his interference in the election of Guigues. Therefore they prescribed an extra year of noviciate.[68] Instead the novice decided to leave and then to propose reforms to the Oblates.[69] Whatever the Oblate concerns, they gave him a testimonial.[70] For his part, Chiniquy expressed thankfulness for the time spent there.[71]

When he left at the end of November 1847, Chiniquy moved in with his old friend Father Brassard at Longueuil, across the river from Montreal. While in the noviciate, Chiniquy had managed to issue a second edition of his *Manual*,[72] containing multiple episcopal benedictions. This book became an official school text, and, perhaps, the best seller of the century in French Canada. Now Chiniquy applied for work in the Diocese of

---

65. Chiniquy to Cazeau, 6 December 1847 (**AAQ**, DM, H:263).

66. Bp. Bourget to Tellemont, 4 March 1848 (**ACAM**, RLB 4:430-1).

67. According to Trudel, pp. 83-85, Chiniquy fomented trouble there.

68. Carrière, "Une mission tragique aux Illinois" (*RHAF*, 1955), p. 528.

69. Chiniquy to Guigues, 27 November 1847 (quoted in part in Carrière, p. 527); Chiniquy to Cazeau, 6 December 1847 (**AAQ**, DM, H:263).

70. Allard, quoted in full in *50 Years*, p. 454. This is not denied or even mentioned in the thorough Carrière article, but Trudel doubted it. We have found all the letters quoted by Chiniquy to be accurate (except for occasional dates) when checkable. Surprisingly most letters are still checkable. See our Appendix 2 for the list.

71. Chiniquy to Guigues, 7 December 1847 (quoted in Carrière, p. 529).

72. Ares, ch. 2, analyzes its contents. See the résumé in print in Louis Rousseau and Frank Remiggi, *Atlas historique des pratiques religieuses: Le Sud-Ouest du Québec au XIXe siècle* (Ottawa, 1998), 235 p. See also the historiography in our Appendix 1.

1. A RISING STAR IN QUEBEC

Montreal.[73] While he waited Chiniquy worked on "a short work of apologetics" and asked Quebec Diocese not to recall him before he was done.[74]

Temperance crusades

Bishop Bourget had already been enthralled by Chiniquy's temperance successes and quickly appointed him as roving temperance missionary for Montreal Diocese. This important responsibility was given despite Bourget's stated reservations about Chiniquy's conduct towards the Oblates.[75] From April 1848 until April 1851 Chiniquy led his triumphant Temperance Crusades.[76] In his autobiography Chiniquy atypically underplayed his own importance. Trudel and particularly Ares give elaborate, totally positive accounts of his temperance efforts.

Chiniquy's phenomenal success was due to many factors. Most of the English, the *rouges*[77] and the clergy agreed that alcoholism was disastrous. Chiniquy's own position of total abstinence was simplest to define and manage and so came to predominate. His *Manual* provided directions to establish an organization. He personally provided dynamic energy, stunning eloquence, simple emotional stories, a strategy of periodic repeat visits to areas, and the Temperance Society organization. Publicity came abundantly and with enthusiasm through the *Mélanges religieux* and even *l'Avenir*. Before long Bishop Bourget named Chiniquy the Apostle of Temperance, a parallel to Ireland's Father Mathew.

Most of Chiniquy's time was spent inside Montreal Diocese, particularly in the rural areas. Without preaching everywhere, the temperance crusader came close enough to every parish so that anyone in the

---

73. Chiniquy letter to Bp. Bourget, 24 November 1847 (**ACAM**, 402.102, 847-1).
74. Chiniquy to Cazeau, 6 December 1847 (**AAQ**, DM, H:263). Carrière, p. 530, claims that Chiniquy applied without success to Quebec. I found no evidence to confirm this.
75. Bp. Bourget to Bp. of Marseilles, 10 April 1848 (**ACAM**, RLB 4:459).
76. Ares provides the most detailed account of the organization, popularity and durability of this campaign.
77. See our prologue.

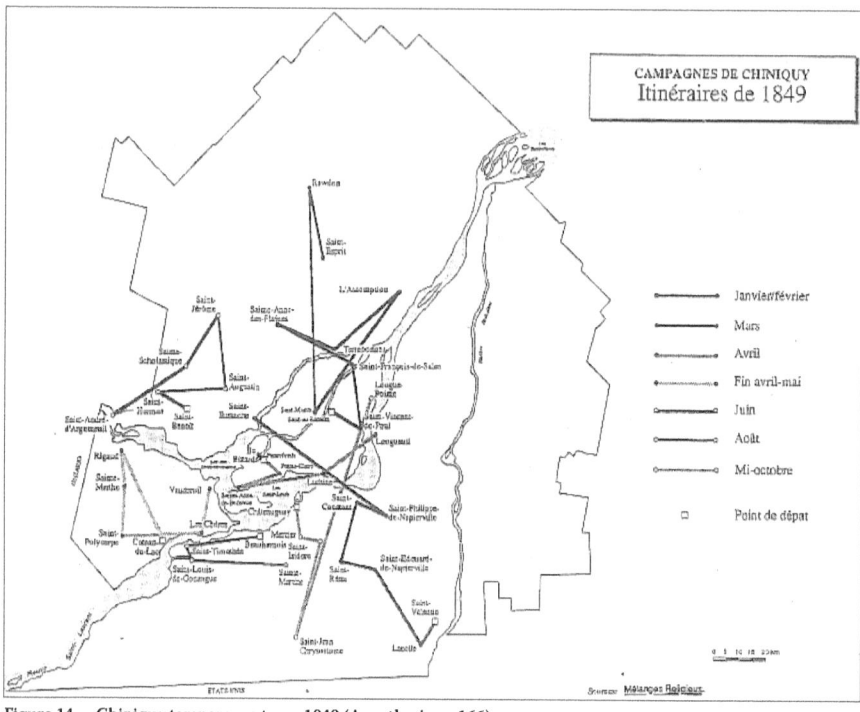

Figure 14   Chiniquy temperance tours 1849 (Ares thesis, p. 166)

Diocese could travel a short distance to hear him.[78] Temperance activity peaked in Montreal Diocese just as Chiniquy finished his crusades.[79] We can confirm[80] the estimate of Hector Langevin of 200,000 conversions to Temperance in 18 months work.[81]

The nationalist content of Chiniquy's temperance preaching was unusual. While not blaming the English for their woes, temperance was extolled as a nationalist cause for French Canadian progress and prosperity. "Renounce [alcohol] for the love of our brethren, our country and our

---

78. See the map above from Ares and others at pp. 158, 166, 175 and a summary on p. 230.
79. Ares, p. 226, has a graph for the 1840 to 1881 period.
80. Ares, pp. 177-188.
81. His preface to the *Manuel* was reproduced in *LQO*, p. [10].

1. A RISING STAR IN QUEBEC

God."[82] Irish patriots Daniel O'Connell and Father Mathew were cited in the *Manuel* as heroes for God and country.

Jan Noel demonstrates that Chiniquy provided the dynamism to regain the popular trust and unity for the Church that had been lost in the 1837 Rebellions.[83] The Apostle of Temperance pulled the people together in a cause which, though nationalist, was neither political nor anti-English. Europe was being shaken by revolutions while Chiniquy's cause was non-threatening to authorities. Moreover, it was of immense value to the Church that a popular priest was directing this nationalist cause.

Figure 15   Lithograph of Hamel painting **AP** 04-002

The Church led the way with honours for Chiniquy. Pope Pius IX examined the *Manuel* and sent his benediction for the work of an "apostle of temperance".[84] Bourget presented a crucifix from the Pope. Several gold medals, as well as a portrait of their hero Chiniquy by Théophile Hamel, were awarded at massive public meetings in his honour. From this painting, thousands of lithographs were produced. These adorned the walls of most temperance supporters, alongside their black cross.[85] The love of ceremonial, which Chiniquy had cultivated in Beauport, went well with the triumphalism of ultramontane liturgy. Vast processions and

---

82. His closing words in the *Manuel*, p. 173 (my translation).
83. Noel, *Canada Dry* (Toronto, 1994), pp. 167-169.
84. Charles Baillargeon to Chiniquy 18 August 1850 (**LAC** MG 24, J 20).There were other apostles of temperance but in Canada only Chiniquy was referred to as **the** Apostle of Temperance.
85. The black cross is credited to him by *La Presse* of 14 January 1899, p. 1; and Voisine, "Les croisades de tempérance" (Montreal, 1979), p. 47; but it is denied by those trying to minimize any positive role for Chiniquy e.g. Trudel, p. 34.

Figure 16 Temperance black cross **AP** 15 (2) 025

elaborate ceremonies accompanied each visit of the Apostle of Temperance.

As support multiplied, someone, quite possibly Chiniquy, suggested petitioning Parliament to limit liquor licences.[86] Most politicians were hesitant at first. The avalanche of petitions and Chiniquy's own interventions in a parliamentary committee in Toronto swept objections aside. Victory was complete. In the summer of 1850, at the instigation of an English Protestant MP, the Canadian Parliament voted a highly unusual gift of £500 for the Apostle of Temperance. The popular temperance law that Chiniquy promoted proved to be so strict that it was unenforceable. In 1851 a weaker bill replaced it.[87]

In private, Bourget often wrote to Chiniquy. These letters combined overall appreciation and praise but also occasional strong critiques of excesses[88] or potential doctrinal errors.[89] Chiniquy's tendency to simplify, his extreme devotion to the cause, and his overpowering energy were both his key assets and his liabilities.

Two problems noted by his first bishops were the danger of pride and excessive polemical language. After a Chiniquy temperance sermon in 1850, a riot was sparked in St. Hyacinthe that culminated in the burning of a distillery. This brought strong criticism from Chiniquy's opponents.[90] In addition Chiniquy was accused of eating meat and not fish on Fridays

---

86. Others promoted the idea at a giant rally for Chiniquy in Montreal (*Av*, 11 October 1848, p. 2) and a sample petition was included in a Circular letter of Bp. Bourget's on 25 March 1850 (*MEM*, vol.2, p. 108).

87. Voisine, "Les croisades", p. 150.

88. E.g., Bp. Bourget to Chiniquy, 3 May 1849 (**AAQ**, 7 CM, E.U., VII:200, p. 7).

89. 12 points in Bp. Bourget to Chiniquy, 26 October 1848 (**ACAM**, RLB 5:48-52). Also see Bp. Bourget to Chiniquy, 3 March 1849 (RLB 5:148-150).

90. *Av*, 13 November 1850, p. 2; *MW*, 11 November 1850, p. 356.

and of making potentially heretical statements.[91] In the midst of extreme adulation, some friendly criticism was needed.

Overwork recurred as a problem. In the summer of 1849, and again in February 1850, Chiniquy's exhaustion resulted in severe illnesses. Each time complete rest for about one month was necessary. In addition, the first of Chiniquy's many financial crises surfaced in April 1850. This followed his prolonged illness and substantial loans to his brother. The *Minerve* took up public fundraising for the Apostle of Temperance until Parliament decided on the grant previously mentioned.[92]

Other crusades

Chiniquy enjoyed the support of the *Institut canadien* members since temperance was interpreted as a patriotic cause. In April 1849 he was invited by Pierre Blanchet to lecture at the *Institut* on either "the Canadian economy and industry" or on any other subject of his choice.[93] Chiniquy accepted and prepared the lecture for May 3, in the midst of his frantic schedule. It never took place.

After his acceptance but prior to the date of the lecture, Chiniquy began a series of critical letters to the *Avenir*. These broke his friendly ties to the reform group. Chiniquy's ultramontanism had not prevented him from sympathising with progressive political causes. In 1849 he supported abolition of the seigniorial system[94] and he continued to subscribe to the *Avenir* after certain Catholic papers decried it. However, he could not allow the Pope's temporal authority over the Papal States in Italy to be attacked with impunity.

---

91. Bp. Bourget to Chiniquy, 26 October 1848 (**ACAM**, RLB 5:48-52); Bp. Bourget to Quintal, 20 April 1849 (RLB 5:174).

92. The *MW* and G. Barthe criticized this. See Chiniquy's defence in *MW*, 10 February 1851. Even the Governor General sent a contribution (Bp. Bourget to Lord Elgin, 11 May 1850, **ACAM**, RLB 6:74-5).

93. Blanchet to Chiniquy, 6 April 1849 (**UCT**, Charles Chiniquy papers).

94. Georges Baillargeon, "A propos de l'abolition du régime seigneurial" (*RHAF*, 1968), p. 383.

At first Chiniquy was somewhat diplomatic, suggesting that the *Avenir* editors reconsider their position. His language was nevertheless strong enough, or patronizing enough, to infuriate several writers. Even so, Chiniquy might have gone ahead with the lecture at the *Institut* but for the disruption caused by the burning of the Parliament buildings in Montreal on April 25th, 1849. It is unlikely that Chiniquy intended to bait the anti-clericals but, nevertheless, he unleashed the most vehement anti-clerical attack in years.[95] He produced a heated correspondence against: "the anti-Christian and anti-social phrases: ['] out of date texts from the Councils ... worn-out threats of excommunication ... abuse of spiritual power by Pius IX ['] - which should never have appeared in your paper."[96]

Chiniquy's letters to the *Avenir* continued regularly until June 9th and effectively polarized matters. *Avenir* correspondents became infuriated at the priest's interference in a political matter for which he had no expertise. Chiniquy in turn was furious at the correspondents for their questioning of Catholic spiritual leaders: the Pope and bishops.[97] Although this ultramontane crusade against anti-clericals was a side issue for the Apostle of Temperance it began to play a noticeable part in his preaching. However this did not prevent him from visiting Louis Joseph Papineau who, for the most part, was impressed by Chiniquy.[98]

The platform of the apostle of temperance began to be used for other ultramontane causes. In March 1851, Chiniquy tried unsuccessfully to derail a rural political meeting that was promoting annexation to the United States. Again Chiniquy's ultramontanist and pro-authority stance

---

95. Fréchette, *Mémoires intimes* (Montreal, ²1977), p. 113: "He was the first Canadian priest who denounced the liberals from the pulpit" (my translation). This is also stated in a biography of Barthe from *La Patrie* (copied in *CFA*, 19 August 1893, p. 11).

96. Letter to *Av* that appeared 18 April 1849, p. 2, the same day as news of a huge Montreal meeting to honour Chiniquy (my translation).

97. *Av*, 27 November 1850, p. 2, mentions a Chiniquy sermon to dissuade Catholics from subscribing to the *Avenir*.

98. L.J. Papineau letter to his wife, 24 June 1850 (**LAC** MG 24, B2, microfilm C-15791 p. 4537).

1. A RISING STAR IN QUEBEC

clashed with the the *Avenir* group. Each of his interventions further polarized the situation. Even Bishop Bourget tried to curb his overzealous temperance preacher.[99]

Still we have found no record that Bishop Bourget expressed regret over Chiniquy's debates with French Protestants. Chiniquy had begun similar debates previously in his Quebec City days. Now he entered the thick of this fight, going to the two major centres of French Protestant activity. At the end of January 1850, he attacked the 'Swiss' in a sermon against the FCMS at Pointe aux Trembles.[100] A year later he debated Louis Roussy, one of the pioneer GL missionaries at St. Marie or Marieville (not far from Grande Ligne).[101] Both encounters were reported at length in the *Montreal Witness*. Each time Chiniquy incited laity to minor violence against his opponents. From the Marieville debate emerged very contradictory pamphlet accounts by Chiniquy and Roussy.[102]

Protestants saw this as a planned aggression by the right hand man of Bishop Bourget. Chiniquy's autobiography supports this assessment and implies that the Apostle of Temperance volunteered for such an assignment.[103] His anti-Protestant activities even extended to New York State.[104] Chiniquy claimed later that he had helped to encourage and finance the

---

99. Bp. Bourget to Chiniquy, 31 March 1851 (**ACAM**, RLB 6:388).

100. *MW* accounts spread over 11, 15, and 25 February and 4 March 1850.

101. *MW*, 17 February 1851, pp. 52-3. Two recent articles analyze this debate: Christine Hudon, "Le prêtre, le ministre et l'apostat. Les stratégies pastorales face au protestantisme canadien français au XIXe siècle" (*SCHEC, Études d'Histoire religieuse*, 1995), pp. 81-99 ; and more specifically Pierre Rannou, *Confrontation entre Chiniquy et Roussy à Sainte-Marie-de-Monnoir, le 7 Janvier 1851* (Longueuil, 2001), 36 p.

102. Chiniquy, *Le suisse méthodiste confondu* (Montreal, 1851), and L. Roussy, *Récit de la discussion entre M. Chiniquy et M. Roussy* (Napierville, 1851). See the pamphlet covers in our Figures 32 and 33.

103. *40 Years*, p. 69.

104. *MW*, 20 October 1851, p. 357.

firmly ultramontane Montreal *True Witness* in order to counter Protestantism.[105]

Chiniquy's vigour for the Temperance Crusade seems to have gradually declined. His energy could not be squelched but was, instead, rechannelled. As he visited the French Canadian community in Troy, New York and then continued on to Boston to meet Father Mathew, a new plan or crusade came to mind. Chiniquy decided that emigration to the United States could not be prevented. The French Catholic emigrants would surely lose their language and religion if not guided by the clergy. Factory work and urban life would destroy Catholic values.

One of Chiniquy's letters came to be frequently quoted by the reform group for its understanding of the reasons for emigration: "food, space and freedom" were available in the United States, as opposed to Canada.[106] Even Chiniquy's brother, Achille, went to California to find work. The need for a rural French Catholic colony in the United States was confirmed for Chiniquy during his 1851 temperance lecture tour of Detroit, Chicago and rural Illinois.

Chiniquy's plan for preserving the faith of emigrants did not even remotely carry the day in French Canadian clerical circles. All the French bishops and Catholic journalists viewed emigration as so disastrous for French Canada and for the Catholic faith of emigrants that they steadfastly opposed it. The apostle of temperance wrote a public letter on August 13th, 1851 promoting colonization of Illinois from French Canada. For the first time, he received attacks in the newspapers from hostile clerics. Chiniquy was confirmed in his resolve to move to the United States when his motives were misconstrued[107] and a misguided optimism of leaders about keeping all French Canadians in Canada continued.

---

105. *MW*, 27 October 1877, p. 2. A press debate soon followed over his role after the Catholic *True Witness* denied his claim.

106. Chiniquy to *Mélanges religieux*, 16 October 1849 (quoted in *Av*, 26 March 1851, p. 2, and in *SC*, 10 April 1851).

107. While he alleged that he wanted to gather the emigrants already in the United States, he was viewed as trying to stimulate Canadian emigration.

1. A RISING STAR IN QUEBEC

Suspension

Meanwhile much more serious problems arose. Chiniquy was suspended on September 28, 1851. Unfortunately neither the suspension order nor Chiniquy's written response, supposedly a confession, was preserved.[108] Bishop Bourget quoted alleged extracts from these letters much later[109] but Chiniquy gave another version. A woman clearly charged Chiniquy with sexual harassment. In contrast to all sexual accusations publicized much later but relating to previous alleged incidents, Chiniquy himself admitted this allegation. Nonetheless he denied the charge and claimed that the woman later confessed that it was a fabrication.[110]

Looking back there is some evidence of previous charges. Father Brassard made a trip to Kamouraska in 1848 to check out some kind of allegations. He cleared Chiniquy. This did not keep Bishop Bourget from fearing that the *Avenir* would get the real story on Chiniquy one day.[111] In January 1851, Brassard wrote to his bishop to plead in favour of Chiniquy. In Brassard's opinion "his unfortunate story from Kamouraska is not known except by his superiors and maybe by a few priests" and Chiniquy "has already paid dearly for his fault".[112] Perhaps this response stemmed from a Kamouraska letter relaying news of another Chiniquy scandal there.[113]

---

108. Trudel, p. 131, claims to quote from a letter from Chiniquy to Bp. Bourget of 4 October 1851, but no copy of this exists at **ACAM** or elsewhere.

109. Bp. Bourget to Bourbonnais, 19 March 1857 (in *Cour*, 7 April 1857).

110. For his full response see Chiniquy to Bp. Bourget, 18 April 1857 (*Av*, 1 May 1857, pp. 2-3).

111. Bp. Bourget to Bp. Turgeon, 21 August 1849 (**ACAM**, RLB 5:279-280). There is no reference here to any particular offence but, whatever it is, it is viewed as scandalous.

112. Brassard to Bp. Bourget, 26 January 1851 (only a transcript exists in **AAQ**, 7 CM, E.U., VII:200, p. 13; my translation).

113. Letter from Kamouraska to Quebec Diocese, 19 May 1850 (formerly **AAQ**, Kam, II:48, now at St. Anne de la Pocatière Diocese archives).

THE CONTROVERSIAL CONVERSION OF CHARLES CHINIQUY

In May 1851, Bishop Bourget provided guidelines for Chiniquy's trip to Chicago, including that he must avoid ostentation and respect all local priests. His first guideline was to "take strict precautions in your relations with women."[114] At the time Chiniquy responded by complaining of "calumnies" about himself relayed by Bourget to Brassard. In this letter to the bishop, he implied that he was innocent without making an outright denial.[115]

Bishop Bourget six years later declared:

> for a long time, the guilt of Mr. Chiniquy was known to me, when a certain girl came to testify against him. She expressed a repugnance to meet him. According to our regular procedure, this testimony was not recorded for canonical trial. We limit ourselves then to saying to this gentleman that in addition to all that had been reported against him, a certain girl had recently brought another complaint against him.[116]

No specifics are thus available for this Montreal charge. Chiniquy's autobiography claimed that the reason of suspension had to remain intentionally vague and therefore impossible to refute: an unnamed criminal action with an unnamed person.[117]

It was standard Catholic practice in 19th century Quebec[118] that most sexual charges against clergy were treated as fleeting and were corrected by prayer and vigilance. For repeat offences the penalty was suspension plus one year of probation in residence with, and under the surveillance of another priest. The repentant priest was gradually reintegrated into

---

114. Bp. Bourget to Chiniquy, 7 May 1851 (**ACAM**, RLB 6:440; my translation). This last phrase was the usual ecclesiastical term used for adult females. It would be an unusual warning for an experienced priest.

115. Chiniquy to Bp. Bourget, 13 May 1851 (**AAQ**, 7 CM, E.U., VII: 200, p. 19).

116. Bp. Bourget pastoral letter, 18 April 1857, p. 4 (**ACAM** 402.102, 857-27; my translation).

117. *50 Years*, p. 523. See closer to the time period, the letter Chiniquy to Bp. Bourget, 18 April 1857 (in *Église de Rome: réponse de Révérend Charles Chiniquy...*, 1870, pp. 9-12).

118. Lemieux, *Les années difficiles* (Montreal, 1989), pp. 134-5.

1. A RISING STAR IN QUEBEC

his duties. Generally, correspondence surrounding such cases was not recorded, making it virtually impossible to retrace details.

One might explain Chiniquy's year with the Oblates as being an obligatory year of probation. Of course we cannot know the reality of any of the charges, especially when no thorough investigation or hearing was ever performed. Bishop Bourget appears to have been unusually lenient in letting Chiniquy leave Montreal with no supervision. The bishop's correspondence reveals a concern, above all, to give Chiniquy another chance, but also to protect the Apostle of Temperance for the sake of the Church's reputation.

Chiniquy's account counter-charged that, since his enemies opposed his views on temperance and emigration, and were jealous of his success, they tried to frame him. We do know of the opposition of his Uncle Amable Dionne. Apart from this opposition and understandable jealousy of some priests, Chiniquy's conspiracy theory, in this case, is improbable. In any event, his scenario lacks any evidence.

Chiniquy's written response after this suspension, which is now missing, would help resolve the issue. We have Bourget's declaration that his priest confessed against Chiniquy's denial. Bourget's account is strengthened by several Chiniquy letters that mention his exile to Illinois and his unfulfilled desire to return to Canada.[119] I conclude, provisionally, that Chiniquy was suspended privately, after at least two unproven and virtually uninvestigated sexual allegations against him. Further, Chiniquy was allowed to go to Illinois as a concession, a decision much regretted later by Bishop Bourget.

---

119. Chiniquy to J.C. Chapais, [Autumn 1852] and 28 March 1856 (Barnard, *Mémoires*, vol. 2, pp. 88-89, 131).

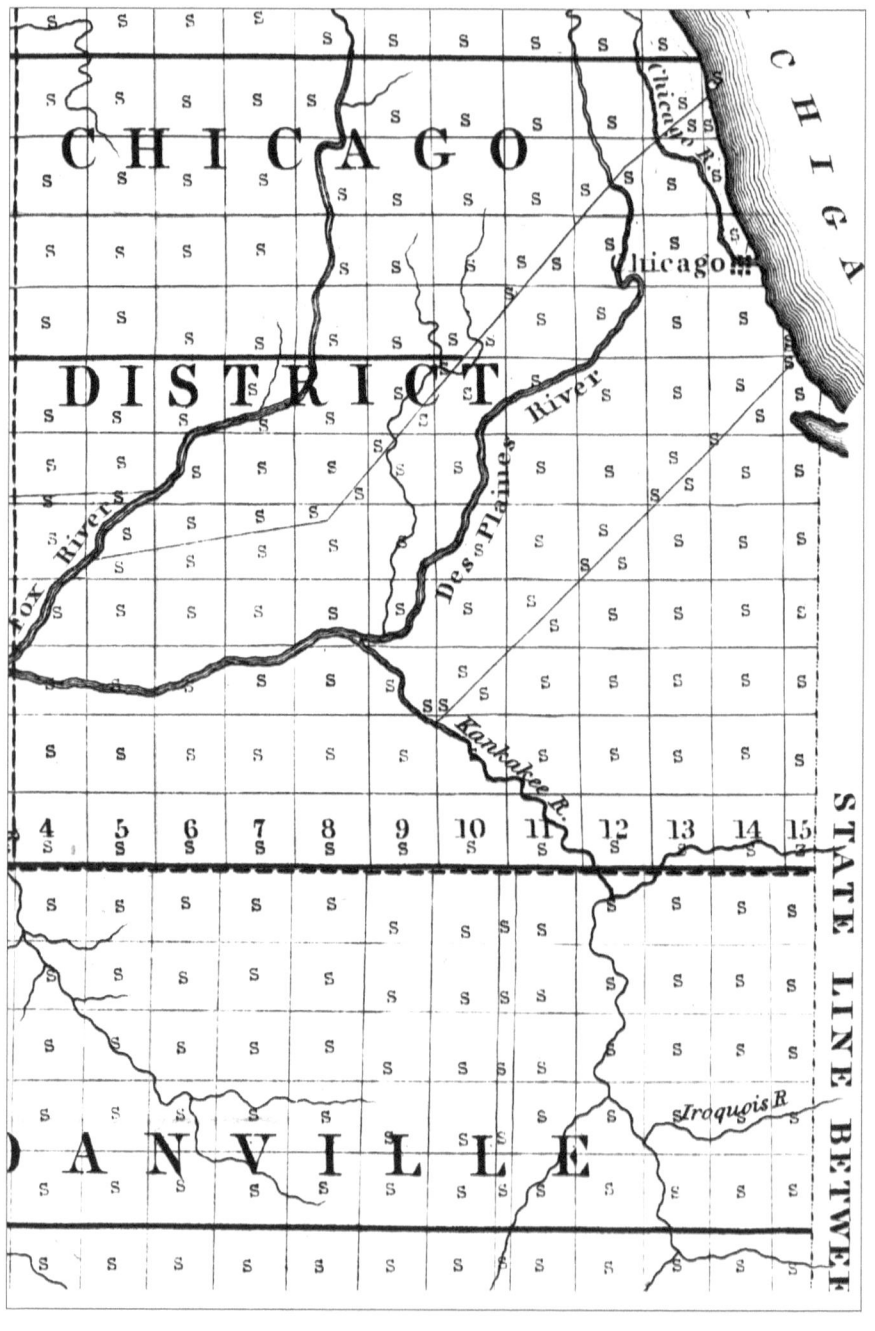

Image 2 Illinois map, 1845   AP 15-027

2

PIONEER IN ILLINOIS (1851-55)

KANKAKEE COUNTY

In 1851, Chiniquy moved to rural Illinois as a colonizing priest.[1] He came to an area with a long history of French presence but with only a recent settlement by French Canadians. Sixty miles south of Chicago lay a Pottawatomi Indian reserve, the only one left in Illinois after 1832. A fur trader, Noël Levasseur, persuaded its last residents to sell it to him and leave in 1836.[2] Levasseur then moved to what became Bourbonnais Grove, on the Kankakee River. He began a campaign to persuade others from Lower Canada to emigrate. Several families came after the 1837 Rebellions and a larger group in 1848.

As Bourbonnais filled up, a few settlers moved away from the river to higher ground. The new community of Beaver Mission, several miles from Bourbonnais, was situated on heavy black soil. To the east there was sandy soil. The entire region was still frontier with virtually empty

---

1. This was a concept that became more popular later. Priests led and supervised groups of landless Quebecers to settle *en bloc* in new agricultural areas of Canada.

2. See E. A. Senesac, *Centennial Anniversary of the Church of the Maternity of the BVM* (Bourbonnais, 1947), pp. 10-31.

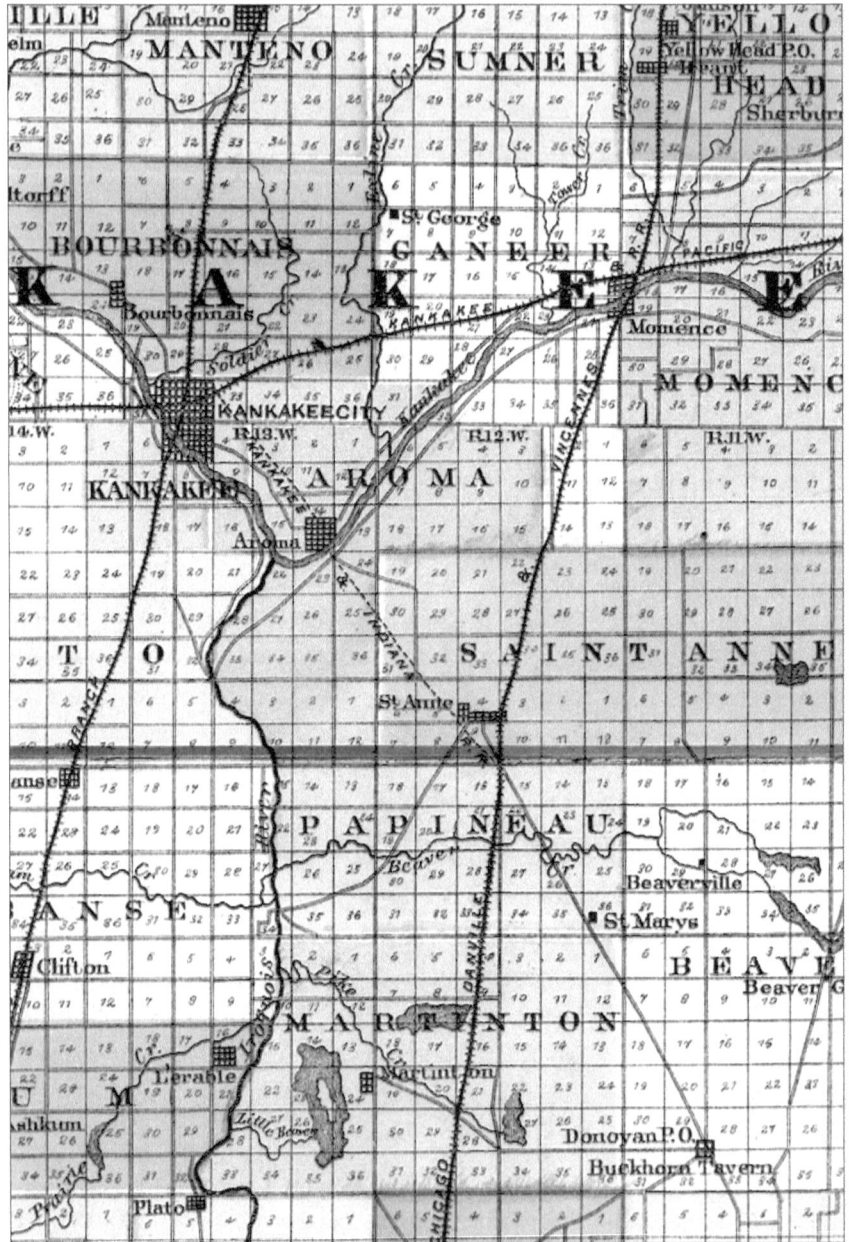

Figure 17   Part of Kankakee Co. (Warner & Beers Illinois Atlas, 1874)   AP 15 (2) 027

2. PIONEER IN ILLINOIS (1851-55)

Sketch of first St. Anne church   Pioneer cabin   Sketch of first St. Anne school
Figure 18, 19, 20 (*Heritage of St. Anne*, 1950)

prairies, when Chiniquy chose Beaver Mission for his new settlement. He highlighted the French-Canadian roots by renaming the village St. Anne.

At first the travel route from Canada had to pass by water through the Great Lakes to Chicago and then along the Kankakee River. Before the railways bypassed this earliest village and changed the axis from East-West, along the river, to North-South, Bourbonnais formed the centre of French population. Bourbonnais furthered its dominant French character by founding a large Catholic high school around 1865.[3] However Bourbonnais regressed and became the suburbs of a newer town, Kankakee.

After the Illinois Central Railroad arrived in 1853, Kankakee town became the commercial and government centre of Kankakee County. Its residents formed a mixed population of French and English. The county court house and jail, often referred to in Chiniquy documents, were situated there.

St. Anne remained more rural and isolated. It was unable to acquire its own direct rail link to Chicago until 1870. However it did develop some small industry (brick and tile factories), which helped to retain its children and to balance the rural base. In 1880 the town population

---

3. St. Viateur College was founded by the Viatorian order and was until 1920 the only seminary for Chicago Diocese priests. There was also a girl's school founded by the Sisters of our Lady in Bourbonnais in 1860.

was still only 412.[4] To this day the village remains small, serving the larger thriving rural area.

Who were the settlers of Bourbonnais and St. Anne? They do not appear to have been predominantly anti-clericals seeking to escape the Catholic hierarchy. In fact, Chiniquy advertised St. Anne as a Catholic bastion with a rural francophone identity.[5] The diverse population came from France, Belgium, Ontario and all over Quebec. Many had already lived in New England or New York. No pattern emerges from an initial examination of the biographies of immigrants. All ages, all areas and all backgrounds were represented.

The decision to emigrate from Quebec soon became a very controversial one. After 1852, those who left Quebec were often called traitors by the Quebec press, who also provided plentiful negative publicity about Illinois agricultural conditions. At the same time, the Belgian Consul in Chicago, apparently, bought land around St. Anne to settle Belgian immigrants and devout Catholics from France.[6]

Later, after the Civil War, land in Kankakee County became scarce. Several bad harvests and the high price of land resulted in major departures of French groups from St. Anne[7] to Kansas and Wisconsin. Still, new French surnames kept appearing in St. Anne records of the 19th century to replace the names of those who left. Emigration from Quebec must have continued at a slower rate. At the same time gradual anglicization occurred among the French immigrants. Civil War service often resulted in anglicized surnames. As Dutch, German and Americans moved to the area, English was increasingly used for education and

---

4. Census for 1880-1900 reported in Kenaga and Letourneau, *History of Kankakee County* (Chicago, 1906), p. 691.

5. Chiniquy letter to a workers' organization in St. Hyacinthe, 9 February 1852 (*Le Pays*, 22 March 1852).

6. *Montreal Weekly Witness*, 24 October 1855, p. 374.

7. *Minutes of the 1869 CPC Synod*, appendix, p. lxx. Bristol, *Atlas of Kankakee County* (Chicago, c1883), p. 21 also reports that at least 1,200 families from the St. Anne Presbyterian Church had migrated West.

2. PIONEER IN ILLINOIS (1851-55)

conversation. The French school in St. Anne finally dropped French as its primary language in 1888.[8]

THE CATHOLIC DIOCESE OF CHICAGO

A new outlook on the Chiniquy story comes from a study of the state of the Catholic Church in Illinois. Chiniquy's clashes were far from being the only ones that the first three Chicago bishops faced during the mid-19th century. Each of these bishops encountered strong opposition from numerous priests.

Chiniquy's first Chicago bishop was Bishop Van de Velde (or Jacques Olivier) who eventually sought reassignment due to the bad climate but also due to "having later become involved in difficulties with a few of his clergy over the title to certain pieces of ecclesiastical property, which they were retaining in their own name."[9] He finally went directly to Rome to lobby to escape Chicago. This unusual request was first refused but eventually granted in 1853.[10] He proved to be the last French-speaking bishop in the diocese.

Prior to the resignation of the next bishop, Anthony O'Regan, the *Chicago Tribune* provided a steady barrage of criticism from Protestants and a few Catholics denigrating the "Irish tyrant". After anonymous Catholic priests with inside knowledge publicly decried the lack of accountability on

Figure 21 Bishop Van de Velde (Garraghan, *The Catholic Church*, p. 137a)

---

8. Against the wishes of Chiniquy who predicted the end of French worship there (*A*, 28 April 1900, p. 7). See anthropologist Caroline Brettell's examination of St. Anne in her "From Catholics to Presbyterians: French-Canadian Immigrants in Central Illinois" (*Am. Presby*, 1985), pp. 285-298.
9. Garraghan, *The Catholic Church in Chicago* (Chicago, 1921), p. 161.
10. He died of yellow fever after several years as bishop of Natchez.

the part of their leader, Bishop O'Regan was, in fact, forced out of office. Even so, like his predecessor, he had to go directly to Rome to plead to be relieved in 1858.[11]

Next came Bishop Duggan. He had even greater problems. His bizarre actions and summary suspensions eventually resulted in him being declared insane. One of the priests suspended by Bishop Duggan stated very candidly:

> the Diocese of Chicago has received three successive bishops from St. Louis who have all failed in their administrations and there will be no confidence placed by either the clergy or the laity in any new selection that may be made by the Archbishop of St. Louis.[12]

The next bishop, Thomas Foley, had to act as administrator for one year until, in 1870, the insane Duggan was finally released from his bishopric. Chicago clergy had requested a Father McMullen as the new bishop but his previous contesting of a Duggan action precluded him. As usual Archbishop Kenrick of St. Louis directed the choice. Bishop Foley had little to do with Chiniquy, who was now openly a Protestant, except for continuing court battles about property rights. He is the last Chicago bishop mentioned by or about Chiniquy.

What are we to make of the quality and impartiality of the Chicago bishops who faced Chiniquy? Without showing any awareness of Chiniquy, the historian Gaffey concluded that there was a problem of inbred St. Louis leadership. An ageing archbishop chose only those who promoted his interests as Chicago bishops. Local Chicago needs were ignored. Gaffey also suggests that the appeal system was hopeless since Archbishop Kenrick automatically defended his bishops.[13] Chicago

---

11. He retired to England, though still young, with an honorary episcopate.

12. Father John McMullen to Archbp. Spalding of Baltimore (quoted by Gaffey, "Patterns of Ecclesiastical Authority: The Problem of Chicago Succession" (*Church History*, 1973, p. 262). Father McMullen PhD was President of the Catholic University of St. Mary of the Lake and later became Vicar-General of Chicago.

13. Ibid., p. 269.

2. PIONEER IN ILLINOIS (1851-55)

clergy rebels were remarkable for their courage in appealing to Rome rather than just conforming or leaving.[14] Certainly, being a successful bishop of Chicago would require great administrative skill, strong local support and a firm but fair hand to produce unity. Those do not seem to have been Archbishop Kenrick's criteria for selecting bishops.

In the diocese primary ethnic loyalties (whether Irish, French or German) were a constant problem, particularly when applied to the questions of property and choice of priests. Efforts to consolidate all church property under the bishop's name proved quite difficult in Chicago. The main contentious properties were those of St. Mary's University, the French church in Chicago (St. Louis) and Chiniquy's church in St. Anne. As we will see later the opposition in each case came from clergy, with Chiniquy as the ringleader in two of the three cases. The St. Mary's dispute was probably more significant because it had broad clergy support.[15] Unlike the St. Anne schism, it was resolved with time.

Accusations of corruption, against Bishop O'Regan, or immorality, against several of the bishops, lack convincing evidence. On the other hand, Protestant charges of centralizing all money and building a large bishop's palace are quite true. As for administrative skill, Van de Velde had some difficulty while O'Regan and Duggan definitely had major problems apart from Chiniquy. Their overbearing authority was repugnant to local Catholics reared in a democracy in which accountability was expected. Chiniquy was not faced with complete incompetents but he did have to deal with intransigent bishops who felt very threatened by any questioning of their decisions.

Could it be possible that Chiniquy played a major role in driving two bishops to request retirement after just a few years and one to go insane? That would probably be too strong a claim. The former priest of St. Anne's certainly played a major role in the demise of O'Regan.

---

14. Ibid., p. 268.
15. See all of Gaffey's article.

Probably all these bishops, who knew that they lacked episcopal talents, and who tried to avoid the job, were delighted to be done with Chiniquy and other independent Illinois clerics.

SUMMARY OF THE ILLINOIS CONTEXT

Rural northern Illinois was a place where few took off their hats to a superior, where amusements were simple and few, where great debates between Lincoln and Douglas drew huge crowds, where all groups mixed but political and religious beliefs were held firmly and even violently, where newspapers relished a conflict, where foreigners were numerous but suspect if they tried to do anything un-American, where traditions from the East or from the "old country" were often jettisoned, but where Canadian links were often strong and Canadian news well-publicized. Many of these Illinois characteristics facilitated the schism in St. Anne.

COLONIZING PRIEST

Chiniquy arrived in Illinois in late 1851 as a pioneer of the type of colonizing priests who founded new communities far from their home region. Prior to his arrival, it is not clear whether Chiniquy was urged to come by the bishop of Chicago[16] or whether the bishop reluctantly accepted the disgraced priest.[17] A letter of Bishop Van de Velde in which he agreed to give Chiniquy a chance, after Brassard's urging, favours the second position.[18] Chiniquy's account includes a transcript of a much earlier letter from Van de Velde.[19]

---

16. *50 Years*, pp. 497-8.
17. Trudel, p. 132.
18. Bp. Van de Velde (Olivier) to Bp. Bourget, 15 October 1851 (**ACAM** 402.102, 851-5).
19. Bp. Van de Velde to Chiniquy, 1 December 1850 (*50 Years*, p. 497). This early letter has been decried as a forgery by Catholic authors. The main objection to this early letter is its mention of the possibility that Chiniquy would become the bishop's successor. Given the public reputation of Chiniquy at the time such a possibility is not inconceivable. In all other points the alleged letter corresponds to the natural goal of maximizing the strength

2. PIONEER IN ILLINOIS (1851-55)

Probably Van de Velde invited Chiniquy in the quoted early letter. When then Chiniquy's subsequent visit to Illinois in early 1851 was a success he planned to return soon. The sexual allegations in Montreal complicated matters. While Brassard encouraged the now reluctant Chicago bishop to take Chiniquy, Bishop Bourget facilitated the matter and wrote notes to Van de Velde that expressed expectation that Chiniquy would be a success in Illinois.[20] Chiniquy departed hastily from Montreal after a final address of thanks to the Apostle of Temperance in Longueuil (the sexual accusation was never publicized).

Chiniquy arrived in Bourbonnais, Illinois at the beginning of November 1851,[21] when Chicago Diocese was only seven years old. He began his service under the only non-Irish bishop of Chicago prior to 1915. Jacques Olivier Van de Velde was a multilingual Belgian Jesuit who had been a professor in St. Louis before his appointment as second bishop of Chicago (1849-53). He continued his predecessor's policy of accommodating the many immigrants to Chicago through the provision of national or ethnic parishes. To this end he recruited, among others, French priests for Chicago and the Bourbonnais area.

The unstable nature of virtually all of the early French priests is striking: alcoholism, immorality or incompetence resulted in short-lived tenures but replacements were hard to find. Although in 1833 the French still formed the majority in Chicago, a large migration of French

---

of the Catholic minority. There is abundant evidence elsewhere of similar appeals, by Van de Velde and other bishops, for priests from Quebec to come and help them e.g. Bp. Van de Velde (Olivier) to Bp. Bourget, 4 March 1850 (**AAQ**, 7 CM, E.U., VII:200). In addition my research has not uncovered any forged letters or evidence of changes in any letters quoted by Chiniquy, which can be verified.

20. Bp. Bourget to Bp. Van de Velde, 18 October 1851 (**ACAM**, RLB 7:12).

21. At this point, one would normally turn to the archival material from Chicago Diocese. Unfortunately such material is missing. However Catholic envoy Grand Vicar Mailloux managed to faithfully copy many of the relevant letters, particularly any that favoured the Catholic interpretation. Again I find Mailloux to have been an accurate scribe, when letters can be verified. See his **ASQ** collection.

Métis soon left few French speakers.[22] The situation changed again with French Canadian immigration in the late 1840s and the 1850s.

Meanwhile Bishop Van de Velde was beginning a long series of battles with clergy over property titles. Historian Patrick Carey found that, in other dioceses, trouble over church property generally developed between bishops and well entrenched lay trustees.[23] However, in Chicago there was no such pattern of traditional local elite who demanded control. Rather, this was a frontier diocese, led by inexperienced bishops who enforced rules that still were being defined. Here, the local clergy were the representatives of stability and local involvement, against the incoming foreign bishop. The short tenure of these earliest bishops and the fact that they were parachuted in from the St. Louis seminary, did not contribute to peace.[24]

In 1851 Bourbonnais was already established, with its own priest, when Chiniquy moved twelve miles southeast to Beaver Creek, to serve a handful of families settled there. For a while he lodged with Peter Spink, a French Canadian storekeeper[25] whose sons attended College back in St. Hyacinthe, Quebec. Spink was a very ardent Roman Catholic who, with the blessing of the Chicago bishop, had pleaded with Bishop Bourget since 1845 to send priests to protect the faith and language of the Catholics in Bourbonnais.[26]

Chiniquy bought some Beaver Creek property in his own name in December 1851 and soon had work begun on the chapel. When Bishop Van de Velde visited in April 1852, Chiniquy had to rewrite the eccentric

---

22. Garraghan, *The Catholic Church*, p. 149.

23. See the excellent treatment in Carey, *People, Priests and Prelates*, (South Bend, 1987). He, however, never refers to Chicago Diocese or to Chiniquy.

24. Gaffey, p. 268.

25. Despite his English name. *Av*, 20 November 1856, p. 2 mentions that he was a rebel at St. Charles (Richelieu) in 1837.

26. Spink to Bp. Bourget, 15 September 1845 and 30 March 1846 (**ACAM** 195.119, 845-2 and 846-1).

2. PIONEER IN ILLINOIS (1851-55)

deed although he still included a qualification that the property was to be used for the good of the local Catholic citizens of St. Anne.[27]

Before long Chiniquy clashed with other Illinois priests. Apparently Father Courjault of Bourbonnais wrote letters under a pseudonym that were blamed on Chiniquy.[28] Chiniquy sided with the Bourbonnais parishioners to have this priest ousted for immoral acts. Next the French priest in Chicago, Isidore Lebel, and Chiniquy clashed[29] in Quebec newspaper correspondence. The issue was whether or not Illinois was a good location for emigration.[30] Bourget and Lebel wanted Chiniquy to stop attracting Canadian emigrants while Van de Velde took a mediating position that perhaps Chiniquy had exaggerated the ease of emigrant life somewhat.[31] Neither Lebel nor Chiniquy capitulated[32] but the emigration controversy died down eventually.

This controversy made for strange alliances. In a major reversal, the reformers' *Avenir* publicized Chiniquy against the Quebec clergy. Chiniquy was now very daring in favouring the side of emigration, leaning to Republicanism and publicly critiquing some clerics.[33] The *Avenir* approved the contrast that Chiniquy drew between, on the one hand, liberty and economic prospects in the United States ("bread, space and liberty") and, on the other, the Canadian government's inaction as to economic reform. Chiniquy was even invited to speak at the *Institut canadien*. Ironically (for the future) he declined due to the

---

27. Price, pp. 56-7.
28. Bourget to Van de Velde, 20 March 1852 (**ACAM**, RLB 7:223); *50 Years*, p. 543.
29. Chiniquy cites a letter of warning from Van de Velde about Lebel in *50 Years*, p. 554.
30. See *Le Pays*, 22 March until 18 June 1852; editorial in *Av*, 11 August 1852, p. 2. Then again in the May-June 1853 period when *Minerve* attacked Chiniquy's position. There were formidable witnesses on both sides.
31. Bp. Bourget to Bp. Van de Velde, 14 April 1852 (**ACAM**, RLB 7:771).
32. This was despite Bp. Van de Velde's statement that he had more than once encouraged Chiniquy to modify his descriptions (Bp. Van de Velde to Bp. Bourget, 28 December 1851 (**AAQ**, 7 CM, E.U., VII:200, pp. 30-1).
33. *Av*, 11 August 1852, p. 2.

Institut's refusal to obey their bishop and remove the Protestant paper, *Le Semeur canadien*.[34] While Chiniquy was respected by virtually all concerned as a colonizing priest, the bright picture he painted of Illinois immigration was not appreciated by government or clerical leaders in Canada.

In June 1853, the Bourbonnais church burned down while Chiniquy was in charge of both it and St. Anne's. Nothing came of this at the time but much later, after Chiniquy's apostasy, certain Catholic priests accused Chiniquy of having torched his own church. This precipitated a successful slander suit by Chiniquy. The priest of St. Anne blamed the fire on the former priest, Courjault, who had threatened in a letter to burn the church.[35]

The truth lies clouded in two propagandas. Both accusations of arson appear to be weak in their alleged motives. Besides, almost every building in Bourbonnais, St. Anne and even Chicago had burned down at least once. In this situation of extreme conflict both Catholics and Protestants regularly accused each other of arson.

When Chiniquy appealed for donations from French Canada, the new Bourbonnais priest wrote to Bourget claiming that Chiniquy pocketed the funds.[36] These constant clashes with other French priests in Illinois, as well as with the Quebec newspapers, had already produced a full-blown conspiracy theory in Chiniquy's mind.[37] He felt that individuals in Quebec were aiming to destroy his reputation. At this point the bishops were not included as part of the perceived conspiracy, at least not in the version he suggested to Bishop Bourget.

In the midst of this almost constant conflict, Chiniquy wrote back to J.C. Chapais in Kamouraska. As always, Chiniquy was keeping up with the political questions of the day in Lower Canada. He gave advice

---

34. L.J. Papineau to the *Institut Canadien*, 25 November 1852 (**LAC**). Papineau would have liked to hear Chiniquy but advised a position of no compromise.
35. *50 Years*, p. 555 even provides a date for the letter.
36. Chiniquy to Bp. Bourget, 12 November 1853 (**ACAM** 402.102,853-2).
37. Ibid.

2. PIONEER IN ILLINOIS (1851-55)

about laws to stem emigration but he also stated that his goal was to protect immigrants from Protestantism, which was like "the vulture that devours the small defenceless bird".[38] The priest of St. Anne spoke fondly of Kamouraska while comparing attacks against himself to the political position of Chapais:

> You have seen, by experience, that the higher one mounts on the horizon, the more one is battered by the storms which result from constantly shifting human passions. But the trees with vigorous roots, instead of being toppled by the storm, only become stronger.[39]

Following another collapse from exhaustion[40] Chiniquy acquired more land from Peter Spink.[41] That same month Spink took exception to an apparent slander during a sermon and sued Chiniquy, his own priest. Chiniquy won the trial and the first appeal.

Being a man of many projects, with a special interest in education, Chiniquy decided to build a convent and a college.[42] For this purpose he continued to purchase land in his own name.[43] As a colonizing priest he also negotiated with the railroad to acquire land.[44] Meanwhile D'Arcy McGee, the Irish Catholic journalist and future Father of the Canadian Confederation embraced Chiniquy's vision of rural Catholic colonies. However when McGee convened a conference in January 1856 to encourage rural Catholic immigration, Chiniquy was disappointed not

---

38. Chiniquy to J.C. Chapais MPP, [autumn 1852] in Barnard, *Mémoires Chapais* (Montreal, 1961) vol. 2, pp. 88-9 (my translation).
39. Ibid.
40. *Le Pays*, of 6 September 1853 reported him as near death.
41. The notarized warrantee deed of 12 November 1853 (**UCT**, Presbyterian Board of French Evangelization, 79.215C, file 1-14).
42. Chiniquy to Quebec Diocese, 10 May 1854 (**AAQ**, CE,1:167).
43. Chiniquy warrantee deed, 5 May 1855 (**UCT**, Presbyterian Board of French Evangelization, 79.215C, file 1-14).
44. Chiniquy to Roswell Mason, 9 January 1853 (**Kankakee County Historical Society**, Chiniquy collection).

to receive an invitation.⁴⁵ The French-Canadian priest did manage to persuade the Belgian consul to finance land for Belgian Catholic immigrants around St. Anne.⁴⁶ Even Bishop Bourget came to appreciate Chiniquy's vision of emigration enough to promise to seek nuns as teachers for the St. Anne school.⁴⁷

Because of his goal of protecting Catholic immigrants Chiniquy naturally fought the political Know-Nothing movement.⁴⁸ In a letter to American Catholic newspapers he commented favourably on armed resistance and ambushes for revenge against anti-Catholics:

> The morning after, two corpses of well-known Orangemen were found lying on the broken columns [of the Catholic church, which they had been desecrating]. I do not [have] to tell you that since that day the Catholics of Kingston have been left in peace. I will then say bravo!⁴⁹

Let it be noted that this letter appeared only months before Chiniquy's excommunication.

Meanwhile Chiniquy had survived cholera in 1855 and by early 1856 was again fund-raising and recruiting priests.⁵⁰ Another letter back to Kamouraska reveals the pressure he felt over the emigration question (besides his other problems):

> [prior to your kind letter], I had thought genuinely that for my devotion and sacrifices that I made to save our unfortunate immigrant compatriots, my country had rejected me ... all that

---

45. *50 Years*, p. 668 mentions an 1852! conference and *40 Years*, pp. 307-9 refers to an 1853! conference. The best source remains Mary G. Kelly, *Catholic Immigrant Colonization Projects* (NY, 1939), chapter 8 and especially p. 194.

46. *MW*, 24 October 1855, p. 374. Perhaps this was actually the Austrian-based Leopoldine mission, which financed much Catholic immigration. See Kelly for details.

47. Bp. Bourget to Chiniquy, 2 April 1856 (**ACAM** RLB 9:315).

48. See my chapter 5 and Higham, *Strangers in the Land* (NY, 1955).

49. Quoted in *MW*, 20 February 1856, p. 60.

50. *Le Pays*, 15 January 1856, p. 3.

2. PIONEER IN ILLINOIS (1851-55)

you have suffered is nothing compared with what has happened to me on leaving for Illinois.[51]

While enumerating the miraculous successes of the St. Anne colony, Chiniquy also longed for more contact with home after "the bitter bread of exile" shared by all French-Canadian immigrants.

If the fact that Bishop Van de Velde drank alcohol horrified Chiniquy, the St. Anne priest's propaganda for immigration embarrassed his superior. Nevertheless I find no evidence, at the time, of major problems between Chiniquy and his first bishop of Chicago. Life never remained calm for long around the dynamic priest. His battles against the Quebec newspapers, his clerical colleagues in Kankakee County and his parishioner, Peter Spink, prepared the way for much more serious conflict.

---

51. Chiniquy to J.C. Chapais, 29 March 1856 (Barnard, *Mémoires*, vol. 2, p. 129).

Image 3 Temperance Medallion 1849 **AP** 05-002

3

REBEL PRIEST (1856-58)

THE SPINK TRIALS

Chiniquy's tempestuous character along with his insistence on justice often led him to the civil courts. His legal trials began in Illinois[1] in January 1854 when the St. Anne priest announced in a sermon that Peter Spink was lying to his clients about land sales.[2] Spink sued his priest for slander. Chiniquy won the first round[3] but Spink pursued an appeal and had the trial moved downstate to the Circuit Court in Urbana.

At that point the Springfield lawyer and politician, Abraham Lincoln, agreed to represent Chiniquy. A hung jury[4] resulted in one final trial in October 1856.[5] After this again resulted in deadlock, Lincoln

---

1. There are also reports of laity going to court in Kamouraska in 1845 due to Chiniquy pressuring them to produce false oaths (Trudel, p. 66).
2. George, "The Lincoln writings" (*Jounal of Illinois State Historical Society*, 1976), pp. 22-3.
3. May 1855 in Kankakee.
4. In May 1856.
5. Most of the evidence was given in French and then translated by an interpreter (Whitney, *Life on the Circuit with Lincoln*, Caldwell, 1940, p. 74).

Figure 22   Lincoln photo (Wikimedia commons)

helped to negotiate an out of court settlement where each party paid his own court costs and Chiniquy rescinded the original accusations as hearsay.[6]

Later Chiniquy claimed that he was protecting the poor from an unscrupulous land speculator, whose court cases were financed by Bishop O'Regan in order to ruin Chiniquy.[7] In fact Spink was a very committed French Catholic[8] who was able to afford a prolonged court case, employing the same lawyers as the Catholic Diocese of Chicago and having a priest testify on his behalf. According to four witnesses whom St. Anne parish sent to the bishop, O'Regan admitted to relocating Chiniquy, in part, to stop the court case.[9] If the priest had moved, Spink would likely have won the case.

BISHOP ANTHONY O'REGAN (1854-1858)

Anthony O'Regan was the bishop whose name is most commonly associated with Chiniquy's. Like Van de Velde he had been a director of the St. Louis seminary, but he was born and educated in Ireland. Despite

---

6. Houde, "Chiniquy's Revolt" (Chicago, 1968), pp. 110-111; George, pp. 22-3. Resther (manuscript, 1884), p. 4 claims that Spink agreed only conditionally but Chiniquy did not respect the conditions. Chiniquy did claim victory since he was not found guilty but, in fact, he had to retract his statements. See **ASQ** 50:14c for a copy of the court record of the results. Most critics have ridiculed this conspiracy idea.

7. *50 Years*, p. 566; Chiniquy letter to Bp. O'Regan in *Av*, 18 December 1856, p. 2; Chiniquy to *Journal de Québec*, 2 February 1857, p. 5 (**ASQ** 50:1j).

8. For example he was chosen to read the address to the Bishop on his visit to Bourbonnais (*CT*, 11 June 1857). In a strange twist, Mailloux, who arrived later, described Spink as a Scot who persecuted all the Illinois priests (see his notes to the Lambert memoire, **ASQ** 50:7a, p. 6).

9. *Av*, 20 November 1856, p. 2; *50 Years*, p. 637. Pierre Gendron in *Av*, 20 and 27 November 1856 supports the Chiniquy contention of a Spink-O'Regan alliance.

3. REBEL PRIEST (1856-58)

his reluctance to accept, O'Regan was consecrated bishop of Chicago in 1854. His was another short episcopal term of four years marked by quarrels with clergy. At the end he made repeated requests to be discharged of the episcopacy.

After the more minor struggles under Van de Velde, O'Regan bulled ahead to fully implement the decrees of the 1829 Baltimore Council. These forbade trusteeism. Even loyal Catholic historians can admit that while he was reputed to be an ecclesiast, scholar and director of young men,

Figure 23   Bishop Anthony O'Regan
(Garraghan, *The Catholic Church*, p. 167a)

> nature had not, it would appear, fitted Bishop O'Regan to the task of taking tactfully in hand and administering with success the delicate affairs of this young and unsettled diocese of Western America.[10]

The general critique is not of corruption but rather of authoritarianism and lack of diplomacy. Chicago's own seminary and Catholic University of St. Mary of the Lake was the main focus of controversy, with Chiniquy not far behind. Bishop O'Regan did not hesitate to suspend all clergy whom he deemed rebellious.

PROPERTY DISPUTES

At Chiniquy's first visit to his new bishop, in December 1854, the topic of church property in St. Anne arose. Trust never developed between the two. Instead conflict slowly escalated. In a Chiniquy public letter of 25 October 1856 he addresses his bishop and claims:

> You have, at three different times, threatened to interdict and excommunicate me if I would not give you my little personal properties! and as many times you have said in my teeth, that

---

10. Garraghan (Chicago, 1921), p. 179.

> I was a bad priest, because I refused to act according to your rapacious tyranny! The impious Ahab, murdering Naboth to get his fields, is risen from the dead in your person.[11]

O'Regan replied that this was not a dispute over property since he already had title to the St. Anne properties. Chiniquy contended

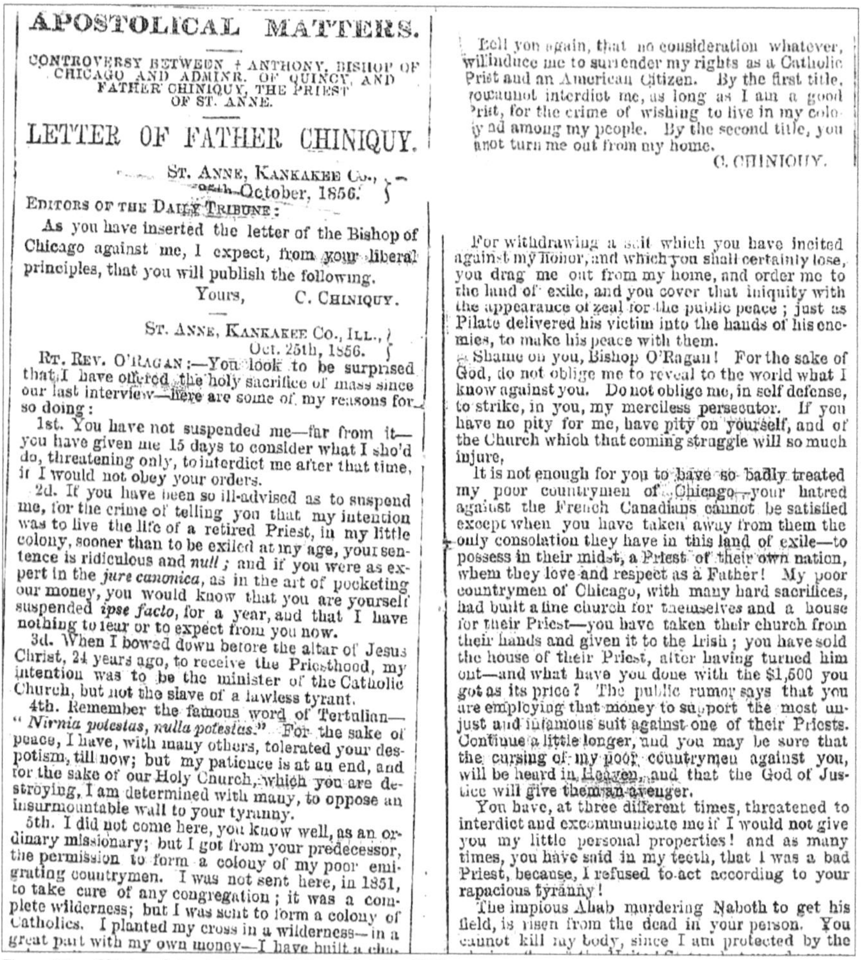

APOSTOLICAL MATTERS.

CONTROVERSY BETWEEN + ANTHONY, BISHOP OF CHICAGO AND ADMINR. OF QUINCY, AND FATHER CHINIQUY, THE PRIEST OF ST. ANNE.

LETTER OF FATHER CHINIQUY.

ST. ANNE, KANKAKEE CO., 25th October, 1856.

EDITORS OF THE DAILY TRIBUNE:

As you have inserted the letter of the Bishop of Chicago against me, I expect, from your liberal principles, that you will publish the following.

Yours, C. CHINIQUY.

ST. ANNE, KANKAKEE CO., ILL., Oct. 25th, 1856.

RT. REV. O'RAGAN:—You look to be surprised that I have offered the holy sacrifice of mass since our last interview—here are some of my reasons for so doing:

1st. You have not suspended me—far from it—you have given me 15 days to consider what I sho'd do, threatening only, to interdict me after that time, if I would not obey your orders.

2d. If you have been so ill-advised as to suspend me, for the crime of telling you that my intention was to live the life of a retired Priest, in my little colony, sooner than to be exiled at my age, your sentence is ridiculous and *null*; and if you were as expert in the *jure canonica*, as in the art of pocketing our money, you would know that you are yourself suspended *ipse facto*, for a year, and that I have nothing to fear or to expect from you now.

3d. When I bowed down before the altar of Jesus Christ, 24 years ago, to receive the Priesthood, my intention was to be the minister of the Catholic Church, but not the slave of a lawless tyrant.

4th. Remember the famous word of Tertulian—"*Nirnia potestas, nulla potestas.*" For the sake of peace, I have, with many others, tolerated your despotism, till now; but my patience is at an end, and for the sake of our Holy Church, which you are destroying, I am determined with many, to oppose an insurmountable wall to your tyranny.

5th. I did not come here, you know well, as an ordinary missionary; but I got from your predecessor, the permission to form a colony of my poor emigrating countrymen. I was not sent here, in 1851, to take cure of any congregation; it was a complete wilderness; but I was sent to form a colony of Catholics. I planted my cross in a wilderness—in a great part with my own money—I have built a chu…

…ell you again, that no consideration whatever, will induce me to surrender my rights as a Catholic Prist and an American Citizen. By the first title, you cannot interdict me, as long as I am a good Prist, for the crime of wishing to live in my colony and among my people. By the second title, you cannot turn me out from my home.

C. CHINIQUY.

For withdrawing a suit which you have incited against my honor, and which you shall certainly lose, you drag me out from my home, and order me to the land of exile, and you cover that iniquity with the appearance of zeal for the public peace; just as Pilate delivered his victim into the hands of his enemies, to make his peace with them.

Shame on you, Bishop O'Ragan! For the sake of God, do not oblige me to reveal to the world what I know against you. Do not oblige me, in self defense, to strike, in you, my merciless persecutor. If you have no pity for me, have pity on yourself, and of the Church which that coming struggle will so much injure.

It is not enough for you to have so badly treated my poor countrymen of Chicago—your hatred against the French Canadians cannot be satisfied except when you have taken away from them the only consolation they have in this land of exile—to possess in their midst, a Priest of their own nation, whem they love and respect as a Father! My poor countrymen of Chicago, with many hard sacrifices, had built a fine church for themselves and a house for their Priest—you have taken their church from their hands and given it to the Irish; you have sold the house of their Priest, after having turned him out—and what have you done with the $1,500 you got as its price? The public rumor says that you are employing that money to support the most unjust and infamous suit against one of their Priests. Continue a little longer, and you may be sure that the cursing of my poor countrymen against you, will be heard in Heaven, and that the God of Justice will give them an avenger.

You have, at three different times, threatened to interdict and excommunicate me if I would not give you my little personal properties! and as many times, you have said in my teeth, that I was a bad Priest, because, I refused to act according to your rapacious tyranny!

The impious Ahab murdering Naboth to get his field, is risen from the dead in your person. You cannot kill my body, since I am protected by the…

Figure 24 Chiniquy letter to *Chicago Tribune*, October 1856

11. Quoted in *Av*, 18 December 1856, p. 2, and *50 Years*, p. 648, but this last contains the wrong date (25 September), which is followed by Trudel and Price (*RHAF*, 1959). "Persécutions" (Montreal, 1857), p. 4 and the *Chicago Tribune* extract above from **AP** 15-C1-F010-01 confirms that the September date is an error.

3. REBEL PRIEST (1856-58)

that the bishop had felt threatened by the phrase in the deed that Chiniquy insisted on inserting: "for the use and in the interest of the congregation".[12] The contentious priest was also accused by the diocese of persuading the neighbouring Manteno congregation to add a similar clause. Leaders in Manteno denied any Chiniquy influence on their resistance to giving unrestricted control of their property to the bishop.

This church property issue was well publicized by anti-clericals[13] and Protestants.[14] The American episcopal drive to centralize all church property in the hands of the bishops was ridiculed by dissenters and unsympathetic media, as being inspired by greed. In fact it was the officially approved alternative to American Protestant-based "trusteeism" and prevailed everywhere in the U.S. by the 1860s. In the U.S. however the centralization also attempted to eliminate traces of the universal Quebec practice of local village administration by a parish council.[15]

A large meeting of French Canadians in Chicago agreed to protest Chiniquy's punishment:

> We know that if Chiniquy is persecuted today it is because he refused to approve the despoilment of our church - he was the first to publicly point out the injustice of the bishop towards us; and the hate which he has borne because of his generous defence of his oppressed brothers and the courage with which he has pleaded for our rights in the realm of public opinion are sufficient reasons for us to assure him of our eternal gratitude.[16]

---

12. *Av,* 15 March 1857, p. 2; also Chiniquy to Rev. Matthew Dillon: "for the use and benefit of the Catholics of St. Anne" (*CT,* 13 April 1857).

13. *Av,* 15 May 1857, p. 2, suggests that the Assomption parish should have stood up against their bishop as Chiniquy had.

14. *MW,* 30 May 1857, p. 340, quotes *Av* (See previous footnote) on Chiniquy and then says that most of the Catholic church disputes are about property. Hierarchical absolutism is described as the key problem.

15. See Duane Galles, "Canonical restraint on administrators of parish property" (*Christifidelis,* 19, 5, 2001).

16. Assemblée des Français canadiens de Chicago to *Av,* printed 1 September 1857, p. 1 (my translation). This address, signed by hundreds, provides a thorough, if

For Bishop O'Regan the more minor irritation of the St. Anne properties, hardly compared with public interference in this diocesan matter.[17] Just after the Chicago French Catholics had first written to the papers, in September 1855, Chiniquy raised the matter privately with Bishop O'Regan. The St. Anne priest, having investigated the allegations, offered his help to resolve the matter. Chiniquy proposed that O'Regan make several concessions.[18] His bishop was not amused by the suggestions. Later, after his suspension, Chiniquy again raised the grievance of the Chicago French Canadians.[19]

This matter further fuelled conflict between the two clerics. O'Regan made public retraction by the rebel priest of all these charges a prerequisite for later attempts at reconciliation.[20] On his part Chiniquy insisted on resolution of the Chicago French church conflicts prior to his own submission.[21] This nationalist stand brought substantial support from French Canadians in Chicago[22] and Kankakee County, besides the sympathy of the *Avenir*. Even Bourget's envoy Desaulniers pointed out that O'Regan was biased against French Catholics, in that he did not provide a good priest or a place to worship in Chicago.[23]

O'Regan appears to have been maladroit and authoritarian in introducing the new system of episcopal ownership.[24] The legitimacy of

---

biased, account of their grievances. An earlier letter (22 January 1857), covering similar ground was printed in *50 Years*, pp. 752-7.

17. Bp. O'Regan's explanation is provided in his letter to Facile, 27 October 1856, pp. 3-5 (**UND** III-2-i-8 or 5239).

18. *50 Years*, pp. 619-622.

19. Chiniquy letter of 25 October 1856 to the newspapers (see footnote 55).

20. *50 Years*, p. 749.

21. Ibid., p. 743; Mailloux notes, c25 June 1857 (**ASQ** 50:2L verso).

22. Chiniquy letters to *Av*, 15 February, 15 April, 15 June, 1 September and 1 December, 1857. Most of these were also sent to the *CT*.

23. Desaulniers to Bp. Bourget, 26-7 October 1856, p. 8 (**ACAM** 402.102, 856-17a).

24. See the previous section on Bp. O'Regan for his problems with others, in particular with property matters.

3. REBEL PRIEST (1856-58)

the charges by Chicago French Catholics[25] is not clear but manifestly Chiniquy was willing to risk his already vulnerable position to defend them. O'Regan's manner of refusing all discussion simply hardened the opposition.

When "property" was mentioned in this overall conflict it usually referred to the property of Chicago French Catholics rather than to that of St. Anne.[26] Chiniquy often mentioned this issue as the precipitating factor, sometimes in veiled terms: "I publicly protested against ... a thing done by the bishop, and which I considered to be against the laws of God and of man. The result of this was that we were all to be excommunicated."[27]

It is hard to believe that Chiniquy was preparing for future legal battles, early on, when he insisted on a clause furthering congregational ownership of property. This clause proved of great importance in court cases. As trust disappeared with the bishop over the Chicago properties and the Spink trial, Chiniquy suspected that O'Regan was determined to steal all French properties.

Property matters were not the direct cause of the excommunication.[28] Nonetheless, the escalation of conflict resulted primarily from opposing approaches to the question of local ownership of church

---

25. Trudel, pp. 176-8, however, assumes that any episcopal announcement, declaring that this was not a true issue, resolves all doubt in such matters.

26. For the common property problems of ethnic Catholic churches see Carey (South Bend, 1987), pp. 143-6. For the St. Louis and then Notre Dame French parish of Chicago see Garraghan (Chicago, 1921), pp. 149-50, 198.

27. From an 1860 lecture in Ireland contained in Mary Bird, *A Few Reminiscences* (Leeds, 1878), p. 15. Chiniquy often simplified his story with this or similar terms. Sometimes it was further specified that Bp. O'Regan had sold the cemetery soil, including bodily remains.

28. Price, "Aux origines" (*RHAF*, 1959), p. 73, quotes Bp. O'Regan and qualifies the bishop's statement that property had nothing to do with the discipline. It is noteworthy, on the other side, that a lengthy defence of Chiniquy against O'Regan never mentions property matters (P. Gendron in *Av*, 20 November 1856, p. 2).

property.[29] The bishop's view of property and obedience led him to attempt to get rid of the rebel troublemaker while Chiniquy's suspicions and sense of justice kept him from submitting.

After Chiniquy's final break with Catholicism, the property remained at the centre of conflict between the parish and the diocese. The rebel group and its priest retained the church building. Loyal Catholics were taken to court by Chiniquy's group to oblige them to pay pew rents.[30] The desecration of a Catholic church for schismatic and then "heretical" purposes horrified Catholic leaders. Would this not encourage other rebels to take over their churches from a powerless hierarchy?[31]

This church property in St. Anne[32] remains in Presbyterian hands to this day. Many expensive rounds of court battle finally resulted, in September 1874, in technical victory for the Catholic Diocese. To avoid endless appeals, the properties were left with Chiniquy's group, who had then possessed them for many years. Another lot was granted in compensation to the Diocese.[33]

SUSPENSION AND EXCOMMUNICATION

In 1856 trouble was closing in around the rebel priest. He inquired about returning to Montreal Diocese, complaining of Irish persecution,[34] but the blow struck before he could receive a response.

Charles Chiniquy was suspended "for canonical causes" on August 19th, 1856. The interdict was read on August 24th and then he was

---

29. The Toronto correspondent in *MW*, 16 March 1859, p. 173, was disappointed that the whole issue of Chiniquy's conflict seemed to be "who is to own this and that building?"
30. Mailloux to Dillon, 27 October 1857 (**ASQ** 50:3).
31. Mailloux to Bp. Duggan, 19 November 1858 (**ASQ** 50:11v).
32. The deed from Spink can be found in **UCT** (Presbyterian Board of French Evangelization, 79.215C, file 1-14).
33. Stephen Moore to Chiniquy, 26 November 1893, p. 6 (**SL** c.1/3).
34. Chiniquy to Bp. Bourget, 9 August 1856 (**ACAM** 402.102, 856-3).

3. REBEL PRIEST (1856-58)

excommunicated on September 3rd.³⁵ The pastoral letter announcing the excommunication reads in part:

The said M. C. Chiniquy, notwithstanding this suspension has wickedly presumed to exercise the functions of the sacred ministry, to preach, administer sacraments and say mass, and has thus formally placed himself in open opposition to the authority of the Church and became schismatic. The said M.C. Chiniquy, thus formally admonished by me by letter and by verbal instruction, having publicly and obstinately persisted in his violation of the laws of the Church and disobedience of its authority is hereby excommunicated; and I caution all Catholics against having any communication whatever with him in spiritual matters. Should any catholic become refractory to this order, he also becomes excommunicated.³⁶

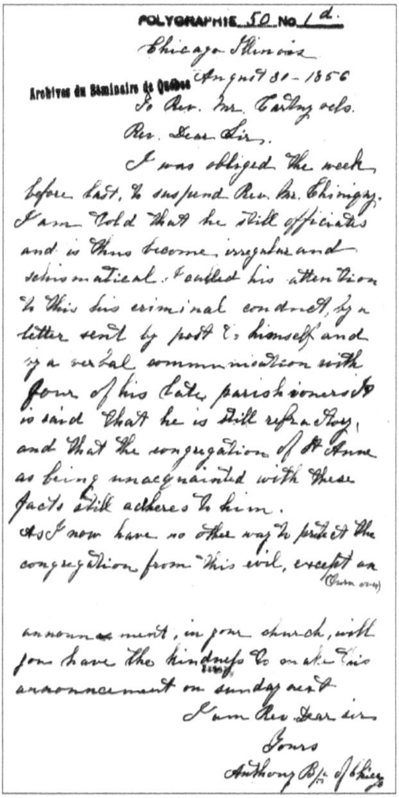

Figure 25 Bishop O'Regan letter, August 1856 (**ASQ**)

The term, "for canonical causes" is deliberately ambiguous. Once Chiniquy had become so rebellious and schismatic that he had to be excommunicated, the original causes became irrelevant to the bishop. Most Catholic biographers have taken the term to refer to unnamed sexual offences.

---

35. This summary comes from Mailloux letter to Auclair, June 1858 (**ASQ** 50:19f).
36. Pastoral letter of Bp. Anthony O'Regan, 3 September 1856 (**ASQ** 50:1b).

81

Chiniquy's account interprets the words "for canonical causes" as a cover for the bishop's arbitrary, and unjust, removal of the independent priest. He maintained that since no specifics would have held up in an investigation, generalities with innuendo were used instead. The suspension would facilitate the seizure of more property.

O'Regan himself reported:

> [Bishop Van de Velde] cautioned me against him. He told me he would one day cause a schism and that he found it impossible to manage him and the French Canadians in this Diocese. I soon found all this and much more to be true.[37]

My reconstruction concludes that there was an a multiplicity of misdemeanours, which added up to an unacceptable trouble-making priest. Bishop O'Regan had heard some evidence of sexual allegations, had seen the scandalous court trial of a priest against his parishioner, and had resented Chiniquy's attitude to church property in St. Anne, besides his championing of the Chicago French Catholics against their bishop.

In order to stop the trial and to distance Chiniquy from his power base, the bishop ordered him to move immediately to the other side of Illinois (Cahokia). Chiniquy tried unsuccessfully to present compromises but finally refused to move, primarily because of the upcoming court case. O'Regan may have given him two weeks to report to his new posting.[38]

Chiniquy claims that on his return to St. Anne he reversed his position and decided to submit. By that time the bishop had sent out public notification of the suspension. Believing this to be not only unjust, but also a breaking of the promise of time to reconsider, Chiniquy ignored the suspension and carried on. Four representatives from his congregation visited O'Regan and confirmed Chiniquy's version of his last encounter with the

---

37. Bp. O'Regan to Facile, Superintendent of the Christian Brothers in Montreal, 28 October 1856 (**UND** III-2-i-8 5239).

38. *50 Years*, p. 633. Bp. O'Regan denied having given time to report before an interdict would take effect.

3. REBEL PRIEST (1856-58)

bishop. According to their testimony the bishop had no solid evidence of sexual misbehaviour but simply wanted Chiniquy to move. Furthermore they claimed that O'Regan was still willing to reassign Chiniquy if the priest submitted.

With the backing of most of his parish, Chiniquy wrote a protest to Archbishop Kenrick of St. Louis, without making a formal appeal. In all likelihood this was a wise tactical move. The archbishop naturally backed his bishops, unless there was incontrovertible evidence against them.[39] However, such a formal appeal was the normal procedure that the Quebec bishops insisted must be used by loyal Catholics.[40] Chiniquy did make a lengthy direct appeal to the Pope, with a copy to Napoleon III of France. Nothing came of this, although Chiniquy claims that it caused O'Regan's removal.

Figure 26   Chiniquy at age 50 (Meir, *The Saga*, p. 7)

It was astonishing at the time that a Catholic priest should defy his bishop and yet insist that he was a faithful Catholic. To Protestants this would be startling, for its rare occurrence, while to Catholics the rebellion unquestionably attacked a basic foundation of their beliefs, i.e., hierarchical authority. Chiniquy proposed an apologetic for

---

39. See the account of another appeal in Gaffey, "Patterns of Ecclesiastical Authority" (*Church History*, 1973), pp. 260-262.

40. Bp. Bourget to certain St. Anne inhabitants, 4 October 1856 (**ACAM**, RLB 9:406-7) and in his pastoral letter of 6 May 1857 (**ACAM** 402.102, 857-32, p. 5).

defiance of unjust episcopal orders based on Canon Law, Jerome, Pope Gregory, Thomas Aquinas and Scripture.[41]

With the battle lines drawn there seemed to be no room left for manoeuvre. In order to resove the conflict either the bishop or his excommunicated priest would have to swallow his pride. The bishop continued to insist on a thorough and public act of repentance by Chiniquy.

The rebel priest maximized the impact by adding several other accusations against his bishop. In his initial meeting with O'Regan, Chiniquy claimed to have received a threat of suspension rather than a declaration of suspension. Therefore his continuation of priestly duties was not in violation of a suspension. Furthermore the notice of excommunication was unsigned and posted by "unfit" (drunken) priests. From all points of view, he concluded that the excommunication was "a nullity" and thus should be ignored.

The sexual allegations must not be overlooked in explaining the excommunication, even if theological principles have been shown to play the major role. We have seen that there had already been accusations in Canada. During this excommunication period we have two accounts of horrendous charges over a broad period and involving many women.[42] The credibility of these charges is central to understanding Charles Chiniquy.[43] A 1993 play "Chiniquy, God's Liar"[44] was based firmly on one of these accounts (Lambert). Inevitably it depicted a seductive charlatan who was interested in nothing but sex, money and power.

These sexual charges were believed by Quebec envoy Alexis Mailloux[45] and were circulated privately among the Quebec bishops, who also believed them. Mailloux tried to persuade the Chicago and Quebec

---

41. *50 Years*, pp. 649-50, 652, 765.
42. Memoirs transcribed by Alexis Mailloux of Mrs. Marie Lambert (Descormier), 29 June 1857, 7 p. (**ASQ** 50:7) and Godefroi Lambert, 22 May 1858, 56 p. (**ASQ** 50:7a).
43. I will leave evaluation of this to the last section of Chapter 8.
44. "Chiniquy, menteur de Dieu", a play by Jean Guy lasted only a few days in Quebec City in March 1993.
45. For more on Alexis Mailloux (1801-77) see *DCB*, 10, pp. 488-489.

3. REBEL PRIEST (1856-58)

bishops to hold a church trial for Chiniquy based on these charges, even in absentia. Unfortunately, his overtures were not taken up. Without any formal investigation the truth remains obscure. We conclude however that sexual charges had almost nothing to do with the excommunication, since they were never specified, nor stressed by O'Regan. An alternative explanation claims that the bishop could not specify the charges due to civil law[46] or to confidentiality.

Chiniquy was suspended for not moving to Cahokia and was excommunicated for carrying on in his functions after his suspension. In other words, disobedience of clear directives by his episcopal authority was the primary cause of the suspension and the sole cause of the excommunication. Although property matters, sexual allegations, non-cooperation with local priests[47] and the court case were not the direct cause of suspension, they were the direct causes for the forced move to Cahokia.

Why was there so much pressure to move at **this** point in time? Only the Spink court case seems to provide an answer. The bishop hoped either to achieve social peace or to humiliate Chiniquy, by having the case abandoned or won by Spink. Chapter 8 will examine the reasons for Chiniquy's defiance.

From O'Regan's letters, one learns that he primarily objected to Chiniquy's disobedience of episcopal decrees: "I was obliged to suspend him due to his obstinate disobedience, his language and the excessive violence of his conduct; his subsequent schism led to his excommunication."[48] This was certainly a valid reason in canon law for suspension and excommunication. Both disciplinary actions, according to the canons, are to be used with the pastoral intention of obliging

---

46. Father L. Courjault in *Av*, 18 December 1856, p. 2.
47. This last was listed as the first stated cause by the four witnesses who visited the Bishop. See *50 Years*, p. 637.
48. Bp. O'Regan to Bp. Prince, 20 November 1856 (in *Av*, 4 December, 1856, p. 3). The violent language and conduct refers primarily to his press accusations of October 1856, **after** the excommunication. Schism was also, in effect, disobedience.

the offender to repent and be restored to the church. Notwithstanding, the one accused by the bishop was assumed to be guilty until proven otherwise.[49]

From the Roman Catholic viewpoint Chiniquy became a 'schismatic' by separating himself from the unity of the Church. This separation was shown by persistent disobedient acts such as continuing to celebrate the mass after the excommunication was announced. His group claimed to be Christian but did not recognize episcopal authority. Therefore, true Catholics were advised to cut off all spiritual ties with the schismatic leader and his followers.[50]

EXTERNAL SUPPORT

The threats of excommunication against Chiniquy and his followers had very little effect. His supporters addressed a supportive speech to him immediately after the announced excommunication.[51] A subsequent protest meeting by his supporters in Kankakee on September 21st approved a private letter to the bishop.[52] Meanwhile, Chiniquy advertised in the local paper that all his personal effects were to be put up for sale in order to finance his court case with Spink.[53]

Within a month and a half of the excommunication being announced, the Chiniquy point of view was prominent in American and Canadian press headlines. Until the Spink case was resolved in late October,

---

49. This aspect has been updated in the revised Canon Law of 1983. Historically, most Protestant churches have had similar procedures of church discipline. Each church has an appeal system or hearings which, at their best, protect the one disciplined from injustice or misunderstanding. Every church is left in a quandary if the accused eschews the appeal system and instead takes his case to the press, as Chiniquy did.

50. The consequences of excommunication were spelled out by Archbp. Baillargeon in an 1856 letter quoted by Bp. Larocque in his 15 February 1857 circular letter (*Mandements des évêques de St-Hyacinthe*, vol. I, pp. 293-4).

51. *50 Years*, pp. 643-646.

52. Ibid., pp. 446-447.

53. In the *KG*, 18 September 1856 quoted in Houde, "Chiniquy's Revolt" (Chicago, 1978), p. 111.

3. REBEL PRIEST (1856-58)

Chiniquy could not concentrate on publicizing his side of the excommunication story.

Most of the protests were by laity. One might legitimately suspect that the St. Anne priest coordinated these protests. The ideas, and at times the wording, strongly reflect Chiniquy's own. Initial publicity came in response to O'Regan's explanation of the excommunication in the *Chicago Tribune*. The St. Anne laity sent a letter accusing the bishop of persecuting their honourable priest. They vowed their support for Chiniquy in his appeal to Rome. The letter, addressed to O'Regan ended by hoping:

> that your Lordship will not persist in your decision, given in a moment of madness and spite; that you will reconsider your acts, and that you will retract your unjust, null and ridiculous excommunication, and that by these means avoid the scandal of which your precipitation is the cause. We then hope that, changing your determination, you will work for the welfare of our holy religion, and not to its degradation, in which your intolerant conduct would lead us ... that we shall have in the Bishop of Chicago, not a tyrant, but a father, and that you will have in us not rebels, but faithful children.[54]

This strong language was typical of Chiniquy from 1856 on, even when addressing his bishops.

Chiniquy's letter of October 25th caused a sensation in Chicago.[55] The letter called his bishop a lawless tyrant, a fool, and a Judas who stole the French church and pocketed church funds:

> Now seeing that the more humble I am before you the more insolent you grow, I have taken the resolution to stand by my rights as a Catholic priest and as an American citizen ... Do not be angry at these harsh words which you find in this letter. Nobody but I could tell you these sad truths, though every one of your priests ... repeat them every day. By kind and honest proceedings, you can get everything from me ... but you will

---

54. *50 Years*, p. 645. Also in *Av*, 30 October 1856.

55. For some reason it was not published in Quebec until December 18, after many other developments.

find me an immovable rock if you approach me as you have always done with insult and tyrannical threats.[56]

Many of these points will be analyzed in Chapters seven to nine. For the moment, notice the fascinating combination of vicious polarizing comments mixed in with pleas for peace. The holy war approach and terms, honed through battles with brewers, Protestants and anti-clericals, were now applied to a bishop.

POLITICIZED PUBLICITY FOR THE SCHISM

Such rebellion caught Protestant attention. The *Chicago Tribune* opened up its columns to Chiniquy's side in early 1857. A survey of the *Chicago Tribune* for 1857 and 1858 reveals an interesting mixture of politics and religion. As an official Republican paper, one would expect frequent references to Lincoln, slavery and the elections. However, tied into these subjects one finds the following themes: religious tyranny and slavery versus trusteeism and liberty. Catholic bishops and particularly Bishop O'Regan were identified with the foreign (predominantly Irish) intrusion of despotism.[57]

> There is danger that the liberties of the country will be crushed between the upper and nether millstones of American despotism - Catholicism and Slavery. The first wages incessant war upon the right of private judgment in matters of religion and upon the doctrine of toleration, made by our fathers a part of the civil polity of the Republic ...In a word, this amalgamation of all that is worst in Catholicism - its ignorance, prejudice, intolerance and pauperism and hate - and all that is most odious in slavery - its arrogance and its blood-thirstiness [must be fought].[58]

> Catholics of the United States are, almost without exception, members of the Pro-Slavery or Democratic party...with the

---

56. Chiniquy to Bp. O'Regan, *50 Years*, pp. 647, 650. As usual this is faithful to contemporary printed versions e.g. *Av*, 18 December 1856, p. 2.
57. See chapters 5 and 9 where I examine anti-Catholicism.
58. *CT*, 30 July 1857, p. 2.

3. REBEL PRIEST (1856-58)

> religious features of Catholicism we find no fault. The faith of its votaries, though never so lifeless and absurd, does not concern us. But Catholicism is more a system of politics than religion.[59]

Catholicism was also portrayed as being guilty of promoting Irish Democrat goons in the political machines of Chicago, Boston and New York.

The *Chicago Tribune* of these years actually opposed the Know-Nothings and nativism,[60] while praising "the majority" of non-Irish immigrants who became American citizens and voted Republican. Protestant news was prominent in this paper and causes such as temperance were often affirmed. Nevertheless political coverage remained its primary focus.

Chiniquy's cause was championed by the *Tribune*. However it relied on correspondence and sent no reporter to nearby St. Anne. News of Chiniquy was usually found on the front page while columns were opened for letters from Catholics or Protestants supporting Chiniquy. Editorials urged support for this "champion of liberty".

O'Regan was attacked constantly either by correspondence of dissident Chicago Catholics or by editorials:

> For possessing this spirit of religious independence, they are persecuted by the Irish Bishop with a malevolence that is shocking and insufferable. These French Catholics have made their appeal to the great American Public, for justice and sympathy.[61]

The Republican paper's proposed solution was the initiation of state laws protecting the laity from having its property "stolen" by the bishops. This torrent of anti-O'Regan material, doubtless, played a major role in the bishop's resignation.

---

59. *CT*, 1 August 1857, p. 2.
60. An American anti-ethnic movement in the 19th century.
61. *CT*, 27 January 1857. See also its editorial on 31 March 1857.

However, after St. Anne voted Democrat in the November 1858 election, Chiniquy was immediately dropped by the *Tribune* as an ungrateful turncoat.[62] Although the Chicago Tribune was openly anti-Catholic[63] in this period, its anti-Catholicism was dependent on politics. Unfortunately for Chiniquy, the competing *Chicago Times* strongly opposed Chiniquy and continued to refuse his correspondence.

Voting returns show that Kankakee County as a whole consistently supported Republican presidents from 1856 until 1904.[64] Other factors complicated the matter. What of the Democratic St. Anne vote of November 1856? In this same time period the *Kankakee Gazette*, which was Republican and mostly anti-Chiniquy, clashed with the *Kankakee Democrat*, which was Democratic, Protestant and pro-Chiniquy. Some of Chiniquy's lawyers were Democrat candidates. It is important to take into account the political and partisan nature of much of the press when examining evidence about Chiniquy.

The *Montreal Witness* demonstrated a more theological interest in expressing its wish:

> that [Chiniquy] might seek shelter from the persecution of the Hierarchy, in the freedom of the Gospel and throw off the degrading claims of Rome. The issue he has raised with the Hierarchy leaves him in spite of his professed attachment to the church of his youth and of his palmy days, no other alternative but to submit in abject humiliation, or to allow himself to be cast overboard. May his trials lead him to see that he can become a faithful servant of Jesus Christ, and yet at the same time be like our blessed Reformers, an outcast of Rome, loaded with her curses.[65]

Unfortunately copies of the only French Protestant journal, the *Semeur canadien*, have been lost for these years. However, we find one quote

---

62. *Chicago Times*, 8 December 1858. *Chicago Press and Tribune*, 2-3 December 1858.

63. Keefe, "The Catholic Issue in the Chicago Tribune before the Civil War", (*Mid-America*, 1975), pp. 227-45.

64. Kenaga-Letourneau, *History of Kankakee County* (Chicago, 1906), pp. 691-2.

65. *MW*, 28 February 1857, p. 132.

3. REBEL PRIEST (1856-58)

from it in the *Journal d'Illinois*. This deplores the bishops' insistence on total submission even in the face of probable injustice.[66]

The Chiniquy conflict resulted in the radicalization of anti-clerical papers. At first the liberal Republican editor of the local Kankakee paper, the *Journal d'Illinois*, tried to remain neutral. When the Bourbonnais priest attacked this neutrality in April 1857, the editor's anti-clerical stance was inflamed and, henceforth, the Chiniquy cause was allotted much ink. No Chiniquy sermons or letters were printed, perhaps reflecting the anti-clerical stance. However militant lay protests against the bishop, by the French in Chicago or in St. Anne, were its regular source. Thus lay supporters presented the Chiniquy viewpoint. In the same way as the *Tribune*, this French newspaper served Chiniquy and his supporters well as a forum for their ideas between early 1857 and April 1858. Then either because of the lacklustre Republican support by Chiniquy's supporters or perhaps because of the danger of losing Catholic readers, this paper dropped all mention of the former priest.

By April 1858, the paper had backed away from Chiniquy:

> Often we have praised Mr Chiniquy because often Mr Chiniquy spoke in favour of liberty and development, of learning and enlightenment, and we will continue to praise him whenever he shows himself to be a man of progress ... The rest ... does not interest us. We do not care to get involved in a dispute between a priest and his church superiors. We only attacked the opponents of Mr Chiniquy because they attacked us.[67]

Shortly after this disavowal, the French paper had to close temporarily due to so many unpaid subscriptions. Probably these were Chiniquy supporters. The *Journal d'Illinois* closed definitively in January 1859. In its attempt to remain neutral in religion and to avoid mention of the local conflict, it had managed to alienate both sides.

---

66. *JI*, 17 July 1857, p. 1 ('From a Montreal religious newspaper').

67. *JI*, 30 April 1858, p. 2 (my translation). This was to protest being lumped together by the *Journal des débats* of Toronto. Chiniquy was never mentioned again in the *JI* by the editor.

We find then in Illinois, a context where the language of politics and religion often mixed and the themes of "tyranny, slavery, battle and liberty" were common emotive terms. Flag-waving could be used in religious battles or politics inserted into religion. Being a 'true American' was promoted by Republicans to embody certain religious beliefs or at least to deny absolutism.

Back in Quebec, the *Avenir* pressed the excommunicated priest to go further:

> What would happen if Mr Chiniquy who formerly, in the name of the Canadian clergy fought a ferocious war against the *Avenir*, were now to excommunicate Mr O'Regan.[68]

The paper began to champion Chiniquy and his followers, both in their nationalist cause, as well as in their resistance to oppression of their property rights. Not only did editor Pierre Blanchet print all available material favouring Chiniquy, he also reprinted much of the material in pamphlet form and then personally visited St. Anne. On the one hand, the *Avenir* profited from the clerical directives (which all other French papers obeyed) not to publicize the affair.[69] On the other hand, the *Avenir* profited from the keen public interest in French Canada to know the details of the conflict. P. Gendron became the regular *Avenir* correspondent in St. Anne.

While the *Avenir* needed a popular cause and regular new developments in order to expand its circulation, Chiniquy required regular publicity lest he be isolated from French Catholics. In 1857, the *Avenir* reported that it had 500 subscribers, in Quebec but also including a large proportion in the United States. Chiniquy news undoubtedly spurred this interest. Ultimately, Chiniquy benefited from the association. However, at the end

---

68. *Av*, 23 October 1856, p. 3 (my translation).

69. Bp. Bourget to Baillargeon, 4 February 1857 (**ACAM** RLB 10:31) requested that all good papers be told not to mention Chiniquy. *MW*, 11 April 1857, p. 228, affirms that this was successful among French papers except for the *Av* and the *SC*. The *Courrier de St. Hyacinthe* had been reprimanded for its news and so ceased all mention of Chiniquy. Even *Le Pays* decided to remain silent.

3. REBEL PRIEST (1856-58)

of 1857, ecclesiastical pressure forced the *Avenir* to close. Blanchet was defiant despite the obvious negative results of associating himself with the Chiniquy cause. In May 1858, he opened up again for one last issue or Extra which contained nothing but Chiniquy material.[70]

Media coverage is essential for the survival and growth of a dissident group so Chiniquy benefited from the interest. At the same time he provided a colourful personality for the newspapers that adopted the rebel priest; his pen and lectures provided frequent denunciation, while he relished continual polemics. This was wonderful material to sell newspapers.

CLERICAL SUPPORT

More surprising was the endorsement of Chiniquy that came from other Catholic priests. It was easier in Illinois than in Quebec to survive contradicting the bishop. Several persons who claimed to be priests, and who apparently had inside knowledge and theological education, wrote anonymous critical letters to the *Chicago Tribune* concerning Bishop O'Regan.[71]

Chiniquy maintained that he had the support of many progressive priests and people. In Quebec, the *Avenir* published the letters of "CT" from St. Pie, who was knowledgeable about canon law, and "Sacerdos" from Montreal Diocese.[72] "Sacerdos" was only silenced by the closing of the *Avenir*, it seems. The identity of these priests or theologically educated laity remains a mystery. Some at the time believed that

---

70. *Av*, 25 May 1858. This linkage of Chiniquy and the demise of the *Avenir* is a glaring omission by Bernard's *Les rouges* (Montreal, 1971), Eid's treatment of ultramontanism (Montreal, 1976) and all other analysts.

71. *CT*, in 1857: 25 August p. 2; 2nd and 16 September, p. 2; 10 October, p. 3, plus many who described themselves simply as 'a Catholic'.

72. "CT" in *Av*, 9 January 1857, p. 1; "Sacerdos" on 15 October 1857, pp. 1-2, and 22 December 1857, p. 1.

Figure 27   Moise Brassard
(Soc. d'histoire de Longueuil)

Chiniquy wrote them himself.[73] These letters tended to praise Chiniquy's role in temperance and immigration while critiquing Bishop O'Regan for his racism and persecution. They pleaded with other bishops to stop interfering and supporting the evil bishop of Chicago.

Besides these anonymous priests, several clerics took a more direct part in the conflict. Some were, eventually, obliged to publicly retract their support. However each had backed Chiniquy, even though he was excommunicated.

Rev. Louis Moise Brassard defended his protégé in Longueuil several times prior to Chiniquy's departure from Montreal. When news came of the excommunication he volunteered to be part of an effort to reconcile Chiniquy to the Church.[74] He encouraged Chiniquy with three private letters after this peace mission failed.[75] Finally on April 9th, 1857, Brassard wrote a public retraction. Sydney Smith maintained that this public letter shows that the private letters, attested to by Chiniquy, were frauds.[76] Printed extracts from these private letters were quite critical of the bishops.

Once again, I maintain that Chiniquy's printed and dated letters are reliable. Nevertheless, where they are mere extracts, he could have easily distorted the picture. Chiniquy was correct when he accused Bourget of

---

73. Mailloux thought that he found the Chiniquy style in an anonymous letter from St. Michel d'Archange (**ASQ**, 50:1 4b); see Mailloux notes in the margin). It is certainly not Chiniquy's handwriting and it is not likely from him.

74. See the next section of this chapter.

75. Chiniquy gives extracts in *50 Years* from these yet undiscovered letters dated December 1856, [March 1857] which arrived 1 April and 29 May 1857. It is not surprising that the originals have not been found since virtually all his early papers were destroyed in the 1892 burning of his home.

76. S. Smith, *Pastor Chiniquy* (London, 1908), pp. 48-9.

3. REBEL PRIEST (1856-58)

dictating the Brassard retraction.[77] In any event he lost the support of his friend, if Chiniquy printed the supposed letters from Brassard, despite the latter's requests that they be kept confidential. Brassard was forced to make a choice. Naturally he chose his church and calling.[78]

In 1855 the Brothers of Christian Schools were persuaded to take charge of the new school in St. Anne. When the initial excommunication of Chiniquy occurred, the Brothers were put in a quandary. Although Bishop O'Regan insisted that they leave, cutting all ties with Chiniquy, the teachers tried to act as peacemakers. Brother Facile,[79] their superior in the United States, wrote a forthright letter to O'Regan.[80] He expressed readiness to assist in moving Chiniquy out of St. Anne.

However, Facile thought that O'Regan had insulted his order and included them as part of a plot. Along with Brassard, and even the initial assessment of Desaulniers, Facile believed that the authoritarian bishop was most concerned to do things his own way, even at the expense of demolishing the future for the parish. Facile also expressed sympathy with the plight of the French Catholics in Chicago. The Brothers waited until the spring of 1857 to leave St. Anne.[81] There appears to have been no retraction by Facile despite O'Regan's complaints.

The third cleric to support Chiniquy was an Irish priest in Chicago, Dennis Dunn. Chiniquy recounts that they had an initial rapport because they both supported temperance.[82] Chiniquy's autobiography pictures Dunn as more sympathetic to Bishop Van de Velde than to

---

77. *50 Years*, p. 764 for the accusation; Bp. Bourget to Brassard, 1 April 1857 (**ACAM** RLB 10:78-9).

78. A letter to Mailloux in 4 April 1859 (**ASQ** 50:16j), shows that Brassard was disillusioned with Chiniquy's obstinacy yet still protested the handling of him by Church authorities. He also had decided not to talk about Chiniquy to any one.

79. His name before taking orders was Bernard Rabut (1800-1877); see Voisine, *Les Frères des Écoles Chrétiennes*, vol. 1, (Quebec, 1987), pp. 220-24.

80. Facile to Bp. O'Regan, 19 February 1857 (**ACAM** 402.102, 857-13).

81. Trudel, p. 191.

82. *50 Years*, p. 605-6.

O'Regan,[83] even though O'Regan appointed Dunn as Vicar General for Chicago Diocese.

Dunn next appears in the Chiniquy story long after the excommunication. He visited Chiniquy to attempt reconciliation in 1858, during the interregnum that followed O'Regan's departure. While the exact details remain unclear, there is no doubt that Dunn was very sympathetic to Chiniquy's suffering. Vicar General Matthew Dillon of Chicago privately called his fellow Vicar General, Dunn, "a great Chiniquy man and a man in whom you can have no confidence."[84] Dunn's enthusiasm for the reconciliation, and especially his public declaration of peace in St. Anne, horrified Mailloux and Dillon.

When the reconciliation ultimately failed, Mailloux attacked Dunn's compromising actions.[85] Dunn's acts of support for Chiniquy had been cited in the newspapers.[86] Quebec's envoy felt that Dunn should lose his title of Vicar General and even be excommunicated.[87]

Dunn never retracted his actions, intended to support an apparently mistreated cleric, but he did dissociate himself from any open rebellion.[88] The new Bishop Duggan again appointed Dunn as Vicar General, only to end up in a disastrous conflict with him.[89] Tragically Dunn died an excommunicated Catholic after his own rebellion.[90]

It would be fruitless to estimate the numbers of Catholic clergy who supported Chiniquy. Certainly he was not without clerical sympathizers ready to question the bishop's opinion, in the early days of his excommunication. Eventually it boiled down to a choice between the opinion of one man and the entire Catholic Church. No priest left with Chiniquy.

---

83. Ibid., p. 606.
84. Dillon to Mailloux, 30 March 1858 (**ASQ** 50:19i).
85. Mailloux to Bp. Duggan, 24 July 1858 (**ASQ** 50:11u).
86. *Av*, 25 May 1858, p. 1; *SC*, 28 May 1858 p. 2.
87. Desaulniers to Champeaux, the Saturday before Easter [1858] (**ASQ** 50:2).
88. Dunn to Godefroi Lefevre, 10 August 1858 (**ASQ** 50:13ad).
89. See the closing section of this chapter.
90. See Gaffey, "Patterns" (*Church History*, 1973) for a vindication of Dunn.

3. REBEL PRIEST (1856-58)
RECONCILIATION ATTEMPTS

In the 1850s, just prior to the costly American Civil War, battle imagery was ready at hand in Illinois. The St. Anne historical booklet of 1976[91] uses the intriguing comprehensive categorization of "Local and National Civil War" to comprise both the local schism of Chiniquy and the War between the Union and the Confederacy.

Yet several times Chiniquy expressed a loyalty to the Catholic Church and the desire "to make all the sacrifices possible to achieve peace, except for those sacrifices which would require me to betray my conscience or my character."[92] The Catholic hierarchy in Canada was also praying for such a settlement. These were hopeful signs.

A first peace delegation sent by Montreal Bishop Bourget was composed of Chiniquy's old friend Brassard and a former Nicolet schoolmate, Isaac Desaulniers,[93] then director of the St. Hyacinthe seminary.[94] This pair went first to Bishop O'Regan and then to St. Anne at the end of November 1856.

Stunning results were achieved. Desaulniers wrote out a submission in French, which proved acceptable to Chiniquy. The excommunicated Chiniquy then copied it into English with minor adjustments. At a public meeting to celebrate the peace, Chiniquy agreed that he would leave St. Anne and attempted to get the laity to sign a submission as well. According to Brassard[95] and Chiniquy, the three priests agreed

---

91. Meier, *The Saga of St. Anne* (St. Anne, 1976), p. 51.
92. Chiniquy to Brisard, 16 March 1856 (**ASQ** 50:1). This refers to the Spink conflict but the idea was repeated several times in different contexts of this 1856-8 period.
93. Chiniquy mentions the friendship in *Av*, 26 May 1849, p. 1. See *DCB*, vol. 9, p. 465. Lesieur-Désaulniers, Isaac-Stanislas.
94. *50 Years*, p. 738, agrees that this was an excellent choice.
95. Brassard to Mailloux, 24 March 1857 (**ASQ** 50:2b). This letter is very critical of Desaulniers and Bp. O'Regan. It supports Chiniquy's version while decrying his rebellion.

that if the submission failed, all three would go together to appeal to the Archbishop in St. Louis.

To the despair of the delegation, O'Regan refused the submission because he thought it expressed inadequate repentance. Desaulniers' pleaded to accept the submission, at least provisionally, and get Chiniquy out of St. Anne. The bishop declined. Instead O'Regan expected Desaulniers to return to St. Anne and achieve total success, clearing O'Regan's name completely. Desaulniers complained in private to Bishop Bourget but in the end the Quebec emissary had to obey. He had no expectation of success.[96] Chiniquy immediately refused the new comprehensive retraction proposed by O'Regan since it contained "lies".[97]

This first attempt at reconciliation in 1856 served only to envenom the situation. Chiniquy supporters branded Desaulniers a Judas and a traitor. His continued presence at Bourbonnais as interim priest enraged them. From a reluctant servant of the bishop, Desaulniers soon became a determined warrior against the Chiniquy schism. The failed submission became public. Both sides provided ample interpretation of the motives of all concerned.[98] A confused public became even more perplexed.

Chiniquy initiated a reconciliation plan through Bishop Pinsoneault in May 1857.[99] In June, Mailloux proposed one creative reconciliation plan. Then he served as reluctant intermediary for another conditional submission by Chiniquy.[100] Nothing came of those attempts. Both Chiniquy and the Quebec Bishops (primarily Bourget) professed a desire for peace but maintained their aggressive language. By the time a peace letter arrived, often another action or statement had widened the

---

96. Desaulniers to Bp. Bourget, 28 November 1856 (**ACAM** 402.102, 1856-18).

97. Chiniquy to Moreau, 26 February 1857, p. 42 (**ASQ** 52:5f). The retraction can be found as the undated document held by the **ACAM** (402.102, 858-9) which has been classified, mistakenly, with 1858 documents.

98. For example, *Av*, 26 December 1856, pp. 1-2; 1 May 1857, pp .2-3.

99. Chiniquy to Bp. Bourget, 10 May 1857 (**ACAM** 402.102, 857-34).

100. See the undated account [c23 June 1857] of his interview with Chiniquy (**ASQ** 50:14L), and, for the conditions which Chiniquy insisted on, see **ASQ** 50:2L verso.

3. REBEL PRIEST (1856-58)

gap. Throughout this process O'Regan was not only inflexible but was rankled by any advice or initiatives from Quebec.

O'Regan went to Rome to attempt to resign. Meanwhile the interim administrator for Chicago managed to play an important role in the Chiniquy affair. Bishop Clement Smyth[101] of Dubuque, Iowa had jurisdiction of Chicago for only six months in 1857-1858. He was another fairly young Irish bishop replacing a pioneer French bishop.[102] In Dubuque, Smyth, like O'Regan, ran into problems with French clergy who felt displaced. He also faced pressure in his own diocese for his strong stance favouring the Union side.[103]

According to Vicar General Mailloux, Smyth possessed a pastoral rather than a disciplinary character.[104] His distance from the context of St. Anne, on the one hand, and, on the other hand, his open ear were very important elements in the Chiniquy crisis.

The final peace plan was a project of Dennis Dunn or possibly interim Bishop Smyth.[105] Profiting from O'Regan's departure, the Vicar General offered to accompany Chiniquy to Dubuque in order to submit to Bishop Smyth. Again Chiniquy signed a submission and peace was seemingly made.[106] Dunn announced the good news on March 28th,

---

101. 1810-1865. He was a Cistercian superior before becoming Bp. of Dubuque in May 1857. From November 1857 until early June 1858 he was the designated administrator of Chicago Diocese (*Catholic Encyclopædia*, 5:180 and *New Catholic Encyclopædia* (Toronto, 1967), v. 4, col. 1084).

102. This was a trend shown in the 1850s in the dioceses of Dubuque and Chicago and later in Detroit.

103. In 1865, shortly after his stagecoach was set on fire by anti-Unionists, Bp. Smyth died.

104. Mailloux notes appended to letter from Father Louis Cartuyvels of 28 May 1858 (**ASQ** 50:11f). This tendency was seen as a weakness for the conflict with Chiniquy.

105. *50 Years*, pp. 776-7.

106. See Trudel, p. 193 for the content. For the original see **ASQ** 50:14h. *50 Years*, p. 778, gives a truncated version.

1858 to the St. Anne parish, and then Chiniquy went off for a retreat at Notre Dame, Indiana.

Once again the public announcement of reconciliation appeared just before denials by the bishop. Testimonials given for Chiniquy's character were now deemed insufficient. A fresh accusation of murder or at least being an accessory to a murder arose so the original excommunication still applied. Once again the accusations surfaced that the other side was just playing a game of either mock submission[107] or mock acceptance[108] in order to embarrass the other. Would the confusion never cease?

In retrospect, it seems that a reasonable peace could have been maintained if O'Regan had accepted the Desaulniers-Brassard plan. This probably would have salvaged the priest and his parish. O'Regan would not have had to restore Chiniquy to St. Anne. Perhaps back in Quebec, with greater supervision, Chiniquy could have found some place in the Catholic Church.[109] Instead the reconciliation attempts turned into Catholic missions to undermine Chiniquy's credibility and influence.

CATHOLIC ANTI-CHINIQUY MISSIONS

The quelling of the Chiniquy schism was of utmost importance for the Quebec church. Bishop Larocque feared "Chiniquyism" even in St. Hyacinthe.[110] In Illinois, Bishop O'Regan was out of favour with the local French Catholics as well as being chronically short of French priests. While he wanted total control, O'Regan often pleaded with Quebec bishops for reinforcements. Finances and personnel were perpetually lacking for these requests despite the general acknowledgement of the

---

107. Mailloux to Thomas Biggs, 11 March 1861, p. 5 (**ASQ** 50:20).
108. *MW,* 19 May 1858, p. 316. Chiniquy gives his full account in Chiniquy to Cazeau, 8-22 April 1858 (**AAQ** EU VII 140).
109. However this outcome would seem unlikely. See Chapter 8.
110. Bp. Larocque to Mailloux, 19 April 1858 (**ASQ** 50:11L).

3. REBEL PRIEST (1856-58)

vital importance of this schism for the Church in Quebec. In their letters to Illinois Quebec bishops offered, instead, many prayers and good wishes along with requests for the latest news.

Isaac Desaulniers, after having agreed to a short embassy to St. Anne, was conscripted as Bourbonnais priest from November 1856 until June 1857. He provided a continuous stream of letters to Bourget about the situation. Desaulniers was caught between O'Regan and Chiniquy.[111] The rebel priest's impenitent aggressive attacks on Bishop O'Regan incensed Desaulniers enough for him to defend the bishop. Brassard blamed his former partner, Desaulniers, for declaring war on Chiniquy, and using just the method that would harden the rebel priest in his resolve.[112]

Nevertheless slowly the St. Hyacinthe cleric, Desaulniers, recuperated followers of Chiniquy in the surrounding area and relieved them of their excommunication.[113] For his efforts, Desaulniers shared the accusations hurled at the Chicago bishop.[114] After his departure, there were diametrically opposed accounts of his triumphant or ignominious farewell.[115]

Finally Desaulniers was relieved as priest by Jean-Baptiste Champeaux and Vicar General Alexis Mailloux. The former did not last long and attracted even more venom than his predecessor.[116] He managed in particular to alienate the local French paper, the *Journal d'Illinois*.

The arrival of Mailloux indicates the high importance accorded to the mission.[117] Mailloux had been a fellow worker for Temperance with

---

111. See his letters of 26-28 November 1856 (**ACAM** 402.102, 856-18).
112. Brassard to Mailloux, 24 March 1857 (**ASQ** 50:2b).
113. A total of 100 was reported in *Av*, 1 April 1857, p. 1.
114. *Av*, 1 June 1857, p. 3. These are resolutions from a public meeting in Kankakee. Also *CT*, 6 June 1857 from the French group in Chicago.
115. Compare *CT*, 11 June with 22 June 1857.
116. Mailloux to Quebec Diocese, 27 March 1857 (**AAQ**, 7 CM, E.U., VII:2), found him to be unsuited to the task.
117. Archbp. Baillargeon to Mailloux, 11 February 1857 (**ASQ** 50:13y) for his commissioning; Bp. Prince to Mailloux, 19 January 1858 (ASQ 50:13t); Bp. Larocque to Mailloux, 19 April 1858 (**ASQ** 50:11L).

Chiniquy and shared an interest in colonization.[118] Like his predecessor Desaulniers, Mailloux became mired in Illinois, with no one to relieve him. His term lasted five long years until 1862.

The confusing, tense, and prolonged battle with Chiniquy required someone with knowledge of Chiniquy, pastoral experience, determination, irreproachable morality and the confidence of both the bishop of Chicago and the bishops of Canada. Mailloux matched this description. Also he provided a needed continuity, as the responsibility for Chicago Diocese was transferred from Bishop O'Regan to Smyth to Duggan. In addition, Mailloux provided a needed encyclopaedic documentation of the conflict.[119]

French-Canadian bishops kept in close contact with Mailloux and all assured him that there would be rewards in heaven for his great efforts to stem the schism. The Vicar General, known for his ultramontanism, his temperance crusades, his colonization and his anti-Protestant manual (the same interests as Chiniquy), became the focal point in the battle for the hearts of French Catholics in the American midwest.

Apart from the brief reconciliation effort previously mentioned, Mailloux engaged in both a defensive and an offensive battle with the rebel priest. He gathered data of Chiniquy's misdemeanours and wrote articles for the *Courrier du Canada* to counteract pro-Chiniquy material. Organized pressure was coordinated against the Chiniquy supporters in the form of social isolation of schismatics, heart-rending pleas from Canadian relatives, and repeated proclamations of the terrible eternal effects of excommunication.

Chicago French Catholics asked Desaulniers and Mailloux to help them resolve their problems with the bishop. They were disappointed when

---

118. Chiniquy complains about Mailloux's emigration position in his letter to J.C. Chapais, 29 March 1856 (Barnard, *Mémoires*, vol. 2, p. 130). The Mailloux plan to colonize the Eastern Townships of Quebec however received episcopal approval.

119. His collection, found in the **ASQ** 50-54 (the last two have been removed or lost), remains the main source for this period, since Chicago Diocese conserved no file on the rebel priest and Chiniquy's own collection was burned.

3. REBEL PRIEST (1856-58)

the members of the French Catholic mission to Illinois consistently took the bishop's side.[120] Mailloux was accused of turning emigrants away from Illinois, bribing witnesses to testify against Chiniquy and even collecting the lies of prostitutes.[121] Chiniquy supporters viewed the Quebec mission to Illinois as the source of all the divisions in the County. At the same time Bishop Smyth reproached Mailloux for conspiring with Dillon to censure the bishop's actions in reconciling Chiniquy.[122] At points, Mailloux felt isolated and desperate.[123]

In general, Mailloux appears to have engaged in an honest uncompromising battle.[124] He agreed with the hard line of Bishop O'Regan that Chiniquy could not be trusted and that he must repent of all his errors, in writing, before resolution was possible. Mailloux scuttled the Smyth-Dunn attempt to resolve the issue by sending a letter that pointed out Chiniquy's previous offences in Quebec.[125]

Mailloux's most remarkable documentation was his transcription of sexual allegations by Godefroi Lambert and his wife Marie. When Mailloux raised this issue locally, there was hostile reaction from Chiniquy supporters. From that point on, the allegations were circulated only in private among the bishops.[126]

Mailloux did have setbacks. He failed to convince the bishops to charge Chiniquy in a religious court. He also failed to recover Chiniquy or the St. Anne parish. Nonetheless, he did firmly re-establish the

---

120. *Av*, 15 October 1857, p. 1.

121. *Av*, 12 December 1857, pp. 1-2.

122. Bp. Smyth to Mailloux, 7 April 1858 (**ASQ** 50:14j).

123. He even imagined a Catholic conspiracy against him in his notes after the letter Cartuyvels to Mailloux, 28 May 1858 (**ASQ** 50:11f). Also see Trudel, p. 234, footnote 47.

124. Brassard however disliked his inquisitorial approach: Brassard to Mailloux, 4 April 1859 (**ASQ** 50:16j).

125. Mailloux to Bp. Smyth, 28 March 1858 (**ASQ** 20i).

126. Auclair to Mailloux, 5 August 1858 (**ASQ** 50:9b) gives the reactions of Bp. Baillargeon and then states their reasons for not publishing the allegations.

Roman Catholic church as the primary allegiance for almost all the French in Bourbonnais and many others in Kankakee County.

By the time Mailloux left, Chiniquy had moved from being a dissident Catholic to a Christian Catholic to a Chicago Presbyterian to a Canadian Presbyterian. Mailloux promoted an extraordinary anti-Chiniquy coalition: Rev. Moses Staples of the evangelical Kankakee Presbyterian church, Rev. Thomas Biggs - a high Anglican from England - and himself. Mailloux contributed the copious records needed to accuse Chiniquy in English newspapers.[127]

Faced with all this Chiniquy demonstrated either tremendous courage or demonic determination according to one's viewpoint. He writes of the apostate situation:

> the poor suspended Priest! Alas! What will become of him? The laughing stock of the ungodly, mocked by children, a public scandal. He no longer has a place in society; death would be a blessing for him; he ardently desires it. This priesthood, so great, so sublime ... for which he has sacrificed all ... Dreadful despair haunts his soul ... Where will this suspended Priest find Friends! And when we think that a host of excellent Priests are suspended each year on the basis of vague suspicions, accusations without evidence and even more often for having spoken truth to a bishop!![128]

Most individuals would have crumpled long before the end. Threats, accusations, apparent betrayals, and almost unanimous Quebec pressure did not stop Chiniquy as he faced a new bishop.

Bishop James Duggan,[129] the fourth bishop of Chicago, was its most problematic bishop. Irish born, he had been administrator of Chicago Diocese after Van de Velde and before O'Regan. He was chosen as bishop

---

127. Mailloux to Biggs, 11 March 1861 (**ASQ** 50:20) provides a good summary of the situation from Mailloux's viewpoint.

128. Chiniquy to the *Journal de Québec*, 2 February 1857 (**ASQ** 50:1j), p. 22 (my translation). It is also found in the *Persécutions* pamphlet.

129. Duggan (1825-1899) was Chicago bishop 1858-70 (*Catholic Encyclopædia*, 2:654-5; *New Catholic Encyclopædia*, 3:560).

3. REBEL PRIEST (1856-58)

of the troublesome diocese in 1858, only ten years after his ordination, at the age of 44.

Duggan retained popular Dennis Dunn as Vicar General. In 1866 the bishop closed St. Mary of the Lake University after recurring problems. In response, Dunn, Father McMullen and the rest of the board pursued a protracted and dangerous appeal to Rome against their bishop.[130] This resulted in the suspension of Dunn and three other priests. Dunn refused to retract and lived his last days in disgrace, poverty and in an excommunicate state. He was even harassed on his deathbed by Duggan.

Figure 28 Bishop Duggan (Garraghan, *The Catholic Church*, p. 181a)

Meanwhile Duggan attempted suicide twice and was finally committed to a mental asylum from 1869 until his death in 1899. Archbishop Kenrick attributed the insanity to the conspiracy of clergy against Duggan.

In his role as the new Chicago bishop, James Duggan visited St. Anne in August 1858, accompanied and scripted by Mailloux. The rebel priest had claimed for two years that he had not been suspended nor validly excommunicated. Duggan read out the original notification from 1856 and declared that in any event, he now definitively excommunicated Chiniquy and all his supporters. This brave performance was Duggan's only real contact with Chiniquy. He did cut through past confusion to force a choice on Chiniquy and his St. Anne parishioners. All avenues of appeal had led to nothing. Would they humble themselves and return to the Catholic church?

---

130. We follow Gaffey for most of this account of Bp. Duggan.

THE CONTROVERSIAL CONVERSION OF CHARLES CHINIQUY

4

FRANCO-AMERICAN PROTESTANT (1858-87)

CATHOLIC CHRISTIAN (1858-59)

Bishop Duggan came to St. Anne on August 3, 1858 and pronounced a definitive sentence of excommunication on Chiniquy and his followers. On the 22nd of the same month, the *Église catholique chrétienne* (Christian Catholic Church) was founded.

The traumatic events of the second failed submission back in April of the same year had prepared the Chiniquy group for a complete break. Chiniquy claimed that he had a conversion experience just after that Dubuque meeting in April. Chapter 8 will examine that claim. Whatever the St. Anne pastor reported to his congregation after Dubuque, there was outrage and widespread determination to resist.[1] While Chiniquy expressed some hope of reconciliation in May,[2] he was not prepared to concede anything.

---

1. Chiniquy to *Av*, 18 April 1858, p. 2 (printed 25 May).
2. Chiniquy to *JI*, 6 May 1858 (copied in *MW*, 19 May 1858, p. 316).

Montreal Witness
September 4, 1858

FATHER CHINIQUY ESTABLISHING A NEW CHURCH NEITHER PROTESTANT NOR ROMAN.

Last month, just about the time that Father Chiniquy and the newly-appointed Bishop Duggan were confronted publicly at Ste. Anne of Illinois, two priests were on their way from the Diocese of Quebec,—the Rev. Messrs. Alain and Gingras, to labor against the schism. From these gentlemen we have now, in the *Courrier du Canada*, a full statement, from the Roman Catholic side, of the exciting scenes recently enacted amongst the French Canadian colonists of Illinois. The important announcement is first made that "since Sunday, the 22nd of August last, the schism of Illinois has become the heresy of Illinois ¡" a new development for which the priests bless God as rendering Father Chiniquy hereafter far less dangerous to the faith of French Canadians. To understand the importance attached by Romanists to the alleged change, one should bear in mind that a schism relates only to the discipline of the church, while a heresy touches the doctrine. Hitherto Mr. Chiniquy had ever professed his attachment to the Roman Catholic Church, and indeed, but two or three months since, in a public document, he professed a blind submission to the Council of Trent, which is the official embodiment of all the worse features of Romanism. He would be a better Catholic than the Bishops themselves, whom he accused only of unfairness in certain proceedings towards himself. As he retained in principle the whole of Romanism, he and his party could not be accused of heresy, but only of schism. But now for the first time, on Sunday before last, he has publicly renounced the Roman Catholic Church and her doctrines, thus becoming a heretic, and as such he would be lawful game to burn at the stake if Rome had the power.

But let us hear the Quebec priests. We translate from the *Courrier* :—

"Since Sunday, the 22nd August, the schism of Illinois has become the heresy of Illinois, for on that day the unfortunate Mr. Chiniquy has declared in a public meeting called by himself in the Court House of Kankakee, that he separated himself from the Roman Church to found a new sect which he calls the Christian Catholic Church, separated from Rome and Bishops. If we deplore from the bottom of our soul, the loss of Mr. Chiniquy and of the poor victims he carries along with him, it is on the other hand salutary in the interest of truth and religion that Mr. Chiniquy should have resorted to an extremity which can leave no doubt in the least penetrating minds and the least candid hearts."

After stating how Bishop O'Regan went to Rome to resign a charge which the irritation of French Canadians had rendered impracticable to him, and how the "Apostate Chiniquy" was constantly and make penance, go and expiate the abominations and sacrileges of which you are guilty ¡ and if your penitence be sincere and genuine, I promise that God will forgive and the church receive you as a lost child found again.

"Monseigneur Duggan was interrupted several times, but calm, coolness and dignity never forsook him, he did not fear threats nor even death. After thus fulfilling his mission the Bishop moved towards the steps of the scaffold in order to withdraw, but at that time he was surrounded by the partisans of Mr. Chiniquy who were shouting and insulting him. The Bishop remained impassable until the Sheriff stepping forward, took him under his protection, and secured his departure against violence.

" A few days after this scene, on Sunday, 22nd August, Mr. Chiniquy in the court-house justified his past conduct before a public meeting composed mostly of Protestants. He renewed all his former insults against the Bishops of Canada and their priests, flattered the prejudices of his hearers, and told them that the Church of Rome is not the religion of Jesus Christ, but the religion of Bishops,— that it was only during his childhood that he shared the ideas which Catholic priests and bishops impart to the people concerning Protestants and Protestantism ¡—that only one consolation remained to him, the Bible, and only one thing to do, to separate himself from the Bishops and the Roman religion. He said, moreover, he was consummating an immense sacrifice, as people would call him Protestant—a name not in favor amongst his country people ; and he added that since he was no longer a Roman Catholic, he would be called a Christian Catholic."

The Quebec priests have brought back with them statistics of the numerical strength of the schism in Illinois. At Bourbonnois there are about 500 French Canadian families ; all now, without exception, are Roman Catholic, and Mr. Chiniquy has not there a single partisan left. At Ste. Anne, the stronghold and head-quarters of Father Chiniquy, 200 families follow him, while 70 are Roman Catholic. At Kankakee, 25 families are for Mr. Chiniquy, and 25 against. In each of three other small localities, Mr. Chiniquy can reckon about 10 families, all the rest being sound. Moreover, the two Quebec priests assert that the schism and heresy are daily and rapidly losing numbers.

Father Chiniquy cannot expect any amount of success in the establishment of a new Catholic Church not Roman. Many priests, such as the notorious Abbé Chatel, have attempted it before him and failed. A contest between a priest and his bishop, however damaging it may be to Romanism, is powerless to raise a living Church to God. It is only the great ideas of faith, gratuitous salvation and other fundamental truths of Christianity which can effect any permanent good, and which were the main springs at the time of the great Reformation. But on these Chiniquy has been thus far silent, and we have the unsuspected testimony of his adversaries, that up to a few days, and throughout his contest, he professed no heresy, and was fully agreed with Romanism on all doctrines. It is only after this Hierarchy have hopelessly cut him off that he disagrees with Romish doctrine, and this should repress too sanguine hopes of the heretic priest, until new evidence is supplied of the evangelical soundness of his schism. Before he can be initiated to the confidence of the evangelical community as a decidedly converted and trustworthy man, some explanation will be required on his part concerning the grave charges of insincerity and systematic falsehood proffered so publicly

Figure 29   New of the "Catholic Christian Church", 1858

4. FRANCO-AMERICAN PROTESTANT (1858-87)

Later in the summer of 1858 Quebec Baptist leaders Narcisse Cyr and Theodore Lafleur visited Chiniquy, incognito. They attempted to show the excommunicate that his true home lay in Protestantism.[3] This visit was known to Mailloux. To him it confirmed Chiniquy's apostasy and his subsequent dangers to Catholicism.[4]

Another crucial element in the story of the schism took place in 1858 with the first of three consecutive years of poor harvests in St. Anne. Many debts were called due by loyal Catholics, which bankrupted some of Chiniquy's followers. Who could help in these financial difficulties? Chiniquy travelled to the Eastern United States and eventually raised over $1,200 for relief from Protestant sources. This came principally from Philadelphia where he attended the inter-denominational prayer meeting, known for promoting evangelical revival.[5] Thus began a fundraising campaign that reached all over the United States and even to France.[6]

All those who joined the new Catholic Christian church were now aware that they were personally excommunicated from any Roman Catholic Church. They were therefore deprived of the sacraments, marriage, spiritual contact with any other Catholics and, finally, Catholic burial.[7] The final break was facilitated by two years of uncertainty and independence, in between the questionable excommunication and the definitive one.

---

3. Mailloux to Quebec Diocese, 27 July 1858 (**AAQ**, 7 CM, E.U., VII:3 4). *40 Years*, p. 185-6, credits Lafleur with great influence for his conversion. Lafleur, *Historical Sketch* (Montreal, 1885), pp. 29-30, provides the best, though skimpy, detail on the relationship; also *GL Annual Report* (Montreal, 1899), p. 11.

4. Mailloux to Quebec Diocese, 27 July 1858 (**AAQ** EU VII 34), p.10 refers to them as "Swiss" and fears a visit to Quebec sponsored by them.

5. *SC*, 19 August 1858, p. 2.

6. See *Presby*, 31 December 1859, p. 2 (a diverse list of contributors), and also 7 January 1860, p. 2.

7. Édouard Langevin to St. Anne Catholics, 31 October 1856 (**ASQ** 50:1f; a copy appears in *Av*, 18 December 1856, p. 2).

The new denomination was deemed suspect by some Protestants.[8] At the same time for Catholics, as expressed for Bishop Larocque, the poor sad Chiniquy had descended to the level of mud along with the foreign heretics (often labelled the Swiss), whom Chiniquy had formerly done violence to.[9] Chiniquy himself contrasted the religion of the bishops with that of the Gospel or the Bible.[10] He was undeterred by insults with the term "Protestant".[11] Unfortunately, the basis of the new Catholic Christian Church, including the articles of belief and the organization, do not seem to have been recorded for posterity![12]

We do have a transcription from a document one year later:[13]

"Christian Catholic Church at St. Anne, State of Illinois, Kankakee County

At a meeting of the (French-Canadian) inhabitants of St. Anne in Kankakee County, State of Illinois, on the 3rd day of September 1859, in (accordance with) a former notice given at the Chapel of the Christian Catholic Church of St. Anne, for the purpose of organizing a religious society,

• on a motion of Reverend Charles Chiniquy, seconded by Désiré Drolet, Louis Mercier was unanimously elected President;

• on a motion of Moise Langelier, seconded by Michel Drolet, Georges Gauthier was elected Secretary;

---

8. *MW*, 4 September 1858, p. 564.
9. Bp. Larocque to Mailloux, 6 September 1858 (**ASQ** 50:13ah).
10. *MW*, 15 September 1858, p. 588.
11. *MW*, 4 September 1858, p. 564; *CT*, 4 December 1858, p. 1.
12. Among the principal sources the *JI* does not mention the new group, *Av* had ceased to exist and *CT* had dropped Chiniquy in its preoccupation with the American election while the copies of *SC* have not been discovered yet. *MW* is available but it relied on news from the other four newspapers.
13. Serge Thériault, *Msgr. René Vilatte: Community Organizer of Religion (Berkeley, 2006)*, p. 218-219. "Record of the Christian Catholic Church", filed 13 September 1859 at Kankakee Court House names the trustees one year after inception (from a copy among Chiniquy papers in the possession of Lois Meier of Kankakee).

4. FRANCO-AMERICAN PROTESTANT (1858-87)

• *on a motion of Joseph Martin, seconded by Anselme Robillard, it was unanimously resolved that this society be known and designated as the Christian Catholic Church;*

• *on a motion of Abraham Pelletier, seconded by Achille Chiniquy, it was unanimously resolved that there be elected for the government and management of this said Church Society, ten trustees, whose term of office shall last for one year from this day and until their successors in office shall have been elected by this said Society;*

• *on a motion of Magloire Desmarteaux, seconded by Louis Mercier, the following persons were proposed and unanimously elected for the management and direction of the Christian Catholic Church:*

Reverend Charles Chiniquy, Michel Allais, Louis Mercier, Anselme Robillard, Thomas Lortie, Moise Langelier, Abraham Pelletier, Joseph Martin, Michel Drolet, Achille Chiniquy.

The above named persons having accepted the said office of trustees have hereunto set their hands and seal: Charles Chiniquy, Anselme Robillard, Louis Mercier, Moise Langelier, Abraham Pelletier, Michel Drolet, Joseph Martin, Michel Allais (being absent has not signed), Louis Mercier, President, Achille Chiniquy, Secretary.

REVEREND CHINIQUY ELECTED PRESIDENT OF THE BOARD

At a meeting of the Board of Trustees, on the 10th day of September 1859, the Reverend Charles Chiniquy was elected President unanimously.

FILED FOR RECORDS IN KANKAKEE COUNTY, DISTRICT COURT, ILLINOIS *Subscribed and sworn before me this 13th day of September 1859.*

Philip Worchester, Clerk"

By November 1858, Mailloux was becoming very disturbed at the "sacrilege" occurring in the St. Anne church. Catholic practice was being distorted there with impunity. Mailloux tried to convince the bishop to seize the building, which, by rights, belonged only to the

Catholic Diocese and to its obedient followers.[14] Loyal Catholics had even been threatened with lawsuits to force them to pay their pew rents.[15]

Among the gradual transformations were the disappearance of auricular confession, statues, holy water, Latin masses, fast days and vestments. No longer did they believe in purgatory, indulgences, mediation of the saints including Mary, and papal infallibility. Bible studies became prominent in many worship gatherings. The Bible evaluated every doctrine and practice with, presumably, the input of Protestant interpretations. Already in 1852 the precedents were present in St. Anne for group Bible study and critique.[16] Now there were no external restraints.

This transformation was not as rapid as some reformations[17] but it followed very much in the line of Protestant developments.[18] Chiniquy spoke of his inspirations: "In order not to be guided by my own experience, which is nothing at all, and my spirit ... I studied what the great Reformers had done, and tried, as well as I could, to follow them."[19] As Chiniquy appealed for Protestant funds, the parish had to pass closer scrutiny. The Catholic Christian Church impressed most of the initially sceptical analysts. An official for the American and Foreign Christian Union (AFCU) wrote:

> I consider most of them as genuinely converted; many others are reading the Bible with the earnest desire to discover the way of salvation; I had feared that the movement was motivated mostly by hate against bishops and priests, but I found, on the contrary,

---

14. Mailloux to Bp. Duggan, 19 November 1858 (**ASQ** 50:11v).

15. Mailloux to Dillon, 27 October 1857 (**ASQ** 50:3). This paralleled actions in Quebec against Protestant converts.

16. *50 Years*, pp. 552-3.

17. Marsault, *De Rome à l'Évangile* (Paris, 1908), p. 96 compares St. Anne with Guillaume Farel's reformation in Switzerland in 1530.

18. *The Life and Labours* (Glasgow, 1861), pp. 19-25, provides an early account of the process with Chiniquy trying not to move too quickly for the congregation. Also see *50 Years*, pp. 802-808.

19. *Life and Labours* (Glasgow, 1861), p. 19. *50 Years*, p. 805 mentions the influence of Calvin and Knox.

4. FRANCO-AMERICAN PROTESTANT (1858-87)

very different motivations. In fact, I regard this community, as a whole, as superior in its spiritual aspects to most of our Christian communities.[20]

It was reported that over 1,400 attended the first communion in St. Anne where both bread and wine were served. 500 of them partook of the elements. 300 attended Sunday School that day.[21]

It seems that Chiniquy himself rapidly adopted a generic evangelical Protestant theology. There is no record that he questioned any Protestant belief after 1858. Nevertheless he was in no rush to align his group with any particular Protestant denomination. Many different groups had helped in the community's financial needs. There was great confusion as to which Protestant denomination was best.[22] Roman Catholic leaders feared that he wanted to start a new denomination to steal away French Canadians.[23] This is quite possible. Chiniquy always retained the term Father or *Père* despite evangelical objections[24] but solely to facilitate evangelism - to relate better to Catholics.[25]

The great contest anticipated by Protestants[26] and feared by Roman Catholics came in early 1859. Chiniquy returned to Lower Canada (Quebec)[27] aiming to win the French populace over to his new cause, the evangelical gospel. While the GL Mission seems to have organized

---

20. Rev. Paillard quoted in *Le père Chiniquy: Le réformateur canadien* (Melun, 1860), p. 10 (my translation). This provides a good early summary. However another evangelical writer described Chiniquy as falling between Catholics and Protestants in *MW*, 12 January 1859, p. 28.
21. [Louis Auger] letter to *SC*, 7 October 1859, p. 3.
22. See the illuminating debate over this issue with Chiniquy's insightful evasion in *40 Years*, pp. 120-125.
23. Jérome Sasseville to Mailloux, 11 February 1859 (**ASQ** 53:1, now missing but reported in Trudel, p. 212).
24. He, himself, opposed it on doctrinal grounds (*MW*, 2 February 1870, p.1).
25. *CC*, 5 (1888), pp. 39-40.
26. *SC*, 28 May 1858, p. 2. Also *Av*, 15 September 1857, p. 1.
27. See "Lettre des Catholiques de Ste. Anne de l'Illinois à leurs frères du Canada" (**AAQ** DM XI-3) announcing the meetings.

much of the lecture tour, a group of young liberal francophones, the *Francs frères*, acted as bodyguards.

Perhaps the two propagandas are at their most contradictory regarding this tour. For Trudel, this was the time of utmost humiliation and rejection for the defrocked priest who had to flee to save his life. For the Anglican Hellmuth[28] and in Chiniquy's interpretation, the power of the Quebec bishops was now broken. This conclusion was drawn from the huge crowds, many converts and large numbers who accepted bibles. Many Catholics did break the bishop's order to not listen to Chiniquy. Some were convinced by Chiniquy's arguments and a few joined a Protestant church. Chiniquy aroused enormous interest, gathering large crowds in Montreal and Quebec, as well as many who visited his hotels for individual talks.

Still Chiniquy did not come close though to breaking the Catholic grip on Quebec. Nor did he spark a new movement. In his parting speech, Chiniquy interpreted the attempts on his life during the tour as a sign of Catholic weakness. He predicted a revolution of the people against their oppression.[29] The ultimate failure of the ex-priest's impact is evident beause it was to be eleven more years before he came back again for an extended period. The expectations had been too high after his amazing success in Illinois.

Besides the debate about how many Chiniquy drew to the Protestant faith, the question of religious liberty arose. Chiniquy encountered death threats, rock throwing and a knife on his tour. Bishop Bourget had written in his pastoral letter to be read in all churches:

> persons have slipped into our midst whose aim it is to propagate this evil spirit which, like a cancer, eats away at the interior of all societies. It is up to you to **oppose, by all the means in your**

---

28. Hellmuth letters, reprinted in *Father Chiniquy, the Reformer of the Far West* (London, c1859), pp. 9-11.

29. Chiniquy to *SC*; printed also in *MW*, 30 March 1859, p. 201.

4. FRANCO-AMERICAN PROTESTANT (1858-87)

power, this flood that threatens to drag us towards a bottomless pit.[30]

Protestants were outraged that another critic of Catholicism was not allowed a chance to speak after Catholic riots had chased away Gavazzi.[31] Long after the events Catholic clergy rejoiced at the violence done to Chiniquy.[32] The Protestant acting mayor of Quebec was condemned by Catholic aldermen and by the papers for having provided an armed escort for Chiniquy. These issues followed Chiniquy for all of the many lecture tours he undertook: the issue of public blasphemy[33] versus freedom of speech, and that of provocation of riots versus the provision of police protection by the municipality. Both sides felt that the legal authorities should put their opponents in prison for their actions. Should the "blasphemer" or those who attacked him be arrested?[34]

In rural areas, Chiniquy was even less successful during this tour. When pressed by sharp advocates to declare if he was a Protestant, he could find no effective answer. Rural priests exploited his association with the 'Swiss' Protestants effectively.

---

30. "Pastoral Letter denouncing Mr. Chiniquy, priest as an apostate", 4 February 1859 (*MEM*, vol. 3, pp. 423-4). The translation and accenting with bold characters is mine. Archbp. Baillargeon was less emotional and more specific in his "Circular Letter against the apostate Chiniquy", 5 February 1859 (*MEQ*, vol.4, pp. 329-30).

31. In 1853. See Sylvain, *Alessandro Gavazzi* (Quebec, 1962).

32. For example Mailloux to Biggs, 11 March 1861 (**ASQ** 50:20), pp. 10-11; Trudel, pp. 213-223.

33. Salman Rushdie would provide somewhat of a modern parallel in Islam although the highest Roman Catholic authorities never explicitly condoned violence. Rather it was deemed understandable, given the situation. The *MW* view was similar for **some** Orange Order violence.

34. Again parallels could be drawn to modern debate over speeches by very militant minority groups or by those militantly opposed to more immigration. It proves very difficult to delineate fair limits to the right of free speech.

Back in Illinois, more controversy was developing. Critics deemed the harvest failures described by Chiniquy to Protestant donors[35] to be frauds. While some Kankakee non-francophones organized a public letter of protest and accusation against Chiniquy's humbug,[36] others claimed that they had investigated and confirmed all his claims.[37] Both sides produced reputable witnesses.

Eventually a mediating explanation was brought forward. This held that exorbitant interest rates on the land were the true problem.[38] Since the emigrant farmers took time to adjust to new conditions, setbacks were common. However, even minor harvest setbacks were devastating due to the debt loads. Over $34,000(U.S.) from Protestant donations was spent for debt relief and provisions, up until September 1860.[39]

Undoubtedly, many St. Anne area residents were in very poor financial straits due to three years of bad harvests.[40] This situation became an opportunity for extensive Protestant involvement in the community. The financial aid broke through suspicions of both the ex-Catholics and the English Protestants. Chiniquy's ability to produce aid strengthened his position.[41]

Another associated conflict was given wide press coverage in Canada. Chiniquy sued an Oblate priest, Father Auguste Brunet, for libel. The

---

35. See for example, in the brochure *Father Chiniquy, Reformer of the Far West* (London, c1860).

36. *KG*, 28 November 1859 and 8 December 1859.

37. *MW*, 10 September 1859; *SC*, 7 October 1859, p. 3; *MW*, 21 December 1859; *KD*, 25 January 1860. Chiniquy's letter in the *Presby*, 24 December 1859, p. 2, summarizes his eminent witnesses.

38. *MW*, 7 January 1860, p. 11. Mailloux himself confirmed the harvest failure (Mailloux to Quebec Diocese, 27 July 1858, **AAQ** EU VII 34, p. 4).

39. The audited statement appears in *Presby*, 29 September 1860. When funds spent on church construction are included, the amount came to $40,804.07.

40. Even Mailloux admits this in Mailloux to Biggs, 11 March 1861, pp. 3, 14 (**ASQ** 50:20). Chiniquy is blamed for encouraging them to come.

41. See Brettell, "From Catholics" (*Journal of Presbyterian History*, 1985), p. 297, for a Roman Catholic accusation of Chiniquy bribing the destitute into his church.

visiting missionary apparently repeated the old accusation that Chiniquy had burned the Bourbonnais church in 1854. A prolonged court case with appeals ran from December 1858 until April 1860.[42] In the end, Brunet lost. He was given a long prison sentence after he refused the alternative of paying a fine. After four months, local Catholics, outraged at the injustice, broke into the prison and smuggled him across the Canadian border.[43]

With each skirmish Chiniquy dropped in the estimation of loyal Catholics outside St. Anne. He managed to conserve most Protestant support however. He also developed the reputation of being constantly harassed and persecuted by Catholic authorities for his new convictions.

AMERICAN PRESBYTERIAN (1860-62)

Chiniquy and his group composed but a few independent congregations and still possessed the name Catholic. Pressure grew on them to join one of the established denominations, if they wished to secure further financial aid. Throughout his Protestant years, Chiniquy exhibited a common evangelical trait of being somewhat indifferent to denominations. He maintained contacts with many groups, and stressed the need for evangelical unity.[44] Due to his open views, he was falsely reported to have joined both the Baptists[45] and the Anglicans.[46]

---

42. For the legal details see Moore to Chiniquy, 26 November 1893 (SL c.1/3), pp. 7-8 and *KD*, 25 January 1860.

43. Carrière (*RHAF*, 1955), pp. 537-555, is the best account of Brunet's time in Kankakee County.

44. See for a good resume Chiniquy to *Presby*, 29 September 1859 (printed 15 October, p. 2) and in *40 Years*, ch.9.

45. Chiniquy to the *Standard*, 16 April 1873, reproduced in pamphlet form (SL c.1/12), contains Chiniquy's refutation.

46. *MW*, 22 October 1859, p. 676, for Chiniquy's refutation.

Finally, Chiniquy opted for the Presbyterians. This was based on several factors.[47] Apparently the rebel priest had been inspired by Augustine's writings and was surprised to find that the Presbyterian Confession of Faith matched many of those ideas.[48] Calvin and the Huguenots provided a French link in the Presbyterian family. This was important for evangelism of French Catholics in the U.S. or Canada.[49] In addition, the Presbyterian Church was a very strong force in Illinois. It had already helped finance mortgages for the St. Anne property.

On January 31, 1860 Chiniquy, plus his St. Anne and Kankakee congregations, were received into the Chicago Presbytery (Old School).[50] Chiniquy and the congregations insisted on an important concession - that they should swear allegiance only to the Bible, rather than to the Westminster Confession.[51] They also successfully resisted presbytery's suggestion of rebaptism.[52] A Presbyterian committee took over full control of money raised for relief or mission work in St. Anne. In May the ex-priest impressed with his speech at the General Assembly of the American Presbyterians.[53] Then his articles to the *Presbyterian* resulted in donations from virtually every American state.[54]

A honeymoon period lasted for most of that year. However, competition did develop in the form of new congregations of French Episcopalians in Kankakee and French Baptists in St. Anne. Most of these members came from among Chiniquy's converts.

---

47. *MW*, 18 February 1860, pp. 108-9.

48. *Presby*, (Philadelphia) 3 March 1860, p. 2.

49. One could imagine the difficulty for French work in Quebec, of being part of the Anglicans, known as the English church.

50. This was a division between American revivalism and traditional Scottish Presbyterianism. The Chicago Presbytery by majority vote remained in the traditional group which tended to be pro-slavery though most Chicago members opposed slavery.

51. *40 Years*, ch. 18. They did agree with the Confession but did not want to recognize tradition above the Bible.

52. *40 Years*, p. 250.

53. *Presby*, 9 June 1860, p. 1.

54. See the list in *Presby*, 30 June 1860, p. 2. Many were from the Southern US.

4. FRANCO-AMERICAN PROTESTANT (1858-87)

After all his draining experiences, the ex-priest accepted invitations to Scotland and France. Travelling often proved to be Chiniquy's primary source for restoration of health and energy. By August, replacements were found for spiritual guidance in St. Anne and the ex-priest set out by ship for Europe.

For over six months Chiniquy gave talks about the Catholic Church and his own situation. Among others he addressed the Edinburgh meeting for the Tri-Centenary of the Reformation in Scotland,[55] and the *Synode des Églises libres* (Free Church) in France.[56] He managed to speak in 85 localities of Great Britain and in Ireland, as well as to visit Switzerland and Italy. Once again Chiniquy returned with abundant financial donations for his mission, totalling over $10,000.[57]

While Chiniquy was gone, the St. Anne situation fragmented. Theodore Monod, his replacement, accused Chiniquy's brother Achille of shady financial dealings and profane language. When Charles returned to defend his brother, the congregation split. Monod became pastor of a new Second Presbyterian Church of St. Anne but he was not yet finished. He brought charges before Chicago Presbytery against Rev. Chiniquy himself. As usual with Chiniquy, there was a prolonged battle (from May 1861 until June 1862) and no generally accepted decision. Chicago Presbytery acquitted Chiniquy of the charges twice but never pronounced him innocent. The third time he was found guilty and was suspended in June 1862.

These charges never involved sexuality. He allegedly exaggerated (or lied) about his St. Anne school. Chiniquy had called it a college or "seminary" and said that pastoral candidates were being trained there, while in reality it was a secondary school. This wording stems from common usage in French Canada but it was deemed deceptive for

---

55. This was organized by the Scottish Reformation Society for August 1860.

56. This evangelical group led by Théodore Monod Sr. broke away from the official Reformed Church (*Église réformée*). It had links with the Free Church of Scotland and the Evangelical Alliance.

57. Chiniquy letter in *KG*, 17 January 1861.

English donors. Besides these "lies" for fundraising, Chiniquy had been involved in several court cases against Presbyterian clergy. Presbytery's earlier acquittals of Chiniquy had been due to insufficient evidence. These acquittals were overturned when the St. Anne pastor finally became quite obstreperous and refused to cooperate with the committee in a third hearing on the same charges. None of the individual charges look very serious, nor does the accumulation of charges quite accord with Presbyterian polity.

It appears that the central problem was Chiniquy's conspiracy theory about the neighbouring Presbyterian pastors, Moses Staples and Monod.[58] Staples became convinced of financial irregularities going on in the French congregation and cut off funding of St. Anne. Chiniquy was outraged since he himself had done the fundraising. Slanderous letters by St. Anne laity[59] and then a court case against Staples exasperated the presbytery. Chiniquy was a most difficult man to oversee and direct. Other congregational members expanded on his inflammatory ideas and words until virtually irreconcilable divisions developed.

Finally on 10 June 1862, Presbytery deposed Chiniquy as pastor for various charges, summarized as "contumacy", besides the fact that he did not attend the hearing. In fact, on that date Chiniquy was in London, applying to the Canada Presbyterian Church for admission. He had sent his resignation to Chicago Presbytery. A lengthy account was published by a Canadian team of investigators. They detailed their findings, the attempted reconciliations and their eventual acceptance of the "innocent" Chiniquy.[60] Chicago Presbytery protested and planned to issue a rebuttal.[61] After one of Chiniquy's supporters proposed that they allow him

---

58. *50 Years*, p. 821.
59. Felix Masson to the *KG* (against Staples), printed 29 May 1862.
60. Kemp, *The Rev. C. Chiniquy, the Presbytery of Chicago...* (Montreal, 1863). Chiniquy also published his own *Address...on his defence before the Presbytery of Chicago* (Sandwich, 1862).
61. L.M. Stevens, John Faris and Théodore Monod, no title [Prospectus of a book defending Chicago Presbytery against Chiniquy] (Chicago, 1863), 8 p.

4. FRANCO-AMERICAN PROTESTANT (1858-87)

to leave,[62] the Presbytery must have reconsidered, deciding that it was better off without the troublemaker. Time managed to heal the wounds so that, long after, in 1895, Chicago Presbytery received Chiniquy as a speaker. By that time the two Presbyterian congregations in St. Anne had been rejoined and reincorporated into Chicago Presbytery.[63]

Naturally, Catholic accounts emphasize this suspension for insubordination in Chiniquy's first Protestant body.[64] By now he was aged 53 and, whatever the extenuating circumstances, he had been suspended from two (at least) different dioceses, by multiple bishops, and now also by a Protestant presbytery. Alphonse Villeneuve in his usual graphic language comments:

> Even in this sect where corruption reigned and everything was permitted, Chiniquy was found to be too corrupt, too rebellious, too unreasonable. So Chicago Presbytery excommunicated him.[65]

Besides this suspension, Chiniquy chose a dubious tactic designed to clear his name. In the process he united the local French Baptists, Episcopalians and Second Presbyterians against him.[66] Pressure came also from the circumstance that, once again, his church property officially belonged to a church body that had rejected Chiniquy.

PASTOR OF ST. ANNE (1862-87)

Very prominent figures in the Canada Presbyterian Church were appointed to investigate the Chiniquy conflict: Knox Professor W. Caven and Rev. Alexander Kemp. Dr. R. F. Burns was also

---

62. This was the idea of Rev. Alfred Hamilton, a long-time Chiniquy supporter, cited in *Cour*, 27 June 1862, p. 2.
63. Meier, *The Saga* (St. Anne, 1976), p. 11.
64. Trudel, p. 233, notes the parallels with the Bp. O'Regan conflict and also that Protestant biographies are strangely silent on this incident.
65. [Villeneuve], *Honte et mépris* (Montreal, 1875), p. 5 (my translation).
66. *KG*, 6 March 1862. He sent a messenger to trick them into signing a petition which he then twisted to vindicate his statement about the college and candidates for the ministry. Chiniquy justified the trick in *KG*, 13 March 1862.

instrumental in the final acceptance of Chiniquy. Principal Willis of Knox was appointed to the Chiniquy committee along with Caven, Kemp, and W. Gregg, after Chiniquy was accepted as a minister in 1863.[67] While mortgage questions dragged on and full reconciliation with Chicago Presbytery was encouraged regularly by the Synod, the basic status of Chiniquy and his congregation was resolved.[68]

The ex-priest became a standard figure at Canadian Presbyterian synods, recounting stories of converts and pleading for moral and financial support for French work. He was never again to be disciplined (or even charged) or to change denomination. In terms of internal church matters, Chiniquy entered an astonishing, long period of calm and stability.

For most of the rest of his life, Chiniquy was pastor of the St. Anne Presbyterian congregation.[69] No other major crises developed in the Illinois village church life. In 1864, he was married to Euphémie Allard. The couple adopted a daughter and then eventually Euphémie conceived two other daughters.[70] Their residence was expanded so that they could welcome ex-priests for counsel and practical aid.

The St. Anne congregation became one of the biggest churches in the Canadian Presbyterian Church and probably produced more candidates for pastoral or mission work than any other.[71] A local French Protestant school was maintained and financed with Presbyterian money. Eventually, in 1871 the Roman Catholics regained a church base in St. Anne when Father Letellier became the resident priest.[72] No further major local incident was reported between the two faiths.

---

67. *CPC Synod Proceedings*, 1863, pp. 52-6.
68. Summary in *CPC Synod Proceedings*, 1869, pp. lxix-lxx, lxxv.
69. He lived there from 1862-70, 1870-74 and 1880-92.
70. The first baby Charles Jr. died shortly after his birth on February 12th, 1867.
71. 14 missionaries according to *A*, 16 July 1909, p. 5.
72. Meier, *The Saga*, p. 67. See also Savaète, *Mgr Ignace Bourget* (Paris, 1916), pp. 250-252 for Bp. Bourget's successful strategy to recuperate most Kankakee County Catholics. He recruited the St. Viateur Order and the Sisters of the Congregation of Notre Dame to set up schools, turning the county eventually into a centre for Catholic activities.

4. FRANCO-AMERICAN PROTESTANT (1858-87)

Court cases did continue, especially the one over the St. Anne church property. This was finally resolved by a wise compromise in 1874. In addition, months before his marriage, Chiniquy was charged by another woman with "breach of promise to marry". The suit was withdrawn.[73] Then there were several failed suits by Chiniquy's sexton for failure to pay his salary. Achille Chiniquy was arrested for burning the schoolhouse but acquitted. In 1888 when the Chicago, Danville and Vincennes Railway Company tried to get the St. Anne people to pay up for their railroad, the St. Anne pastor gave a speech, which apparently defeated the railway's suit.[74] Chiniquy claimed that there was a pattern of legal harassment by the Catholic Diocese through all these court cases. At any rate he kept his lawyers busy.

A very high proportion of the community moved west to Kansas, Wisconsin or to the west coast of the U.S.[75] Yet the St. Anne congregation remained fairly stable. Chiniquy's reports to Synod concentrated more on his visits to, or correspondence with, Catholics in other parts of the U.S. or Canada. Most of his recorded converts for these years came from outside the Kankakee County area. During these visits away from home he also raised most of the considerable funds needed to finance the congregation and school.

After Chiniquy's stint in Montreal and again after his South Seas tour, St. Anne requested his return as pastor. Chiniquy's ministry to ex-priests took high priority but he was also highly praised as a pastor. His

---

73. Roxanna Crow vs Chiniquy in December 1863. See Moore to Chiniquy, 26 November 1893, p. 11 (**SL** c.1/3). This same Moore letter describes the following cases.

74. Brettell, "From Time to the Other: An Alternative to the Assimilation Model of Immigration History" (unpublished, c1990), p. 18.

75. Bristol, *Atlas of Kankakee* (Chicago, c1883), p. 21, estimates that 1,200 families associated with Chiniquy's church had moved West.

reputation was outstanding for being very generous to both the poor[76] and to the general community.[77]

There have been widely differing accounts of how many Kankakee County parishioners followed Chiniquy out of the Roman Catholic fold. I have found two detailed estimates. In 1860 Chiniquy counted 886 French Canadian families or 6,200 individuals who had left the Roman Catholic Church.[78] Mailloux provided a counter-estimate in early 1861. Excluding other French Protestants who had originally left with Chiniquy, he posited a total of 310 families or 1,553 individuals in Illinois who were Chiniquy Presbyterians.[79] Both sets of figures are no doubt distorted in opposite directions. The time differential and the fact that different groups were tabulated add further complications. The proportion of views pro and con varied considerably, according to the most recent developments.

Initially Chiniquy had massive support from the majority of French Canadians in Kankakee County. Subsequently there was sizeable slippage of support outside of St. Anne. The villagers of Bourbonnais generally remained loyal to the Catholic bishop. The French in the larger town of Kankakee appear to have been split on the question of the schism. St. Anne itself remained predominantly Presbyterian but the move out west by a large group left remaining Protestants and Catholics on more even ground. In addition, viable French Presbyterian congregations were established in Kankakee and Chicago, not to mention French Episcopal, Methodist and Baptist congregations in the area.[80]

---

76. Bruneau, "Le père Chiniquy comme je l'ai connu" (Montreal, c1915), pp. 8-9 (**AP** 15-C2-F102).

77. *St. Anne Record*, 6 August 1909, p. 1, reports a talk on "Father Chiniquy as a Benefactor", by Rev. Beauchamp.

78. Cited with approval by Rev. Baird, *The French Canadian Mission in Illinois* (AFCU, 1860), p. 3: St. Anne 375 families, Bourbonnais 40, Kankakee 100, Chicago 125, Petites Isles 30, Momence 50, Middleport 35, St. Marie 20, Érable 15, Barren 16, Ava 50, Chateauville 30.

79. Mailloux to Biggs, 11 March 1861 (**ASQ** 50:20), p. 13: St. Anne 200 families, Bourbonnais 4, Kankakee 36, Chicago 10, Petites Isles 1, Momence 7, Middleport 6, St. Marie 7, L'Érable 2, Manteno 0, Bend 8, others 30.

80. Only the last continued beyond a few years (Meier, *The Saga*, pp. 75-8).

4. FRANCO-AMERICAN PROTESTANT (1858-87)

Chiniquy had been encouraged by Chicago Presbytery to be rebaptized at his entrance into the Protestant denomination. He had refused, deeming his Catholic baptism to be valid. However on August 12, 1874, he decided, on the spur of the moment, to be baptized. He was attending a Methodist revival camp meeting in St. Anne at the time. This decision indicates his spiritual concerns, as well as a lack of denominational attachment. His issue was baptism by a valid Christian church and not adult versus infant baptism. Questions were raised in Presbyterian circles about his sudden baptism but no one pursued the issue.[81] Chiniquy's published response to concerns has recently been examined.[82]

Among the most controversial chapters of Chiniquy's two autobiographies are those concerning his relationship with Lincoln. There is no dispute that the future President was his lawyer. However, virtually all Lincoln biographers have disputed Chiniquy's claims to an intimate friendship between the two. Neither do they credit Lincoln's supposed comments to Chiniquy about faith or the Jesuits.[83] Yet Chiniquy reported specific dated incidents and quoted long conversations. He even claims that "There is no man living who had so good an opportunity of knowing Mr. Lincoln, under most trying circumstances, as I had."[84] Chiniquy's reporting of oral conversations is much more subject to embellishment than letters. His quotation marks notwithstanding, few mortals remember long conversations from years ago with such accuracy.

Joseph George provides a strong argument for dismissing the Chiniquy accounts completely but he based his case on an argument from silence. The fact that other sources do not mention the friendship can never prove that Chiniquy is a liar. Among the meagre witnesses

---

81. *40 Years*, pp. 250-55. *CPC Synod Proceedings*, 1874, App. p. 64.

82. *Why Father Chiniquy was rebaptised* (St. Anne IL, November, 1873), 8 p. **AP** 01-27. This was incorporated into the *40 Years*, ch. 24. See Jason Zuidema's upcoming article in *Westminster Theological Journal* (2009) on the lack of depth of Chiniquy's Presbyterian allegiance.

83. The most comprehensive is George, "The Lincoln Writings of Chiniquy" (*JISHC*, 1976).

84. *40 Years*, p. 207.

Figure 30   Emma, Joseph Morin and Rebecca, Charles and Euphemie (Kankakee Co. Hist. Soc. P3753)

supporting Chiniquy there appears a report that Judge Starr, an early Kankakee resident, mentioned that Lincoln consulted Chiniquy during the Civil War.[85] Within the Chiniquy family archives we find two

---

85. Bruneau, pp. 7-8.

4. FRANCO-AMERICAN PROTESTANT (1858-87)

important letters to Chiniquy from Lincoln's son. The first states that his father had "made many friends in his life but plainly none were more than yourself". The other requested Chiniquy not to raise the matter of his father's death any more, for the sake of social peace.[86]

Chiniquy produced most of his writing while in St. Anne, relying on Chicago publishers. The ex-priest attributed the remarkable string of burned proofs of his books to Catholic conspiracy. His early books seemed to produce financial losses. *The Priest, Woman and the Confessional*, his first Protestant work, was commissioned by evangelicals in England to counter an attempt by Ritualists to reintroduce auricular confession into the Church of England.[87]

Since Chiniquy lectured most often about his own experiences, it was natural to proceed to autobiography. *Fifty Years in the Church of Rome*, first published in 1885, proved to be his most popular production, with its intermingling of exciting narrative and apologetics. Much of the book was compiled from previous writings[88]. An extract from *50 Years* that reconstructed the assassination of Lincoln "by the Jesuits" proved to be popular and durable in American circles.

Except for a term in 1870 when Chiniquy worked in Montreal, he lived in St. Anne from 1851 until 1874. He then returned to St. Anne in 1880 and remained there until 1888 as pastor. Even after his retirement, he stayed on until he moved to Montreal in 1892.

---

86. Robert Lincoln to Charles Chiniquy, 10 September 1885 (**AP** 07-187) and the latter reported orally by Samuel Lefebvre but not found either in **SL** nor **AP**.

87. 50 Years, p. 822; AP 07-15. Laverdure, "The Religious Invective" (McGill, 1984), pp. 41-42, suggests that, although the English version was published one year earlier, the French version was the original as stated by the *Times* of London obituary on Jan. 17, 1899, p. 10. In 1892, Chiniquy affirmed that he wrote his books in English and then translated them into French (*MW*, July 5, 1892, p. 6).

88. Chiniquy's son in law, Joseph Morin translated to produce *Cinquante ans dans l'Égise de Rome* the same year, but copies of this have always been rare. The only complete version dates from 1902 and comes from Europe, with no re-printing. This shorter version is also less lively than the English original.

"SOUND AN ALARM!"

AN APPEAL TO PROTESTANTS.

―――:0:―――

"It is high time to awake out of sleep."

―――:0:―――

The following Appeal, by Pastor Chiniquy, from the "Christian Times," of April 20, 1869, is affectionately commended to the earnest consideration of the Church of Christ.

DEAR BRETHREN. –In a few months a General Council will be held in the City of the Seven Mountains, on which the Mother of Harlots and abominations sitteth. The Pope has called the generals of his almost inumerable legions to meet at the headquarters of his empire.

I have been twenty-three years tied at the feet of the Man of Sin.

When among his blind and devoted slaves, I have had every opportunity to know his dark and giant plans, and I feel that if this does not give me the right, it imposes upon me the duty, of raising my warning voice at the approach of this portentous event.

The Pope has a mission, a most terrible mission to perform towards you, my brethren. The Pope does not make a secret of his mission; he boasts of it—since more than a thousand years he proclaims it in every way. His mission is to curse your Bible, and destroy it every time he can lay his hands upon it:— His mission is to blot out the Word of God from the hearts and intelligence of men, to make room for his traditions; his mission is to shed the blood of the disciples of Christ. Here is the law: "Let the secular powers be warned . . that they publicly take an oath that they will study in good earnest TO EXTERMINATE, to their utmost power, from the lands subject to their jurisdiction, all heretics denoted by the Church."

"And the Pope made public rejoicings in Rome for the slaughter of the thousand heretics thrown down from the top of the high mountains of Piedmont on the naked stones. And the Pope got all the bells of Rome rung, and all the cannons of the city fired, in public tokens of his gratitude to God when he heard that 75,000 Protestants had been slaughtered in a single night (the night of St. Bartholomew) in France!

The Pope has repeatedly proclaimed that 'his mission is to destroy 'liberty of conscience'; and I know what I say, my brethren, when the Pope will find his opportunity, the Roman Catholics will destroy "liberty of conscience," if they have to walk to their knees in your blood.

We have too much TALKING ABOUT the power and intelligence of the Protestiants, as a security against the general apostacy of which we see so many signs in the horizon. No human power, no human intelligence, will stand, when God, in order to chastise His own children, will take away their lamp to deliver them into the hands of the merciless instrument of his vengence, the Pope.

What eloquent phrases have we not heard these fifty years about the intelligence and power of the English people being a bulwark against Popery! But see how the God of the Gospel is, to-day, extinguishing the lights in the midst of

5

ANTI-CATHOLICISM

AN EVANGELICAL VERSION

The most in-depth recent study of Chiniquy prior to this book came from Paul Laverdure. He noted the continued use of Chiniquy writings and focused on the author primarily as a propagandist for anti-Catholic hate through speeches and literature.[1] This is natural because virtually any modern person who picks up Chiniquy's writings is offended by the sweeping condemnations of Catholicism. Despite the many insights of Laverdure's work, this approach should be modified in light of the historical and theological context of anti-Catholicism.

Right at the beginning of the Reformation, Protestant writings began to counter Roman Catholic politics and ideas. A ferocious fight provoked vicious propaganda on both sides. Usually the term "anti-Catholicism" refers to movements or spokesmen who engaged in polemics against the Roman Catholic Church, its power and its doctrines. The themes that are presented to show the dangers of

---

1. Notice the title of his MA thesis "Religious Invective of Charles Chiniquy, anti-Catholic crusader 1875-1900" (McGill, 1984).

Catholicism and the superiority of Protestantism have not changed much over the years despite the thousands of writings.

Until recently most historical research on anti-Catholicism has sought a completely hostile indictment. it has minimized the diversity, the causes and any positive theological aspects of this anti-Catholicism. For a long time, only Catholics using counter-propaganda tackled the subject. When other analysts more independent from Catholicism began to examine anti-Catholicism[2], they were still most dismissive of their subjects and their writings because of the polemics. Recent analyses[3] have barely qualified this perspective.

Protestant historians have been too embarrassed about Protestant excesses to challenge the dominant assessment. Historical treatments seem virtually unanimous. They view anti-Catholicism as rank ethnic and/or political bigotry, which simply uses religious terms for effect. This starting point tends to superficial treatment of Chiniquy.

There has been a more helpful contribution by Karl Keating[4] the director of Catholic Answers. He seeks to understand and counter anti-Catholic fundamentalists. He finds that Catholics leave their Church for doctrinal reasons. They need to be taught and challenged about doctrines. If they receive no adequate answers they will leave. So Keating tackles the

---

2. Billington, *The Protestant Crusade* (Chicago, 1964); Myers, History of *Bigotry in the United States* (New York, 1960).

3. Norman, *Anti-Catholicism in Victorian England* (London, 1968); Higham, *Strangers in the Land: Patterns of American Nativism*, 1860-1925 (NY, 1968), pp. 3-139. Klaus suggests that Victorian sexual neuroses are partly to blame in his *The Pope, the Protestants and the Irish* (NY, 1987), p. 294.

For the Canadian scene see J. R. Miller, "Anti-Catholic Thought in Victorian Canada" (*CHR*, 1985), 474-494; "Bigotry in the North Atlantic triangle: 1850- 1900" (*Studies in Religion*, 1987), 289-301; "Anti-Catholicism in Canada: From the British Conquest to the Great War" IN *Creed and Culture* (Montreal, 1993), 25-48. Unfortunately Miller fails to show any redeeming and, hence, human quality among anti-Catholics. This caricature of bigoted ignorance leads us either to simply despise anti-Catholics or to question the motivation of the analyst.

4. Karl Keating, *Catholicism and Fundamentalism: the Attack on 'Romanism' by 'Bible Christians'* (San Francisco, 1988), 360 p.

5. ANTI-CATHOLICISM

issues and shows how anti-Catholics misrepresent Catholic doctrine. Keating mentions and dismisses Chiniquy's credibility in passing. He is more thorough in looking at theologian Lorraine Boettner and modern exponents: Jimmy Swaggart, Bart Brewer and Jack Chick. This post-Vatican II defence of the faith or apologetic approach could permit reconsideration of the Chiniquy debates while consciously eschewing counter-propaganda. Keating admits that it is hard to distinguish fundamentalists from the broader evangelicals. He sticks with the former and advances understanding of their beliefs and methods.

I maintain, following David Bebbington[5], and in more depth John Wolffe[6], that anti-Catholicism was an inevitable component of 19th century evangelical theology. That does not mean that all anti- Catholicism was theologically based, or that all evangelicals with these theological principles would agree on the best methods for expressing them.

Bebbington has provided a helpful summary of four evangelical essential traits. These have remained constant across cultures and across the centuries (at least since John Wesley[7] if not since the 16th century Anabaptists):

> Conversionism - the belief that lives need to be changed; activism - the expression of the gospel in effort; biblicism - a particular regard for the Bible; and what may be called crucicentrism, a stress on the sacrifice of Christ on the cross.[8]

All these are paralleled in Catholicism. However conflict with Catholicism and other ideologies increased the evangelical distinction of these traits.

---

5. Bebbington, *Evangelicalism in Modern Britain* (London, 1989). See e.g. pp. 101-2 among others.

6. Wolffe, *The Protestant Crusade in Great Britain, 1829-1860* (Oxford, 1991).

7. Also see *Blackwell Dictionary of Evangelical Biography, 1730-1860*, ed. Donald Lewis (Oxford, 1995).

8. Bebbington, p. 3.

In an evangelical context **conversionism** means that every person, whether baptized, ordained, born into a Christian family or other, whatever their confessional status, must be born again, or have a life-changing personal experience of salvation through Jesus Christ. Everyone would need that knowledge, including Catholics. Those who denied this most would be, therefore, those who had most need of salvation. Catholic reaction and their denial of what they perceived as "proselytism", confirmed to evangelicals the profound error of Roman Catholicism. Any Catholic pressure brought to bear on converts led to evangelical outrage about freedom of thought and freedom of religion.

Activism tended to mean that causes such as temperance, Lord's Day observance, universal education, abolition of slavery, and opposition to gambling were seen as imperative Christian causes. Catholic opposition or neutrality on these issues provoked strong anger among evangelicals about the perceived support of immorality or illiteracy.

Biblicism proclaims that the Bible is the ultimate authority, above every civil or religious ruler or tradition. Counter-claims that the Pope was the unchallenged mouthpiece for God were unacceptable. An important corollary followed: no person or group should be allowed to use civil or religious authority to coerce believers to disobey perceived biblical commands. Any bishop or priest who demanded obedience without a clear biblical mandate had to be resisted. Private judgement had to be defended against arbitrary church authority. Evangelicals believed additionally that they must resist any exclusive state church.[9] Further, the key means of Roman Catholic control - their separate schools and the confessional - had to be countered.

Crucicentrism among evangelicals rejects any other mediators or salvation through good works, as inimical to true faith. Catholic prayers to saints, dependence on holy objects, penance and stress on physical observances: all these were seen as biblically unfounded. In practice, they

---

9. Certain Anglican evangelicals in England did promote Anglican privilege but they did not intend to infringe on the freedoms of other Protestants.

5. ANTI-CATHOLICISM

are diversionary from the heart of true faith. The Catholic mass came to be seen as the centre of a pagan idolatry.

Evangelical apologists clashed with Deists and liberal theology as well. However, until the late 19th century, their greatest battles proved to be against Catholicism, whether in France, England, French Canada, English Canada, the United States, Australia or New Zealand. The causes dearest to evangelicals were repugnant to Roman Catholics (and many High Church Anglicans) and vice versa. Perceived need to unite against Catholicism was a major factor in the formation of the international and interdenominational Evangelical Alliance in 1845.[10] This and other evangelical trans-Atlantic and trans-Pacific networks shared news and projects.[11]

Anti-Catholicism was constant as an evangelical theological tenet throughout pre-Vatican II history. However the general public (usually with a non-evangelical majority) adopted anti-Catholicism as a cause only at political crisis points. At those points, politicians and non-evangelical spokesmen often became the champions. Very different motivations and means surfaced in this broader form of anti-Catholicism. This has tended to confuse analysis.

I support the conclusion of Wolffe that:

> [evangelical] anti-Catholicism was neither a superficial
> prejudice nor a coherent ideology, but rather a frame of mind,
> an integral part of religious, political, and social belief and
> experience, ingrained into the consciousness of individuals in
> diverse ways that led inevitably to conflicting assumptions and
> aspirations. It was inextricably linked with the urge to promote
> spiritual revival, social and political advance, and controlled
> civil liberty. It was a crucial strand in an evangelical world-view

---

10. This was the first successful international co-operation of members of most Protestant churches. Individuals rather than denominations became members. It was a forerunner of both the World Council of Churches and the World Evangelical Fellowship. Wolffe, "The Evangelical Alliance in the 1840s..." IN *Voluntary Religion* (Oxford, 1986), pp. 333-346.

11. See Rawlyk and Noll eds., *Amazing Grace: Evangelicalism in Australia, Britain, Canada and the United States* (Montreal, 1994).

that made far-reaching connections which seem strange to a later age with different presuppositions but which had an inherent logic of their own. [12]

Why did anti-Catholicism flourish in Britain and the Western (mostly Anglo-Saxon) world?[13] Wolffe relates it to

> the universal human tendency to prejudice and paranoia, the development of militant Ultramontanism, the Irish Catholic diaspora, and a pervasive sense of political and social crisis. However the crucial factor linking these impulses together was evangelical Christianity. In a culture in which religious idioms were widespread even in those places where committed evangelicalism only had a limited appeal, the resulting ideology found receptive soil, especially in connection with patriotic and nationalist emotions.[14]

In North America and Australian, the context was not so different from Great Britain. In times of pessimism about the national ability to assimilate Irish or other Catholic emigrants, religious beliefs fuelled mounting socio-political pressure for government to curb Catholicism.[15]

The Converted Catholic, an evangelistic journal that we would define as anti-Catholic, in fact disclaimed the title.[16] It wished to distance itself from political and scandal-oriented spokesmen in order to pursue its goals of addressing Catholics and "converting them to Christ". Rare are the historians who acknowledge the claimed distinction between

---

12. Wolffe, *The Protestant Crusade* (Oxford, 1991), p. 143.
13. Ibid., pp. 318-9, lists the Protestant Societies in 19th-century Britain.
14. Ibid., p. 316.
15. Higham, pp. 39, 58.
16. *CC*, 14 (1897), p. 198 (editor ex-priest James O'Connor in New York). See our p. 255.

5. ANTI-CATHOLICISM

political nativists[17] and those who wanted to evangelize (or proselytize) Catholics.[18]

There exists then, an evangelical version of anti-Catholicism with a theological base. This is the context in which Chiniquy is best understood.

ANTI-PROTESTANT PROVOCATIONS IN ULTRAMONTANE QUEBEC

Evangelical conversionism entailed a particular interest in missions in non-Protestant areas. As missionary fund-raisers have always known, it is difficult to maintain long-term interest in a remote cause. One unerring way to get attention is to provide accounts of either spectacular conversions, preferably numerous, or of persecution of the missionaries and/or their converts. A secular analogy can be found in the general eagerness for accounts of atrocities prior to, and during, wars. These accounts promote outrage and action.

Reports of a broader conspiracy to eliminate or muzzle missionaries inevitably incensed committed evangelicals. The Evangelical Alliance, from its formation, brought broad pressure to bear in order to protect fellow evangelicals living in more vulnerable areas. While Communism was a main culprit for most of the 20th century, and Islamic states are seen as the primary offenders at present, Catholicism dominated in the 19th century.

It seems that while Catholic theology left its believers more vulnerable to bogus stories of miracles or relics, evangelical theology predisposed many to accept propaganda about the millennium and about Catholic conspiracies. Evangelicals believed in the reality of a demonic

---

17. *DCA*, p. 801. Nativism refers to an American 19th-century movement that aimed at the ban or limit of immigration and the rights of immigrants. This was usually tied into anti-Catholicism since most immigrants who were not Anglo-Saxon (and thus had more difficulty assimilating) were Catholic.

18. Higham, p. 5 rejects Billington's oversimplified equation of nativism and anti-Catholicism.

realm that fought against God's people throughout history. Such a realm would, according to the New Testament, use persecution, distorted theology and deception. It was claimed that, in Catholicism, distorted theology was obvious, persecution of Protestantism was growing and deception was only to be expected.

Pope Pius IX and his ultramontane spokesmen felt themselves to be threatened by various influences. They responded with the declarations on Religious liberty, the Syllabus of Errors (opposing all republican, nationalist or modern ideas), and increased mention of the Index of prohibited books. This facilitated Catholic orthodoxy in Catholic nations. On the other hand it increased Protestant anger in England, Canada and the United States (not to mention republican France and nationalistic Italy).

Following news of such Vatican statements, any sign of Catholic intolerance in word or action was widely reported and deplored. An appetite grew for such news, and especially by eyewitnesses of persecution. In times of general crisis and increased public interest in anti-Catholicism, such stories were in great demand.

In the trans-Atlantic evangelical world, several situations for such intolerance were repeatedly publicized. Accounts of seduction by Catholic clergy were frequent. Stories of abortions and forcible retention in convents, though seemingly baseless, surfaced regularly in Canada, the United States and Britain. The fictional Maria Monk[19] account of 1836 was widely believed and sold well. On the other hand, certain trials of evangelicals in Catholic countries were quite real[20], if often enhanced. Evangelical journals frequently mentioned stories of Catholic intolerance to Protestants in Austria, France and Spain.

---

19. *DCB*, 7: 624-6.
20. Wolffe, *The Protestant Crusade* (Oxford, 1991), pp. 267-8. See Alessandro Gavazzi, *Father Gavazzi's Lectures in New York* (NY, 1883); Anne Lohrli, "The Madiai: A Forgotten Chapter of Church History" (*Victorian Studies*, 1989), 28-50. The Madiai family became famous after being imprisoned in Florence in 1852 for convening a Protestant religious meeting.

5. ANTI-CATHOLICISM

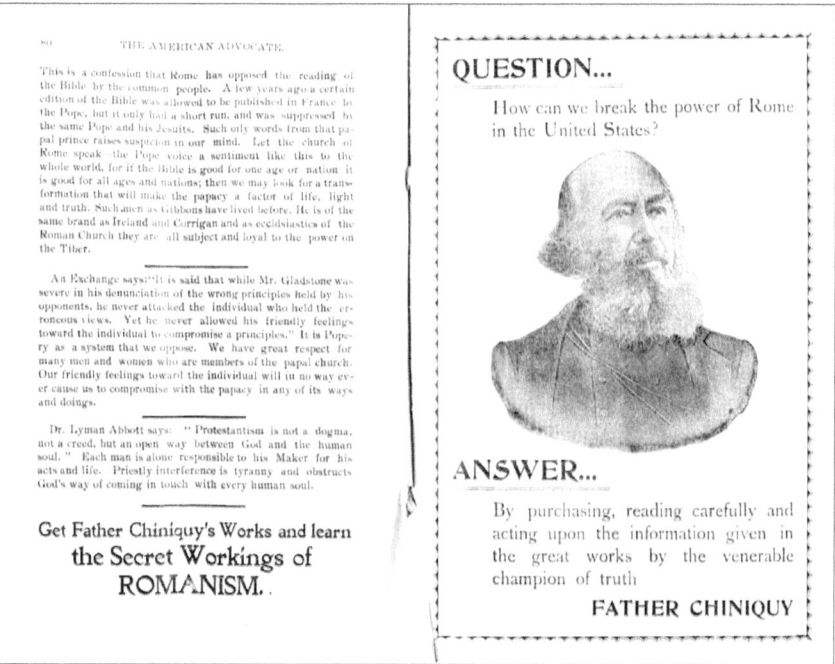

Figure 31   *American Advocate*, Feb. 1899   **AP** 15 C1 F023 08

For a North American element in these accounts of persecution, evangelical papers turned to French Canada. Events in ultramontane Lower Canada provided ample opportunity to document Catholic exclusiveness in pastoral letters as well as in the persecution of evangelists in French mission. Many notable evangelical leaders resided in Montreal, allowing corroboration and rapid publicity of any Catholic offences. Any verbalized anti-(French) Protestantism of Catholic leaders[21] was publicized. Any threats of violence, job loss or censorship became known around the evangelical world. French Canada became the visible case study of Catholic culture - exposed to Protestantism and English freedoms, but, according to the evangelical mind, powerless to progress due to the total political and social control by its church leaders.

---

21. Ruddel, *Le protestantisme français au Québec 1840-1919* (Ottawa, 1983), pp. 1-13.

Of particular importance for this evangelical study were the stories of persecuted non-Anglo Saxon converts from Catholicism. These persons were seen to demonstrate that the gospel was needed in all races and also that the Catholic Church would not recognize freedom of conscience. Any difficulties the convert had were, in the polemical context, attributed directly to the priests or bishops. The quest for social and political control in ultramontane Quebec became the paradigm for true Catholic goals everywhere. It appeared to conclusively prove much of the Catholic conspiracy theory.

Demonstrations of religious intolerance by governments of Catholic countries were deemed to necessitate curbs on any Catholic attempts for further political power in Protestant countries. Both Catholic anti-Protestantism and evangelical anti-Catholicism sought to exclude or control foreign elements. Protestants felt that ultramontane Catholics could not fail but be disloyal to their country since their true ruler was the Pope. Anti-Catholicism successfully promoted British, American[22] and Canadian nationalism as it opposed foreign interference by the Pope.

Catholic leaders, particularly in French Canada and wherever they constituted the state church, encouraged anti-Protestantism[23] and intolerance. This provocation provided an important stimulus to anti-Catholic organization. The theory of worldwide Catholic conspiracy was given credibility by Vatican pronouncements and stories of ultramontane Canada. Promoters of anti-Catholicism were quick to seize on the power of emotive stories of intolerance. Chiniquy was perfectly situated to be a participant in this debate.

A POLEMICAL AGE

The language of Chiniquy's books is offensive to most religious and secular readers today. It needs to be seen in historical perspective.[24]

---

22. Wolffe, pp. 308-11 on Britain and p. 315 on the USA, views it as formative of nationalism.

23. Jean Baubérot and Valentine Zuber, *Une haine oubliée: l'anti-protestantisme avant le 'pacte laïque' 1870-1905* (Paris, 2000).

24. Wallace, *The Rhetoric of Anti-Catholicism. the American Protective Association, 1887-1911* (NY, 1990). His historical work is less impressive, including his mangling of

5. ANTI-CATHOLICISM

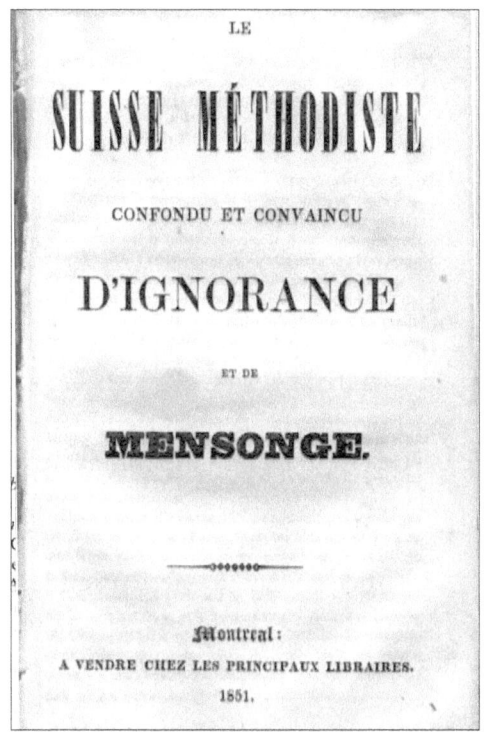

Figure 32   Chiniquy's Anti-Protestant pamphlet **AP** 01 062
(Trans. The Swiss Methodist proven to be ignorant and a liar)

Polemics have always constituted a popular literary and oral form for politics and sometimes for other subjects. Those who use polemics virtually always distort quotations, exaggerate and seduce. Polemical writing does not attempt to reveal the truth or to provide detached analysis. It seeks to interest, persuade the unconvinced and reinforce the convinced through propaganda. Social or political causes justify their propaganda or polemics by the necessity of undoing the propaganda of the other side. At the beginning of the 21st century, Western society denounces religious polemic but uses polemic in many other ways. If we admit that the polemical genre is simply human and is justifiable under certain conditions, then perhaps we can look at this religious form more dispassionately without immediately falling into the indignation it so easily provokes.

A glance at Catholic papers such as the *Freeman's Journal* of New York, the *Boston Pilot*, the *Shepherd of the Valley* of St. Louis, the New Zealand *Tablet*, the Montreal *True Witness* or the Quebec *Courrier du Canada* would show us the extent of anti-Protestant polemic. The

---

Chiniquy's name into Chaniquay. The work is hampered by the bias of his sources toward the antiquated Billington-Myers line of thought while it is amazing that he could find no sign of rhetoric used in America against the anti-Catholic American Protective Association (APA)!

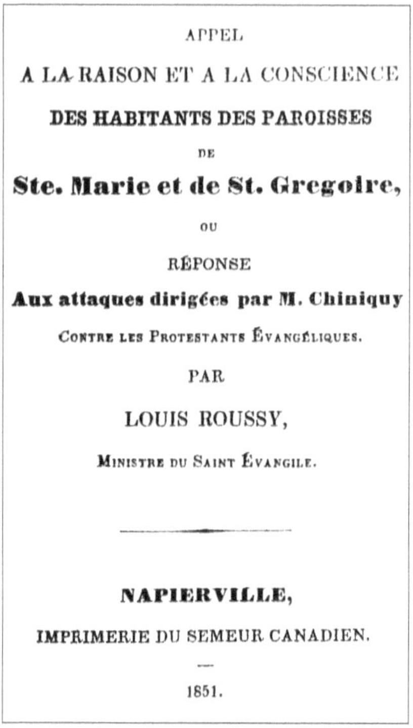

APPEL
A LA RAISON ET A LA CONSCIENCE
DES HABITANTS DES PAROISSES
DE
Ste. Marie et de St. Gregoire,
OU
RÉPONSE
Aux attaques dirigées par M. Chiniquy
CONTRE LES PROTESTANTS ÉVANGÉLIQUES.
PAR
LOUIS ROUSSY,
MINISTRE DU SAINT ÉVANGILE.

NAPIERVILLE,
IMPRIMERIE DU SEMEUR CANADIEN.
—
1851.

Figure 33 Trans. "Appeal to reason and conscience or a Response to the attacks of Mr. Chiniquy against evangelical Protestants"

reason for the foundation of many of these Catholic papers, and for much of the polemics they contained, was to react to prior anti-Catholicism. Notwithstanding, they contained many unguarded polemical statements against Protestants. In Britain, the angry *Dublin Tablet* proved to be an embarrassment to the more moderate English Catholic bishops.[25]

In French Canada, both Protestants and Catholics considered themselves to be besieged minorities. Here the polemics on both sides are too evident to need examples. Both anti-Catholic and anti-Protestant newspapers shared opposing pressures. On the one hand, vivid language and controversy tended to arouse interest and to help sell papers. On the other hand, causes could easily lose ecclesiastical and general support, and forfeit wider press coverage if they became too belligerent.[26]. This did not tend to apply to French Quebec.

Naturally, anti-Catholic sentiment spilled over into political activity. Politicians and anti-Catholic enthusiasts tried to harness each other. In the long-term it was always the politicians who triumphed, returning to a more tolerant policy as times changed. Republicans in the United States, the Tories in Britain and the Liberals in Quebec (in a much more qualified way) were the main exploiters of anti-Catholic sentiment. American Nativism also used anti-Catholicism for its associated ends.

25. Klaus, p. 23.
26. Higham, p. 86 and Wolffe, p. 293.

5. ANTI-CATHOLICISM

Polemics are seen most clearly in the religious debates or réunions contradictoires of the 19th century. In Britain[27] and America such debates generally followed provocative anti-Catholic lectures. Sometimes both sides planned them. At other times, disruptive elements transformed a lecture into a debate. The key debates for French Canada held at Pointe aux Trembles and Marieville, both involved Chiniquy as the Catholic spokesman. Later the Protestant Chiniquy still liked this format and constantly challenged Catholics to debate. Despite some Catholic successes with debates in England,[28] this tactic was generally abandoned by the Roman authorities. It was believed that debate proved less productive than ignoring the attacks.

French newspapers in Quebec alternated between vitriol and the silent treatment against Chiniquy. In response Chiniquy used his cultivated talent for polemics in lectures or print, the weapons of choice in this conflict.

CLERGY CONVERSIONS AND APOSTASIES

Who could describe the inner working of the church better than someone who had been called to the ministry in it? For information and polemical purposes, ex-priests, ex-nuns, and on the other side ex-Protestant pastors were pre-eminent. While the manner of recounting ranged from the erudition of John Henry Newman[29] to the innuendo and gory details of *Maria Monk*, the impact was considerable.

Everyone seemed to want to know the reasons why clergy had left and what they could now reveal about the errors of their former church. The new church rushed to trumpet news of the convert while the former church rushed to point out the disloyalty, contradictions and, hopefully, immorality of the apostate. Each conversion was proclaimed

---

27. Wolffe, p. 110-111.
28. Ibid., p. 52-4, 60.
29. However he lost a libel case against Giacinto Achilli, another ex-priest.

as the ultimate proof of the truth of the convert's new faith. If dignitaries were involved, the triumph was so much the greater.

Eventually lists of clergy converts were compiled to counteract the lists of the other side.[30] Such tabulations still continue in Protestant circles with ex-priest Emmett McLoughlin's biographies of 17 ex-priests.[31] Almost inevitably the accounts of conversion turned into bitter propaganda that insulted the former church of the clergy convert. It was thought expedient by Catholic authorities to list apostates with the "real story" of their departure.[32] Thus one propaganda provoked counter-propaganda in order to castigate the apostate or "pervert".[33]

This clergy conversion phenomenon applied to both camps. Among the best known ex-priests of the 19th century were the Italians, Giacinto Achilli and Alessandro Gavazzi[34]; the Americans, William Hogan, Pierce Connelly,[35] and James O'Connor; the German Johann von Doellinger; Miguel Hidalgo[36] and Antonio Martinez[37] of Mexico; Félicité de Lamennais, Father Hyacinthe and Bishop Léon Bouland, from France; and the Canadian Chiniquy.

---

30. Close, *Why 854 Priests Left the Church of Rome* (London, ²1936), is the most comprehensive so far, but is still highly inaccurate. See his preface for his sources and the polemical context. For a list from France see Meillon, *L'Ancien prêtre et le ministère évangélique* (Cahors, 1901), p. 101.

31. McLoughlin, *Famous Ex-Priests* (N.Y., 1968), 224 p. This is still in print. He differs from the others in including famous priests who became agnostics and atheists, in addition to those who became evangelical Protestants.

32. Lucey, *The Business of Vilification Practised by 'Ex-Priests' and Others*, post 1905, 43 p.

33. Ibid.; Chiniquy, *The Perversion of Dr. Newman* (Montreal, ³1896). This latter is also ch. 41 of *50 Years*. Also see Klaus, p. 20.

34. Hall, "Alessandro Gavazzi: A Barnabite Friar and the Risorgimento", *Church, Society and Politics* (Oxford, 1975), pp. 303-356; Sylvain, *Alessandro Gavazzi 1809-1899*, 2 vol., (Quebec, 1962).

35. Paz, *The Priesthoods and Apostasies of Pierce Connelly. A Study of Conversion and Anti-Catholicism* (Queenston, 1986).

36. McLoughlin, pp. 51-62.

37. Ibid., pp. 82-94.

5. ANTI-CATHOLICISM

Considerable instability may be noted in the lives of some of these ex-priests.[38] Quite a few ex-priests returned to the Catholic Church, either for reasons of belief or to resolve problems of finances or social isolation. Joseph-René Vilatte began and ended in the Roman Catholic clerical world with many years in between spent with groups separated from Rome. He constantly was looking for bridges between.[39]

Several ex-priests were notorious for their foul stories and constant demands for more pay. Probably their vulnerable financial situation encouraged the latter. Despite historians' assumptions nobody appears to have become rich through the ex-priest lecture circuit.[40] Some, such as Achilli, were dumped when they were found to be frauds or sexually immoral.[41]

Pressures were considerable. For the first time these ex-priests faced pressures of making many new independent decisions, finding a stable source of income, developing a whole new network of friends, and choosing a new denomination, while forming a fully evangelical doctrine and lifestyle. This pressure proved too much for many priests. In fact the French Protestant paper the *Aurore* included a broad generalization about ex-priests: "What confidence can we have in ex-priests after this? I know hardly any, apart from Father Chiniquy, who have remained faithful to themselves and to evangelical Christianity."[42] The writer had been disappointed too many times by unstable or immoral

---

38. Marsault, *De Rome à l'Évangile* (Paris, 1908), ch. 2, gives a helpful though polemical view of the strong and varied pressures which a priest faced on leaving the Catholic Church.

39. *New Schaff-Herzog Encyclopedia*, vol. 12 (1912), 187-9 describe an unstable personality but see Serge Thériault, *Mgr J.René Villatte: Community Organizer of Religion, 1854-1929* (Ottawa, 2006).

40. Kinzer, *An Episode in Anti-Catholicism: The American Protective Association* (Seattle, 1964), p. 246.

41. Wallace, p. 114.

42. *A*, 11 August 1894, p. 9 (my translation). Under the pseudonym *lutteur* (wrestler), Chiniquy wrote a defence of ex-priests and their precarious situation in *A*, 25 August 1894, pp. 11-12.

characters. Ex-priests had to maintain credibility and integrity in order to continue to receive evangelical support.

At the turn of the 20th century, an ex-priest from France, Félix Meillon, who had become a Reformed pastor, contributed a careful study of the phenomenon of ex-priests.[43] He chronicled the development of the *Oeuvre des prêtres*, starting with the inspiration of the Chiniquy model in St. Anne.[44] Meillon was well aware of the multiple reasons for leaving the church, a minority of which related to the spiritual life. He discounted both the Protestant propaganda, that there was a sweeping movement from Catholicism to Protestantism, and the Catholic propaganda, that lust, pride or vice inspired all ex-priests.

Addressing himself to French Protestant authorities, Meillon pleaded first for a retreat house for the few ex-priests who had a genuine spiritual attraction to Protestantism. Then, in order to provide credibility and to prevent hasty, pressured decisions, he counselled a prolonged interim period, involving study and supervised placements, before any move was allowed from the Catholic priesthood to the fundamentally different Protestant pastorate. Such a measured policy was rarely followed due to the temptation of publicizing a new celebrity convert.

The International Catholic Truth Society (ICTS) took as one of its tasks to refute the allegations of ex-priests. Pamphlets discrediting Chiniquy were distributed at some of his lectures in England in 1896.[45] Among the Society's 20th century critiques of Chiniquy are found Sydney Smith's restrained biography[46] and Hull's solid refutation on the subject of the confessional.[47] A different tone is set in an American ICTS pamphlet dating from the APA heyday of the 1890s. Lucey[48] sought to prove that

---

43. Meillon, *Les anciens prêtres* (Cahors, 1900), 101 p.
44. Ibid., p. 43. This was a retreat house in France for ex-priests.
45. The pamphlet *Pastor Chiniquy DD. A Reply to Accusations circulated by Roman Catholics* (England, c1896) **SL** c.1/2 0.
46. S. Smith, *Pastor Chiniquy* (London, 1908), 64 p.
47. Hull, *Maria Monk, Chiniquy and Jovinian* (Bombay, 1912), 39 p.
48. Lucey, *The Business* (Brooklyn, 1905).

5. ANTI-CATHOLICISM

ex-priests were all a depraved lot who had never entered the Catholic fold (the frauds) or had been expelled (the immoral). In Lucey's view the latter followed the pattern of Judas Iscariot, betraying for money.[49] They always spoke in towns far from home, in order that their credentials could not be checked.[50]

Indignant loyal Catholics felt helpless when a so-called "ex-priest" came to their town. "If they express their righteous resentment, their expressions are construed as a menace to free speech. If they resort to violence, the law very properly interferes".[51] By the time they found any true information about the person, he had left the area. So Lucey compiled a pamphlet with documentation of the 'true' lives of these ex-priests. At least for Chiniquy, the information is anecdotal and highly misleading.[52] None of the other ex-priests mentioned by Lucey were known outside the United States. In general, these ex-priests were accused of profiteering from their invented stories and having been dismissed from their Catholic posts for immorality or drunkenness.

There has been little historical or theological writing of substance about ex-priests. Basil Hall's article[53] contributes a more sympathetic reading but does not widen its scope beyond Gavazzi. Paz tackles the subject but loses objectivity. He suggests various reasons for why Connelly left the Catholics: insanity, narcissistic personality disorder or a desire for power and fame.[54] A theological basis is dismissed summarily. It is unfortunate that Paz, in unmasking one propaganda, appears to fall unwittingly into counter-propaganda.[55]

---

49. Ibid., p. 3.
50. Ibid., p. 4.
51. Ibid., p. 5.
52. Ibid., pp. 41-2.
53. Hall, "Alessandro Gavazzi".
54. Paz, p. 218.
55. Ibid. He is very derogatory to his subject Pierce Connelly, claims that there is no moral or theological judgement implied in his own constant use of the term

Some of the conclusions of Paz are compatible with ours: churches were often eager to welcome converts as leaders and ordain rapidly (this changed with time); leaving the priesthood was a very major step[56] which required sacrificing financial security; apostates to Protestantism were greatly pressured to become anti-Catholic performers (although converts do tend to justify their choice); the Atlantic Ocean was a highway rather than a barrier for these trends.[57]

Ex-priests were a needed source of affirmation and morale building for anti-Catholic circles. They evoked much curiosity but also great hostility among loyal Catholics. Unconsciously, they were led to become more virulent in order to maintain financial support. Interest tended to die out unless fresh revelations of Catholic horrors or incidents of Catholic persecution surfaced. Keen evangelical insight was not expected nor sought from these speakers. Low expectation increased the possibility of frauds.

Nevertheless integrity was not optional. Ex-priest conversion stories were, for the most part, naively believed at the start. If local Catholic authorities raised serious critiques of these persons, the allegations were usually checked. Evangelical anti-Catholic groups quietly dropped any ex-priests who were proven to be fraudulent or immoral.

Catholic denigration of these 'apostates' was expected by Protestants and tended to follow a predictable pattern of accusations: the priest had been dismissed and did not leave voluntarily; he was sexually immoral, a drunkard and/or an embezzler. That is to say, Catholic counter-propaganda was obviously biased and therefore suspect in the eyes of Protestant leaders. Had not Luther, Calvin and virtually all Reformation leaders been slandered with similar charges? Protestants, in general, would give

---

'apostate' for ex-Catholics (only), and provides a highly unbalanced list of converts in the two directions. Paz apparently has never heard of Chiniquy!

56. See for the modern situation: F.A. Dellacava, "Becoming an ex-priest: the process of leaving a high commitment status" (*Sociological Inquiry*, 1975), 41-49.

57. Paz, pp. 228-30.

5. ANTI-CATHOLICISM

the benefit of the doubt to ex-priest's propaganda rather than to Catholic propaganda.

It is this polemical context that is very relevant to a study of Chiniquy. In Quebec, tirades against apostate priests were much more abusive than in the United States or Britain. However in each country there were numerous charges and counter-charges related to ex-priests. Propaganda from the other side was only to be expected and so it was discounted.

ANTI-CATHOLIC LITERATURE

A huge market for anti-Catholic literature allowed for a wide range of material. These included reprints of Reformation works, *Foxe's Book of Martyrs*, histories showing God's providence acting through Protestants, and contemporary doctrinal studies.[58] Not much controversy resulted from these works but they fed the anti-Catholic passions of Anglo-Saxon Protestants.

Small cheap pamphlets called 'tracts' were the written material of choice for evangelicals in early 19th century Britain.[59] By 1842 the Protestant Association had distributed over 750,000 tracts to bolster the faith.[60] Not all of these were anti-Catholic but anti-Catholicism was a popular topic. Both pro-Chiniquy and anti-Chiniquy camps frequently employed one-penny tracts for wide distribution.[61]

By the late 1830s, there was a tendency among anti-Catholics in Britain to choose periodicals over tracts and pamphlets.[62] In the 1850s, Britain was swamped with recently established newspapers. While the mainline press such as the *Times* was pressured to raise the no-Popery

---

58. Wolffe, pp. 111-112.
59. Klaus, pp. 228-232.
60. Wolffe, p. 158.
61. The Sydney Smith biography and Chiniquy's *Life and Work* (London, 1897).
62. Wolffe, p. 158.

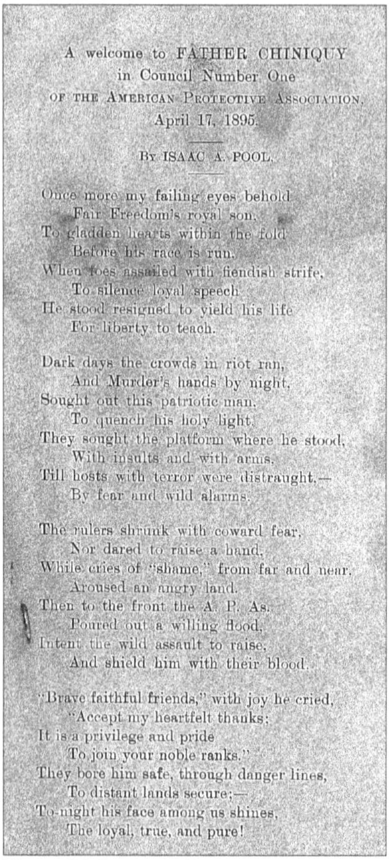

A welcome to FATHER CHINIQUY
in Council Number One
OF THE AMERICAN PROTECTIVE ASSOCIATION,
April 17, 1895.

BY ISAAC A. POOL.

Once more my failing eyes behold
Fair Freedom's royal son,
To gladden hearts within the fold
Before his race is run.
When foes assailed with fiendish strife,
To silence loyal speech
He stood resigned to yield his life
For liberty to teach.

Dark days the crowds in riot ran,
And Murder's hands by night,
Sought out this patriotic man,
To quench his holy light,
They sought the platform where he stood,
With insults and with arms,
Till hosts with terror were distraught,—
By fear and wild alarms.

The rulers shrunk with coward fear,
Nor dared to raise a hand,
While cries of "shame," from far and near,
Aroused an angry land.
Then to the front the A. P. As.
Poured out a willing flood,
Intent the wild assault to raise,
And shield him with their blood.

"Brave faithful friends," with joy he cried,
"Accept my heartfelt thanks;
It is a privilege and pride
To join your noble ranks."
They bore him safe, through danger lines,
To distant lands secure;—
To-night his face among us shines,
The loyal, true, and pure!

Figure 34 American Protective Association tribute **AP** 10-55

cry,[63] many specifically Protestant or anti-Catholic papers were established.[64]

The trends of using tracts and starting exclusively Protestant newspapers, were both repeated in North America.[65] Newspapers like John Dougall's *Montreal Witness* outsold all local papers. Each newspaper passed on information about Catholic intolerance and anti-Catholic speakers to their informal network. Some newspapers constantly printed anti-Catholic material while others were less committed to the cause and more selective.[66] In the United States there were regular complaints that the secular press did not report Catholic intolerance[67] and avoided the APA.[68]

American ingenuity and a strong political message brought new forms of communication. In order to publicize its message the APA innovated secret distribution of handbills at night. Circulars were also sent out to selected

63. Klaus, pp. 221-2. This was truer in the 1830s than the 1850s.
64. Lists in Wolffe pp. 158, 322-3 and in Klaus pp. 226-7, 345-7.
65. Wallace provides a list on p. 104. Kinzer gives another list on pp. 327-30.
66. Wallace, pp. 104-5.
67. This was also a constant refrain of the Protestant papers in Quebec.
68. Wallace, p. 106.

5. ANTI-CATHOLICISM

community leaders.[69] One influential though more rare APA tactic was the production of bogus encyclicals and forged Catholic documents.[70]

A few literary scholars produced anti-Catholic materials.[71] Generally the apologetics productions were more straightforward. *Maria Monk*'s revelations continued to be reprinted into the 20th century though they had been discredited back in the 1830s even by Protestant authorities. Accounts of convent immorality or oppression were popular, along with commentaries on the political threat of Catholic conspiracy. Ex-priest accounts and evangelistic books, aimed at Catholics, round out the main categories of anti-Catholic literature.

Undoubtedly Chiniquy's work deserves the attribution of number one anti-Catholic bestseller status.[72] He managed to publish his own ex-priest autobiography in two volumes, as well as conspiracy theories about the assassination of Lincoln,[73] doctrinal works on Mary and the Confessional, sexual allegations, persecution accounts, sermons, debates and critiques of 'perverts' like Cardinal Newman. In fact, Chiniquy managed to insert almost all of this into his *50 Years*. One stands amazed at his ability to handle so many of the anti-Catholic genres.

COOPERATION WITH ANTI-CLERICALISM

Anti-clericalism was not a major theme in the 19th century Anglo-Saxon world. Doubtless there were some nominal Protestants who joined the anti-Catholic cause for anti-religious motives, just as there were those who joined for entirely political motives. However we are interested in anti-clericalism in majority Catholic areas. In fact the

---

69. Wallace, pp. 101-2.
70. Kinzer, pp. 81-2. Wallace, pp. 106-111. Thanks to John Wolffe who pointed out that this was presaged by the 1836 'False Bull' affair in Britain.
71. Klaus, pp. 233-6. Browning, Kingsley, Macaulay, Thackeray and Tupper are mentioned in his sketchy list.
72. Kinzer, p. 31, referring to *50 Years*.
73. George, "The Lincoln Writings of Chiniquy" (*JISHS*, 1976), pp. 17-34.

Figure 35   Anti-Catholic cartoon, 1894 **AP 09 240**

term 'anti-clerical' originated in France around 1850 to refer to those who opposed the power of clergy.[74] Anti-Catholic exponents tried to

---

74. É. Fouilloux, "Les églises contestées" IN *L'histoire religieuse de la France, XIXe-XXe siècles* (Paris, 1975), pp. 143-157 on anti-clericalism.

5. ANTI-CATHOLICISM

cooperate with those who had socio-political differences with the Catholic Church, without supporting the latter's hostility to religion in general. Such entente was most easily accomplished with Catholic immigrants, far from the authorities that they resented.[75]

In Ireland it appears that attempts to achieve cooperation between anti-Catholics and anti-clericals failed because of the greater need for nationalists and Catholics to stay united. Even in Italy, where nationalist forces opposed the Pope, and Gavazzi personally combined anti-clericalism and evangelical anti-Catholicism, no true cooperation occurred. Probably cooperation was greatest in France between liberal Protestants and anti-clericals, on the question of public schools. This did not bear evangelistic fruit however.

In Quebec[76] as in Ireland, there was nationalistic resistance to cooperation with the English. What happened then with the small French Protestant community? There were examples of limited cooperation between French Protestants and Catholic anti-clericals. The *Montreal Witness* helped to publicize the *Institut canadien* and encouraged fundraising for the *Institut* in the 1870s. French Protestants Cyr and Lafleur joined and lectured in the *Institut*. In return, the majority in the *Institut* refused to ban the donated Protestant *Semeur canadien* from their premises. Since even this small demonstration of religious tolerance was extremely controversial, no greater cooperation developed.

The anti-clerical *Avenir* of Pierre Blanchet certainly played a major role in publicizing Chiniquy's conflict with his Illinois bishops. However the *Institut canadien* itself refused all comment. Chiniquy mentions that several young Catholics from a group called the *Francs frères*, including Joseph Guibord, acted as his bodyguards during his 1859 visit to Montreal.[77] Apparently though Chiniquy was embarrassed that anti-clericals helped him.[78] The *Institut*, in turn, had nothing official

---

75. Wolffe, p. 190.
76. See our Prologue.
77. *LQO*, p. 409.
78. Ibid., p. 412.

to do with him. It even refused to host him during a visit to Montreal in January 1860.[79] This did not stop the ultramontane *Courrier du Canada* from castigating the 'democratic' papers in Quebec for their support of Chiniquy in 1859.[80]

One 1876 Protestant report[81] accused Chiniquy of sponsoring the short-lived, and rabidly anti-clerical, *La liberté* newspaper.[82] Chiniquy's words in his *50 Years* show that this would be an uncomfortable alliance: "Though I am in favour of liberty of conscience, in its highest sense, I think that the atheist ought to be punished like the murderer [i.e., the death penalty] and the thief - for his doctrines tend to make a murderer and a thief of every man."[83]

Pierre Blanchet and Joseph Doutre were two of the exceptions to the lack of cooperation between anti-Catholics and anti-clericals. Blanchet allowed the *Avenir* to be driven into the ground rather than to stop publicizing Chiniquy. Doutre served as a lawyer for Chiniquy's associate,[84] appealed to the ex-priest for funds for the Guibord case,[85] served on the Civil Rights Alliance with Chiniquy,[86] and wrote letters of appreciation for the *Montreal Witness*.[87]

Later we see a greater parting of the ways as Calvin Amaron, in order to stimulate interest for the French Protestant *Aurore*, mentioned that there was a need for an edifying French paper to oppose the French

---

79. Clipping from a French newspaper, 26 January 1860 (**ASQ**, Polygraphie 52, 4).

80. *Cour*, 27 July 1859, p. 2. It did not require hearty support in order to offend the *Courrier*.

81. Court, *The Story of my Connection with the Chiniquy Movement in Montreal of 1874-77* (Montreal, 1877), pp. 15-16. The newspaper was denounced by *A*, 1 April 1876.

82. This newspaper of Gegeor Melchi however never mentioned Chiniquy, preferring scandalous writings such as *Maria Monk* and *The Wandering Jew* which the *MW* (1 April 1876, p. 1) considered to be fundamentally anti-Christian.

83. *50 Years*, p. 305. These comments were prudently dropped in the French translation *50 ans* and in the edition of *LQO*.

84. *MW*, 27 April 1876, p. 3.

85. Joseph Doutre letter to Chiniquy, 8 May [1874] (**UCT**, Chiniquy Personal Papers).

86. *G*, 5 December 1877, p. 4.

87. *MW*, 17 January 1876, p. 1.

5. ANTI-CATHOLICISM

Figure 36 Whole family in front of St. Anne, Illinois house **AP 04-80**

anti-clerical press.[88] Quite possibly ultramontane pressure prevented real cooperation. However, despite the frequent lumping together of evangelical anti-Catholics and anti-clericals by Catholic conservatives, the links seem to have been very weak and rare.

---

88. *CFA*, 30 March 1893, p. 11.

CONCLUSION

In summary, Chiniquy belongs to the version of anti-Catholicism, which has evangelical roots and generally evangelical goals. His goals were neither ethnocentric nor aimed to conserve Anglo power. While his conspiracy mindset verged on paranoia, Chiniquy genuinely saw it as his duty to warn all Protestant countries lest they should fall under the social, political and religious control which he had experienced in French Canada. As he saw it, progress, liberty and education demanded political measures to curb Catholic conspiracy. At the same time, evangelism was needed for those who had been duped. Chiniquy strove after these two goals of politics and evangelism with energy and vision.

The anti-Protestantism and social control of ultramontane Quebec helped form Chiniquy's vision. Reaction to his apostasy cut off positive contact with Catholics. This inspired him to provide a retreat centre that assisted ex-priests financially and spiritually in their isolation. Chiniquy's experiences of social isolation and mob violence as well as his ex-priest status provided him with a ready Protestant platform outside Quebec.

In this polemical age, Chiniquy thrived and became a Protestant champion. He mastered many of the forms of polemical literature in French and in English. In the process he managed to convince all the leading evangelical leaders in the Western world that he was a genuine evangelical. Probably many questioned his methods, but none seem to have questioned his faith publicly.

6

A PROTESTANT CHAMPION

SENTINEL

Evangelist and polemicist in Montreal (1870, 1875-78)

Outside Illinois the other primary location for Chiniquy's Protestant ministry was Montreal. Chiniquy's Montreal mission began during several months in 1870 and then a prolonged period from January 1875 until the summer of 1878. Unlike his later Protestant ministry in St. Anne, there was constant controversy in Montreal. As he came to oppose Catholicism in its stronghold, outrage was provoked. Chiniquy preached on general biblical topics each Sunday morning. Controversial apologetics dominated his lectures on Sunday or other evenings. Chiniquy always found eye-catching, confrontational titles: The conflict of Rome with Christianity, Flee idolatry, The virgin Mary - neither mother of God nor intercessor, Liberty of conscience, The Jesuits - their anti-social and anti-Christian principles, Why does the Church of Rome hate public education?, Jesus Christ and not the Pope is our authority, The priests of Rome - the true murderers of Abraham Lincoln.

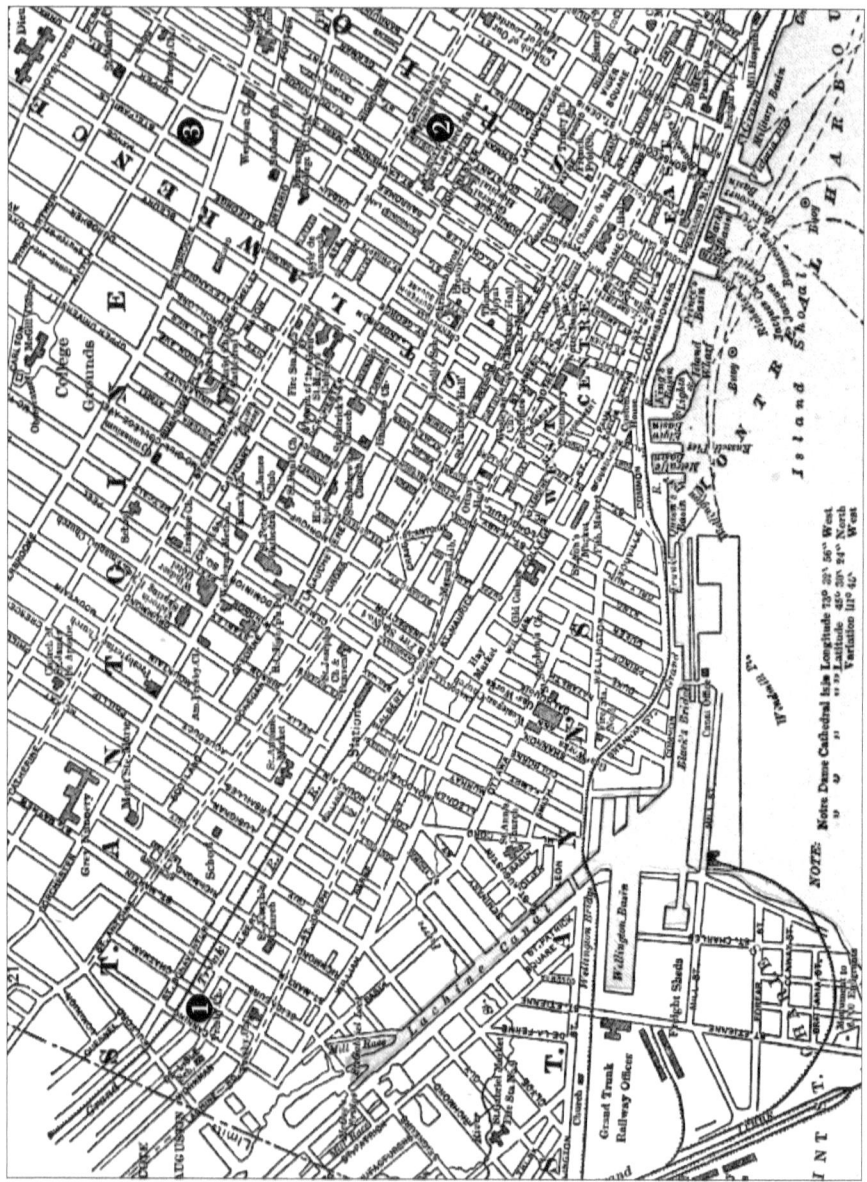

Figure 37   Detail on 1891 Montreal map   **AP** 15 (2) 027
1. St. Saviour's Presbyterian Church, 1877-78
2. Russell Hall, 1875-76
3. Retirement home 3458 Ste. Famille St., 1892-99

6. A PROTESTANT CHAMPION

Bourget viewed Chiniquy's lectures as apocalyptic portents. He condemned his former friend as a wolf in sheep's clothing. In a 1875 pastoral letter the bishop renewed the 1859 denunciation of Chiniquy and warned the faithful to avoid all contact because of his apostasy, his excommunicate state, and his gross distortions of Catholic beliefs. Bourget's emotions are summarized in his repeated phrase, "how have you fallen from Heaven, Lucifer (or angel of light)?"[1] In addition the bishop's imprimatur appeared on a series of pamphlets that refuted specific points of Chiniquy's allegations.[2]

Probably Chiniquy's publication of a series of lists of alleged converts was part of the rationale for Bourget's counter-attack. However the lists kept appearing after the Catholic denunciations. Astounding numbers were listed in rosters of those abjuring Catholicism between November 1875 and June 1876. According to MacVicar's tabulation at Presbyterian Synod, the *Montreal Witness* published 2,043 names in this period.[3] Chiniquy himself claimed 7,000 converts in four years spent in Montreal.[4]

Naturally those statistics were disputed. There were nowhere near 7,000, nor even 2,000 new French Protestant members. Yet few on the list were challenged as frauds. Doubtless, Chiniquy did make a major impact, first with his lectures, and then as he counselled day and night. He was particularly successful with immigrants from France who felt marginalized by the more conservative French Canadian Catholics. Abjuration from Catholicism was not equivalent to a conversion to

---

1. *Quomodo cecidisti de coelo, lucifer?* in Bourget pastoral letter "pour dénoncer de nouveau Mr. Ch. Chiniquy et défendre aux Catholiques de lire le Daily Witness…", 19 March 1875 (*MEM*, vol. 7, pp. 107-25).

2. Villeneuve, *Contre Poison. Faussetés, erreurs, impostures, blasphèmes de l'apostat Chiniquy* (Montreal, 1875), 2 vols. Villeneuve in the same year also produced another pamphlet on Chiniquy, *Honte et mépris,* 8 p., under the pseudonym of XYZ.

3. *PCC Synod Proceedings,* June 1876, p. 179. 220 more converts were listed as a result of his tours outside Quebec.

4. *50 Years,* p. 822.

Protestantism. Nevertheless, abjuration became a costly act when publicized. Even allowing for exaggeration in Chiniquy's figures, it is hard to imagine how so many francophone abjurers, could continue without a trace in Montreal. If the abjurations were legitimate large numbers must have lapsed or have left the province, as many French Protestants tended to do.[5]

The most shocking of Chiniquy's provocations came in January 1876. He consecrated a wafer, using the Catholic liturgy and the irreversible power that, according to the Catholic Church, all those once-ordained still retained.[6] After this he pierced the wafer with a knife, crumpled it and ground it under foot. Catholics in England later wrote of him:

> there is one thing at which [Catholics'] blood boils and which they cannot and will not stand, and that is the travestying of the sacred ceremony ... at which our Lord instituted the Sacrament of the Eucharist. If the law does not prevent it, then the person who indulges in this awful profanity does so at his peril.[7]

Bourget's circular recommended that the Church celebrate a Mass of Reparation:

> At the mere mention of this horrible attempt, this unheard of sacrilege, this frightful profanation, there can be but one sentiment of grief throughout the entire Diocese ... the Lamb of God, full of mercy and sweetness, allows himself to be immolated and held up to mockery by the hands of an apostate and sacrilegious priest, see if there be a sorrow equal to mine (says Jesus).[8]

---

5. There were groups of Chiniquy converts who helped found Namur, Quebec with others reported at Mattawa, Ontario and many in New England. Chiniquy often pleaded for jobs for new converts who were put out of work due to their new beliefs (e.g. *MW*, 15 November 1877, p. 2). He also mentioned in a 17 September 1877 letter that many had emigrated (Butler, *The Reformation in Canada* (London, 1877), p. 11).

6. There was a subsequent debate between Bp. Bourget and the Toronto Catholic bishop who denied that apostates conserved the power (*MW*, 16 February 1876, p. 2).

7. *Catholic Times*, in England, as quoted by J. Moore, *Rev. Charles Chiniquy's Recent Tour Abroad*, [1897], p. 4.

8. The Montreal Catholic paper, *True Witness*, 11 February 1876, p. 6; *MEM*, vol. 7, pp. 308-10.

This action was apparently a Chiniquy innovation.[9] However it followed the pattern of Old Testament actions against Baal practices, Boniface against the holy oaks,[10] and missionaries against African or Amerindian animism. In each case the most central objects of "idolatry" were physically destroyed, in order to demonstrate that they had no power against the supreme God of the Bible. The Protestant papers seemed uncomfortable with Chiniquy's radical action but they rejected the accusation of mockery. Evangelicals defended the action since it had a Biblical basis.[11] They noted that the design was to first shock, but then to stimulate reformulation of one's faith.

Since 1859, even before this aggressive act, Chiniquy had faced violence.[12] Often he provided provocative fresh material in his well-publicized lectures at the Annual meetings of various evangelical societies of Montreal, which were concentrated in the same week in January.

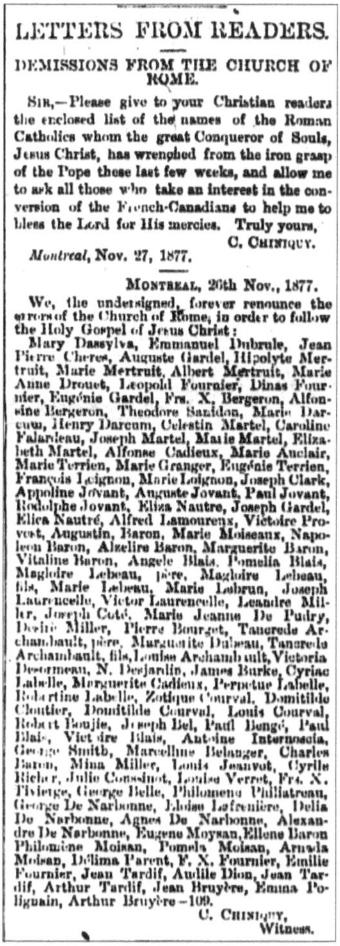

LETTERS FROM READERS.

DEMISSIONS FROM THE CHURCH OF ROME.

SIR,—Please give to your Christian readers the enclosed list of the names of the Roman Catholics whom the great Conqueror of Souls, Jesus Christ, has wrenched from the iron grasp of the Pope these last few weeks, and allow me to ask all those who take an interest in the conversion of the French-Canadians to help me to bless the Lord for His mercies. Truly yours,

C. CHINIQUY.

Montreal, Nov. 27, 1877.

MONTREAL, 26th Nov., 1877.

We, the undersigned, forever renounce the errors of the Church of Rome, in order to follow the Holy Gospel of Jesus Christ:

Mary Dassylva, Emmanuel Dubrule, Jean Pierre Cheres, Auguste Gardel, Hipolyte Mertruit, Marie Mertruit, Albert Mertruit, Marie Anne Drouet, Leopold Fournier, Dinas Fournier, Eugénie Gardel, Frs. X. Bergeron, Alfonsine Bergeron, Theodore Sanidon, Marie Darcuw, Henry Darcum, Celestin Martel, Caroline Falardeau, Joseph Martel, Marie Martel, Elizabeth Martel, Alfonse Cadieux, Marie Auclair, Marie Terrien, Marie Granger, Eugénie Terrien, François Loignon, Marie Loignon, Joseph Clark, Appoline Jovant, Auguste Jovant, Paul Jovant, Rodolphe Jovant, Eliza Nautre, Joseph Gardel, Elica Nautré, Alfred Lamoureux, Victoire Provost, Augustin, Baron, Marie Moiseaux, Napoleon Baron, Alzelire Baron, Marguerite Baron, Vitaline Baron, Angele Blais, Pomelia Blais, Magloire Lebeau, père, Magloire Lebeau, fils, Marie Lebeau, Marie Lebrun, Joseph Laurencelle, Victor Laurencelle, Leandre Miller, Joseph Coté, Marie Jeanne De Pudry, Desiré Miller, Pierre Bourget, Tancrede Archambault, père, Marguerite Dubeau, Tancrede Archambault, fils, Louise Archambault, Victoria Desormeau, N. Desjardin, James Burke, Cyriac Labelle, Marguerite Cadieux, Perpetue Labelle, Robertine Labelle, Zotique Courval, Domitilde Cloutier, Domitilde Courval, Louis Courval, Robert Boujie, Joseph Bel, Paul Bengé, Paul Blais, Victoire Blais, Antoine Internoscia, George Smith, Marcelline Belanger, Charles Baron, Mina Miller, Louis Jeanvot, Cyrille Richer, Julie Conssinot, Louise Verret, Frs. X. Piviege, George Belle, Philomene Philliatreau, George De Narbonne, Eloise Lafrenière, Delia De Narbonne, Agnes De Narbonne, Alexandre De Narbonne, Eugene Moysan, Ellene Baron Philomine Moisan, Pomela Moisan, Arnela Moisan, Délima Parent, F. X. Fournier, Emilie Fournier, Jean Tardif, Audile Dion, Jean Tardif, Arthur Tardif, Jean Bruyère, Emma Polignain, Arthur Bruyère—109.

C. CHINIQUY,
Witness.

Figure 38 Abjurations (*Montreal Daily Witness*, Nov. 28, 1877, p. 2)

9. This was repeated at least one other time in Burlington VT in 1878. See Ruddel (Ottawa, 1983), p. 54-55.

10. Thanks to the late John H. Yoder of the University of Notre Dame for his reminder of this connection.

11. *MW*, 7 February 1876, p. 2; 18 March 1876, p. 4; R.F. Burns, *Our Modern Babylon* (Halifax, 1876), pp. 17-18.

12. The major Montreal riots were on 9 January 1870 at the Craig St. Church; numerous times in January and February 1875 at Craig St. and Côté St. churches; and in November 1884 at Canning St. Church and St. Jean Church.

In Quebec most of those arrested or suspected of violent opposition against Chiniquy's lectures were French. Outside Quebec most were Irish. Strong-arm tactics were transferable from politics to religion especially in Irish circles. When municipal, often Catholic, police proved untrustworthy or slow, the Orange Order offered its services to maintain the peace. At other times a bodyguard was formed from the students of Presbyterian College. It is almost certain that without these bodyguards, Chiniquy would have been killed.[13] Chiniquy carried a heavy blanket to protect his shoulders and head. Several times he escaped, relying on his calm and ruses.[14]

Each act of violence or disruption against Chiniquy helped solidify evangelical Protestant support for his right to freedom of speech.[15] Neither the *True Witness'* appeals for calm[16] or parish sermons[17] stopped the violence nor did they dissuade Chiniquy from believing that the Catholic hierarchy was directly responsible for the violence. Nevertheless, contrary to some American anti-Catholic lecturers, no act of violence against Catholics ever followed a Chiniquy lecture.

Chiniquy worked for the FCMS in 1870, using the Craig St. Church in Montreal as his base. When he served the Presbyterians from January 1875 on, he was given the use of Russell Hall on St. Catherine Street. It soon proved too small for the crowds so a new St. Sauveur Presbyterian Church with seating for over 600 was opened in January 1877 on Canning Street

---

13. *MW*, 25 February 1875, p. 1, pointed out the constant cries of "kill him" and the futility of waiting for the police.

14. Joseph Morin, "Charles Chiniquy, the apostle of French evangelization", handwritten manuscript, p. 26. **AP 12-34**

15. Note the disproportionate space given to these riots in Campbell, *A Concise History of French Protestant* (Montreal, 1898) and also in the French Protestant histories of Duclos (Montreal 1913) and Villard (Toronto, 1928).

16. Their editorial is quoted approvingly in *MW*, 18 February 1875, p. 3.

17. *MW*, 15 February 1875, p. 3.

6. A PROTESTANT CHAMPION

in the West end.[18] This was prudently situated across the street from a police station.

The lists of abjurations diminished in frequency and numbers after mid-1876. Riots also diminished, as the means of protection were standardized. This did not mean a period of stability for Chiniquy. His name appeared in the *Montreal Witness* and other newspapers almost constantly. There were descriptions of violent incidents, spectacular lectures or letters to the editor. Court cases also continued.[19] A French Protestant convert, LeMettayeur Masselin, alleged that Chiniquy had conspired to defame him.

The only example of a lengthy evangelical Protestant critique of Chiniquy is found in connection with this case. James Court[20] had been a pioneer in organizing French evangelization with the FCMS and then with the Presbyterian Church. His son, W. B. Court,[21] published a pamphlet about the French Presbyterian mission. The younger Court had worked with Chiniquy and became very critical of his authoritarianism, his inflated convert lists and his willingness to use unscrupulous means and people. Court also accused Chiniquy of helping to fund a scurrilous anti-clerical paper, *La liberté*, whose editor eventually turned on the ex-priest.

Court Jr. was even more critical of the Presbyterian Board of French Evangelization leadership and called for a review. No review occurred. Instead the Board, including his own father and virtually all involved in French ministry, exonerated all those named by Court. The son's criticisms were attributed to mental imbalance by some. W.B. Court was neither prominent enough nor were his charges specific enough to

---

18. *MW*, 15 January 1877, p. 2, provides a description of the church building and its official opening.

19. The following was the thirty-fourth trial according to Chiniquy in *MW*, 29 November 1877, p. 2.

20. See "James Court" in Jean-Louis Lalonde, *Belle Rivière*, 1840-2006 (Montreal, 2007), p. 475-490.

21. Court, *The Story of My Connection* (Montreal, 1877), 18 p.

make a dent in Chiniquy's reputation.[22] Among the insights in Court's pamphlet we learn that Chiniquy eventually alienated at least some of the European converts with his aggressive ways and that most of those on his lists later abandoned the Protestants.

While other French Protestants undoubtedly disapproved of Chiniquy's methods, public criticism was deemed unwise. Catholic propaganda was ever on the lookout to discredit French Protestantism and its prime target, Chiniquy. Although a Chiniquy supporter usually, Baptist leader Theodore Lafleur did comment in 1885 to his denomination:

> there is just now a larger, though more outward and superficial agency at work in the presence and preaching here [Montreal] of Mr. Chiniquy. Crowds gather whenever he speaks; the mass simply from curiosity and lawlessness; a good number with a settled purpose of preventing him from speaking, and a few to listen and learn what he teaches. Without endorsing his mode of attack, now that he is here we must stand for the liberty of speech and of religious worship, and in those troubled meetings endeavour to scatter the good seed of the Word ... so that a few at least may be enlightened and saved.[23]

Chiniquy took every opportunity to visit and speak in outlying areas of Quebec and other parts of Canada or the United States. Because he rejected very few invitations, periods of complete exhaustion regularly interrupted his plans. He required sick leaves every year he served in Montreal. When he visited rural Quebec he made no money[24] but he did encounter great physical dangers. Chiniquy aimed to encourage local French Protestants of all denominations,[25] as well as to make new converts. While he ended up greatly irritating committed Catholics,

---

22. The *MW* (15 September 1877, p. 4) agreed with having a review and provided a quite objective evaluation of the charges.

23. GL Report in *Baptist Year Book*, 1885, pp. 93-94.

24. Catholic analysts deemed this the only reason for his travels.

25. He returned to St. Marie, for example, in order to apologize to the Baptist, Louis Roussy and to repudiate his own former stance in the debate.

6. A PROTESTANT CHAMPION

those who wavered had an opportunity to hear and discuss an alternative faith.

Chiniquy did not neglect political action to stem Catholic power. He helped organize the Protestant Defence Association,[26] opposed public funding of Catholic schools across Canada,[27] hosted the Bismarck Lodge #4 of the International Protestant League,[28] and encouraged the Civil Rights Alliance to become more aggressive.[29] In other words, he associated himself with the party line for militant Protestants. This does not mean that he was a partisan for any political party. Chiniquy was always suspicious of the primary desire of politicians to use Christians for political ends.[30]

On the road

Each decade Chiniquy was invited to Britain by Protestant organizations. In January 1874 he began a six-month tour, starting with speaking engagements at St. James Hall and Exeter Hall before many dignitaries.[31] Lord Russell was prevented by sickness from presiding over one meeting but the Dean of Canterbury, Arthur Kinnaird MP, Sir Robert Peel, Sir John Murray, Lord Alfred Churchill and the well-known pastor P.T. Forsyth attended. A special reception was held for Chiniquy and the German Ambassador at the National Club.

In January 1883 he returned to Great Britain for lectures sponsored by the Protestant Educational Institute and its director G.R. Badenoch.

---

26. *MW*, 29 December 1875, p. 1. This was designed to protest treatment of Protestant natives in Oka, Quebec.
27. *MW*, 20 September 1876, p. 1 (here in Prince Edward Island).
28. *MW*, 12 December 1877, p. 5.
29. *MW*, 5 December 1877, p. 4.
30. For example he criticized the *MW* for supporting the Liberals (*MW*, 15 November 1877, p. 2).
31. Badenoch, *Ultramontanism. England's Sympathy with Germany* (London, 1874), pp. 111-117, 146-153.

This time recognition came in the form of an invitation by the most notable evangelical leader, Lord Shaftesbury, to address the Bible Society in London and to become a life member. Chiniquy used his influence in this group to persuade them to provide Catholic translations, such as the De Sacy, but with alternative readings in the margins.[32] He also successfully overcame strong pressure against printing versions of the Bible with the Apocrypha.

In the summer of 1878 Chiniquy took a one-year health leave from Montreal, on his doctor's advice. As usual a sea voyage restored him and he commenced a gruelling schedule of lectures. This time he headed to the Western United States and then to Australia. Again he travelled alone on the trip.

In Australia the Orange Order provided bodyguards but Chiniquy still encountered riots by Irish emigrants, particularly in Hobart Town, Tasmania.[33] Pastors of all Protestant denominations sponsored Chiniquy's lectures. Predictably, Chiniquy condemned 'Ritualism' (High Church Anglicanism) as well as the allocation of any political or educational power to Catholics. Chiniquy crossed Tasmania, New South Wales, Victoria, South Australia, Queensland and finally in 1880, New Zealand. Apparently he stimulated support for the Orange Order in all these areas.[34]

Besides his trips abroad, Chiniquy regularly visited French Protestants in New England and the Maritimes. What stands out most in Chiniquy's and others' accounts of these trips are the periodic riots. There were assaults on Chiniquy and/or the churches he addressed in Antigonish, Nova Scotia (July 1873), Halifax (March 1876), Hobart Town in Tasmania (July 1879), Rimouski, Quebec (June 1883), Quebec City (June 1884), and Montague, Prince Edward Island (August 1886). All became part of the

---

32. *Pastor Chiniquy at the Bible House* (London, c1883), 4 p.

33. There is a whole list in *50 Years*, pp. 823-828, and then in *40 Years*, ch. 34 and 35. For Hobart see the lengthy account in the *Mercury*, Australia, July 7, 1879 **AP** 15 (3) M 07-07b.

34. By 'a member of the Order', *Orangeism in Ireland and Throughout the Empire* (London, 1939), vol. 2, p. 526.

6. A PROTESTANT CHAMPION

Chiniquy lore. During a tour of New England in 1886, the ex-priest could not find any English church willing to take the risk to host him.[35] Nevertheless in 1885 he spoke at Hartford Seminary and in August 1888 he was invited by the evangelist Dwight L. Moody to speak at his Northfield, Massachusetts conference.[36]

ANTI-CATHOLIC FRIENDS AND CONTACTS

What kind of people welcomed and promoted Chiniquy? Were they noted more for being evangelical or were they the most rabid anti-Catholics? What denominations and organizations did he work with? What newspapers publicized his doings and sayings? Who published his books? A study of Chiniquy's contacts in various localities helps reveal his basic tenets.

We amassed an extensive chronology and list of correspondence. It is very important to begin to list and analyze Chiniquy's international connections.[37] No diary or continuous record of Chiniquy's life has yet been discovered. Inevitably then such a compilation will be incomplete.[38]

In Quebec, after he became a Protestant, Chiniquy gained the respect of all French Protestants. All Protestant leaders were close to him: the Baptists Lafleur, Therrien, and Cyr, the Presbyterians Duclos, Amaron, Doudiet, Bourgoin and Coussirat, the Congregationalist Provost, the Methodists Massicotte, Thomas Dorion, and Villard, and the French Anglicans. None of them publicly criticized Chiniquy. All praised him. Their newspapers, the *Semeur canadien* and later the *Aurore*, were uniformly positive and united behind their champion.

Almost every English-speaking evangelical in Quebec supported Chiniquy at some point in time. Although it was very evangelical and

---

35. *CC*, 3 (NY, 1886), p. 36.
36. *CC*, 5 (1888), p. 303, contains the speech text.
37. See our Appendix 5 for a preliminary list.
38. Some key friends have doubtless been neglected because of the sources or period covered. Others mentioned may have supported him only for a short period.

anti-Catholic, the *Montreal Witness* did question Chiniquy on occasion about his fund-raising or his extremes in anti-Catholicism. These rare and limited critiques in a controversial life point to support as being the general rule. The *Witness* always treated Chiniquy as "one of us", who on occasion needed to be challenged. Similarly Chiniquy occasionally critiqued the *Witness* for being too moderate, though he usually praised it.

The English Quebecer closest to Chiniquy was certainly Principal Donald MacVicar of Presbyterian College. At the same college Professor John Campbell was another friend and colleague on the Presbyterian Board of French Evangelization. Strong Chiniquy supporters from the FCMS included the Congregationalist pastor Henry Wilkes, Principal Dawson of McGill, John Redpath, James Court and Rev. Robert Ferrier Burns (Free Church). All of the evangelical elite in Montreal offered their financial and public support at points, or even acted as bodyguards. All these supporters were known to be evangelicals committed to French mission. The only evangelical criticism came from W.B. Court, the son of James, in 1877.[39] Chiniquy's reputation was deemed so crucial to the evangelical cause that W. B. Court was attacked by all Protestant leaders, including his own father.

The other English newspapers in Montreal were not evangelical in viewpoint and were therefore much more critical of Chiniquy. They preferred not to give him any publicity. They deemed him to be destructive to racial and religious harmony. Although non-evangelical Anglican Bishop Fulford opposed Chiniquy and any evangelization among the French,[40] the predominantly evangelical students of the Anglican Montreal Diocesan College turned out in force for Chiniquy's funeral.[41]

In the rest of English Canada, Chiniquy's was most strongly supported by Free Presbyterians, for example, Rev. George Sutherland of Prince

---

39. Court, 18 p.
40. Black, "A Crippled Crusade" (U. of Toronto, 1989), ch. 5.
41. *G*, 20 January 1899, p. 1.

6. A PROTESTANT CHAMPION

Edward Island. Evangelical Anglican leader Isaac Hellmuth[42], eventually bishop of London, was one of the first Protestants to help Chiniquy financially and with publicity. He was disappointed in his eager hope of drawing Chiniquy into the Anglican fold.[43]

Those who were most involved in evangelical organizations and were mission-minded tended to favour Chiniquy's cause. His earlier temperance work attracted further support. Presbyterian papers and the *Sentinel* in Toronto provided him with all the publicity he needed. The Orange Order was one largely non-evangelical group who also promoted Chiniquy speeches and material.[44]

As the power base for Presbyterians gradually shifted from Montreal to Toronto,[45] greater distance from the 'Catholic menace' made English evangelicals less aggressive. Those of the small but influential liberal evangelical school of thought followed George Grant, Principal of Queen's University, Kingston, in criticism of the Chiniquy polarization and anti-Catholic rhetoric.[46]

In the United States, as in Canada most of Chiniquy's close acquaintances were evangelicals. His Illinois lawyer, Stephen Moore had a conversion and joined the Methodists. Rebecca Snowdon and George Stuart were lay philanthropists linked to the revival in Philadelphia. Editor-pastor James O'Connor was one of a host of evangelical ex-priests who looked to Chiniquy for inspiration. Chiniquy was financed by various evangelical organizations. Among these were the American and Foreign Christian Union and the American Tract Society. He maintained close links with the French mission in the

---

42. Richard Vaudry, *Anglicans and the Atlantic World: High Churchmen, Evangelicals, and the Quebec Connection* (Montreal, 2003); *DCB*.
43. Black, pp. 330-335.
44. Perry, *Lectures* (Toronto, 1892). See our Chapter 9 for more on his Orange connections.
45. See Fraser, "The Christianization of Our Civilization" (York University, 1983), p. 109.
46. *40 Years*, pp. 294-302.

College protestant français of Springfield, Massachusetts and with the mission to Catholics of the Pauline Propaganda.

Prior to his adoption of Protestantism, Chiniquy, as a member of a minority ethnic group of Catholics, naturally expressed alarm at the anti-Catholic Nativists and Know-Nothings.[47] However much later the Loyal Women of American Liberty, a political rather than religious group, financed one of Chiniquy's pamphlets.[48] After Chiniquy spoke at several "patriotic" rallies in Boston, combined Catholic and Unitarian pressure resulted in the exclusion of a Chiniquy book at the Boston Public Library. In reaction, a 'Christian patriotic' meeting was organized in Boston. The book was successfully reinserted.[49] These activities provide evidence of broader anti-Catholic support for Chiniquy.

One most crucial question remains: did the APA actually ever pay Chiniquy? Several polemical Catholic pamphlets affirmed that the APA did so.[50] These pamphlets provide no supporting evidence. This makes the affirmation quite suspect. In Kinzer's thorough study[51] nothing of this is mentioned; nor is it in any neutral commentaors in Chiniquy's time.

There seems to be little question that Chiniquy approved of the APA initiatives in general. He favoured political initiatives to block Catholic power. In Chiniquy's view, Catholic secret societies were extremely dangerous but Protestant societies were essential.[52] Still there is at most

---

47. *MW*, 20 February 1856, p. 60. The Know-Nothings were so called because, as a secret society they pledged to vote only for the approved Protestant candidates. They always replied to queries of outsiders with 'I know nothing about it'. See Billington for more information.

48. *Mr. Chiniquy in California*, (San Francisco, c1878), 4 p.

49. J. Moore, *Boston Public Library rejects Father Chiniquy's 'Forty Years in the Church of Christ.'* (Boston, c1900), 8 p.

50. *Chronology of the Life of 'Pastor' Chiniquy*, n.d., p. 10 (**UND**) and Lucey, p. 42. See also George p. 20 and Wallace pp. 33, 54.

51. Kinzer, *An Episode in Anti-Catholicism: The American Protective Association* (Seattle, 1964). He does state that Chiniquy's works inspired them (pp. 31-2).

52. *MW*, 18 December 1877, p. 2: "I like secret societies because they are just the only ones by which God's purposes are accomplished." He pointed to Jesus, the apostle

6. A PROTESTANT CHAMPION

a minimal link between Chiniquy and the APA. This contrasts with the abundant evidence that reputable, and often initially suspicious, evangelicals cooperated with Chiniquy.

One would expect the APA patriotic press to publicize Chiniquy.[53] He had links with several of the journals that Kinzer associates with the APA.[54] Nevertheless, Chiniquy gave his plaudits and financial donations to the *Citoyen franco-américain* and the *Converted Catholic*.[55] These papers distanced themselves from those who were anti-ethnic or who were aggressive against individual Catholics. Chiniquy and the writers of these journals wished to maintain positive relations with lay Catholics in order to convert them.[56]

Probably Chiniquy would have agreed with a letter to the *Converted Catholic* from Detroit which said: "the APA and other bodies seem to have a mission in relation to political Romanism, but your method of work for the enlightenment of Roman Catholics as well as Protestants seems to be destined to have the most durable success."[57]

In Australia the same pattern is evident. Chiniquy's sponsors, publishers and greatest supporters were committed evangelicals. Although it was announced that Chiniquy's trip to the Antipodes between 1878 and 1880 was sponsored by the Orange Order, the Order acted as bodyguards rather than as organizers or speakers. Presbyterian pastor and editor George Sutherland knew Chiniquy when he had lived in Sydney,

---

Paul, and all military generals as examples showing the necessity of secrets.

53. An excerpt from Chiniquy's *50 Years* is found as "President Lincoln's assassination traced directly to the doors of Rome" *APA Magazine*, 1,6 (Nov. 1895), 547-561.

54. Kinzer, p. 256. See e.g. *Protestant Standard* of Philadelphia, the *Boston Citizen* and the *Primitive Catholic* of New York. The last however had religious priorities.

55. See for example his typical letter to the *CC*, 12 (1895), p. 63, which calls it the most revealing journal about Catholic intentions.

56. *CC*, 12 (1895), p. 295, critiquing the Orangemen, and 14 (1897), p. 198, opposing anti-Catholicism.

57. Ibid., 11 (1893), p. 39. A recent discovery will likely shed light on the discovery when examined: *A Welcome To Father Chiniquy*, American Protective Association, 1 p. **AP** 10-56. See Figure 34 on our p. 148.

Nova Scotia. This was the person who invited Chiniquy to lecture in Australia. In HobartTown there was a notable absence of Anglican support but the Dean of Melbourne and other Anglican evangelicals did commend Chiniquy's work.[58]

So far as we know little research has been done on Chiniquy's links in Australia and New Zealand. Still, those contacts we know about were all evangelicals. As in the United States, Canada and Britain, Chiniquy acquired broad evangelical support. Often the Free Presbyterians took the lead, but Chiniquy's message appealed to the full spectrum of evangelicals. Though his tirades against Ritualists inflamed many Anglicans, the sentiments appealed to most evangelical Anglicans.

Much more is known about Britain's religious and political scene than that of the colonies. In the Victorian era religious conflict was also an intensely political and religious issue. Who invited Chiniquy and who publicized him? Once again it was evangelical, anti-Catholic bodies such as the Scottish Reformation Society, the Protestant Educational Institute and the Protestant Alliance. These groups wished to lobby rather than to be politically partisan. They sought conversions of Catholics.[59] Lord Shaftesbury, the Baptist orator Charles Spurgeon Jr., Lord Roden of Ireland, Rev. Grattan Guinness and other evangelical celebrities welcomed Chiniquy.

Chiniquy's keenest British supporters included less well known individuals such as G.R. Badenoch -the Scottish Reformation Society secretary who invited him to Scotland in 1859, Mesac Thomas - Colonial Church and School Society secretary in London in 1860 (later the Australian bishop of Goulburn), Montagu Russell Butler - a fund-raiser and tract writer, the fervent editor Mrs. Faulkner Bird of Leeds and A.H. Guinness - the Protestant Alliance secretary who invited him in 1896. Each of these combined impeccable evangelical credentials with staunch anti-Catholicism.

---

58. *Mercury*, July 7, 1879 **AP** 15 (3) 07-07b-05.
59. Wolffe, *The Protestant Crusade* (Oxford, 1991), pp. 161-2, 318.

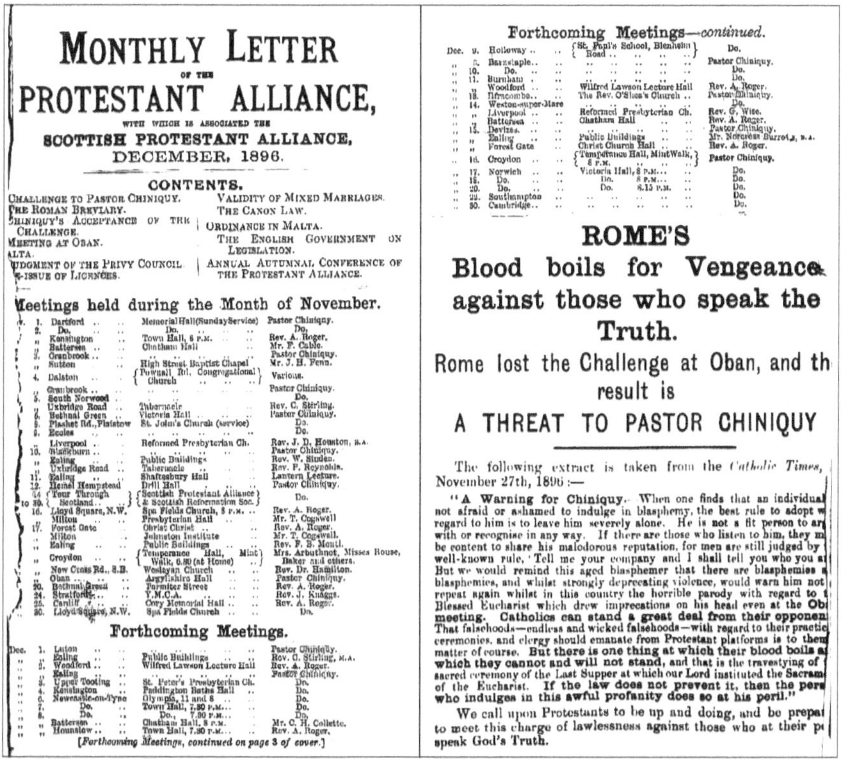

6. A PROTESTANT CHAMPION

Figure 39 Heavy schedule in England (Monthly letter, Dec. 1896) AP 15 C1 F020 08

Chiniquy's press coverage, at least that which he collected for a scrap book,[60] is solely from the identifiably Christian press of Britain: *The Record, The Rock, The Christian,* the *Protestant Alliance Monthly Newsletter, The Bulwark* and the *Christian Herald.* There were articles in the *India Watchman* from Bombay, and from France in the *Bulletin du monde chrétien,* the *Chrétien évangélique* and the *Chrétien français.* Key evangelical leaders such as Eugene Reveillaud of France and Alessandro Gavazzi of Italy called Chiniquy a good friend.[61] No evidence has been found that he had a comparable relationship with any social or political leaders.

---

60. **SL** c.2/20 also **AP** 15 C1-F011-F023.
61. Reveillaud in *Cinquante ans* preface; Gavazzi in a letter printed in *MW,* 4 April 1870.

THE CONTROVERSIAL CONVERSION OF CHARLES CHINIQUY
GRAND OLD MAN (1888-98)

Finally at the age of 78, on January 1st, 1888, Charles Chiniquy retired from the pastorate of St. Anne's. He decided to invest considerable time in reuniting the two Presbyterian churches in St. Anne under the new pastor. Then he stayed on in St. Anne until his fine residence burned down in 1892. This brought an end to his American base for lecture tours and annual visits to the Canadian Presbyterian Synods.

Chiniquy was now the Grand Old Man of Protestantism. The *Converted Catholic* referred to his "sweet and venerable face": "For the last 40 years ... [he] has been the foremost champion of Protestantism on the American continent. His fame is worldwide. Though 87 years of age, Father Chiniquy still enjoys good health."[62]

In many newspaper accounts Chiniquy's strength, health and stirring oratory were noted with comparisons to the undimmed eyes of Moses:

> For his age, his physical and intellectual strength are fantastic ... Though he does not perform miracles, he is himself a living miracle. His hand does not tremble and he reads at age 85 without glasses. Rome certainly is justified in fearing this man whom it has not been able to destroy by hate, jealousy or its infernal plots. Let Rome know then that it is useless to fight those who are protected and delivered by the God of Daniel.[63]

Thus even his health became an aspect of the propaganda war. The "grand old man" himself wrote:

> I ascribe my long life under God to my abstaining from the use of intoxicating liquors, and general observance of the laws of health. No doubt my habitual state of mind has had a great influence on my bodily health. My strong confidence in my God and the peace and joy I have felt ... have tended to promote health and length of days.[64]

---

62. *CC*, 12 (1896), p. 3.
63. *A*, 5 May 1894, p. 7. Also see Trudel, p. 279.
64. *40 Years*, p. 476.

6. A PROTESTANT CHAMPION

The *Aurore* pleaded, unsuccessfully, with French Protestants not to invite Chiniquy to so many events. He seemed incapable of saying 'no', and he was too old to wander around the country by himself.[65] There were still crisis points in Chiniquy's life,[66] e.g. when Chiniquy announced publicly that he had no intention of a deathbed repentance and returning to Rome.[67] Rumours of his death surfaced regularly but news of a startling, complete recovery followed.[68]

While the ex-priest's health was good, his finances were more precarious. Despite Trudel's allegations[69], the fire in St. Anne obliged Chiniquy to share an apartment with his son-in-law, Professor Joseph Morin in Montreal. Many of Chiniquy's letters during these years speak of financial straits that he blamed on fires or dishonest publishers. Usually his tours involved fundraising but the proceeds seem to have virtually all gone for French Presbyterian evangelism.

In Montreal the ex-priest settled in as a parishioner at the French St. Jean Church and occasional preacher in the surrounding area. The elders of the church were very proud of their hero who raised funds for the new church and then laid the cornerstone.[70] Nevertheless, they requested that, for his lectures, Chiniquy not display any polemical titles that would antagonize Roman Catholics.[71]

In 1893, Chiniquy was honoured with a Doctor of Divinity degree from Presbyterian College in Montreal. This was awarded by his great friend Donald MacVicar. The title was proudly used to show Protestant recognition. Chiniquy wrote often for the *Aurore* and recruited for it. Unlike the *Montreal Witness* this newspaper never maintained any

---

65. *A*, 3 November 1894, p. 4.
66. June 1892, May 1893, October 1894, December 1895, February 1897.
67. See especially his letters to Archbp. Fabre in *40 Years*, ch. 40.
68. See for example *A*, June 25, 1926 recounting an incident in Worcester MA in 1889.
69. Trudel, pp. 280-281 claiming great wealth from his tours.
70. *A*, 25 August 1894, pp. 3-4.
71. Elders' register for the Église St. Jean, 14 January 1894 (**UCM**). This relates to the Papineau conversion (see below).

Figure 40   French Protestant picnic (SHPFQ *Bulletin,* Sept. 2006, p. 5) AP 12-123-304.

critical distance from their French Protestant champion.[72] Its correspondents always defended Chiniquy when attacked. His talks were a highlight of the annual French Protestant picnics held outside of Montreal. The Duclos history includes a photo of all the French Protestant leaders at a picnic with Chiniquy in the centre of the pioneer missionaries.[73]

When Louis Amadée Papineau, son of the famous leader of the 1837 rebellion, Louis Joseph, became a Protestant in January 1894, he requested that Chiniquy officially receive him. This provoked another vicious propaganda war in Montreal.[74] It also provided the Protestant picnic with a new site at the Papineau grounds of Montebello.

Chiniquy's age did not stop either his aggressive lectures or the assaults against him. On a fundraising tour among Southern Ontario

---

72. *MW* (e.g., 16 April 1875, p. 2) often encouraged more love and moderation in his letters and lectures. This resembles earlier advice from Bp. Bourget to Chiniquy. *MW* always defended Chiniquy's freedom of speech but this was "in no way dependent either upon [his] character, opinions or course." (*MW,* 23 March 1875, p. 3).

73. Duclos (Montreal, 1913), vol.2, p. 303. Also in Ruddell (Ottawa, 1983) and Rocher (Quebec, 1993). See *Le Bulletin,* Société d'Histoire du Protestantisme Franco-Québecois, Sept. 2006, p. 5 for identification of the faces.

74. *A,* 3 February 1894, pp. 7-9, refutes the *Minerve,* 15 January 1894, p. 2. See Trudel, pp. 267-71.

6. A PROTESTANT CHAMPION

Figure 41   The elderly Chiniquy at Elgin Rd cottage **AP** 15 C1 F026 03

churches in December 1895, Chiniquy did not heed moderate voices. He made blatant political references to the Manitoba Schools question that resulted in one cancellation and then rest for exhaustion and discouragement.[75] Still Chiniquy adamantly opposed any separate rights for Catholic schools.[76] In 1896, Dr. Chiniquy took part in a lecture series by experts in French evangelization. His topic, inevitably, was

---

75.   *A*, 21 December 1895, p. 6, and 28 December, pp. 12-13.
76.   *Minerve*, 12 June 1896, p. 2.

the most controversial: "Why did England Conquer Canada?". From his other works we know that he believed that God chose England in order to re-establish religious and political liberty in Canada.[77]

His writing continued as well with Chiniquy's important refutation of a Catholic pamphleteer, "Kentucky Ben". In this Chiniquy demonstrated that he had enjoyed widespread Protestant support.[78] Encouraged by the Presbyterian General Assembly of 1889, Chiniquy began work on a second volume of his autobiography. This was published posthumously as *Forty Years in the Church of Christ*.

After rewriting his will, Chiniquy set off alone for his last voyage across the Atlantic in September 1897. Another National Club reception awaited him with many anti-Catholic notables.[79] At Chiniquy's request the Protestant Alliance arranged a devastating schedule for him of almost daily lectures of several hours, moving constantly around England and Scotland.[80] He also spoke to groups such as the Calvinistic Protestant Union.

The tour included a speech at the National Protestant Congress at Exeter Hall, organized to protest against convents. Other engagements included the Protestant Alliance Congress in Shrewsbury, a huge rally at Blackheath Concert Hall and finally a lecture at Queen's Hall, London in connection with the Grand United Protestant demonstration for the Queen's Diamond Jubilee. In the midst of this trip, exhaustion struck again. After an enforced rest Chiniquy carried on in May and June, to Luther sites in Germany, and to visit Holland and France.

---

77. *MW*, 20 January 1877, p. 1, as one example.

78. *Father Chiniquy to Kentucky Ben* (Minneapolis, 1892). This can also be found as chapter 38 of *40 Years*.

79. See "Welcome to Pastor Chiniquy", a clipping from an unidentified British paper of October, 1896 (**SL** c.1/20).

80. See the schedule on the covers of the Monthly Newsletter of the Protestant Alliance, November 1896 and February 1897 (**SL** c.1/19 and 1/20), and *Life and Work of Charles Chiniquy*, 1897. **AP** 15-01 provides extensive coverage of the tour.

6. A PROTESTANT CHAMPION

One newspaper reporter induced Chiniquy to recount his honest views of English politics. Never one to avoid controversy the ex-priest stated that he had found England to be strongly Protestant, but that it had been betrayed by its Ritualist nobility and upper classes, including William Gladstone and Lord Salisbury. The current pope, like all his predecessors, was the anti-Christ, according to Chiniquy.[81]

On his return to Canada, Chiniquy continued preaching until the autumn of 1897 but then became too weak to walk until the next summer.[82] This allowed him time to write and revise his autobiography.

HIS LAST DAYS (1898-99)

Chiniquy again made a strong recovery and preached in June 1898, for the first time in eight months. He celebrated his 89th birthday at his Elgin Road retreat. The old warrior continued to preach occasionally up until December. After he developed bronchitis in January 1899, Chiniquy was bed-ridden. Gradually he deteriorated and for the last two days was often unconscious. Several hours before his death he recovered enough to recognize his family and then passed away peacefully in his Montreal home, on January 16th, 1899.[83]

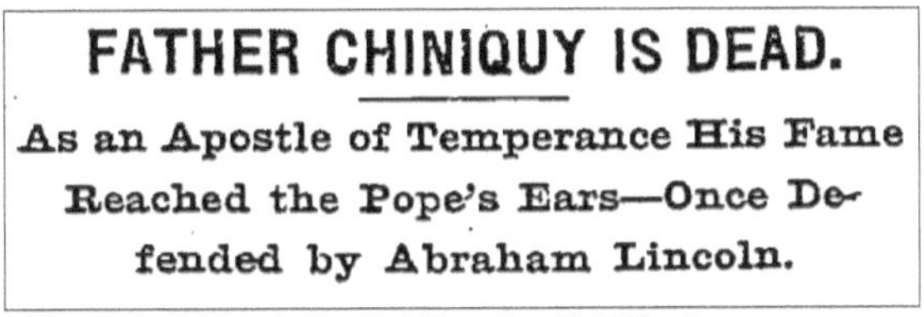

FATHER CHINIQUY IS DEAD.

As an Apostle of Temperance His Fame Reached the Pope's Ears—Once Defended by Abraham Lincoln.

Figure 42   Obituary in *New York Times*, Jan. 17, 1899, p.1

The funeral of Chiniquy was well attended by a broad range of evangelical Protestants and, according to several accounts, by many Catholics. All the funeral sermons have been preserved.[84] Everything proceeded peacefully despite the estimated 10,000 mourners.[85] The

---

81. *Christian Commonwealth*, London, 4 January 1897 (**SL** c.1/20).
82. *A*, 30 April 1898, pp. 7-8.
83. *In Memoriam: Charles Paschal Télesphore Chiniquy* (Montreal, 1899), pp. 5-6 for most of the last 2 paragraphs.
84. Ibid., 1899, pp. 15-39, 59-70.
85. *G*, 20 January 1899, p. 5.

day concluded with interment at the Mount Royal Protestant cemetery in Montreal. Surprisingly, no one has ever knocked over the large gravestone inscribed in French. To cope with the huge crowds unable to hear the funeral, several memorial services were held in Montreal and in St. Anne.[86] Many French Protestants were stunned. They had assumed that once again their hero would be restored.

Controversy did not pass away with Chiniquy's death. Archbishop Bruchési's offer to see the ex-priest on his deathbed was refused. This caused anger on both sides.[87] After Chiniquy's death his last will and testament was published in thousands of copies and presented to Bruchesi. Catholic anger was fuelled. What to Protestants seemed to be a clear statement of faith, which removed any misunderstanding, was to Catholics a last aggressive act.[88]

In his will, the ex-priest asked for a coffin costing no more than $10 and for a sum of money to be distributed to the poor and to Pointe aux Trembles school.[89] Apparently not much money was left in his estate. His heirs, the Morins, continued to live in a small apartment and lacked financial resources.[90]

The fascinating diametrically opposed obituaries raise the question of 'who was the real Chiniquy?'. Next we will examine the contrasting analyses in order to understand the heart of both.

---

86. *A*, 11 February 1899, pp. 5-6; 24 February 1900, p. 10; 3 March 1900, pp. 11-12; Meier, *The Saga* (St. Anne, 1976), p. 11.

87. *A*, 2 February 1899, pp. 5-6, states that the offer was an insult to a pious man while, in Catholic circles, the rebuff was seen as interference by Chiniquy aides.

88. Bp. Bruchesi to the notary George Lighthall, 1 February 1899 (**ACAM** RLBr 1:23), and Bruchesi complaint to the *G* (**ACAM** RLBr 1:21).

89. *A*, 4 February 1899, pp. 7-8.

90. This stems from oral family information by Samuel Lefebvre.

7

WHAT KIND OF CONVERSION?

OPPOSING MYTHS ABOUT CHINIQUY

Extreme statements about Charles Chiniquy abound. Very few remain detached in their assessment of him. Two conflicting images developed quickly and endured, with only a few elaborations, for over 100 years.[1] These images were not designed to convince the neutral but rather to perpetuate the memory of, on the one hand, an overwhelmingly evil or, on the other hand, a saintly figure. For both sides Chiniquy became a larger than life type, a model or a foundational image. In this book "myth" is used to describe a portrait determined more by the ideology of the propagandists than by reality. These images of Chiniquy were emotive and religious, demanding that followers give total consent to each detail, in order to avoid being accused of treason themselves.

Prior to investigating Chiniquy's conversion period let us listen to the opposing interpretations from their points of view, through a composite of their own words. In this next section critical evaluation will be avoided in order to understand and experience the emotions

---

1. See p. 4 and 191 for diagrams that summarize and compare.

expressed. Let it be clear that neither interpretation fits my opinion either as a historian or as a Christian believer.

CATHOLIC INTERPRETATION

The infamous apostate of St. Anne publicly attacked his bishop after his excommunication in 1856.[2] Because of Chiniquy's fame Catholic interpreters in Quebec were obliged to formulate an explanation of the situation. By the time of his definitive excommunication in 1858, Mailloux's input had helped the development of a clear image. Later Catholic accounts inevitably simplified the complex accounts and suggested further scandals.[3]

From the standpoint of church discipline, Chiniquy was first an excommunicated schismatic,[4] then later an apostate[5] and, finally, a heretic.[6] The term 'apostate' was the one most employed for Chiniquy and other ex-priests. Bishop Bourget declared of the former Apostle of Temperance: "he was not only an apostate and a heretic but also leader

---

2. The following is the traditional interpretation followed faithfully by Trudel's original book and more sensationally by Pierre Berton (Toronto, 1976).

3. See e.g. H. Plante, *L'Église catholique au Canada* (Trois Rivières, 1970), p. 366; Lucey, *The Business of Vilification* (Brooklyn, n.d.), p. 41.

4. Someone who breaks the unity of the Catholic Church after Catholic baptism, but does not embrace heresy: Raoul Naz, "Apostasie" IN *Dictionnaire de droit canonique* (Paris, 1935), vol. 1, col. 640.

5. In Canada this has been interpreted as one who makes a formal renunciation of the Catholic faith. The standard authority, Naz, in vol. I, col. 642 however makes the distinction that apostasy means total abandonment of the Christian faith so that "apostates are no longer Christians; heretics and schismatics are no longer Catholics."

6. One who has abandoned part of the Catholic doctrine. This formerly applied to all non-Catholic Christians (Borras, *L'excommunication dans le nouveau code de droit canonique* (Paris, 1987), p. 39).

7. WHAT KIND OF CONVERSION?

of a new sect[7], and thus a veritable arch-heretic who incurs stiffer ecclesiastical punishment and more dreadful anathema."[8]

It was mind-boggling that someone, especially an inspirational priest from Catholic Quebec, could leave the true Church for a sect.[9] The problem must stem from personal flaws. Chiniquy was obsessed by the ancient trio of tempters: money,[10] sex[11] and power. Blessed by God for the sole purpose of turning Canada to temperance, he thought the power was his own. His pride[12] cut him off from contact with God so that every vice now became attractive. In this fallen angel[13] serious underlying weaknesses, given no restraints, developed into gross sins. Since he had sold his soul to the Devil, any sin was not only possible but also likely.[14]

In particular, Chiniquy had always wanted to make his own rules. The Illinois situation permitted him to expose his most serious trait of insubordination. To facilitate his rebellion he turned to chronic invention or exaggeration. A long list of lies by the impostor has been enumerated.[15] After repeated suspensions in the Catholic Church even

---

7. The Christian Catholics who had disappeared 15 years before this statement but were re-established by others since.

8. 19 March 1875 (*MEM*, vol.7, p. 110).

9. *Cour*, 14 August 1900, p. 2: "a Catholic who abandons this Church commits a crime" (my translation), was the response of Thomas Chapais to the overly tolerant obituary by Louis Fréchette.

10. *NY Pilot*, 23 July 1859 (**ASQ** 52:4); *Cour*, 11 January 1861, p. 2: "The job of an apostate has its disagreeable aspects; but it is lucrative" (my translation).

11. P. Resther letter to England, 25 February 1884, 7 p. (**ACAM** 402.102, 884-1). Also Savaète, *Mgr Bourget* (Paris, 1916), ch. 11.

12. *La Presse*, 14 January 1899, p. 1: "From this day Chiniquy was lost to the demon of pride, the most terrible of demons" (my translation); L.O. David, "Chiniquy" (Montreal, 1926), p. 73; XYZ, *Honte et mépris* (Montreal, 1875), p. 4.

13. 19 March 1875 (*MEM*, vol. 7, pp. 108-110).

14. This made any legend or accusation *ipso facto* credible, e.g., the report of paedophilia in Barrett, "Pastor Chiniquy" (Mundelein, 1958), p. 42.

15. S. Smith, *Pastor Chiniquy* (London, 1908), pp. 47-56.

the Chicago Presbytery turned him out. Respectable Protestants also despised Chiniquy for his fraud and his violence.[16]

Chiniquy was a Judas who betrayed the Church for money. Like Gavazzi and all apostates, he was consumed with hatred for his mother church although she had disciplined him for his own good. He then became a ravening wolf, masking his identity to search for stray sheep.[17] His calumny, which was intended to pander to anti-Catholics worldwide, revealed him to be a scurrilous scoundrel.[18] Chiniquy's distortions have been multiplied by repeated reprinting of his obscene hate literature.[19] Along with Voltaire and the Republicans of the world, he supported unlimited freedom of expression including blasphemy and immorality. His apostasy made it even too shameful to consider debate with him.[20]

The faithful could not endure the blasphemy and sacrilege of the apostate priest, culminating in desecration of the host.[21] Quebec had been so badly stained by the horrors of Chiniquy's apostasy and sacrilege that reparations were needed.[22] All Catholics were required to treat any contact with him or his productions as loathsome because of the abomination of his acts and words.[23] His very name invoked the dreadful memories of an unparalleled rebellion against God.[24]

Chiniquy provoked riots everywhere by defaming the faith of others. This was particularly reprehensible in areas of the British Empire or America where Catholics were a small persecuted minority. God had clearly withdrawn the preaching power he had formerly possessed. Only

---

16. See Chiniquy's response in *40 Years*, ch. 38.
17. Bourget pastoral letter, 4 February 1859 (*MEM*, vol. 3, p. 422).
18. *Cour*, 11 January 1861, p. 2 provides a necessary debunking of Chiniquy's exaggerations and broad generalizations about his trip to Europe.
19. *True Witness*, 19 May 1876, p. 4, quoting a Protestant from Halifax.
20. Bourget pastoral letter against Chiniquy and the *Daily Witness*, 19 March 1875 (*MEM*, vol. 7, p. 115).
21. Trudel, p. 251, reflects Catholic orthodoxy in calling it a "criminal act".
22. The newspaper *Minerve* quoted in *40 Years*, pp. 421-422.
23. Biblical texts cited included II Tim. 3:1-9 and II Jn. vv.10-11.
24. *MW*, 28 January 1876, p. 1, recounts one nun's reaction.

7. WHAT KIND OF CONVERSION?

fools listened now. In St. Anne, the coercion of his *Tondeurs*[25] was all that prevented the whole group from abandoning the depraved priest.

Chiniquy was a traitor to the French Canadian people.[26] He appealed to English or American Protestants for publicity, funds and protection. He publicly opposed separate schools and any Roman Catholic involvement in government programmes. In Quebec he became a leader with the ministers of error, "the Swiss".[27] This attempt to drive a wedge into the religious, cultural and linguistic unity of French Canadians would have been disastrous if it had not been blocked.

Chiniquy was effectively countered so that he had no impact on French Canada. The *Montreal Witness* lists of abjurations were either pure inventions or composed of Catholics who had decided to profit temporarily from Protestant money. Virtually all of Chiniquy's so-called "converts" returned to the fold when they understood his true nature.[28] Like Luther and Calvin, his impact was minimal and his ultimate fate would be horrible.[29] The apostate had soiled the Chiniquy name.[30] Despite all this, as long as he lived, Catholics should pray for his recovery and repentance.

Writings about Chiniquy contain recurring phrases such as "the unfortunate" and "poor Chiniquy" but also "vomiting abuse",

---

25. A violent secret society only mentioned by Mailloux, in a letter on 3 November 1857 (**ASQ** 50:4m).

26. *La Presse*, 14 January 1899, p. 1: "The religious apostasy of Chiniquy was combined with a treason to his nation for which the disgrace often brought on him ... the spontaneous loathing of French Canadians" (my translation).

27. *MEM*, vol. 3, p. 421; *Cour*, 27 July 1859, p. 2. On the Swiss see Lalonde, p. 105; *A* 28 July 1887, p. 4.

28. Têtu, *Notes biographiques sur l'apostat Chiniquy* (Quebec, 1900), p. 5; L. David (Montreal, 1926), p. 74; Fréchette, (Montreal, ²1979), p. 111. It was often reported that Chiniquy's followers in Illinois were abandoning him. Each time the next report would tell of the group's continued obstinacy and a consequent need for increased Catholic money and workers.

29. *Le Canadien*, 3 September 1858, quoted in Trudel, p. 207.

30. *L'Événement*, 17 January 1899, quoted in Trudel, p. 291.

"excrement",[31] Anti-Christ.[32] Alphonse Villeneuve surpassed even the *Courrier* and *Minerve* with his colourful vocabulary describing Chiniquy as a brute, imbecile, wretch, vile henchman of Hell, criminal, immoral and base scoundrel, hypocrite, sad fool, "a lying machine, for raving and vomit, which the spirit of Satan directs ... Soon no one will speak any longer of this man: Ridicule will crush him; shame and contempt will be his shroud."[33]

EVANGELICAL PROTESTANT INTERPRETATION

"High Church" Anglicans[34] and Protestants with either liberal or nominal tendencies were rarely admirers of Chiniquy. Most Protestants kept a distance from Chiniquy during his Illinois fights of 1856. However, when he visited Lower Canada in 1859 they saw both that the Catholic hierarchy radically opposed him and that Chiniquy was courageous in advocating the Bible as the basis for Christian faith.

Those Protestants most convinced of the truth and necessity of the Reformation doctrines of *Sola Gratia*, and *Sola Biblia* and who promoted evangelism (i.e. the evangelicals) soon came to sympathize with Chiniquy in much that he did. These evangelicals were very influential in late 19th century English Canada. Virtually all French Protestants in North America and most evangelicals elsewhere adopted the following interpretation,[35] though they did not approve of all of his methods.

Chiniquy was viewed as a committed Catholic, touched from his youth by the Bible's power. He promoted the primarily Protestant battle of temperance and swept through French Canada with his eloquence. His combination of Bible knowledge and independent thought gradually made him frustrated with the Catholic system. The situation exploded

---

31. Resther, p. 1.
32. Bp. Prince to Mailloux, 19 January 1858 (**ASQ** 50:13t).
33. XYZ [Villeneuve], *Honte et mépris*, p. 5-6 (my translation).
34. This is in contrast with evangelical Anglicans who usually supported him.
35. This section will be lengthier since Trudel and those who followed were entirely unaware of this approach, leaving a distorted picture.

7. WHAT KIND OF CONVERSION?

over a trivial property dispute. In this episode, the tyranny of the Chicago bishop exposed the true face of Catholicism. Absolute submission to a mere human was demanded. Chiniquy quite rightly refused. God honoured the tenacity of Chiniquy's resolve bringing him to a conversion to the doctrine of *Sola Gratia*. Some Protestant accounts even omit all mention of property and the initial excommunication, thus portraying a purely theological dispute over Scripture and conversion.[36]

Isaac Hellmuth, a prominent Anglican evangelical, provided an all-important early evaluation of the ex-priest's evangelical credentials in October 1859:

> I believe him to be a really converted man, enlightened by the Spirit of God, and animated by the constraining love of Christ to rescue his dear but benighted countrymen from the tyranny, superstition and idolatry of the Church of Rome.[37]

Biblical archetypes were used to describe Chiniquy.[38] Formerly 'a Saul' who persecuted French Protestants, he had become "a converted apostle Paul",[39] experiencing the same persecution that he had perpetrated. The light of the gospel shone on the French Canadians in Illinois as a group. Like their pastor they converted to Jesus Christ.[40] 'The Moses', who had led his people in Illinois out of slavery to liberty,[41] hopefully would do the same in Quebec.[42]

---

36. See e.g. Villard, *Up to the Light* (Toronto, 1928), p. 107.

37. *Father Chiniquy, the Reformer of the Far West* (London, c1860), p. 3. He is also a "Bible Christian" (p. 11).

38. These were the favourite forms for Victorian evangelical biography: Peterson, *Victorian Autobiography* (New Haven, 1986), p. 7.

39. See Rev. Mowatt's memorial sermon in *40 Years*, p. 494 among many.

40. This rare occurrence, in their circles, of group conversion was very difficult for evangelicals to believe. Nevertheless they came to accept the St. Anne case as genuine.

41. This Exodus typology was the one most commonly used in Victorian autobiography (Peterson pp. 35, 49).

42. A hope expressed as early as the 4 March 1850 edition of the *MW*, p. 68.

THE CONTROVERSIAL CONVERSION OF CHARLES CHINIQUY

As the "Luther of Canada" Chiniquy transformed his community and continued to defy the church of the Anti-Christ. That Chiniquy could play a 'Luther' role was a faint Protestant hope in the early stages of the schism.[43] In those same years Roman Catholics warned of the parallel between Chiniquy and Luther.[44] It was a Catholic who was the first to report that Protestants used the Luther analogy.[45] Likely, Chiniquy would not have encouraged this analogy until after his trip to Canada in early 1859. He knew that the name of Luther, honoured by Protestants, was synonymous with heresy and rebellion for Catholics. It was Hellmuth who popularized the title "Luther of Canada" through his 1859 letters.[46]

In fact there were remarkable parallels between the lives of Luther and Chiniquy: adolescent crises over confession, independent spirit, rebellion with the Bible cited as the final authority, organizational skills, oratorical gifts, determination, impressive debating and writing skills. Mary Bird wrote on her cover page:

> Pastor Chiniquy to whom may be applied most appropriately the cognomen of the Canadian Luther; since it is doubtful whether any other man has been so successful in reclaiming deluded papists from the soul-destroying system of Popery, since [Luther].[47]

Americans also laid claim to their "Luther of Illinois".[48] Others used the less specific term "Canadian reformer".[49]

"There is a special hatred toward Chiniquy, who has done more to shake Romanism than any one since Luther and Knox. There is no name

---

43. *MW*, 8 April 1857, p. 221. Lougheed, "Le Luther du Canada" (*Revue Farel*, 2008).

44. Chiniquy mentions that he was so accused back in his College years (*50 Years*, p. 149). Later he was called by Bp. Signay, "a pint-sized Luther" (p. 249).

45. Catholic priest Rev. Brouillet in Baltimore to Mailloux, 6 June 1859 (**ASQ** 50:20h).

46. Published in *Father Chiniquy, the Reformer of the Far West*, pp. 4, 10, 11.

47. Bird, *A Few Reminiscences* (Leeds, 1878), cover.

48. Barrett, "Pastor Chiniquy", p. 35.

49. *Le père Chiniquy, le Réformateur canadien* (Melun France, 1860), cover; also Provost, "Chiniquy: Sa vie" (n.p., 1899), p. 31.

7. WHAT KIND OF CONVERSION?

that makes the Pope tremble as his."[50] Jesuits were constantly plotting to drag Chiniquy before the courts and bankrupt him. Priests encouraged their flocks to malign or even kill him.[51] Rome never deviated in its intent to eliminate all competition. Clerics sought to convert Chiniquy on his deathbed by underhanded means. They also made false announcements of his reconciliation and, at other points, of his horrible premature death.[52]

Like Samson, Joshua, Daniel and other biblical heroes, Chiniquy never backed down in his causes. His steadfastness was an inspiration for other French Canadians who aspired to break out of their captivity. Prof. Moore's poem expresses the admiration that many felt:

> Our champion in our age has risen,
> Whose name is Chiniquy; not to be driven
> from his bold stand against the Pope ...
> This knight of faith does battle still,
> He works right on with iron will.[53]

Chiniquy was a David sent to fight Goliath. He was the champion of Protestant rights and truth in Ultramontane Quebec. After his victories in Quebec, the British Empire and other parts of Europe appealed for aid in their battles against resurgent Catholicism. The ex-priest was divinely blessed as he revealed the true face of Catholicism and campaigned for both evangelism of Catholics and organized resistance to Catholic political or military plots.

Chiniquy demonstrated the folly of many Catholic beliefs and practices. In particular Chiniquy revealed that church fees were, in effect, extortion, and that the confessional stimulated sexual lust and immorality. Only he, as a former priest, could reveal the inner workings

---

50. J. Moore, *Rev. Charles Chiniquy's Recent Tour Abroad* (Boston, 1897), p. 4. While the popes may very well have heard of the rebel priest no evidence has surfaced yet showing any comment from Rome. One would expect such comments, if known, to have been quoted by Catholics.

51. I remind the reader that in this whole section I am expressing the wording of Protestant writings and not my opinion.

52. XYZ [Villeneuve], *Honte et mépris*.

53. J. Moore, *Rev. Charles Chiniquy*, (Boston, c1898), p. 2.

of Catholicism and communicate them with such clarity, honesty and power.

Chiniquy attacked Catholicism because it destroyed people. He was motivated only by concern for the misled souls of its members. Catholic objections could be summarized as disapproval that he had left the priesthood and that he preached against his former religion. These objections clash with the hero worship given Cardinal Newman for the same 'sins'.

Catholic allegations of immorality against the ex-priest were also pointless. No proof was given. However, if they were true, they showed that the Catholic hierarchy had been negligent. Instead of disciplining Chiniquy they simply relocated him and publicly praised him for his accomplishments. If the allegations were not true, as is more likely, this was typical of the propaganda invented to discredit converts from Rome. The converted priest's integrity was demonstrated by the many commendatory documents prior to his conversion. No sexual allegations were ever made against Chiniquy in his Protestant years. In fact, he waited all of six years after his conversion to marry, at the age of 55.

Chiniquy's generosity for the poor was renowned. His exhausting fundraising trips never enriched him personally. Nor did he seek honours. His joy was to go where he was most needed to stem the tide of Catholic power. As for his personal piety, those who knew attested it as exemplary.[54]

Chiniquy had rough edges due to his polemical Catholic training. In particular, his tongue was too quick. This was understandable and pardonable given the constant provocation, calumny and violence against him. The ex-priest's misunderstanding with Chicago Presbytery was well explained by Kemp.[55] Apart from that minor problem, Chiniquy fit admirably into all churches during his 40 Protestant years. His

---

54. *CFA*, 18 May 1893, p. 5; "Moore's recollection" in *Kankakee Times*, 21 November 1899; Bruneau, "Le père Chiniquy" (Montreal, c1915), p. 3.

55. Kemp, *The Rev. C. Chiniquy, the Presbytery of Chicago...* (Montreal, 1863), 21 p. Also see p. 119-120 of this book.

7. WHAT KIND OF CONVERSION?

submission to the Bible and a love for the Protestant cause controlled his independence of thought.

Chiniquy was a great patriot who cared passionately for his fellow French Canadians. He devoted his life to liberating them from slavery to Catholicism. He stirred people worldwide to pray and to give for the needs of his compatriots. In addition, he was doing great good for all of Canada in diminishing racial hostility. He did this by showing that it was their religion and not their race that made French Canadians backward. The ex-priest's previously expressed his love for his people in his temperance battle. Now he was abused by bishops. They sought to preserve their tyrannical power by isolating the Apostle of Temperance from the people he loved, and who loved him.

Rome's reaction to Chiniquy's very presence provided clear evidence that it opposed freedom of speech and thought. The ex-priest was "the great champion of liberty and the gospel"[56] whose name should be honoured. "Father Chiniquy ... has become the man of the hour [1875] ... by his amazing talent of converting the masses and by his courage in accomplishing his duty in the midst of the greatest perils."[57]

He won the battle to bring religious liberty to Montreal for French Protestants, almost single-handedly. Eventually Catholic riots against him and others ceased. In foreign countries, he roused Protestants from their slumber, sounding an alarm about the true conniving nature of Catholicism: to ask for liberty where it is in the minority and to crush liberty where it had control.

The Grand Old Man of Protestantism had shaken off the curses of Catholicism[58] and prospered in reputation and health for 90 years,

---

56. John Herdt letter to Chiniquy, 17 September 1896 (**SL** c.1/5).

57. *MW*, 16 February 1875, p. 1, in their French column. Primeau-Robert, *La place des protestants dans la nationalité Canadienne-française* (Montreal, 1924), p.37 wrote: "Chiniquy had the utmost value as a fighter ... the Musketeer of the [French] Canadian evangelical church" (my translation).

58. *A*, 1 September 1894, p. 9.

through God's abundant blessing. A writer to the French Protestant paper in New England concluded:

> Most of his persecutors have fallen; he is still standing.
> Hate, like a poisonous ivy attached itself to the old oak in order to cut off the growth; the oak has grown even taller.[59]

After his death a memorial sermon addressed the dead Chiniquy: "Hero of many battles, thou didst fight well in the cause of truth, and now it is the victor's crown."[60]

French evangelical leader Eugene Reveillaud prefaced Chiniquy's *Cinquante ans* with:

> We observe that while Chiniquy was a prisoner of Romanism he already became the apostle of two great causes: temperance and colonization. Afterwards he continued those causes but in addition and above all he became the apostle of the Reformation and of evangelism. This was because he was born an apostle ... He possessed all the apostolic traits: the temperament, the faith, the unselfishness, the courage, the polemics but also the peace-making spirit, the sacred fire, the tireless zeal. As an apostle he also experienced the obstacles, the battles, the disgrace, the frustrations, the wounds.[61]

Others named him the Apostle of French Canada[62] or the Apostle of liberty.[63]

The superlatives about Chiniquy are legion. The *Converted Catholic* declared in 1896 that "for the last 40 years ... [Chiniquy] has been the foremost champion of Protestantism on the American continent. His fame is world wide."[64] A British newspaper claimed that "in the annals of

---

59. *CFA*, 18 May 1893, p. 3.
60. Sermon of Presbyterian pastor Mowatt, *40 Years*, p. 497.
61. *Cinquante ans*, p. [iii-iv].
62. *G*, 20 January 1899, p. 5; Fines, *Album du Protestantisme français* (Montreal, 1972), vol. 1, p. 32.
63. *CT*, 10 August 1858.
64. *CC*, 12 (1896), p. 3.

7. WHAT KIND OF CONVERSION?

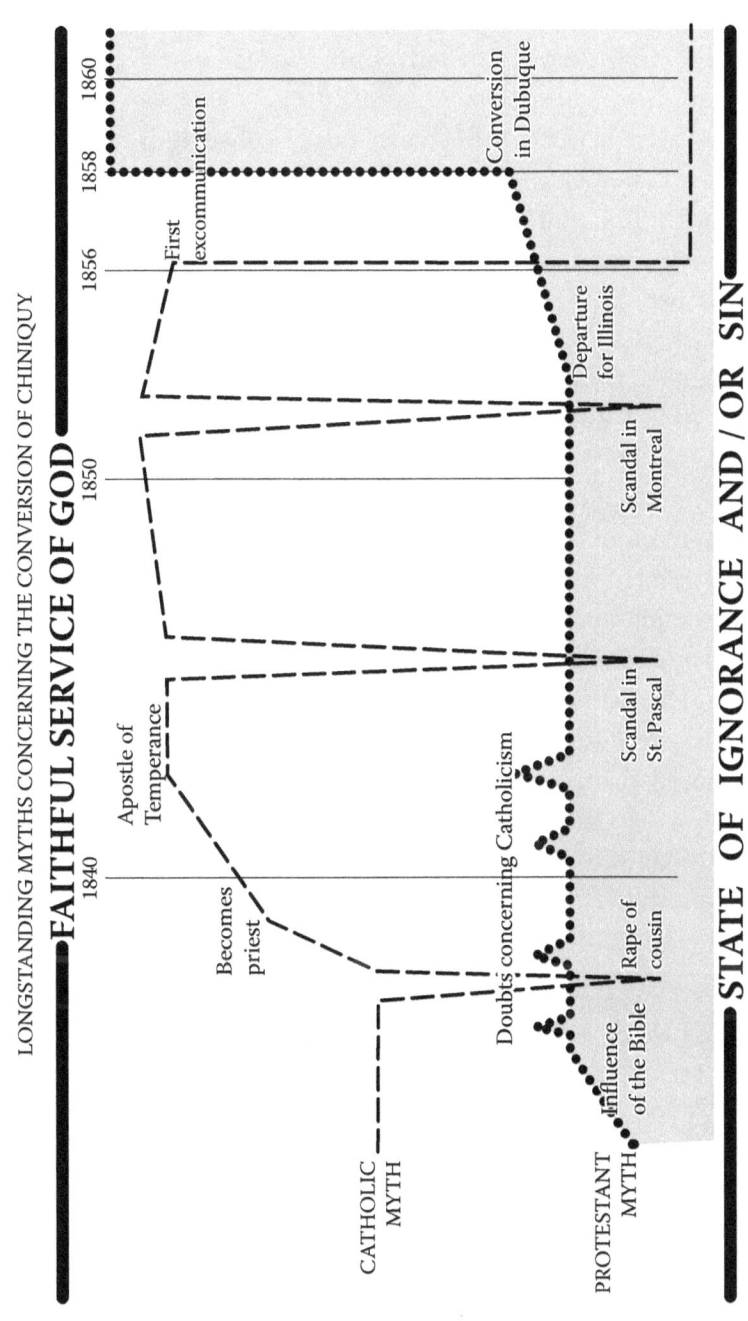

Figure 43   Traditional myths

modern Protestant effort ... there is no parallel to this wonderful lecturer."[65] He was "the most intrepid missionary ... to Roman Catholics since the Reformation."[66]

The *American Advocate* obituary called him "one of [the world's] kingliest men ... His life is without a parallel in this century in his chosen field; future generations will bless his name and crown him as the greatest religious reformer of his country."[67] McLoughlin goes even further: "If it had not been for the dedication, energy, and fearlessness of Charles Chiniquy, the United States would probably now be a Roman Catholic nation"![68]

After Chiniquy's death there was a worldwide demand for more information from his son-in-law, Joseph Morin, about "my hero" and "a latter day saint of God".[69] Protestants thought that Quebec and Canada should be proud of the 'Luther of Canada' and his matchless accomplishments. "The memory of such a valiant leader in the army of Christ should not be allowed to perish from the earth."[70] Chiniquy's colourful revealing books should remain in print for future generations.

Here I conclude my role of summarizing to return to critical analysis. The preceding section did not express my personal beliefs but, rather, a needed exposition of the propaganda of the two contending myths before reconstituting the truth. In a later chapter on the Chiniquy legacy, we shall see that these myths still hold great power, particularly among Protestants.

---

65. "Pastor Chiniquy and the Calvinistic Protestant Union" (England, c1896) (**SL** c. 1/20). He was 86 years old then.
66. Anderson, *Father Chiniquy* (NY, 1946), p. 14.
67. *American Advocate*, Mechanicsville, Iowa, February 1899, p. 76.
68. McLoughlin, *Famous Ex-Priests* (NY, 1968), p. 127.
69. John Leysin of Lanark, Scotland, letter of 13 February 1901; J.P.A. Muhr of Stockholm, letter of 28 May 1908 (**SL** c.2/110).
70. Anderson, p. 38; Seville, "Charles Chiniquy" (*Sunday School Times*, 1953), p. 16, prayed for God to raise up similar "Christian soldiers who will dare to face the attacks on the faith, whether covert or open, by ruthless ismatics - whether Romanists, Communists or other cultists."

7. WHAT KIND OF CONVERSION?

While it is obvious that Chiniquy converted from Catholicism to Protestantism, this movement can be understood in quite different ways.[71] The traditional Catholic myth, above, interpreted this movement as a desperate attempt to change denominations in order to salvage a career. Being a complete hypocrite or humbug, Chiniquy could impersonate a Protestant adequately enough to get recognition and money. According to Trudel:

> Chiniquy's journey from Rome to Geneva was a rapid one with no spiritual component: expelled from the Church of Rome in 1858, left to himself with his small group, the leader of the Catholic Christian church could find nothing better to do for survival than to join a well-established church. Thus he became a Presbyterian in 1859.[72]

In the next chapter I will show the fundamental inadequacy of this interpretation. First let us examine alternative approaches to conversion.

THE EVANGELICAL MODEL OF CONVERSION

Since the Reformation, Reformed Protestantism[73] has insisted on "justification by faith alone" as the centre of the Christian faith. However 16th century Anabaptists and 18th to 20th century evangelicals observed a superficial Christianity (Protestant and Catholic). They concluded that more than good teaching, examples, or the ordinances/ sacraments of the Church was needed to foster genuine faith. Protestant orthodoxy without vitality or enthusiasm was common as churches were even influenced by Unitarians or deists. Breakdown of morality and belief necessitated a counter-cultural commitment and

---

71. See D. Baker ed., *Religious Motivation and Sociological Problems for the Church Historian* (Oxford, 1978) on the conversions of Constantine, Luther and others.

72. Trudel, p. 301. There is no new research or change in explanation in his new account (Montreal, 2004), p. 146-7.

73. That is Lutheranism, Calvinism\Presbyterianism and much of Anglicanism.

transformation. In such crisis situations evangelicalism has generally prospered.

Evangelical theology placed a mandatory experience of conversion at the centre of the Christian faith.[74] Every true Christian is believed to have experienced interior conversion. Drawing from the Hebrew *shuv*, meaning 'to turn around and then to go in an opposite direction', conversion implies rejection of the former life and unbelief. God is the sole author of the associated spiritual regeneration. Humans accept and cooperate in the conversion of the mind, will and spirit.

> In the case of adults ... conversion is absolutely essential [for salvation] ... in the sense that its elements, namely repentance and faith must be present in their lives ... they must, in some form, experience the essence of conversion ... logically conversion follows regeneration ... In regeneration the sinner is entirely passive, but in conversion [he/she] is both passive and active.[75]

Hence conversion includes both conscious elements and subconscious supernatural elements. The Holy Spirit is crucial for providing new power and assurance of forgiveness and faith, leading the newly converted Christian into a dynamic experience of mutual love with Jesus.

The influential 19th century evangelical Anglican Bishop Ryle wrote:

> We maintain that the things which need most to be pressed on men's attention are those mighty works of the Holy Spirit, inward repentance, inward faith, inward hope, inward hatred of sin, and inward love to God's law ... We hold that, as an inward work of the Holy Ghost is a necessary thing to man's salvation, so also it is a thing that must be inwardly felt ... there can be no real conversion to God, no new creation in Christ, no new birth of the

---

74. See Donald Bloesch, "Conversion" IN Walter Ewell ed., *Evangelical Dictionary of Theology* (Grand Rapids, 1984), pp. 272-273; Amand Parent, *The Life of Rev. Amand Parent, the First French Canadian Ordained by the Methodist Church* (Toronto, 1887), 235 p.; Calvin Amaron, *Evangelization of the French Canadians* (Lowell MA, 1885), 15 p.; Louis Beaudry, *Face à face ou luttes mentales d'un catholique romain* (Montreal, 1882), 239 p. and Nathan Beman, *A Plea for the Swiss Mission in Canada* (Troy NY, ²1845), 36 p.

75. Louis Berkhof, *Systematic Theology* (Edinburgh, 1939), p. 491.

7. WHAT KIND OF CONVERSION?

Spirit, where there is nothing felt and experienced within ... We insist that where there is nothing felt within the heart of a man, there is nothing really possessed.[76]

Conversion happens through grace, **from** love of self and rebellion against God, **to** humble love of God as known in Jesus Christ. More simply, conversion is a move from a self-centred to a Jesus-centred life. New birth imagery from the third chapter of John's gospel is often employed to convey the new supernatural start. The evangelical conversion is typically individual,[77] though often encouraged by other individuals or by a group.

According to temperament, age and situation, the stages of evangelical conversion differ. For most people the supernatural experience happens suddenly, or over a short period, and this is the preferred mode of evangelicalism. Statistically, this evangelical type of conversion is most common among adolescents and young adults, becoming rarer after 40 years of age.[78]

There are some individuals with good evangelical credentials who cannot identify a date or sudden transformation, because they grew up in the faith and have always believed. Yet the adage remains: "God has no grandchildren". Children of evangelicals are believed to require conversion as much as anyone else.

While crusades, missions or revivals have been favoured evangelical methods for three centuries, contact by friends or relatives has often had the greatest long-term impact. Depending on the group beliefs about who is eligible for baptism, the new convert receives adult baptism, in order to be integrated into the local and wider church. This

---

76. John Charles Ryle, *Knots Untied* (London, William Hunt, [10]1885), p. 6.

77. Pierre Charles, "Théologie de la conversion" IN *Les Conversions : Compte-rendu de la huitième semaine de missiologie de Louvain* (Louvain, 1930), p. 34, contrasts this with Catholic views.

78. Edwin Starbuck, *The Psychology of Religion* (London, 1899), followed 90 years later, by V. Bailey Gillespie, *Religious Conversion and Personal Identity* (Birmingham, 1979) found the average age of evangelical conversion to be around 16.

is the majority evangelical view in many areas including Quebec today. Alternatively the new convert may become a member after study and on the basis of previous infant baptism. This was the predominant mode in Chiniquy's time. Great care is taken to stress the interior nature of conversion rather than equating conversion with the exterior symbols of baptism, confirmation or any form of penance.

To be recognized as a valid conversion by other evangelicals there need to be 'fruits' (practical results). Typically, evangelicals expect new converts to demonstrate both acknowledgement of guilt and a joyful supernatural experience of having been freed from this burden, by grace. They are urged to announce their conversion publically; to tell friends and family. Other signs of authentic evangelical conversion (at least since the 18th century) include new-found love for the Bible, confidence in God's care and assurance of salvation, initiation of personal devotions, assembling with other evangelicals, and contribution of time and material goods. Lifestyle changes are expected. Obvious sin should be confessed to some responsible Christian, and concrete steps should be taken to avoid similar sin in the future. Some doctrinal confusion is expected in the beginning but it should soon diminish with study.

Evangelical conversion is conversion to Christ rather than to a denomination. Conversion to anti-clericalism or to another denomination (in the Catholic sense of the term) is very different from, and viewed as inferior to, evangelical conversion to Christ.[79] The evangelical notion of the Church is not as strong as in other Christian groups. A new convert typically tries out different churches and denominations before settling on one. The convert seeks a match for his new faith as well as for other various needs. Prolonged 'church-hopping' is deplored as avoidance of commitment and accountability however. Evangelicals

---

79. See the distinct statistics of 25 conversions from Romanism but 50 conversions to Christ in the *Grand Ligne Annual Report* (Montreal, 1900), p. 28. There was assumed to be a time of study and decision between the two. Not all progressed to the second genuinely evangelical stage.

7. WHAT KIND OF CONVERSION?

have always expected loyalty to the wider evangelical world, beyond the denomination and the local church.

This briefly summarizes the primary theological foundations and practicalities of evangelical conversion.[80] We will compare Chiniquy's experience to this in the third section of Chapter eight.

EX-PRIESTS

The conversion of ex-priests[81] has particular features worthy of study. McLoughlin brings an anti-Catholic understanding to his account of political, religious and other ideological conversions of priests out of the Catholic Church. Although not evangelical in approach he contests the popular Catholic opinion that in the past most priests left the priesthood because of a woman. That does not mean that his suggested alternative causes for the production of ex-priests are convincing.[82]

McLoughlin does help us understand the vulnerability of a potential ex-priest in times past:

> He feels, as he has been taught, that only a handful of mavericks, few that he knows, have ever made the step before. Every ex-priest is scared - scared of family, of lost friends, of

---

80. Evangelical theology has always held a warm spot for the conversions of Augustine and, with more qualifications, Francis of Assisi. Saul\Paul, Zaccheus and Levi are among favourite biblical examples.

81. See also the next section.

82. He suggests the following pattern of conversion based on his case studies: 1. Realization of the hierarchy's exploitation of the poor 2. Realization of the immense unchristlike wealth of Rome 3. Realization of the wide-spread immorality of the clergy and their unproductive parasitical living 4. An awakening to the true history of the Church in its interpolation of convenient doctrines and the gradual aggrandizement of the authority of the popes.

These do tend to be the subjects that many ex-priests talked and wrote about. However the first three steps are, for the most part, popular rationalizations rather than the precipitating factors for leaving the Catholic Church. Only the final step of historical reinterpretation would be typical and necessary in order to maintain any lasting change of allegiance.

finances and especially scared of the powerful punishing right hand of Holy Mother Church.[83]

Evangelical converts often experience conflict with family members, who see no need for conversion. Evangelicals especially honoured ex-priests since they faced peculiarly intense hostility and social alienation following their conversions.

PSYCHOLOGY OF CONVERSION

Evangelical conversion is not a psychologically unique phenomenon.[84] Aspects of it may be better understood in the context of certain social sciences. Evangelicals recognize the existence of pseudo-conversions.[85] These may be emotional experiences that lack a focus on sin and forgiveness or that neglect Jesus. These counterfeit experiences are distinguished by their lack of permanence and their doctrinal and practical aberrations. They can be produced by psychological means. In contrast no one psychological factor has been found to adequately explain what are recognized as true evangelical conversions.[86]

In psychology of religion, we start with the classic study of William James. He enumerated the following general stages of conversion: 1) an event or series of events that causes disruption of the previous pattern of thought; 2) confrontation by a different truth claim while the individual is in the problem-solving mode; 3) consideration of this new claim; 4) a moment or period of crisis or encounter; 5) transformation of thoughts

---

83. Ibid., p. 27.

84. Ferm, *The Psychology of Christian Conversion* (Westwood NJ, 1959), p. 50. For surveys of conversion research in many fields see Kilbourne and Richardson, "Paradigm Conflict, Types of Conversion, and Conversion Theories" (*Sociological Analysis*, 1988); Rambo, "Bibliography: Current Research in Religious Conversion" (*Religious Studies Review*, 1982).

85. Biblical examples include the unproductive seeds of the sower and Hebrews 6:4.

86. See Johnson and Malony, *Christian Conversion: Biblical and Psychological Perspectives* (Grand Rapids, 1982), for an evangelical integration of theology and psychology.

7. WHAT KIND OF CONVERSION?

and practice; 6) incorporation in the new group.[87] James demonstrated the importance of the subconscious in all this.[88]

Dean Hogue found that 20th century Catholics who left their church often were seeking democracy and freedom from the rules.[89] That was a more natural motive given their hierarchical church government. He found that most of these dropouts still considered themselves good Catholics and that over half eventually returned. Hogue provided a helpful analogy for apostasy - the breakdown of a committed love relationship. In apostasy as in marriage breakdown there is a predominance of non-rational and inter-personal factors, such as family bonds, experiences of childhood, a feeling of belonging, religious experiences and outside attractions.[90] Such factors certainly appear in accounts of Chiniquy's transitional love-hate relationship with the Catholic Church.

A study of ex-nuns discovered that the doubting of any **part** of the comprehensive convent system resulted in doubting the **whole**.[91] As the nuns began to consider leaving, they experienced a precipitating incident, perceived as an unreasonable demand, which became the justification for a public announcement of departure. Ebaugh concluded that the response of 'significant others' was crucial in the process. Among many adjustments the ex-nun needed to deal with there was her anger towards those who remained in the convent community. For Chiniquy we find a similar precipitating incident. We also find that doubting one point led to doubting the whole system.

---

87. From Ferm, pp. 184-188 and Johnson-Malony, p. 71.
88. William James, *The Varieties of Religious Experience* (NY, 1902).
89. D. Hogue, "Why Catholics Drop Out" IN *Falling from the Faith*, D. Bromley, ed., (Newbury Park CA, 1988), p. 83.
90. Ibid., p. 97.
91. H. Ebaugh, "Leaving Catholic Convents: Toward a Theory of Disengagement" IN *Falling from the Faith*, p. 106.

THE CONTROVERSIAL CONVERSION OF CHARLES CHINIQUY

Its advocates maintain that psychohistory,[92] can only be done adequately by those with psychoanalytical training. Psychohistory is a very controversial field. It has produced enough bizarre and contradictory explanations to make it easy to discount. I will simply relate several of its insights that illumine the case of Chiniquy.

Figure 44   At about age 55 **AP** 04 46

Psychohistorians search for subconscious, often irrational motivation, beyond human control. They seek to explain significant adult actions or attitudes by finding the **one** traumatic childhood experience that determined them. We know that Chiniquy passed through several important crises in his youth. These include the death of his father, separation from his mother as well as the loss of his uncle's funding. More crises followed at age 37 (joining the Oblates), age 42 (suspension in Montreal and move to Illinois) and then especially from age 47 to 49 (the schism). In fact Chiniquy's life seems so full of crises that he must have provoked them unconsciously and then thrived on them. Could his attitude to authorities be explained by the absence of a father to rebel against? Since there is limited information about Chiniquy's infancy, it would require substantial imaginative reconstruction to meet the criteria for psychohistory.

---

92. Lawton, *The Psychohistorian's Handbook* (NY, 1988) is an advocate; David Stannard, *Shrinking History* (Oxford, 1980) is a ferocious critic.

7. WHAT KIND OF CONVERSION?

Psychohistory challenges us to read autobiography critically to discover its motives, which may be subconscious. This might be a profitable area for further study of Chiniquy. There are elements of narcissism, paranoia and repetition compulsions (putting oneself in distressing situations e.g., potential riots) that occurred in Chiniquy's experience. However, it is far more remarkable that the rebel priest demonstrated emotional stability in the midst of his seemingly endless line of severe crises.

During the Illinois schism, a complex of social, political, religious and subconscious elements came together both in Chiniquy and in the group who followed him. Psychohistory reminds us to look for the deeply emotional images, such as Chiniquy's prominent use of the American flag and his word images of "tyranny" and "slavery".

To those psychologists who view any religious conversion as repressive, deviant, pathological or lifestyle-oriented,[93] aspects of the traditional Catholic view of apostates match well. A Catholic professor in France, Maignage first studied the psychology of conversion to Catholicism and then studied the psychology of the closely connected apostasy from Catholicism.[94] There are parallels when one reads of Chiniquy being described alternatively as a great apostate or as a converted Luther. Maignage tries to respond to Diderot's relativism: "the Christian is an unbeliever in Asia, the Muslim in Europe, the papist in London and the Calvinist in Paris".[95] He provides a psychological base for the traditional Catholic approach.

Maignage proposes that "at the origin of every apostasy there was a tendency, an inclination to evil, which was not guarded against nor brought into subjection".[96] The key evils in Christian history have not

---

93. This constitutes the majority of non-practising Christians or non-religious psychologists, according to Johnson and Malony, p. 48.

94. Maignage, *Le témoignage des apostats* (Paris, 1916). This analysis is inevitably marked by the fact that France was then at war with largely Protestant Germany.

95. Ibid., p. 23 (my translation).

96. Ibid., p. x (my translation).

changed much: "selfish passions, uncontrolled appetite for freedom, horror of certainty".[97] Maignage concludes that non-rational and non-doctrinal elements are the cause of all apostasy. These evil impulses make the Catholic susceptible to unbelief and to pride feeling that they have gone beyond Catholicism. Maignage applied his analysis to Luther and to many of the famous apostates in France, whether they became Protestants or atheists.

While Maignage did not choose Chiniquy for analysis, his treatment of Luther probably reflects what he would have done with Chiniquy.[98] Maignage interpreted the German rebel as an extremist under the tyranny of his passions, particularly pride, sensuality, and terror of punishment. Once he realized that his lust was uncontrollable, he turned to "justification by faith alone", in order to live with his own sins. He could now "sin boldly" in Luther's own words. According to Maignage, Luther's greatest sin was to drag so many others with him. This overall analysis would explain the traditional Catholic interpretation of Chiniquy (e.g., Trudel) better than it explains Chiniquy himself.

Neeser, a Swiss Protestant attempted a more objective study of confessional or denominational conversions[99] that occurred in both directions, between Catholicism and Protestantism.[100] First, Neeser separated out all cases of pseudo-confessional conversions. These were actually moral conversions (i.e. change of morality rather than change of belief), precipitated by someone who happened to be from the other confession.

Next he described those conversions that possessed secondary confessional aspects. This included some Catholics who left to seek freedom in morals and worship. It also included many Protestants who turned to Catholicism for aesthetics or contemplative worship. In France some

---

97. Ibid., p. xi (my transl.).
98. Ibid., pp. 80-128.
99. As opposed to the moral conversions of Augustine or George Muller.
100. Neeser, *Du Protestantisme au Catholicisme...* (Neuchatel, 1926). He refers briefly to Maignage.

7. WHAT KIND OF CONVERSION?

turned to Protestantism or Catholicism for political reasons, valuing republicanism or the monarchy respectively.

Finally, Neeser explained truly confessional or denominational conversions based on the following theological principles: **I.** Authority in doctrine is accorded to **either** the Church (by converts to Catholicism) **or** to the individual conscience with the Bible (by converts to Protestantism); **II.** Communion with God is sought **either** through the sacraments and good works **or** through faith alone.[101] Neeser acknowledges both intellectual and experiential motives.

Neeser concludes that Protestants who join Catholicism are often fleeing the dryness of their old faith, in favour of the abundance in Catholic dogma, morality and, above all, involvement of the five senses in worship. Those who convert to Catholicism are usually opposed to individualism and feel a great need for the "real presence" in the sacrament. Often intuitive in temperament, they desire tangible symbols. They also seek a united church body with continuity, security and direction.

On the other hand Catholics who convert to Protestantism often do so because they find rituals hollow. They prefer abstract ideas and words to represent God. They come to have greater confidence in the authority of the divinely inspired Bible rather than church decrees. Frequently they have questioned authorities over scandals or decisions and find that their conscience does not permit them to obey their spiritual directors any more. Protestant converts seek individual liberty in faith and find no great problem in the lack of Protestant organizational unity.[102]

Neeser's analysis and his search for a *via media* certainly betray his Protestant leaning. Nevertheless this neglected work deserves more attention. His model approach incorporates amazing openness especially for his time. At the same time he considered the religious content

---

101. Ibid., p. 99.
102. Ibid., pp. 165-175.

of all the conversions very seriously. Neeser did not attempt to deal with those who move to secularism or to non-Christian religions.

We find Chiniquy's conversion among the detailed examples Neeser studied.[103] The ex-priest is placed in the category of conversions where the confessional or denominational question (confidence in one's Church) is secondary to the quest for greater freedom in morality and liturgy. It is alleged that Chiniquy never had a strong attachment to the Catholic Church, despite his priesthood. According to Neeser, Chiniquy lived by the Protestant principle of Scripture over tradition, from his childhood on. Chiniquy left, not over Catholic doctrine, but over the Church's scandals. The shortcomings that he observed among clergy led him to lose confidence and become detached from Catholic worship and rules. This prepared him for the experience of an evangelical conversion. Neeser admitted that Chiniquy's autobiography left his psychology impenetrable because he avoided nuance and interior thought.

Neeser's categorization of Chiniquy is correct for the most part. However it was not correct that Chiniquy lacked knowledge of, and loyalty to, Catholic doctrine. This conclusion of Neeser's stems from his regrettable restriction to one source: Chiniquy's own conversion account in his *Fifty Years*, written 16 years after the event. Accounts that we discovered which date from immediately after the conversion, do not mention Catholic scandals as motivating factors for the switch.

However, Neeser does admirably demonstrate how converts are pressured to describe their conversion in terms of a change of belief. His description of temperamental and attitudinal differences among converts is very shrewd. The Swiss analyst's categorization of converts might be improved by some adjustment but overall this provides a solid base for future study.

It appears that Christian thinkers ceased analytical study of the psychological aspects of conversion and apostasy between Catholicism and

---

103. Ibid., pp. 59-62.

7. WHAT KIND OF CONVERSION?

Protestantism in 1926.[104] In our more pluralistic age since Vatican II, we have a great need to enter into dialogue. It is imperative that we clearly address the question of why people convert or switch denominations. We must determine what the Churches believe about the spiritual state of these people.[105]

Lane Dennis, an American researcher, used micro-sociology to study a series of evangelical conversions. He concluded that all theories of conversion that were based on one factor (e.g., deprivation, social influence or even the more helpful cognitive belief theory) were deficient. Dennis suggested that there were three areas of social reality which interact in the conversion process: 1. external events and circumstances (the objective world) 2. the external meaning context (the world of ideas or surrounding world views e.g., the meaning system of a friend, the media or a church) 3. the internalized meaning system and process of the subject.[106] All three of these are disturbed when critical questions are raised in a way that the former meaning system, worldview or paradigm cannot resolve. All three must be involved in the conversion or acceptance of an alternative meaning system.

Multiple factors interact, Dennis claims. This appears to correspond to Chiniquy's situation. The external events and difficulties (#1 per Dennis), would be the primary precipitating factor for Chiniquy's conversion. At the same time, the St. Anne priest encountered alternative

---

104. Unfortunately due to time restraints I was not able to consult highly recommended recent books such as Scott McKnight, *Finding Faith, Losing Faith* (Waco, Baylor, 2008), Ruth Tucker, *Walking away from Faith* (Downer's Grove, IVP, 2002), Lewis Rambo, *Understanding Religious Conversion* (New Haven, Yale, 1995) or John Barbour, *Varieties of Deconversion* (Charlottesville, U. of VA, 1994).

105. For example, Protestants deeply resent their new "converts" being called "apostates", when this term conveys abandonment of the Christian faith in Protestant circles while Catholics begrudge the insult of calling those from a Catholic background but with no church attendance "converts from Catholicism".

106. Dennis, "Conversion in an Evangelical context: A Study in the Micro-Sociology of Religion" (Northwestern U., 1980), p. 222 for a diagram.

ideologies around him in Illinois(#2), and needed to find beliefs (#3), which could explain and cope with all the items in his confused life.

Norman Skonovd's sociology thesis, "Apostasy, the Process of Defection from Religious Totalism"[107] presents a helpful examination of ex-cult members. The contention of 'sociology of knowledge' is that knowledge and belief are socially determined or relate primarily to the group. Therefore "religious belief/experience is not as crucial a variable in religious commitment as is religious social involvement ... It is the power of the collective that is primarily responsible for maintenance" in the system.[108]

The defection model of Skonovd examines "religious totalism" in which every part of life is controlled by the religious group. To reject this totalism is a momentous act that alienates the member from his social life and from all the group's visions. The apostate has to abandon all previous hope of salvation and burn all bridges to escape religious totalism. There is no easy exit.

Totalist religion functions by physically isolating its members from outside influence, and by psychic insulation whereby outsiders are demonized. All social and spiritual functions are restricted to the group. Information is filtered so that each member of the group thinks in a similar manner. There is ideological authoritarianism; the inerrant authority must be consulted. Any confusion on the member's part is said to demonstrate ignorance and the need for guidance from the leader. Certainty stems from the authoritative leader rather than from doctrine.[109]

The potential apostate has a strongly independent personality able to resist strong social pressure. The apostasy or conversion first involves deconversion or weakening of allegiances. A crisis is essential to weaken or destroy the religious support structure. Factors that maximize this

---

107. Skonovd, "Apostasy, the Process of Defection from Religious Totalism" (Ann Arbor, 1981), 230 p.
108. Ibid., p. 17.
109. Ibid., pp. 33-49.

7. WHAT KIND OF CONVERSION?

crisis include conflict with other members, physical relocation and isolation from other members. Alternatively, extreme commands from authorities may conflict with deeply held moral or religious beliefs.

At this crisis point, cherished certainties are brought into question and confusion results. Most often the crisis problem is resolved. Occasionally there is "a gestalt switch - the completely different perception of something long seen or the perception of something for the first time which has been in the field of vision for some time."[110]

Apostasy only develops if the confusion and new perspective are not overcome by the efforts of the member and others. Coping mechanisms include repression, avoidance, rationalization, reformation, withdrawal and, if all else fails, escape. Sometimes after one problem is resolved a new crisis arises or a series of crises until the member finally cannot resolve one of them.

As the member decreases social contact with the group, all the group certainties decline in power. If other members become hostile or shun, this makes the questioning member begin a period of testing people outside. The potential apostate may be shocked to find that outsiders are sympathetic.

Even when this dissenter is convinced of the need to leave the community, a major force that restrains the member is fear: fear of damnation, of doubting, of losing community, and of being caught and punished. The departure usually comes after long agonizing. Finally, an even greater fear of staying than of leaving develops. The process is facilitated immensely if the member knows a convincing alternative. Even if the apostate prefers an opportunity for open discussion, proposing this can prove dangerous in a cult.

Skonovd insists that the departure does not end the process. A long reconstruction period is needed after religious totalism, typically six to eighteen months. For a while the ex-member has no identity but that of an ex-member. There is a grieving process with withdrawal symptoms.

---

110. Ibid., p. 64.

Directly confronting the group is the best method to defuse the cognitive and emotive power of the past.[111]

> When the defector has neutralized the cognitive and emotional influence of the group and has begun to re-establish a 'normal' life, he or she is then faced with the problem of accounting for the time and energy expended on what appears to have been a mistake.[112]

Looking back, the ex-member always sees the situation differently from the group, just as separated marriage partners differ in their accounts. These accounts remain fluid for some time, as the apostate continues to reinterpret and assess, and as his emotions vary.[113] Typically, the whole experience of religious totalism is described by the apostate either as brainwashing (so the ex-member is not responsible), **or** as a trial by fire that produced a stronger, more perceptive person.

We will examine how these insights apply to Chiniquy's conversion in the next chapter. First it is necessary to determine whether Skonovd's context of religious totalism matches Chiniquy's context.

TOTAL SUBMISSION TO THE CHURCH

The cults which Skonovd studied bear little resemblance to modern Catholicism. However, there are strong parallels with the religious totalism that 19th century Catholic ultramontanism aspired to. Near religious totalism was most evident where Catholic socio-political power was strongest, as in Quebec.

Bishop Baillargeon wrote to his flock:

> in order to protect you from all danger of losing [the Catholic faith], attach yourself closely to the pillar of truth (I Tim 3:15), to the Catholic Church, which is the depository and the infallible guardian; heed this unique Church of God ... listen then and follow, with religious docility, the pastors which God has given

---

111. Ibid., p. 140.
112. Ibid., p. 165.
113. Ibid., p. 22.

7. WHAT KIND OF CONVERSION?

to instruct and guide you in the way of salvation; and flee these deceitful men who teach another doctrine.[114]

Bishop Bourget appealed:

> In the future, [give] obedience to your worthy bishop, who should be for you another Jesus Christ.[115] The greatest sadness which can happen to a people, is to be carried away by a spirit of vertigo which causes them to not listen any more to those whom [God] empowered to guide, while at the same time, giving blind confidence to the first person who insults those who should be respected and honoured ... [Such people become] nations delivered up to a diabolical spirit.[116]

The noted Catholic convert John Henry Newman, even during his Anglican years, stressed the all-important spiritual authority of the Church:

> to bring our passions into order, to make us pure, to make us meek, to rule our intellect, to give government of speech, to inspire firmness, and to destroy self ... Obedience is the test of Faith ... the whole duty and work of a Christian is made up of these two parts, Faith and Obedience.[117]

Chiniquy, himself, in his days as a loyal priest, insisted that obedience was a prime Catholic virtue and clerical guidance was always beneficial.[118]

At the end of the St. Anne schism, Mailloux translated the pastoral letter of American Catholic bishops in which they stessed obedience:

> asking in return only your docility and ready obedience ... in this age when unfortunately this example of insubordination is so common, where the spirit of revolt and licence have raised

---

114. Archbp. Baillargeon circular letter regarding the 2nd Provincial Council of Quebec, 8 December 1855 (*MEQ*, vol. 4, p. 257) (my translation).

115. Extract from Bp. Bourget to Bourbonnais Catholics, 19 March 1857, found in *Av* of 15 September 1857, p. 3; his pastoral letter of 10 March 1858 (*MEM*, vol. 3, p. 370).

116. My translation of Bp. Bourget pastoral letter, 5 February 1859 (*MEM*, vol.3, p. 423).

117. Quoted in Bowen, *The Idea of the Victorian Church* (Montreal, 1968), p. 59.

118. *Av*, 21 and 23 June 1849.

the flag of rebellion, we view it as our sacred duty to warn you what you owe us.[119]

Because of their public statements newspapers and politicians in Quebec were particularly vulnerable to the requirement for submission. Bishop Fabre refused discussion with the editors of the *Canada Revue* after they criticized some priests. He demanded unconditional submission, if they wished his censure to be rescinded.[120] The furor over the burial of Joseph Guibord again stemmed from the failure to submit to the bishop's decree.

The *Gazette des campagnes* contested the Protestant principle:

> of doing whatever one wants, in spite of what the leader of the sect says or forbids. This conduct demonstrates that either we believe ourselves wiser and more enlightened than our bishop or that his authority is only affirmed in principle while in practice we do not recognize it.[121]

The ideological language of ultramontanism in Quebec: "was directed above all to those emotions (obedience, submission, respect) or else to the imagination, treating the powers of reason as secondary."[122] Submission stemmed both from theology and from social training. It was an act of confidence in the authority rather than in the content of the decree. Neutrality or any discussion, except to receive clarification, was deemed suspect.

As a Catholic Chiniquy had insisted that the pope was immune from criticism. Now he complained that Catholic education trained the mind to avoid exerting itself on any matter on which any member of the Church hierarchy had pronounced:

---

119. Pastoral letter of the Second Provincial Council of St. Louis, September 12, 1858, p. 37 (**ASQ** 50:13a-i). Archbp. Kenrick of St. Louis, Bp. Smyth of Dubuque and Bp. Duggan of Chicago would probably all be thinking of Chiniquy.

120. J. Doutre, *Ruines cléricales* (Montreal, 1893), pp. 106-7.

121. Quoted in Dumont, Montminy and Hamelin, *Idéologies au Canada français, 1850-1900* (Quebec, 1971), p. 159 (my translation).

122. Eid, *Le clergé et le pouvoir politique* (Montreal, 1976), p. 121.

7. WHAT KIND OF CONVERSION?

> Mr. C. illustrated [Catholic Bible study] by supposing that two young men should ask their father's leave to travel to see the world, and he should grant it on condition that they kept their eyes and ears closed the whole way, and went in charge of a priest, who at the end of the journey, would tell them what he had heard and seen for them.[123]

Besides this lack of encouragement to think, the theory that the Church did not change prevented any admission of past error.

From the ultramontane perspective, unconditional submission was required of Chiniquy. His pride had led him to publicly slander his bishop. Then he refused to retract in his "submissions". The rebel priest continued to refuse submission on key points. His desire to be free of restraint was incompatible with Catholic priesthood.

In some ways, evangelical Protestants are similar to ultramontanists. They prefer rural traditional values and advocate church discipline to guard the boundaries of faith and practice. Evangelicals have held their own heresy trials. They have also challenged liberal Protestants who claimed to have the right to teach and preach any autonomous interpretation of faith. Evangelicals would have agreed with much of the 1864 papal Syllabus of Errors. Many evangelicals sympathize with the need, if not always the methods, of recent attempts to maintain doctrinal unity within the Catholic Church. They could have sympathized with the Chicago bishop's need to deal with the rebel Chiniquy. After all, Chicago Presbytery later found him a very difficult person to direct or question.

However, evangelicals have rarely had much socio-political power. They have suffered persecution through much of history, particularly in Catholic nations. Evangelicals, at least in theory, have become convinced that inevitable abuse ensues from absolute power. The human conscience, inspired by the Holy Spirit and the Bible, has to

---

123. *MW,* 24 January 1870, p. 2.

remain free to obey God rather than mere humans.[124] Thus on both historical and theological grounds, no political or even religious authority can command unquestioning obedience from evangelicals.

Furthermore, the plurality of Protestant denominations meant that a person, who was disciplined by one church, could easily join another. Excommunication or expulsion never carried the weight among Protestants that it did for Catholics. While groupthink and pressure are common, it has proved impossible for evangelicals to impose religious totalism in a broader society.[125]

Therefore in Chiniquy's time, rebels who left Catholicism, in opposition to a demand for total submission, could expect to receive evangelical sympathy. The *Aurore* insisted:

> To revolt firstly because of an obvious injustice, or a distortion, for insults to one's reason through the demonstration of intolerable absurdities or for abuse of authority: such revolt is quite natural. If during the battle one opens one's eyes, examines the basis of authority which acts from on high in a cavalier and rough manner, this too is reasonable; and then, if, as a result, one does not wish any longer to submit to that authority, that seems to us in perfect harmony with the teaching of our Master.[126]

When, in addition, rebels to religious totalism invoked Scripture as their authority, evangelicals would rush to their support.

---

124. Acts 5:29. Free thought was even mentioned before justification by faith and Scripture as evangelical principles by A. B. Cruchet in *La révocation de l'Édit de Nantes: discours prononcées à l'occasion du deuxième anniversaire de cet événement* (Montreal, Imprimerie de l'Aurore, 1885), p. 112.

125. There are a few examples among certain fundamentalists and certain conservative Mennonite groups.

126. *A*, 3 February 1894, p. 8 (my translation).

8

THE RELIGIOUS CONVERSION OF CHINIQUY

Chronology of the conversion

ANTECEDENTS

Chiniquy's autobiography, which is virtually the only source about his youth, provides many precursors of conversion. From his childhood Chiniquy with his questioning mind came up against warnings to "just accept" the decisions of Church tradition or leaders.

Young Charles took his faith very seriously.[1] His own father had pursued the priesthood but dropped out at an advanced stage. For the son, the personal intrusion of the confessional and the implications of any priest's misbehaviour weighed heavily. Chiniquy mentions the early influence of a Protestant teacher and of an anticlerical group in his village. He memorized large portions of the Bible, which functioned on occasion as an alternate source of truth. This became problematic with time.

---

1. Laverdure, "Religious Invective" (McGill, 1984), p. 57.

THE CONTROVERSIAL CONVERSION OF CHARLES CHINIQUY

Chiniquy's autobiography does not adequately explain why he became a priest. One may speculate that the prolonged experience at the Nicolet College was a positive one. He was left with no other home after his mother died while he was in college. Since his uncle disowned him Chiniquy had no land or money. Perhaps it was already beginning to be expected that one son should become a priest; this expectation became very pronounced in Quebec by the end of the 19th century, The priesthood provided security and prestige. All these could stimulate a call.

On the other hand any professed call to the priesthood had to be assessed by Church authorities. Since Principal Leprohon later wanted Chiniquy as his assistant at Nicolet, we may presume that the young orphan was encouraged by his teachers.

Chiniquy recorded his recurrent questions about dogma while at college.[2] His superiors responded with warnings. Each time the young student submitted mentally to those who knew more, being fearful of becoming a reformer or heretic. It was reiterated to him frequently that there were only two alternatives: submission or heresy.

Chiniquy became a ringleader priest for various causes in the Quebec area. This attracted the wrath of his ecclesiastical superiors. He received new warnings that he was becoming a reformer,[3] with one foot in the heretical camp. Promoting the One-Mass Society[4] was probably his strongest action. Later his temperance cause differed from Bishop Signay's policy (total abstinence versus temperance). Chiniquy kept on pursuing independent courses until he was restrained (e.g. his political interventions).

In every cause Chiniquy was an extremist, as if fighting a holy war to exterminate the enemy or at least the error. Rallying cries, rather than measured statements, were his strength. He was a master at preparing

---

2. See e.g. *50 Years*, p. 69: "if my reason tells me that the Pope, or some of those other superiors are mistaken... would I not be guilty before God if I obey them?"

3. This was employed as a decidedly negative term. See *50 Years*, pp. 134, 200, 249, 262, 281, 340, 356, 368.

4. See our chapter 1 for details on this and the other events mentioned here.

8. THE RELIGIOUS CONVERSION OF CHINIQUY

others emotionally to accept his logic. His various crusades usually culminated in a call to decision or conversion.

During his years as priest Chiniquy was inspired by Dr. Douglas and encouraged by editor John Dougall. This Protestant support for his temperance cause was an important memory when crises came later. Chiniquy also studied Protestantism in some depth but only in order to refute it. Thus many Protestant concepts were well known to the famous priest before his major conflict in St. Anne.

Chiniquy recorded periodic doubts after his ordination as is natural for any believer. He felt the terrible seriousness of transporting the living God in a communion wafer and an outrage at the unjust or scandalous actions of some priests. Later the ex-priest attributed great importance to one traditional sermon of his own on the subject of the Virgin Mary. Despite its orthodoxy the sermon provoked doubts in him.

Throughout these years, Chiniquy claimed to have heard a probing internal voice that was sceptical of Catholic tradition.[5] Originally he took this to be demonic. Thus he repeatedly rejected doubts, at the recommendation of his confessors. After his conversion, Chiniquy came to view the voice as having been the Holy Spirit, attempting to guide his conscience.

When a Catholic priest, Chiniquy was a zealous believer with serious flaws of violent speech and, probably, sexual misdeeds. His violent language was critiqued but he was never disciplined for it. However, perceived sexual misconduct resulted in the exile of the famed priest to the United States. Godefroi Lambert claimed that Chiniquy abandoned many Catholic practices on arrival in Illinois (e.g., reading his daily prayers and fasting). Nevertheless, no other evidence suggests such rebellion or indiscipline. Chiniquy's own writings actually mention that he had fewer religious doubts in Illinois. He was even criticized by

---

5. *40 Years*, p. 47.

the Protestant press during this period for being a herald of violence against Protestants.[6]

CONVERGENCE OF EVENTS AND INFLUENCES

Chiniquy's traditional ultramontane stance was shaken not by doctrine but by what he perceived as unjust treatment by the bishop of Chicago. Events led rapidly to focus on this fundamental question: should I and can I submit to an unjust bishop? Like the earlier Ultramontane hero in France, Félicité Lamennais, Chiniquy used the press to embarrass his bishop. He hoped that this would bring Catholic pressure to bear on O'Regan. It failed. Instead, most of those who were interested and supportive were Protestants.

In St. Anne Chiniquy disagreed with his bishop first over church property, then much more seriously, over the situation of French Catholics in Chicago. Months before his excommunication and public rebellion Chiniquy offered to make any overtures for peace in his court case with Spink "except for the sacrifices which force me to betray my conscience or my character."[7] This recurring phrase provides a key to the deep-set conflict. Although Chiniquy wanted peace he had limits of principle.

The same month as his peace initiative, Chiniquy wrote of a conspiracy in Quebec against his views on immigration.[8] Chiniquy was bitterly disappointed that Quebec clerical ranks closed against him despite his reasonable faithful position. This dispute also made it harder later to gain Quebec sympathy for his major conflicts.

In August and September 1856, Chiniquy was suspended and then excommunicated from the Roman Catholic Church. The final Spink trial followed in October. Chiniquy was convinced that the bishop was directing the lawsuit. Meanwhile the French Canadians of Chicago and

---

6. *MW*, 20 February 1856, p. 60, with extracts of Chiniquy's letter.
7. Chiniquy to Brisard, 16 March 1856 (**ASQ** 50:1).
8. Chiniquy to Chapais, 29 March 1856 (Barnard, *Mémoires*, vol. 2, p .131).

8. THE RELIGIOUS CONVERSION OF CHINIQUY

St. Anne expressed support for Chiniquy and condemnation of Bishop O'Regan through letters to the French and English newspapers.

The Protestant and anti-clerical press collaborated with their former adversary to combat the "tyrannical" bishop. However the *Montreal Witness* warned that Chiniquy "has no alternative now, but either to bow before the infallible despotism of its hierarchy, which his proud spirit will scarcely allow him to do, or else to submit his case to the decision of the Pope, which can not fail to go against him."[9]

Bishop Bourget attempted to support Bishop O'Regan's hard line and yet achieve reconciliation. In November 1856, Bourget emissaries managed to convince Chiniquy to write an act of submission. Although this was a major feat, Chiniquy had carefully avoided clearing the Chicago bishop of previous accusations. Chiniquy's pride and conscience prevented him from signing Bishop O'Regan's own subsequent submission protocol. This document would have retracted specific "false charges" that Chiniquy was alleged to have made. The failure of this reconciliation hardened positions at the end of 1856, isolating Chiniquy from Quebec clergy.

Nevertheless the excommunicated Chiniquy continued to profess his Catholic orthodoxy:

> I do not want to produce a schism, but it seems that my former friends want to force me into one, by the manner in which they relate to me ... You, our brothers ... curse us because we do not want to submit to such a situation ... the Canadian clergy join the side of the oppressors against the oppressed.[10] .... Oh holy Catholic Church: it was at the entrance of your church that God adopted me as his child; it is you who have opened the gates of heaven to me; it was at the foot of your altars that I received the honor of being raised to the dignity of a priest of the Gospel![11]

---

9. *MW*, 15 November 1856, p. 387.

10. Extracts from Chiniquy "privé" to editor of *La Minerve*, early 1857, pp. 1-4 (**ASQ** 52:5).

11. In a revealing move towards Protestantism, Chiniquy crossed out "of the Church" and replaced it with "of the Gospel" in an earlier version of this letter sent to the *Journal de Québec*, 2 February 1857, p. 23 (**ASQ** 50:1j).

> I would rather die a thousand times than to cease to be your child. Where could I go if I left you? Only you have the words of eternal life. Oh let me devote my final years to defending the weak ... who some seek to oppress even in your midst.[12]

Here Chiniquy simultaneously affirmed that the Roman Catholic Church possessed the sole truth and yet refused to submit to his bishop. The inconsistency is obvious and reveals a long transitional stage as Chiniquy considered alternatives.

In his isolation, Chiniquy readily cooperated with the *Avenir*. They published his side of the controversy in multiple pamphlets in 1857. Meanwhile Brassard warned that tough tactics would only bring tough responses from the St. Anne rebel.[13] Excommunication was not proving salutory.[14] Instead it drove the schismatic closer to anti-clericals.

A Montreal Catholic lawyer wrote to Chiniquy and achieved some moderating effect. Still, in his response, the rebel-priest insisted that Church history revealed many bishops who advanced evil by demanding:

> things contrary to the inviolable rights which the Gospel gives to all people. Do not think that all resistance stems from pride ... Moral resistance to oppression is one of the laws of human nature which J.C. did not come to abolish.[15]

> The Saviour himself had contested the Pharisees' interpretations. From the moment when bishops depart from this divine path of wisdom [justice, love], they become ordinary humans [who even abuse their flocks] ... Maybe I did speak too hastily and too strongly ... but I am alone here, a poor missionary, to fight against

---

12. Chiniquy to *Av* (reprinted as *Persécutions aux Illinois de l'Abbé Chiniquy* (Montreal, 1857), p. 36). This is virtually the same letter as to the *Journal* mentioned above.
13. Brassard to Mailloux, 24 March 1857, p. 1 (**ASQ** 50:2b).
14. This is its intent according to Canon Law and the New Testament (I Cor. 5:5, II Thess. 3:14-15).
15. Chiniquy to Moreau, 26 February 1857, p. 38 (**ASQ** 52:5f).

8. THE RELIGIOUS CONVERSION OF CHINIQUY

so many and such powerful dignitaries. The energy with which I speak and act has its source in my own weakness.[16]

This confession seems to seek reconciliation but his polemics had already done too much damage.

Mailloux's arrival in St. Anne polarized the situation further as he gathered evidence against Chiniquy. Meanwhile the *Montreal Witness* publicly urged prayers for Chiniquy's conversion because, so far, this was:

> only the rebellion of a proud and popular priest against the tyranny and rapacity of his bishop ... A question of Church property is at the bottom of all the contest ... True, Scripture is quoted by the Rev. Father and his friends, but only passages are selected as run in opposition to clerical despotism and the love of wealth.[17]

Chiniquy became increasingly opposed to the episcopate, as such, when all bishops joined ranks to condemn him. "There is one fault which is too common among bishops ... it is to believe themselves personally to constitute the Church".[18] Priests who knew the Scriptures and Canon Law tended to be out of favour, Chiniquy claimed, because they knew that bishops could err:

> The moment when one of these priests is courageous enough to say to his bishop ... 'It is wrong to do that, you should not act like that', he is seen as merely a proud, insubordinate, heretical person, a dangerous man; he is marginalized and treated as someone disgusting ... [But] The Church alone is holy, infallible and without blemish ... you priests and bishops, you are all individually very sinful, weak and fallible ... A human is only infallible when he repeats what Jesus Christ said in the Bible, interpreted by the church ... When we put our passions in place of the holy laws of the Bible, not only do the people have the right to despise our word and our commands, but they are obliged to do so ... another fault too common among the bishops, is to be

---

16. Ibid., pp. 39-40.
17. *MW*, 11 April 1857, p. 228.
18. Chiniquy to Bp. Pinsoneault, 5 March 1857 (in *Av*, 15 April, p. 2).

far too ready to call 'pride', what is actually before God a conscientious conviction.[19]

The *Montreal Witness* promptly and eagerly predicted failure:

> Mr Chiniquy has no right [in the Catholic Church] to interpret the Bible in his own case, he must submit humbly to the interpretation of the Church, as illustrated through Bishop O'Regan or else he becomes, unawares, heretic and Protestant.[20]

In the spring of 1857 sexual allegations against Chiniquy surfaced from the pens of Bourget and Mailloux. The rebel priest responded with fury and counter-charges but he still affirmed Catholic dogma. He invited Bishop Pinsoneault and Brassard for a peace mission[21] but nothing came of this.

In June Bishop O'Regan made a disastrous visit to Bourbonnais that inflamed the situation again. Perhaps it also led to the Bishop's decision to quit the diocese in September. Meanwhile Chiniquy met Mailloux to challenge the content of Mailloux's sexual allegations, and to propose a submission to Bishop O'Regan.[22] In the submission Chiniquy agreed to leave St. Anne but the conditions were designed to benefit the French Catholics of Chicago and St. Anne. By accepting such conditions Bishop O'Regan would have implied that he had erred. So once again the Chicago bishop refused a Chiniquy submission.[23] We observe, on the one hand, that the excommunicate priest desired reconciliation and was willing to submit, despite everything. On the other hand, he refused unconditional submission. Neither the bishop nor his priest would budge from their initial positions.

---

19. Ibid. Notice (in the French original as well) that the Bible is capitalized while 'church' as interpreter is not.
20. *MW*, 29 April 1857, p. 268.
21. Chiniquy to Bourget, 10 May 1857 (**ACAM** 402.102, 857-34).
22. **ASQ** 50:14L and 50:2L verso (dated June 1857).
23. O'Regan to Mailloux, 26 June 1857 (**ASQ** 50:2o).

8. THE RELIGIOUS CONVERSION OF CHINIQUY

In July, the former sacristan of St. Anne, Godefroi Lambert, sent a scathing letter to Chiniquy denouncing the excommunicated priest's previous immorality. Whatever the truth of these allegations, Mailloux and the bishops believed them, while Chiniquy claimed a conspiracy. That same month Chiniquy gave a public lecture on "Liberty of Conscience" which delighted Kankakee Protestants. Presumably it was the same lecture that he gave in Chicago. He praised the Protestant - Washington, and the Catholic - Lafayette, who had joined hands to insist on tolerance and liberty of conscience for both Catholic and Protestant. Chiniquy claimed that America had prospered as a result of such cooperation for liberty.[24]

In October, Chiniquy helped rebuild the Catholic Church building in Kankakee. Although the excommunicated priest wrote less often, his supporters in Chicago and St. Anne continued strong newspaper attacks against the bishop and the local Catholic representative Alexis Mailloux.

The final reconciliation attempt came from Vicar General Dunn after O'Regan left the diocese. Chiniquy's hopes were raised by this friendly supportive act and he was amazed when interim Bishop Smyth accepted his act of submission in March 1858. In this submission he recognized the divine institution of episcopal authority and requested that the St. Anne parishioners be treated as loyal Catholics.[25]

Mailloux was more perceptive. He noted that in this submission Chiniquy neither confessed his offences nor retracted his initial charges against the former Bishop O'Regan. As the Quebec envoy sent to control Chiniquy, he halted the reconciliation by informing the

---

24. *CT*, 19 August 1857, p. 1.

25. *MW*, 14 April 1858, p. 236, printed the submission but commented: "He makes no apology, undergoes no penance" and makes only a broad profession of faith. "No priest in Canada could be restored on such easy terms." The Catholic *Journal des débats* of 15 April 1858, p. 1, was singularly unenthusiastic at the resolution.

Dubuque bishop of Chiniquy's misdeeds in Quebec, and even worse misdeeds in Illinois.[26]

Chiniquy was summoned to return to the interim bishop's Dubuque residence. This directly precipitated his final break with the Roman Catholic Church. According to Chiniquy, Bishop Smyth was most concerned that the wording of this submission made it conditional on the conjunction of the bishop's decrees with the Bible. This had been Chiniquy's intention. Smyth now objected to the phrase "the Catholic Bishop is established by Jesus Christ to lead and govern, **according to the laws of the Gospel, and in conformity to the holy canons of the Church**."[27] Bishop Smyth annulled the recent reconciliation. Then he made Chiniquy's future in the priesthood conditional on unqualified submission to the bishop. This new condition brought an absolute refusal from the still excommunicated priest. It was now apparent that there was no future for Chiniquy in a relationship with any Roman Catholic bishop without total submission.

Chiniquy's autobiography records that on that day, April 10, 1858, he gave in to despair in his hotel room and almost committed suicide. Reportedly, the day finished with a divine vision, a biblical revelation and Chiniquy's acceptance of *Solo Gratia*, salvation by grace.[28] Skonovd and Neeser warn us of embellished conversion stories. Since Chiniquy's autobiographical account was published 27 years after the event let us examine contemporary reports to corroborate the 'conversion'.

The last issue of the *Avenir*, an 'Extra', consisted of a long Chiniquy letter sent April 18, 1858 (10 days after the alleged conversion). Then it

---

26. Smyth to Mailloux, 28 June 1858 (**ASQ** 50:13v); Mailloux to Auclair, 27 June 1858 (**ASQ** 50:19k), on Mailloux's views of the submission. Chiniquy to Cazeau, 8-22 April 1858 (**AAQ** EU VII 140) for his side.

27. Printed in *MW*, 14 April 1858, p. 236 with my addition of bold characters. These two qualifications had been used to defend the rebellion as in a letter of Chiniquy to Brassard, 13 April 1857, printed in *50 Years*, pp. 765 and 769. I presume that the version in *50 Years*, p. 778 is a condensed version of the original.

28. *50 Years*, pp. 791-6.

8. THE RELIGIOUS CONVERSION OF CHINIQUY

discussed the conflict with Bishop Smyth. It mentions nothing about a conversion experience. In part this is a natural omission since Chiniquy is appealing to an anti-clerical readership shortly after the event. The message of this letter concerned the rejection of injustice rather than a gospel of grace. This is also the message of Chiniquy's letter to Quebec Diocese, which overlaps the reconciliation and the new breakdown. He was outraged that the bishop could change his mind so radically without hearing the other side and then demand absolute submission.[29]

A different note was struck by a letter from Chiniquy to the *Journal d'Illinois* on May 6: he is still working "in silence towards enlightening ecclesiastical authorities and bringing them back to the paths of truth and justice, rather than reveal to the world plots of priests ... which I shall not unravel until all other means of conciliation have been exhausted."[30] Chiniquy's attempt to reconcile frustrated some Protestant observers who despaired of him developing any evangelical convictions.[31] French Protestants were more sympathetic and still urged Chiniquy to visit Quebec.[32]

James Duggan was appointed as the new Chicago bishop in June 1858. Mailloux soon brought him up to date on the Chiniquy crisis.[33] Apart from the two published letters, Chiniquy was silent since Easter and through the summer.

Two prominent French Baptists from Quebec, *Semeur canadien* editor Narcisse Cyr and Theodore Lafleur, visited St. Anne in the summer.[34] Lafleur later wrote that "the Grande Ligne Mission may

---

29. Chiniquy to Cazeau, April 8-22 1858 (**AAQ** EU VII 140).
30. This does not seem to have been published according to the former Fraser-Hickson Library (Montreal) collection of *JI*. It appears however in *MW*, 19 May 1858, p. 316.
31. Ibid.
32. *SC*, 28 May 1858.
33. Mailloux to Bp. Duggan, 17 July 1858 (**ASQ** 50:11s).
34. Lafleur, *A Semi-Centennial Historical Sketch*, (Montreal, 1885), pp. 30,53; *GL Annual Report*, (Montreal, 1899), p. 11. Mailloux to Quebec Diocese (**AAQ** EU VII 34), p. 4.

claim the first and large share in the conversion of the most popular priest of Canada ... the strong controversialist against Rome."[35] At Chiniquy's funeral, Lafleur reported:

> He invited me to go and see him [in 1858] and I did so ... After an almost consecutive conversation of fifteen hours, we went down on our knees to pray the invisible Master to direct, enlighten and strengthen him for that sublime moment when the perspective of a reformed faith opened a new world in his astonished soul. I shall never forget his look, and the pallor of his face, glistening with the new celestial light. He had just understood, after many other things, that the God whom we had just addressed in spirit and in truth, was much greater than the one which he professed to have known. The unity of his Church seemed to him very factious and very superficial, yet he feared Protestantism with all its denominations.[36]

Lafleur pointed to this moment as Chiniquy's crucial moment of comprehension, if not conversion. Much later, one of Chiniquy's sons-in-law (a Baptist) declared that though Chiniquy had been baptized a Methodist and had joined the Presbyterians, he had been converted through the Baptists.[37] Chiniquy himself gave partial credit to Lafleur's letters and conversations.[38] These early Baptist contacts seem to have been extremely influential in forming Chiniquy's new views.

In July 1858, St. Anne's financial/harvest problems led Chiniquy to undertake a fund-raising tour of the eastern United States. Eventually, he convinced the evangelical Protestants there to contribute to his community. It took more than anti-Catholicism or dramatizing to convince the sceptical crowds of American evangelicals. They knew that the rebel priest and his flock were still Catholics in name. If Chiniquy was a con artist then he learned the role very quickly. He convinced evangelicals to contribute to his causes for over 40 years.

---

35. *GL Annual Report*, 1899, p. 11.
36. *G*, 20 January 1899, p. 5.
37. Rev. Samuel Delagneau in *A*, 11 September 1909, p. 3.
38. *40 Years*, p. 186.

8. THE RELIGIOUS CONVERSION OF CHINIQUY

Chiniquy claimed in *50 Years* that he gave an immediate evangelical testimony and altar call to his congregation.[39] I was unable to find attestation in the contemporary newspapers. This does not necessarily mean that no such event occurred. However, it suggests that either Chiniquy kept elements secret at the time or, more likely, that he reinterpreted the events later.

When Duggan made the first episcopal visit in years St. Anne, he brought matters to a climax by restating the parish's excommunication in person. This may have had a warning effect on Catholics in Quebec, as Mailloux hoped. Nevertheless, in St. Anne the rebels became more angry and determined.

The *Semeur canadien* was delighted that one vocal speaker at the bishop's visit said:

> it would be better to be guided by the word of God than by words of bishops'. This is a noble statement which has taken a long time to emerge from the mouths of the Catholic people of St. Anne ... we are happy to see that the opposition of the people of St. Anne is not simply a squabble nor due to pure stubbornness nor unbelief; rather it is a serious protest based on the eternal word of God [the Bible].[40]

Two weeks after the final excommunication, the Catholic Christian Church was founded.

SUBSEQUENT INTERPRETATIONS

Both Catholic analysts and the *Montreal Witness* viewed this Catholic Christian church as neither Catholic nor Protestant. For

---

39. S. Smith, *Pastor Chiniquy* (London, 1908), p. 60, finds no announced change until after the excommunication, invalidating, for him, any later claim to conversion. Chiniquy to Cazeau, 8-22 April 1858 (**AAQ** VII 140), p. 14 tells of his report to his congregation of the outrageous actions of his bishop, asking them to choose. The choice mentioned concerns injustice and confidence in Chiniquy rather than a call to follow a different gospel. Certainly the call involves a rejection of this Catholic episcopal authority.

40. *SC*, 13 August 1858, p. 2 (my translation).

Catholics the new name clarified matters. It made the rebellion even worse than simple conversion to Protestantism. Chiniquy was founding an autonomous religion. For Protestants the independent church was a distinct improvement, although many remained suspicious:

> It is only after the Hierarchy has hopelessly cut him off that he disagrees with Romish doctrine, and this should repress too sanguine hopes of the heretic priest, until new evidence is supplied of the evangelical soundness of his schism.[41]

The *Semeur canadien* was convinced of Chiniquy's "evangelical soundness" and managed to sway the *Montreal Witness*.[42] While the *Chicago Tribune* was more interested in Chiniquy's political views, it did report that Chiniquy had announced that: "hereafter his flock would take Scripture as their guide and rule of faith; and if that was called Protestantism, then he and they were called Protestants."[43]

In early 1859 during his visit to Quebec, the former Apostle of Temperance, attempted to profit from the ambiguity of retaining the name "Catholic". The *Semeur canadien* helped to promote his lectures to explain "the truth" about the persecution of French Canadians in Illinois.[44] It seems that Cyr and the other GL Mission leaders who helped organize the tour were satisfied with Chiniquy's theology. They must have hoped for greater influence, if Chiniquy was not openly identified with Protestants from the start.

During this tour Chiniquy developed a pattern. His first lecture in a town recounted his version of events in Illinois. It showed that he had been a loyal but unjustly-treated Catholic. Then, in the second lecture Chiniquy demonstrated a biblical basis for his resistance to a tyrannical bishop and hence the need to read the Bible.[45] Thus Chiniquy used his

---

41. *MW*, 4 September 1858. See Figure 29 for a scan of this. Also 12 January 1859.
42. *MW*, 15 September 1858 translation of *SC* article.
43. *CT*, 4 December 1858, p. 1.
44. *SC*, 4 February 1859 (**ACAM** 402.102 859-6).
45. E.g. in the account in *MW*, 5 February 1859, p. 84.

8. THE RELIGIOUS CONVERSION OF CHINIQUY

reputation and the title "Father Chiniquy" to introduce crowds gradually to an evangelical message. At Napierville, Catholics saw the danger of such tactics and derailed the attempt by continually asking, "are you a Protestant?". This forced Chiniquy out of his ambiguity.[46]

The *Montreal Herald* pointed out that although Chiniquy belonged to an episcopal hierarchy, in his wish to retain a congregational approach to property, he was in contradiction. The conflict of principles required the rebel priest, if honest, to abandon Catholicism and the episcopate.[47]

In Montreal Chiniquy spoke of the mental struggle that followed his refusal of absolute submission. A Bible verse showed him the way out: "You were bought at a price; do not become slaves of men"(I Cor. 7:23).[48] In the autobiographical account of his conversion the Protestant message of salvation by faith alone ("you were bought at a price") was most prominent. However that message is not mentioned in the published report of this 1859 speech. That omission is striking. Instead it is the second part of this verse, "do not become slaves of men", which is emphasized.

In this first tour of Quebec Chiniquy cooperated with the GL leaders and met some FCMS leaders privately. For tactical reasons he used neutral lecture halls, trying to distance himself from English and French Protestants. However he had to resort to English media coverage and physical protection by English evangelicals.

During the tour, Chiniquy was questioned by Rev. Hellmuth of the evangelical Anglican Colonial Church and School Society. Chiniquy responded and related that his flock was moving towards gospel truths as he encouraged them to read the Bible freely and discuss it:

> They have tasted of that fruit of life (the Scriptures) ... and no power in this world now will make them forget that the Holy

---

46. Laviolette to Mailloux, 14 March 1859, p. 7ff (**ASQ** 50:2f). The pastoral letter of Bp. Bourget on 4 February 1859 also called him a Protestant.
47. *Montreal Herald*, 5 February 1859.
48. *New International Version*; *MW*, 5 February 1859, p. 84.

> Scriptures are the most precious treasure of the Christian. [These parishioners were sending him back to Quebec to their relatives] to invite them to give up the human authority of their priests in exchange for the Divine authority of the gospel.[49]

Thus the rebel priest's first step was to take the Bible as his justification for resistance. From this evangelical basis, he steadily grew to accept the other distinctive evangelical beliefs.

By early 1859 it was difficult to detect any remaining non-Protestant theology. In fact, Chiniquy's anti-clerical jibes, fuelled by Catholic violence during his Quebec tour, were already attracting strong Protestant applause.[50] Shortly after the Quebec tour, Chiniquy spoke in Toronto. He stated that his fellow French Canadians had gradually lost faith in their ecclesiastical superiors. Again he cited the I Cor. 7 passage and again he made no mention of a conversion. Rather he spoke of a realization that he should now serve the Saviour rather than the bishop. Nonetheless, Protestants who observed the strong Catholic reaction against him, decided that it was important to support the rebel priest.

One Protestant observer in Toronto regretted that the ex-priest's theological views were not clear and that the whole affair was about the trivial question of property: "This seems to have been the most serious question at issue, at least in the beginning; and one cannot but experience a shade of disappointment that more vital matters were not at stake."[51]

On the other hand an extensive evangelical analysis in a Congregational journal found that Chiniquy had Protestant antecedents in his scripture training as a youth:

> As he frankly acknowledges, God has brought him out of the Church, against his own will. [Each time he felt rebellion was too much and wrote a submission, additional demands were made] ... his manhood [thus] reasserted itself, and by such repeated conflicts he seems at length to have been brought to a thorough renunciation of the Church and the adoption of the Word, as

---

49. Chiniquy to Hellmuth, 18 February 1859 (in *MW*, 25 May 1859, p. 330).
50. From a clipping of an unidentified Toronto paper, 10 March 1859 (**ASQ** 52: 4).
51. *MW*, 16 March 1859, pp. 172-3.

8. THE RELIGIOUS CONVERSION OF CHINIQUY

his guide. There have been so many disappointments with converted priests, that we must needs be cautious, and wait the issue ... We cannot search the heart; but after hearing him in public and in private, we are impressed with the idea that he is a sincere man, - one who loves the truth ... At present he is in a transition state. He has renounced the name of 'Roman', though still calling himself a 'Catholic' Christian. He rejects tradition, transubstantiation, and prayers for the dead; and he holds to justification by faith. ... If it should please God fully to reveal his Son in Father Chiniquy, it may be the means of a great awakening among the French Canadians ... No conversion would be so influential over others as his.[52]

What more did they want of Chiniquy? Perhaps an explicit conversion testimony and membership in a clearly Protestant denomination. The ex-priest's theology already included all evangelical essentials. In addition Chiniquy had attacked Catholic practices of purgatory, indulgences, opposition to Bible distribution, clerical encouragement of violence and use of the Inquisition instead of debate.[53]

In mid-1859 at a Baltimore lecture, Chiniquy was introduced in lavish conversion language. The ex-priest did not object. He was called "the illustrious convert" and recounted his conversion story (in which he again mentioned I Cor 7:23b and spoke of serving God, rather than men).[54] He was introduced as a reformer comparable to Luther, who had produced numerous converts. Still, salvation by grace is not mentioned in the report. The *Semeur canadien* suggested "that he has need of much more progress in understanding and in piety but we are assured that having begun on the true way of practical Christianity," he will do well.[55]

---

52. *Canadian Independent*, April 1859, pp. 294-5.
53. Chiniquy to SC (condensed in *MW*, 30 March 1859, p. 201).
54. Brouillet to Mailloux, 6 June 1859, p. 1 (**ASQ** 50:20h).
55. *Cour*, 27 July 1859, p. 2 (my translation) quoted this. In response the Catholic paper objected that Chiniquy's knowledge lacked nothing while his piety was as poor as was that of all apostates.

Images such as conversion, reformation, and 'a new Luther' became standard in portrayals of Chiniquy after June 1859. His cause was seen as that of the Bible and freedom of conscience versus Catholic traditions and absolutism. Nobody spoke of conversion to a particular Protestant denomination nor was there mention of conversion to belief in God. It was seen as a conversion from the authority of bishops, Pope and Catholic tradition, to the authority of the Bible alone, interpreted by the Holy Spirit.

Although understandable, Bishop Smyth's demand for absolute submission was unrealistic given Chiniquy's temperament and the perception of serious injustice. The St. Anne cleric intuitively found the Protestant evangelical principle. He was encouraged to pursue that principle as his stated basis by his reading of Scripture and GL aid. Lingering doubts among evangelicals about the validity of Chiniquy's conversion[56] tended to disappear after Rev. Hellmuth's affirmation.[57]

REFINED CONVERSION ACCOUNTS

By September 1860, Chiniquy's conversion story had incorporated all the elements of Protestant evangelical experience. He recounted that after having opened his Bible to I Cor. 7:23,

> I was surrounded by a light ... and through that light I saw the way of salvation. Then for the first time I understood the mystery of the Cross of Christ ... I felt that Christ had answered my prayer, that the mountains of my iniquity were gone, and I gave myself entirely and exclusively to Christ.[58]

---

56. Hellmuth to the Record, 17 October 1859 (in *MW*, 7 December 1859, p. 780), and *Father Chiniquy, the Reformer of the Far West* (London, 1860), p. 3.

57. Also Rev. Beaubien in *KG*, 8 December 1859 (**ASQ** 52:4).

58. From a September 1860 sermon in Dublin in Bird, *A Few Reminiscences* (Leeds, 1878), p. 18; also in *The Life and Labours* (Glasgow, 1861), p. 10. Similarly *Presby*, 9 June 1860, p. 1. The mention of "mountains of iniquity" would not imply more than average sins in evangelical testimony.

8. THE RELIGIOUS CONVERSION OF CHINIQUY

He believed that he had been saved from sin and guilt. Thus early on Chiniquy shaped his conversion account and added detail that he had not previously mentioned.

In a conversion account in 1870 Chiniquy adds that he had studied the Bible in Illinois, while a Catholic, in order to refute Protestantism. Now "a new light broke in upon my mind; I felt and believed that I was saved by the blood of Christ alone."[59] This leaves the impression that Chiniquy and his parish were transformed suddenly.

With variations, this post-1860 version became Chiniquy's standard conversion account, particularly in his 1885 autobiography, *50 Years*.[60] There, Chiniquy writes of that same experience:

> In that instant all things which as a Roman Catholic I had to believe to be saved: all the mummeries by which the poor Roman Catholics are cruelly deceived; the chaplets, indulgences, scapulars, auricular confessions, invocation of the Virgin, holy water, masses, purgatory, given as means of salvation, vanished from my mind ... Jesus alone remained in my mind as the Saviour of my soul![61]

Here is an instantaneous rejection of all particularly Catholic beliefs. Prior to this experience he was in great despair and even took steps toward suicide[62] before the light broke in. In this lengthy autobiography the emphasis shifts so that Catholic moral and spiritual abuse are shown, for the first time among his conversion accounts, as a major cause of the conversion.

In an 1893 account Chiniquy did not mention conflicts with the bishop while the evangelical elements in his conversion become much more explicit. He wrote:

> [God] expelled the dark night in which popery had completely drowned my intelligence and my soul till then; He showed me

---

59. *MW*, 24 January 1870, p. 2.
60. *50 Years*, pp. 790-796. See e.g. Duclos, (Montreal, 1913), vol.2, pp. 59-60.
61. *50 Years*, p. 794.
62. Ibid, p. 792.

that 'eternal life' could not be ... the price of my own work and merits ... He showed me that He died on Calvary in order to pay my debts to the last cent and save my guilty soul.[63]

In 1894, Chiniquy described his pre-conversion state: "I was dead and unaware, nothing for God and all for the Pope; one day I read in the Bible of how much Jesus loved me and I devoted myself to him."[64] This complete rejection of his Catholic years is a drastic revision from earlier accounts and attributes a sudden change to Scripture reading.

Chiniquy composed *40 Years* at the end of his life, in part to show "some of the ways through which our merciful God has brought me from the feet of the Pope to those of the Lamb who has made me free and pure with His blood."[65] In the second chapter we see the final development by Chiniquy of his conversion account. Chiniquy condensed the story omitting the incidents in Dubuque. He located the same events (or possibly the Lafleur visit) in his small study at three o'clock on Saturday afternoon.

While much of the account varies from *50 Years*, written 14 years earlier, there is the same prolonged despair, the experience of light and, pre-eminently, the same message of salvation as a gift. A divine voice says: "come out from the Church of Rome. You cannot be saved in that church".[66] Allowing space for a lengthy account of the salvation experience results in minimal mention of property disputes and even of submission to the bishop. Many subsequent accounts of Chiniquy's conversion adopt a similar description of this standardized Protestant evangelical experience.

After his death, Louis Fréchette broke with Catholic orthodoxy in his comments on Chiniquy's conversion: "I can not judge his about-turn. Although it is extremely repugnant to our Catholic convictions, this

---

63. Chiniquy letter printed in *New York Witness*, 14 June 1893, p. 1.
64. *A*, 25 August 1894, p. 5 (my translation).
65. *40 Years*, p. 18. This was actually published posthumously. Also see p. 136.
66. Ibid., p. 48.

8. THE RELIGIOUS CONVERSION OF CHINIQUY

was, I believe, an act of conscience for which he is answerable to God alone."[67]

FRUITS

While a conversion in the sense of mere change of membership is easily proven, such a change has limited usefulness for apologetics or as a model to follow. Protestant evangelicals expect a conversion 'to Christ' rather than 'to a denomination'. A claim of conversion 'to Christ' can be more easily challenged since it is partly dependent on evidence of transformation or, in biblical language, the fruits.

Villeneuve objected, stating that "it is certain ... that the cause of Chiniquy's departure from the bosom of the holy apostolic and Roman Church was twofold; the corruption of his morals and his insane, insatiable pride."[68] Even if this was true, an impressive positive transformation in behaviour could be evidence of a spiritual, evangelical conversion, despite poor initial motives.

Trudel contends that there was nothing spiritual in Chiniquy's preaching or actions, even as a Catholic.[69] That does not match Bishop Bourget's estimation, or Ares' findings, that Chiniquy played a major role in inspiring the mid-century Catholic Revival in Quebec. Was Chiniquy the lifelong hypocrite and fanatic that Villeneuve, Trudel, Berton and others describe?

We have already seen that the rebel priest developed a consistent evangelical theology and doctrine over a relatively short time period. No evangelical in the 19th century seriously questioned Chiniquy's claim to be an evangelical Protestant. This status is already a considerable transformation, given Chiniquy's independent nature and his lack of any formal theological training in a Protestant milieu. The changes

---

67. *Nouveau Monde*, 11 August 1900 (my translation). Fréchette was taken to task for this permissive attitude by the *Cour*, 14 August 1900, p. 2.
68. Villeneuve, *Honte et mépris* (Montreal, 1875), p. 3 (my translation).
69. Trudel, p. 303.

Chiniquy made to his conversion stories over the years followed a typical evangelical model, emphasizing a sudden sin to grace experience.

Chiniquy's piety as a Protestant was hidden, for the most part. Nevertheless the few evangelical references to it are unanimous[70] in praising him. "He is godly, reads his Bible frequently, calling it the most beautiful of books and he prays with all the candour and confidence of a child."[71] His emphasis on the Bible is obvious and his public prayers were so popular that he was often asked to pronounce benedictions at French or English Protestant meetings. There is no good reason to doubt the Protestant accounts of his deathbed, where he demonstrated a strong evangelical assurance in his heavenly future.[72]

Continuity with his Catholic years is shown in accounts of the pastoral care that Chiniquy did as a Protestant and his generosity and concern for finding lost souls. Likewise he maintained an astonishing quantity of energy and enthusiasm, accompanied by striking powers of oratory, from his time as a priest.

During his Protestant years conflicts emerged over money matters, exaggeration/lying and especially over his aggressive tone. Chicago Presbytery expelled him over serious accusations related to money and lying. However, the evidence points to poor money management rather than to personal profit.

Since his early temperance days Chiniquy succombed to the temptation, typical of master storytellers, to exaggerate his stories and actions in order to create the appropriate mood among potential converts. His success in moving crowds led to a lifetime propensity to stretch the truth and put words or thoughts in others' mouths. Usually, but not always, this remained within acceptable limits. Particularly for those in public life exaggeration is often linked with pride.

Many Protestants disliked Chiniquy's aggressive language. Nevertheless they made allowances, considering the provocation of frequent

---

70. E.g. Rev. Amaron's funeral sermon in *40 Years*, p. 486.
71. A letter from 'Chiniquiste' in *CFA*, 18 May 1893, p. 3.
72. *A*, 21 January 1899, p. 4.

8. THE RELIGIOUS CONVERSION OF CHINIQUY

and equally strident statements by ultramontane spokesmen as well as violent acts against the ex-priest. Evangelicals admitted Chiniquy's faults. As had been the case in his Catholic years, these were not seen to invalidate his ministry. It is striking that almost every one of the numerous memorial and funeral sermons at Chiniquy's death mentions 'his faults', only to stress his far greater merit and the forgiving nature of God. Those most committed to French evangelization were the ones most ready to forgive these faults.

As for sexual allegations, there is no record of any new cases during the ex-priest's Protestant years.[73] Chiniquy did marry but only six years after his final excommunication and eight years after his initial excommunication. From the time of his conversion no new scandals surfaced. If we assume that at least one of the previous accusations was accurate, the improvement is striking. If Lambert's horrific accusations were true, the transformation borders on the incredible. While Catholic leaders were convinced of Chiniquy's sexual depravity, Protestants saw no evidence of this.

Chiniquy's actions during his Protestant years conform to the behaviour described in the evangelical model of a convert (see Chapter 7). His theology, piety and concern for evangelism were manifest. Besides these, his ministries apparently converted great numbers. Many ex-priests only lasted a short time in Protestant ministry but Chiniquy's transformation was deep and durable. Evangelicals had strong reasons to be convinced of Chiniquy's conversion: his subsequent evangelical theology and evangelical behaviour.

TRANSFORMATIONS AND CONTINUITY

At the beginning of Chapter 7 we examined the contrasting myths (meaning exaggerated propagandist accounts) of Chiniquy. The traditional Roman Catholics' horror of apostasy informed all aspects of their

---

73. During his Protestant years Catholic accounts repeatedly mention allegations from his past parishes.

evaluation of the apostate. They assumed a critical moment in the late 1840s when the Apostle of Temperance decided to leave the path of faith. Although this was the moment of discontinuity, previous indications of gross sin had preceded it. According to this interpretation, Chiniquy's sinful nature was constant while his changes for the worse began at a critical moment long before the excommunication.[74]

Maignage's analysis might lead us to infer that Chiniquy could not cope with lust while he was in the Catholic Church. However this does not explain why similar problems did not occur in his Protestant years. On the other hand if the sexual accusations were true, an evangelical would have expected a genuine convert to confess candidly to some person (the equivalent of the Catholic confessional). Perhaps this did happen privately.

Years later Chiniquy was reported to assert:

> They say Chiniquy was a rogue. There is more truth in it than they think. Who could be a priest of Rome for twenty-five years without becoming a complete rogue? Let any one before him be surrounded by beautiful women from morning to night, and see what would become of him. He did not come to apologize for Chiniquy and never apologized for him. He would repeat what he had said in his letter to Vicar General Bruyère: 'I was a rogue as you'.[75]

This confirms that Chiniquy was guilty of lust. His book on the confessional assumes that the system inevitably drives all priests, to a similar state of guilt. His refusal to apologize may stem from reluctance to provide ammunition for his adversaries in the polemical context.

On the Protestant side the Chiniquy myth had to explain both change and continuity in his life. In this version all revolved around the ex-priest's courage and his successful leadership following his enlightenment. Chiniquy's pre-existing integrity and openness to God was paired

---

74. See Figure 43, p. 191.
75. *MW*, 12 March 1875, p. 2. This combines first person and third person quotes but all stems from Chiniquy.

8. THE RELIGIOUS CONVERSION OF CHINIQUY

with a critical moment of greater revelation during Illinois battles. According to most Protestant accounts the conversion came instantaneously and brought complete change.

In the Protestant myth, Chiniquy's good characteristics provide continuity while his conversion changed his direction and made him a faithful leader. This occurred after the rejected reconciliation (usually the excommunications are not mentioned). This reading clashes with known facts such as Chiniquy's repeated attempts to return to Roman Catholicism and his problems with Chicago Presbytery.

In the evangelical model of conversion, all humans are viewed as sinful and in need of salvation; sin is only to be expected in the old life before conversion. In this generic evangelical model, the validity of a conversion is determined primarily by the convert's public rejection of his old life and consistent evidence of new life. In Chiniquy's case there was abundant evidence of this transformation in terms of geography, date and denomination. "No Protestant can deny that he is a consistent convert from Romanism."[76] I submit that Chiniquy fits the evangelical model for conversion. His theology definitely was transformed and his ministry proceeded in a Protestant direction while his behaviour did not break any Protestant taboos.

We already have looked at Chiniquy's difficult choice to leave religious totalism.[77] In many respects the ex-priest followed the normal sequence of Skonovd's defection model. In the context of religious totalism Chiniquy had to totally submit or leave. Submission was not so onerous a choice in earlier life. Yet when faced with a perceived injustice (towards the French Catholics in Chicago) combined with a perceived conspiracy (around the Spink trials), the St. Anne priest rebelled. His bishops ruled out any negotiation while official appeals were useless.

---

76. *GL Annual Report*, 1897, p. 7.
77. See Chapter 7 for these theories of Skonovd and Neeser.

Skonovd identified factors that facilitate apostasy. Several of these are seen in Chiniquy's experience: crises of inter-personal conflict, isolation from Catholic colleagues, and distance from the all-encompassing religious totalism of Quebec. His superiors made extreme demands that conflicted with his beliefs. All attempts to resolve the issue failed. How could these possibly work given an inflexible bishop and a priest who had publicly vilified him? The Catholic authorities made all possibility of discussion dependent on the need for total submission. Such a requirement was increasingly unacceptable to someone moving away from the realm of religious totalism.

Within the conversion accounts we find the fear that Skonovd found to be so general among potential apostates from religious totalism. We also can identify the confrontational nature of Chiniquy's anti-Catholicism. As negative as this appears to us, Skonovd found such confrontation, at least on a smaller scale, to be helpful in releasing a person from the power of religious totalism. This is part of the process of constructing a new ideology and life.

Neeser proposed a model of secondary confessional model which fits Chiniquy's case. At first Chiniquy did not object to Catholic theology or practice but rather to a perceived injustice. He was too obstinate to yield on the principles of retaining a French church in Chicago and having the liberty to possess his own property. However my biography of Chiniquy revealed distinct confessional elements that developed in the battle over submission. Who had authority to decree total submission? **Justice** and then **submission** were the initial matters of conflict in Chiniquy's declarations.

The St. Anne priest's obstinacy led him to question the concept of obedience toward episcopal authority. This then led him to investigate a basis for refusal. Far from French friends and colleagues, Chiniquy, moved step-by-step away from the Catholic position. By nature independent and questioning, he was released from the religious totalism, which had previously commanded his loyalty. At the same time, Protestants supported his rebellion by means of letters, newspaper publicity,

8. THE RELIGIOUS CONVERSION OF CHINIQUY

dialogue and finances. Such a contrast in support was obvious to the rebel priest.

The bulk of Chiniquy's theological conversion came gradually, as a process.[78] Two years as a schismatic Catholic, and two more as a 'Catholic Christian' facilitated the transition. His step-by-step movement away from familiar terrain also had the effect of preserving the loyalty of his parish. The pluralist society in Illinois, and the willingness among some Protestants to finance the rebellious group, allowed Chiniquy and his parish the needed time to make a clear choice.

A detailed examination of Chiniquy's conversion process reveals complex factors that precipitated and facilitated the break. The initial publicity for Chiniquy's accusations made later reconciliation attempts almost impossible. He would now have to submit unconditionally and provide a public repudiation of all his initial charges. Although it appears that Chiniquy and the Quebec bishops wanted reconciliation, Bishop O'Regan was intransigent. The conflict intensified as both Catholics and Protestants rushed resources to the crucial battle site.

Neeser described how converts are pressured to transform their accounts into more theological conversions. We see that Chiniquy did much shaping. Skonovd explained how conversion stories are fluid mediums in which the convert/apostate sorts out his past and present. Over time, while Chiniquy's accounts digressed further from some facts, perhaps he understood other elements better. Chiniquy heard others recount his story, while he must have recounted it thousands of times. Inevitably there were changes in the telling.

Chiniquy suffered from the orator's peculiar temptations of embellishment, pride and a sense of being indispensable. Some other evangelical speakers have also faced well-publicized accusations of sexual and financial offences. Chiniquy did not escape such allegations in his polemical setting. Still his guilt remains unproven.

---

78. Allier, *La psychologie de la conversion chez les peuples non-civilisés* (Paris, 1925), tome 1, pp. 547ff.

THE CONTROVERSIAL CONVERSION OF CHARLES CHINIQUY

Chiniquy also bore another mark of many evangelical leaders. He was a crusader. After his initial crusade against alcoholism, he fought against the 'devil's instruments' of Protestantism, liberal anti-clericalism and then American assimilation. In each of these ultramontane causes, 'God and right' were arraigned against 'all the powers of evil', that he found in his opponents. Battle imagery was prominent and compromise was unthinkable. This was Chiniquy's holy war manner of interpreting the world.

As he came into conflict with Bishop O'Regan, the independent priest gradually perceived a need for another crusade against the bishop. Obviously the Catholic authorities could not allow a crusade that demonized the Catholic bishop to proceed within the Catholic fold. Once Chiniquy had polarized the situation, neither he nor the bishops could return to their previous more cordial relationships.

Internal spiritual conversion cannot be proven by human means. This study might be construed as neglecting the spiritual power in conversion through dissection of the process. However, the intricacy and many-faceted aspects of this conversion process make it far more credible and profound.[79] Trudel's disparagement of Chiniquy's claim of conversion stems from that historian's conformity to an ultramontane interpretation. Modern rationalist critique agrees that no conversion happened. Yet, judged on his own terms as an evangelical Protestant converted to a new understanding of Jesus Christ, the evidence supports Chiniquy's claim.

Chiniquy did not convert to Christianity. During his early Protestant years he did not in effect[80] reject all things Catholic. When he joined the Presbyterian Church he chose neither to be reordained nor to be rebaptized.[81] Most of his theology came from his Nicolet College training. It was transformed, however, to completely remove all distinctively Roman Catholic doctrines. Chiniquy's concentrated attack on these distinctive

---

79. See also Allier.
80. Later on his words however did claim this.
81. *Presby*, 7 April 1860, p. 1.

8. THE RELIGIOUS CONVERSION OF CHINIQUY
Chiniquy's Movement from Catholicism to Protestantism

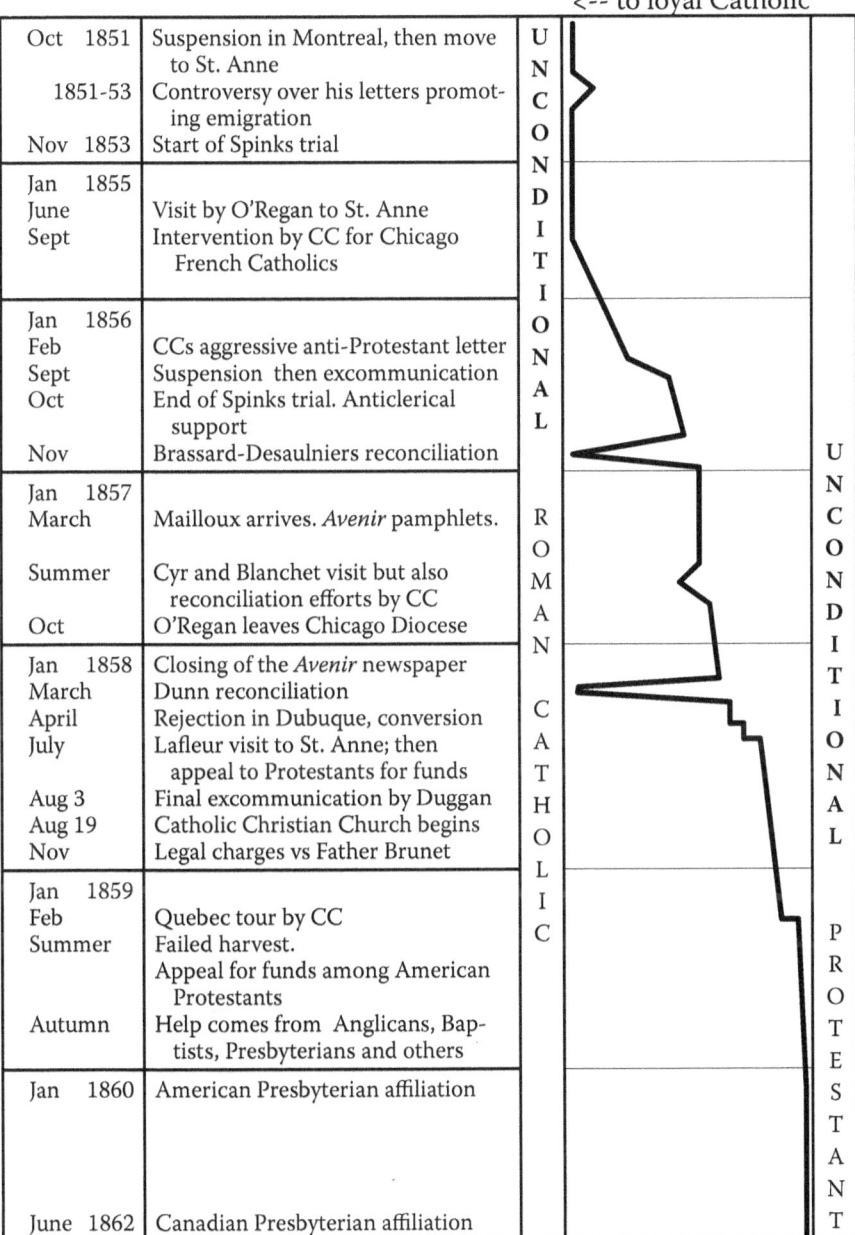

Figure 45

Figure 46 In his St. Anne office prior to 1892 fire   AP 04-016

8. THE RELIGIOUS CONVERSION OF CHINIQUY

doctrines led Quebec bishops to emphasize them even more, developing new ceremonies to celebrate their traditional Catholic faith.[82] The conflict intensified both Chiniquy's Protestantism and Quebec's ultramontanism.

We find many elements of continuity in Chiniquy's temperament and methods. There were also definite transformations in his beliefs. Among the many steps of the Chiniquy conversion three major stages, stand out: 1) his refusal to submit at the first excommunication in 1856; 2) the hotel room experience after his last refused submission in Dubuque in April 1858; 3) the Lafleur interpretations and explanations in July 1858. As can be seen from Figure 45 the failed reconciliations also played a major role in provoking Chiniquy's transformation.

Such complexity of motivation or events would be of minimal importance to evangelicals as they evaluated the validity of Chiniquy's conversion. The essential facts were that Chiniquy provided an acceptable conversion story, maintained a consistent evangelical theology following the conversion, and evangelized with success. Further, there were no more sexual allegations or other flaunting of evangelical standards.

Chiniquy was not an impostor; nor are there signs that he was tormented with doubts after his departure from the Catholic Church. He was not looking for an opportunity to leave the Church of his youth. Nevertheless, certain of his principles and character traits were stronger than loyalty to his Church. Rebellion was possible in a situation far from the Catholic stronghold of Quebec. As Chiniquy learned in childhood, there were only two alternatives for Catholics: submission or heresy. This left no room for half measures. Chiniquy's situation called for a new framework to understand the Christian faith. The GL Baptists and others provided such an alternative. From the evidence of the last 40 years of his life, there remains no doubt that Chiniquy found a niche among evangelical Protestants.

---

82. Bp. Bourget pastoral letter, 19 March 1875 (*MEM*, vol. 7, pp. 122-124).

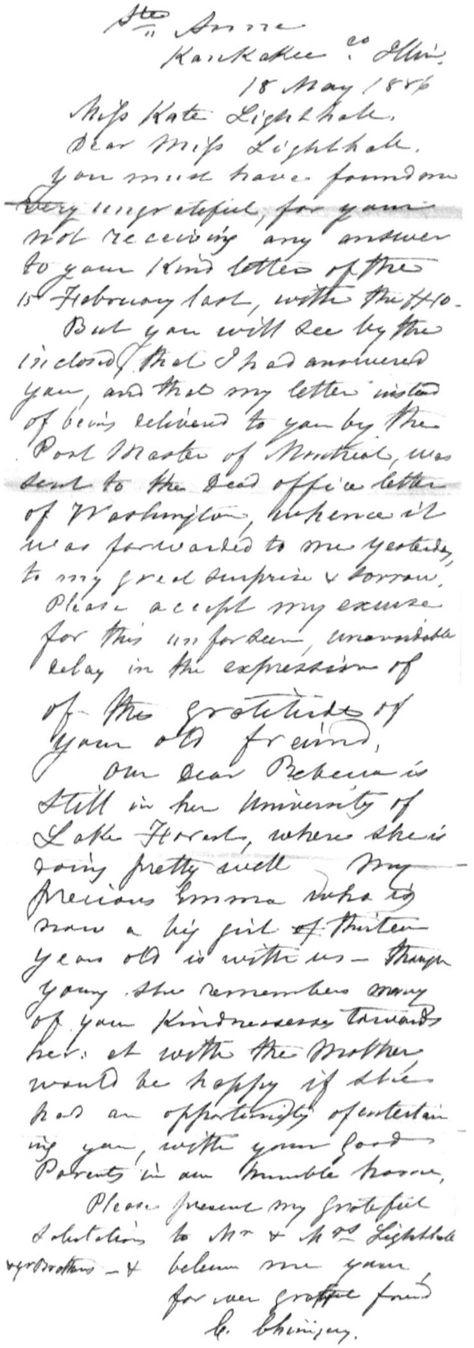

Ste Anne
   Kankakee Co Illi.
      18 May 1886
Miss Kate Lighthall,
Dear Miss Lighthall.
   You must have found me
very ungrateful, for your
not receiving any answer
to your kind letter of the
15 February last, with the $10.
   But you will see by the
inclosed that I had answered
you, and that my letter instead
of being delivered to you by the
Post Master of Montreal, was
sent to the Dead office letter
of Washington, whence it
was forwarded to me yesterday,
to my great surprise & sorrow.
Please accept my excuse
for this unforseen, unavoidable
delay in the expression of
of the gratitude of
your old freind,
   Our dear Rebecca is
still in her University of
Lake Forest, where she is
doing pretty well. My
precious Emma who is
now a big girl of thirteen
years old is with us — Though
young, she remembers many
of your kindnesses towards
her, & with the Mother
would be happy if she
had an opportunity of entertain
ing you, with your good
Parents in our humble house.
   Please present my grateful
salutations to Mr & Mrs Lighthall
& brothers — & believe me your
   for ever grateful friend
      C. Chiniquy.

Image 5 Letter to Kate Lighthall
18 May, 1886 **AP** 03-032

9

THE SOCIAL CONVERSION OF CHINIQUY

Besides the interior spiritual conversion and his new theology, there were dramatic external changes in Chiniquy's life after his excommunication. As an ex-priest leaving religious totalism, myriad adjustments were required. All Catholics cut off ties with him; this meant virtually every person in French Canada and French America. Even before he had definitively decided to leave, most doors were closed to the rebel-priest. His friends, nation, spiritual heritage, and practically all francophones were alienated from him.

SOCIOLOGY OF CONVERSION AND OF APOSTASY

An approach to conversion as a way of socialization has much to contribute to our study:

> the process by which individuals learn the appropriate roles, norms and status assignments of a group; they inculcate the values, beliefs and world view of a group ...; and they acquire a new social identity(s) based upon their group membership ... What distinguishes conversion, however, from other forms of socialization is the focal emphasis on self-change (e.g. a change

in world view) in a religious or quasi-religious setting and the kind of social audience reaction to that self change.[1]

As described in the last chapter, Chiniquy gradually adopted the typical evangelical 'script'. His conversion was soon accepted by the evangelical society since he socialized to the new group.

A related perspective views Chiniquy as only part of a larger change by the St. Anne French community. Anthony Wallace devised an influential 'revitalization' concept from his anthropological perspective.[2] According to this theory, each person possesses a 'mazeway' or worldview, which enables him to limit stress:

> The effort to work a change in mazeway ... so as to permit more effective stress reduction is the effort at revitalization; and the collaboration of a number of persons in such an effort is called a revitalization movement.[3]

The amazing Chiniquy was an agent of revitalization twice. He has been interpreted first as the catalyst of the Catholic temperance movement and its associated Catholic Revival of mid-19th century Quebec.[4] Then this same leader again assumed the role of prophet for another smaller revitalization, leading his Franco-American parish out of the Catholic Church.

The Wallace process begins with a person under pressure whose mazeway does not relieve his stress adequately. He experiences a 'divine' vision which transforms him into a prophet. If the process continues the prophet proclaims the newly revealed message and demonstrates the power of this message. If this charismatic person persuades others to follow he then forms a group. As the revolutionary movement encounters

---

1. Kilbourne and Richardson, "Paradigm Conflict, Types of Conversion and Conversion Theories" (*Soc. Analysis*, 1989), p. 15.

2. See especially Anthony Wallace, "Revitalization Movements" (*Amer. Anthropol.*, 1956), pp. 264-79.

3. Ibid., pp. 266-7.

4. Ares used this Wallace scheme as a basis for his study of Chiniquy.

9. THE SOCIAL CONVERSION OF CHINIQUY

resistance, the leader must be very realistic and canny about conflict, often resorting to political means or force. Very often these revitalization movements counteract newly dominant foreign cultures (such as the Irish here). Success of the new message-mazeway depends on its ability to reduce stress.

Problems arise in applying the Wallace analysis to Chiniquy. There are two contrary revitalizations here: Catholic revival and French Protestant beginnings. In addition where is the evidence for cultural breakdown prior to the Chiniquy schism? It must have been very unsettling for French-Canadian and European immigrants to cope with a new society where plentiful freedom was paired with a rigid church hierarchy controlled by a different ethnic group (Irish). Nevertheless, no great problem surfaced before Chiniquy came. Most likely all would have worked peacefully without him.[5] Alternatively, there was the real crisis for French Catholics in Chicago. Chiniquy stepped into this and then dragged his own parish with him. Perhaps it is better to focus on how the revitalization analysis fits with Chiniquy's personal experience and then to look for some aspects of the model which match the broader parish experience.

The St. Anne parish followed the rebel priest, despite the flood of desperate pleas from their Quebec relatives. That could indicate that his parish shared much of his dissatisfaction with ultramontane Catholicism. The parish had a strange origin: on the one hand, Chiniquy aimed to protect French immigrants by means of a traditional Catholic setting. On the other hand, some parishoners had experienced marked clerical hostility in Quebec to any emigration to the United States. This hostility likely provoked some alienation from clerical views among St. Anne immigrants.

Group psychohistory provides some wisdom about how Chiniquy could lead his parish in such a new direction. This perspective claims that in a group under pressure often 1) the group believes that it exists

---

5. Mailloux to Biggs, 3 March 1861, p. 3 (**ASQ** 50:20).

primarily for the purpose of self-preservation; 2) the leader is seen as defending them from outside hostility and containing problematic members within the group; 3) the leader is treated as larger than life to defend against the fear of abandonment; 4) in larger dissident groups, repressed fears can lead to violence unless the group divides.[6]

Chiniquy was certainly put on a pedestal by St. Anne parishioners. He was their champion against what they saw as an oppressor who aimed to eliminate all traces of French. As the battle eased, though, the St. Anne priest was not able to retain all his followers. The rebel group split several times forming other Protestant congregations in St. Anne.

Apostasy from religious totalism is much easier to accomplish if it is done as a group.[7] In that case there is a built-in support group, providing continuity of friends who share similar doubts and problems. Apostates lack material resources outside the old community and often have trouble in decision-making since they have become accustomed to a totalist environment. Social continuity is an immense support in these circumstances. Standing together with neighbours considerably strengthened Chiniquy and his St. Anne group at the schism. In one way, standing with Chiniquy was the conservative option.

HIS ANTI-CATHOLICISM

It is the belligerent vilification of his former Church that stands out in Chiniquy's social conversion. This made him the object of accolades from the Orange Order but also the object of many furious Catholic rebuttals. What would drive a prominent ultramontanist to become an ardent anti-Catholic? There are multiple causes. Explosive anger is a common characteristic of apostates who 'have found the light'.[8] Chiniquy's letters regularly show his bitterness and excessive violence. He felt betrayed and typically portrayed the Catholic Church in the worst possible light.

---

6. Lawton, *The Psychohistorian's Handbook* (NY, 1989), p. 178.
7. Skonovd, "Apostasy, the Process of Defection" (Ann Arbor, 1981), p. 124.
8. Ibid., p. 163.

9. THE SOCIAL CONVERSION OF CHINIQUY

Protestant and political lecture circuits sought out convincing foes of Catholicism. The list of sermon topics that Chiniquy offered to potential churches or groups shows a broad range of topics.[9] In fact he regularly preached traditional biblical sermons on Sunday mornings. Also worth noting is that he frequently delivered his less controversial temperance lectures. With his remarkable oratory, he could have chosen other less controversial subjects and commanded invitations to more spiritual circles. Yet, wherever he went, the largest crowds came to his Sunday evening or midweek lectures on controversial topics. He quickly realized that bold statements received more applause.

Chiniquy's crusade mentality tended to demonize any opposition. Dubious tactics by Bishop O'Regan, eventually supported by the Quebec bishops, led Chiniquy to believe in theories of Catholic political conspiracy. These were already current in the United States. Once one adopted the view that the Catholic episcopacy could easily justify falsehood in a good cause, it was possible to imagine multiple plots. It became very hard to disprove these. Any evidence for one plot made all the rest credible.

At the same time Chiniquy adopted a Protestant theology that the Catholic Church dismissed as heresy. The excommunicated Chiniquy came to believe that "the more a man is cursed by their tyrannical and idolatrous Church, the more he is blessed by God".[10] This easily led him to intentionally provoke reaction in order to "suffer for the Lord".

In a peaceful setting, perhaps Chiniquy might have carried on as local pastor and written about the virtues of Protestantism. Given the opposition it is not so surprising that he became a strong anti-Catholic. The opposition included constant legal problems, the circulating of endless scandalous rumours, a special Catholic mission nearby to combat him, several rebuffs after he had swallowed his pride enough to write

---

9. See a list of more anti-Catholic subjects in Figure 47 on p. 250.
10. *MW*, 29 March 1876, p. 1.

THE CONTROVERSIAL CONVERSION OF CHARLES CHINIQUY

Subjects of lectures offered by Chiniquy

"1. Why I left the Church of Rome with 45,000 of my Roman Catholic countrymen?
2. Is the Church of Rome a branch of the Church of Christ or is it old Paganism coming back under a Christian name?
3. Rome and the Bible
4. Rome and Purgatory
5. Auricular Confession
6. Why does the Church of Rome hate the American schools and wants to shut them?
7. The education of Protestant girls in the nunneries.
8. Dangers ahead for this country from the Church of Rome.
9. Solemn duties of the Protestant Americans towards the Roman Catholics.
10. The Roman Catholic Church and the last civil war.
11. Can a true Roman Catholic be a good American citizen?
12. The priests of Rome the true murderers of Abraham Lincoln.
13. What does the Church of Rome understand by Liberty of Conscience?
14. The Jesuits! Their anti social and anti Christian principles.
15. Jesus the sinner's Friends [sic].
16. Eternal Life the Gift of God!
17. Temperance

AT THE CHOICE OF THE FRIENDS"
(This is a transcription of a document in the Rare Books department of McGill U. or CHIM 60979.)

This list is obviously American and probably from around 1897. Examples were found of all the lectures except for 9-12 and 14, with the former only of American interest. Number 1 dominated in the years following his conversion with number 17 becoming the most common between 1860 and 1880. Overall numbers 1 and 17 were the most common lecture subjects followed in order by 5, 16, 7, 8, 3, 2 and 13.

Other popular lectures included:
Defence before O'Regan	= #1a
On transubstantiation	= #18 often combined with #2
The Virgin Mary	= #19
Celibacy for priests	= #20
Wafer God	= #21
Financial needs of converts	= #22
His conversion	= #23
Papal power	= #24
Divisions among Protestants	= #25

Figure 47

9. THE SOCIAL CONVERSION OF CHINIQUY

submissions, solidarity of episcopal denunciations, media attacks in Quebec, and frequent physical violence and threats.

He once addressed Bishop Bourget:

> Everyone knows that it is only when a person has no good reasons to bring forth that he indulges in insults. You label me ignorant, an apostate, a hypocrite, an excommunicate, lacking the spirit; you call me damned, cursed, a devil ... Your religion tells you to hate me; mine commands me to love you ... Your religion wants you to despise me; mine leads me to feel sorry for you because of your errors but to respect you even more as a soul needing salvation.[11]

One could throw back Chiniquy's own words about vulgarity as the sign of a weak argument. While the ex-priest was motivated by far more than hate (as was Bishop Bourget's pastoral letter) he seldom hesitated to use his pen and tongue to proclaim what his emotions felt. Chiniquy alternated between abuse, exaggeration and dispassionate logic.

He insisted that his was an "anti-Catholicism with love". However, his love was addressed almost exclusively to laity and doubting priests who had been "duped" by their tyrannical bishops. As indignant as he had formerly been against insubordinate laity,[12] he was now equally vigilant to warn laity of the political intentions of manipulative clergy.[13] His indignation and his polemical bent inflamed Chiniquy's liberation tendencies. The ex-priest became furious with Protestant clergy who stated or implied that Catholics were Christians.[14] Chiniquy eventually described Roman Catholicism as simply a persecuting paganism with a Christian facade.

Those who were most militantly anti-Catholic and yet not anti-French were usually his strongest supporters. Among these was the

---

11. French section of *MW*, 20 May 1875, p. 1 (my translation). This was later published as *Le vrai contre-poison* (Montreal, 1875).

12. *Av*, April-June 1849.

13. *MW*, 31 May 1875, p. 2.

14. See *A Solemn Question? Can the Protestants conscientiously build up the churches of the Pope?*, by Rev. Charles Hodge and Charles Chiniquy (Halifax, 1873); also ch. 26 of *40 Years*.

predominantly Irish Orange Order.[15] In 1856 just prior to his own excommunication, Chiniquy had severely criticized the group.[16] In 1878 he joined this same militant anti-Catholic organization. His *50 Years*, dedicated in part to the Orangemen of the United States and the British Empire, includes a copy of his membership paper.[17] Chiniquy became Grand Chaplain of the Order and was a lifetime member of the Boyne Lodge #401 of Montreal.[18]

What could explain such an apparent treason? Charles Doudiet, a co-worker in Presbyterian French mission who was also Grand Chaplain of the Order in Quebec, likely encouraged membership in the Order. French Protestants were a small minority in Quebec. Despite the law, civil protection was notably lacking. Certain Catholic civil magistrates and police saw no reason to protect apostates. Both French evangelists, and even local pastors, needed occasional physical protection and legal aid. The Orange Order was more than ready to provide both.[19] When these necessities arose it became irrelevant whether one was enthusiastic about the history of Orangemen or their non-evangelical approach.[20]

Probably Chiniquy would have been killed in one of the many riots against him if not for the Orangemen. While Chiniquy presumably joined the Orange Order primarily for protection, he was lavish in his praise: "he owed all his success in the French mission work to the Orangemen ... He was surprised more Protestants were not Orangemen, and hoped the

---

15. 'By An Orange Order member', *Orangeism in Ireland and Throughout the Empire*, vol. II, (London, 1939); Tony Gray, *The Orange Order* (London, 1972); H. Senior, *The Last Invasion: The Fenian Raids* (London, 1991).

16. *MW*, 20 February 1856, p. 60.

17. *50 Years*, p. 3.

18. *G*, 17 January 1899, p. 1. This was the same lodge to which belonged the 'martyr' Hackett (see *MW*, 16-7 July 1877). Because this is a secret society further information is not available.

19. This insight came from Rev. Jacques Smith during a conversation in September 1992.

20. The evangelical *MW* tended to be quite critical of the Order's aggressive attitude.

9. THE SOCIAL CONVERSION OF CHINIQUY

cause would go on prospering".[21] Occasionally the ex-priest upset more peaceful Protestants when he suggested that a few Orangemen were needed to sort out those who were disrupting his lectures.[22]

Rev. Charles Perry in his *Lectures on Orangeism* in 1892, included a chapter on Chiniquy:

> Chiniquy said he considered it to be his duty to join that grand and noble army of Soldiers of Christ [the Orange Order]. A great and noble work was done in Montreal. The great work was due first to God's blessing, and secondly to the efforts put forth by the Orangemen. He could not have preached there only for their protection. He says, "I always found them staunch and true. I consider it a great honour to be an Orangeman. Every time I go on my knees I pray that God may bless them and make them as numerous and bright as the stars of heaven above".[23]

In his *40 Years* he gave a ringing compliment: "many times I have had the opportunity of witnessing the heroic courage and the admirable intelligence and sang-froid of the Orangemen in presence of danger".[24] One of Chiniquy's pallbearers was a Master of the Order while 200 Orangemen from ten different lodges marched in his funeral procession.[25]

On the other side, Irish Catholics comprised the majority of Chiniquy's assailants outside Quebec, whether in Michigan, Australia, Prince Edward Island or Antigonish. It seems that neither Irish Catholics nor Irish Protestants hesitated to join a fight and Chiniquy provided a good occasion. There is no evidence that Chiniquy's presence ever resulted in Protestant assaults on Catholics. However, his disparaging picture of Catholics obviously influenced millions of Protestants.

---

21. *MW*, 13 July 1876, p. 2, from an account of a 12 July rally in Montreal. Toasts were drunk to King Billy (William of Orange) and to Father Chiniquy.

22. *MW*, 10 March 1876, p. 1, concerning a riot in Halifax.

23. Perry, *Lectures on Orangeism and other subjects* (Toronto, 1892), p. 100, part of a whole chapter on Chiniquy.

24. *40 Years*, p. 386.

25. *G*, 20 January 1899, p. 5.

Chiniquy could tailor the message to his Protestant crowds. Sometimes they wanted political comment, strategy and polemics. In such situations he would warn them that the Pope's mission was to exterminate heretics and eliminate liberty of conscience. The Catholics aimed to blot out the Bible to allow traditions that produced mind control and slavery.[26] Alternatively Chiniquy motivated H.C. Taylor by the opportunity to become the new American anti-Catholic leader. "There will be millions of dollars in the book [which Chiniquy would give the plan for], as well as an imperishable name for its author".[27]

If the audience was more evangelical, often they wanted to hear about Catholic doctrinal errors. They preferred the message that Catholicism could only be fought by means of prayer, love, gospel literature, good example[28] and evangelism.[29] Chiniquy would oblige since he also believed that.

Chiniquy was certainly a master at populism. Laity was very affirmative of the ex-priest,[30] frequently insisting that he speak at church meetings and offering prolonged applause for his comments. The 'Luther of Canada' encouraged his troops with hope of a breakthrough in French Canada.[31] At a FCMS meeting in 1875, he expressed his belief "that God

---

26. Chiniquy, "Sound an alarm", letter printed in the *Christian Times*, on 30 April 1869. Later reprinted as a pamphlet (See our p. 128).

27. Chiniquy to H.C. Taylor, copied by E.C. [Euphémie Chiniquy?], 25 March 1892 (**SL** c.1/3). Chiniquy reasoned that he could not make the same impact himself because he was an immigrant.

28. Chiniquy to the influential National Club in England, newspaper clipping "Welcome to Pastor Chiniquy", early October, 1896 (**SL** c.1/20).

29. *MW*, 29 August 1870, p. 1: "The only way not to be slaves in your own country is to convert the French-Canadian people".

30. See his conflict with Rev. Grant (future Queen's University principal) in *40 Years*, ch. 28. Grant rejects his approach while the congregation, allegedly, supported Chiniquy.

31. Hellmuth's 1859 letter in *Father Chiniquy, the Reformer of the Far West* (London, 1860), p. 11; also a comparison with the conversions at the biblical Pentecost in *MW*, 17 February 1876, p. 1.

9. THE SOCIAL CONVERSION OF CHINIQUY

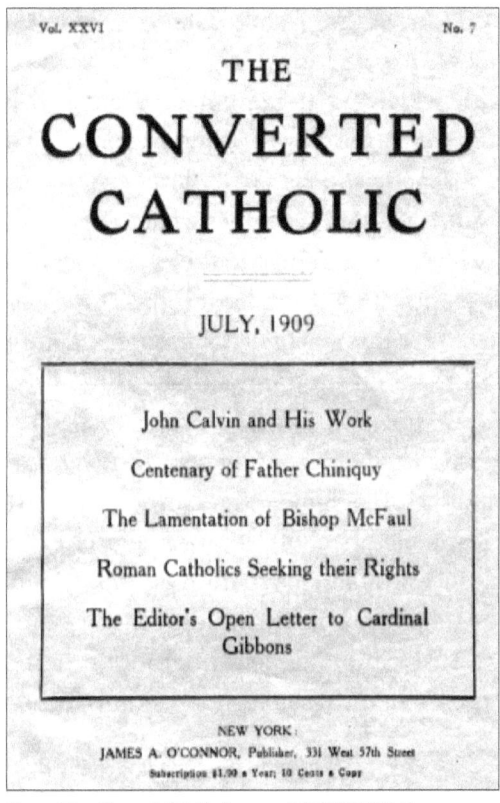

Figure 48   Converted Catholic cover AP 15 C1 F025-01

would not let him go to his grave until he had seen the downfall of Popery in Lower Canada".[32]

In those heady days of 1875-76, with Chiniquy's periodic lists of hundreds of converts, the French editor of the *Montreal Witness* wrote: "in one year, it is obvious that five or six churches like this one will not be sufficient, when Montreal becomes three quarters Protestant". In two years they would be buying the Catholic Cathedral as a church for Chiniquy.[33] Bishop Bourget admitted that "what is certain is that his presence is very harmful especially since he has joined forces with the Witness".[34] "The faith of many is in danger of shipwreck."[35] However Chiniquy exhausted himself and halted his Montreal stay, leaving only one new congregation of converts. The threat was stopped.

Anti-Catholicism was already in decline when Chiniquy was at his peak. He fought to reverse the trend among Protestant leaders. Chiniquy knew Catholicism well and could provide inside partisan information. Through his lectures and especially his books, Chiniquy became the

---

32. *MW*, 29 January 1875, p. 2.
33. *MW*, 2 February 1876, p. 1.
34. Circular letter, 18 March 1875, (*MEM*, vol.7, p. 103, my translation).
35. Ibid., p. 107 (my translation).

interpreter of Catholicism for millions of Protestants. Chiniquy's biblical basis and apparently authoritative explanations of Catholic practices were sufficient for him to become widely popular among evangelicals in the late 19th century. At the same time, the ex-priest knew which points were most controversial within Catholicism. He could write embarrassing public letters to bishops in language that Catholics understood.

One might speculate about whether Chiniquy would have welcomed Vatican II. Those who value the ex-priest's writing most today agree with their hero in being quite sceptical that Rome will ever become less intolerant.[36] It is difficult for them to abandon Chiniquy's final position that Roman Catholicism is paganism. However, Chiniquy did not become an anti-Catholic because of Catholic doctrine in general but because of pre-Vatican II theory and practice of 'religious totalism'. Many of the practices that he saw as the means of this control have been removed: the confessional booth, limitation on Bible distribution, social control, no appeals process and lack of religious liberty. Besides, there is now Catholic-Protestant dialogue so that Chiniquy could debate or, better, discuss the points at issue in a non-polemical setting. Who knows where the Holy Spirit could lead?

HIS NATIONALISM

Prior to his American 'exile' the Catholic Chiniquy identified very much with French-Canadian nationalist causes (then called "patriotic"), with the proviso that patriotic leaders remained loyal to Catholic leaders. At the mass meeting to honour Chiniquy in 1849 held in Montreal's Bonsécours market, Judge Mondelet introduced him as "the greatest patriot in the nation [*pays*]... the first patriot, the saviour of his nation." This

---

36. The fact that I studied in a Catholic theology faculty and had a Jesuit supervisor made my research very difficult with certain French Protestant informants. A few doubted my motives and expected that if the thesis was accurate it would not be accepted. In part this stems from frequent mention in the Chiniquy accounts of Université de Montréal students (then a branch of Université Laval), as his primary assailants in Montreal meetings.

9. THE SOCIAL CONVERSION OF CHINIQUY

elicited prolonged applause from the thousands of French Canadians present.[37]

While Chiniquy in no way advocated political independence for French Canada, his temperance campaign deliberately appealed to patriotic motives to strengthen the social fibre of French Canada. Chiniquy was a forerunner of 20th century nationalist leader Abbé Lionel Groulx when he wrote in 1849: "religion does not forbid us to love our nation [*patrie*]; on the contrary, it hallows and blesses that love ... Should we not be on fire and zealous to destroy all that could ruin or dishonour it?"[38]

Although Chiniquy was in Illinois, the *Avenir* and American immigrants still portrayed him as a nationalist helping French Canadians who were obliged to emigrate.[39] The Illinois priest was critical of the corrupt government of Lower Canada for not taking measures to improve their prospects sufficiently to make emigration unnecessary.[40]

Major difficulties developed between Chiniquy and his bishop, primarily over the welfare of French Catholics in Chicago. Chiniquy's unsuccessful submission of June 1857 contained four conditions. All of these aimed to protect French language worship in Illinois.[41] This nationalist cause against a seemingly biased Irish bishop was not supported by Quebec bishops nor by the press they controlled. The *Avenir* expected, in vain, that "the people know perfectly well that the clergy want to demolish Mr Chiniquy because he is the friend and

---

37. *Av*, 18 April 1849, p. 1 (my translation). Judge Mondelet noted too that the clergy were at this point on the patriotic side.

38. *Manuel*, p. 122 (my translation).

39. J.E. Dorion letter in the *Pays*, 16 June 1852, defends Chiniquy's nationalism in promoting his compatriots' welfare; *Av*, 15 January 1857, p. 1.

40. Chiniquy to J.C. Chapais MPP, [autumn 1852] from Barnard, *Mémoires* (Montreal, 1961), vol. 2, p. 88, and the same message much later in *CFA*, 7 July 1892, pp. 10-11.

41. Mailloux notes, June 1857 (**ASQ** 50:2L verso).

defender of his fellow countrymen, because he does not join with the oppressors of our race [*nation*]".[42]

Instead of becoming a national hero for this new cause, Chiniquy fell to a status similar to that of the American traitor Benedict Arnold. As Chiniquy's hero Lamennais discovered, a nationalism that is independent of hierarchical direction is not acceptable to the Church. Chiniquy was viewed by most of the French press as "a national apostate" for attempting to undermine the religious base of authority.[43] This critique was very much in evidence after his 1859 tour of Quebec.

Those with pragmatic political priorities such as the *Chicago Tribune* or the *Huntingdon Gleaner*[44] were more critical of Chiniquy's lack of political sense and political consistency. But his priorities remained theological. His understanding and consistency were also primarily theological

This does not mean that Chiniquy drew back from political comment. He did not remain quiet any more than he had during his Catholic years, nor was he any less controversial. Chiniquy revived his secondary liberal political tendencies. After his conversion, he praised the 1837 rebels in Quebec who, according to him, had been betrayed by their Church but were at least respected by the English.[45] He venerated Abraham Lincoln as a marvellous leader against slavery and tyranny. Chiniquy now asserted that the Conquest of Quebec by the British in 1759 had been a great event to liberate the French people. It failed in great measure, since the Catholic Church retained power. Thus a new spiritual conquest was needed.[46]

According to the ex-priest, allowing separate schools or any rights to the Catholic Church was disastrous for a free country. Chiniquy often

---

42. *Av*, 6 June 1857, p. 3.
43. *Le canadien*, 7 February 1859, quoted in Trudel, p. 219; also *La Presse*, 14 January 1899, p. 1.
44. *MW*, 27 April 1875.
45. *40 Years*, pp. 448-9.
46. *MW*, 29 January 1875, p. 2; *40 Years*, p. 299.

9. THE SOCIAL CONVERSION OF CHINIQUY

spoke on this subject with grave warnings about the consequences.[47] Any clerical control would be abused to gain the upper hand on tolerant Protestants. Chiniquy insisted that social and religious domination on the Quebec model was the aim of all Catholic leaders elsewhere. Consequently no extra political rights should ever be conceded in these crucial battles.

It was difficult for the ex-priest to refute the charge of treason against French Canada. Contentious Canadian socio-political debates in the late 19th century centred on separate schools outside Quebec and the Métis rebel Louis Riel. The ex-priest was on the 'wrong' or English side each time. As a visionary and organizer, Chiniquy joined the Orange Order, the Civil Rights Association, the Protestant Defence Association, the International Protestant League and the Bible Society. He spoke in defence of Masons, the *Institut canadien*, Joseph Guibord, another ex-priest Alessandro Gavazzi, and any other dissenters. Most French Canadians, following their Church (which had condemned all of these) and valuing their language (which was threatened by English Protestant militants), could hardly approve.

Why were French Canadians poorer than the English? The Apostle of Temperance attributed this to wasting money on alcohol.[48] When he left the Catholic Church, Chiniquy attributed the inequities to the absence of a society based on biblical principles.[49] Eventually, he adopted the anti-clerical stance of blaming Bishop Lartigue for the failure of the 1837 rebellions and the execution of rebel prisoners.[50] With such views Chiniquy's attempt to rouse nationalists made no headway among the religiously controlled press.

Inevitably, Chiniquy became more of an internationalist through his theology and his contacts. The world's enemy was Rome, he warned. Chiniquy supported any patriotism that contested Catholic power,

---

47. *MW*, 20 September 1876, p. 1.
48. See Noel, "Dry Patriotism" (*CHR*, 1990), pp. 200-204.
49. *MW*, 28 January 1870, p. 1.
50. *40 Years*, p. 449.

whether English Canadian, American, British, Australian or that of Bismarck's Germany. He believed that only a strong nation could resist papal interference.

Still the ex-priest continued to promote French ministry and the French language in Illinois. In Quebec he also strove for a strong self-supporting French church.[51] Nevertheless, Chiniquy's nationalist concerns remained secondary to spiritual allegiance, as they always had been (and as they were for the Catholic Church). Chiniquy's nationalism intensified in the Illinois conflict. In becoming anti-clerical and pro-American this nationalism helped marginalize Chiniquy and all French Protestants from French Canadian society and its nationalist causes. Even if his nationalism was not accepted at the time, the evidence shows that Chiniquy was loyal to his language and to his compatriots.

HIS METHOD OF CONFRONTING OPPONENTS

Among Chiniquy's characteristics that did not change following his conversion was his attitude towards opponents. From his aggressive words to the *Avenir* in 1849 to his battles in Illinois, both O'Regan and Mailloux discerned a pattern of calumny against all who opposed Chiniquy.[52] Later, former Presbyterian colleagues Rev. Staples and L'Hôte charged Chiniquy with having produced multiple false accusations against them.[53] While all the facts are not clear in this case, it is certain that Chiniquy did repeat the pattern.

When attacked, Chiniquy usually responded with speed and force. His crusading emotional approach could quickly cast recent friends as newly discovered traitors. The worst was assumed and demonic motives imputed. Probably Chiniquy damaged or destroyed the careers of many former colleagues who disagreed with him. Finally, after being taken

---

51. *MW* promoted this in 29 March 1875, p. 2.
52. Bp. O'Regan to Facile, 27 October 1856, p. 2 (**UND** III-2-i-8); and especially Mailloux notes to Godefroi Lambert letter, 24 July 1857 (**ASQ** 50:11b); also Trudel, p. 237.
53. *KG*, 3 July 1862.

9. THE SOCIAL CONVERSION OF CHINIQUY

under the wing of the Canadian Presbyterian Church, the middle-aged ex-priest began to learn to hold his tongue concerning other Protestants.

From the Catholic viewpoint,

> Mr Chiniquy has abandoned himself, possibly more than any man of his time, to excesses of language towards Catholics and above all concerning the beliefs which they cherish most: the Virgin Mary, the Real Presence, and Confession.[54]

This is why he encountered fury from lay Catholics. Bourget and other Catholic bishops recognized the anger and the potential for violence by certain Catholics against the apostate. They counselled boycott and shunning instead.

Now let us look at the frequent physical and verbal attacks against Chiniquy and the attitude he adopted in response. Shortly after his conversion, the ex-priest was invited to visit Canada. He reckoned that this was suicidal:[55]

> I felt that an implacable war was to be declared against me, which would end only with my life. The Pope, the bishops and priests, all over the world, would denounce and curse me. They would attack and destroy my character, my name and my honor, in their press, from their pulpit and in their confessionals.[56]

By his count, which seems relatively accurate on this point, there were more than 20 attempts on his life by means of stones, sticks, pistols and poison.[57] He was most upset about the August 1876 incident in Prince Edward Island. A threatening crowd surrounded him, his

---

54. *La Patrie*, 17 January 1899, p. 8 (my translation).
55. *40 Years*, p. 148.
56. *50 Years*, pp. 791-2.
57. Ten times his blood was shed, while three times very serious bruises were caused so that death was feared, he reported in the *New York Witness*, 6 June 1893, p. 1. By 1878, 12 stonings, two shootings and three beatings with clubs in Butler, *Abbé Chiniquy* (London, 1879), p. 14. In *50 Years*, Chiniquy reports having been attacked over 30 times and stoned 20 times (pp. 823-4).

wife and two daughters.[58] Normally he travelled alone, presumably to protect his family. Chiniquy often spoke of divine protection but he did not neglect his physical armour; this frequently included a heavy hat tied to his head and a thick plaid blanket on top of his shoulders.[59] These protected against the smaller stones and vegetables tossed at him.

Gavazzi, an ex-priest from Italy was also attacked in Quebec. He wrote: "I hear of dear Chiniquy's finding in Popish Canada the reception I met long ago, and both preserved by God's providence."[60] Chiniquy publicly noted the similarities with the treatment of Gavazzi and the ex-nun Edith O'Gorman in New Jersey.[61] He called these actions a revival of the Inquisition, orchestrated by means of the confessional and violent sermons. He maintained that Catholic authorities were afraid of any discussion so they chose to eliminate opposition.[62]

Napierville Catholics explained that they could not permit Chiniquy to address the audience if he was a Protestant, preaching a new doctrine.[63] So besides the outright violence, the fiery lecturer had to cope with frequent interruptions and attempts to drown out his speeches.[64] The *Montreal Witness* tried to encourage Chiniquy's followers to seek peace as much as possible.[65] It also charged that the bishop was morally responsible in not clearly condemning the disturbances or insisting that all Catholics permit free speech.[66]

---

58. A draft chapter, never included in *40 Years*, called "My life and that of my family in danger" **AP** 15-C2-F046-01.

59. *40 Years*, pp. 241-2.

60. Letter printed in *MW*, 23 April 1870, p. 4.

61. *MW*, 21 April 1870, p. 3.

62. *MW*, 30 March 1859, p. 201.

63. Laviolette to Mailloux, 14 March 1859. p. 3 (**ASQ** 50:20f).

64. *MW*, 12 February 1875, p. 2.

65. *MW*, 11 February 1875, p. 2. Chiniquy's conduct was supported in *MW*, 12 February, p. 2.

66. *MW*, 12 February 1875, p. 3. This concern was addressed indirectly by a strong statement of condemnation of violence and assertion of freedom of speech by the Roman Catholic *True Witness*.

9. THE SOCIAL CONVERSION OF CHINIQUY

Chiniquy also reported a pattern of calumny against himself. This involved a whole array of Catholic spokesmen, who carefully avoided any formal civil or religious trial.[67] Vicious false propaganda was certainly spread by some of Chiniquy's detractors (but also by some of his supporters).

In response, Chiniquy chose as his biblical model the answer of Jesus to the Pharisees: "If I said something wrong, you must give evidence for it. Should you hit a man for telling the truth?"[68] Thus Chiniquy rebuked clerical authorities and demanded that he be proven guilty.[69]

In 1857, Chiniquy blamed his own violent language on the oppression he experienced from an administration that could calmly defame and throw out an innocent priest.[70] His letters reveal a very emotional person. He swayed from peaceful overtures to angry denunciations in the same letter.[71] Mailloux and Trudel interpret this combination as the actions of an unscrupulous man using every arm in his arsenal. Could it not be that Chiniquy genuinely sought peace? However, frequently, when no discussion was allowed, he was overcome by his residual anger. In his later Protestant years there was the same mixture of emotions. For instance evangelical love for those who were 'lost' spiritually was closely associated with holy-war anger against representatives of the institution of Rome.

Chiniquy's evangelical 'liberation theology' was fairly well developed in 1857. He had constructed a biblical base and understood the dynamics amongst those who feel oppressed.[72] Defenceless lay Catholics and spiritual priests were deemed to be victims in a war with the powerful clerical authorities that sought total social, political and religious

---

67. *Av*, 25 May 1858, p. 2.
68. Jn. 18:23 (*New Living Translation*).
69. Chiniquy to Moreau, 26 February 1857, p. 39 (**ASQ** 52:5f).
70. Unpublished letter from Chiniquy to *Journal de Québec*, 2 February 1857, p. 14 (**ASQ** 50:1j). See the quote on our p. 217.
71. E.g. Chiniquy to Mailloux, 29 July 1857 (**ASQ** 50:3f).
72. Chiniquy to Moreau, 26 February 1857, p. 41 (**ASQ** 52:5f).

control. This explains in part Chiniquy's passion, his 'holy war' attitude, his polemics, and his politicization.

Even prior to any threats of physical violence, Chiniquy stated his willingness to give up his life rather than to abandon the cause of justice.[73] He often cited the following Bible passage: "The apostles left the high council, rejoicing that God had counted them worthy to suffer dishonor for the name of Jesus."[74] Suffering was a badge of honour:

> if it has been good to me to suffer those humiliations, to be cursed and threatened with death, to be stoned and bruised, for the Gospel cause, it is good also for you Protestants to have seen these things with your own eyes ... Many of you were sleeping in the false security of a deceitful peace ... Do not think that this is the work of a thoughtless and stupid mob. [These were well-dressed church-going people.] Under the banners of Jesus we are determined to fight, to suffer, to bleed and to die in this battle. We do not ask you, brethren to come and partake our dangers.

Instead he requested prayer and financial aid.[75]

Any Catholic violence that Chiniquy's presence provoked was deemed proof of his thesis (and that of most evangelicals) that Catholicism had not changed in its desire to exterminate any dangerous opposition. In addition

> any injury to Mr. Chiniquy would probably double the income of all the missionary associations now at work in Lower Canada.[76]

> We are certain then that Mr Chiniquy, far from complaining about this thrashing, would like it to happen again.[77]

A close friend reported:

---

73. Ibid., p. 42; also *40 Years*, p. 150.
74. Acts 5:41 (*New Living Translation*).
75. Chiniquy letter in *MW*, 4 February 1870, p. 1 for the whole paragraph above.
76. *MW*, 12 January 1870, p. 2. This came in an article designed to calm Protestant feelings of revenge, especially among Orangemen.
77. French section of *MW*, 13 March 1876, p. 1 (my translation).

9. THE SOCIAL CONVERSION OF CHINIQUY

> 'I enjoy', he told me one day, 'when I receive some opposition, seeing that there are better results.' That was his experience and for a good result he would expose himself to death. No, a thousand times no, he was not scared by danger; the more agitated his meetings were, the happier and more satisfied he was; also the greater and more uplifting were his thoughts and his eloquence.[78]

This same informant recounted one occasion when a bullet narrowly missed Father Chiniquy while he was preaching. Chiniquy continued his sermon, using the shooting as an illustration of Rome's methods.[79] If he were martyred, the point would be most firmly made.

In 1879, Chiniquy wrote from Australia:

> from the very day of my conversion, not an hour has passed when I have not prepared myself for the sacrifice. And the fact is, that I consider it a real wonder that I have not fallen dead under their blows. They have so often attacked me with stones, sticks, daggers and pistols; I have been so often struck and bruised, that the idea of dying under their blows has become as my daily thought - I dare say my daily bread. Besides that, at my age - 70 years - death has absolutely lost all its terrors for me. It would be such a sure cause of an eternal joy - I would be so sure of my crown in heaven - if I could give the last drop for my dear Saviour's sake, and die for Him as He died for me.[80]

One hostile obituary claimed that "the thought that he never was even once killed in a religious riot must have embittered his last hours."[81]

Like the Catholic bishops, the Protestant[82] Chiniquy never counselled violence or revenge.[83] Nevertheless, as was the case for his Catholic anti-Protestant statements, Chiniquy's polemics incited persons who were already inclined to violence. Among Chiniquy supporters violence

---

78. Bruneau, "Le père Chiniquy" (Montreal, c1915), p. 10 (my translation).
79. Ibid., pp. 10-11.
80. Chiniquy letter to *Sydney Witness*, 19 April 1879, p. 1 (clipping in **SL** c.1/12).
81. *Buffalo N.Y. Express*, 17 January 1899 (**CBA**, Charles Chiniquy Obituaries).
82. Note the 1856 letter while he was still a Catholic on p. 68 of this book.
83. He opposed retaliation in *MW*, 4 February 1870.

seems to have been limited to acting as bodyguards and confronting those who harassed the ex-priest. According to my research, none of Chiniquy's bodyguards were ever arrested and no Catholic property was ever damaged in the wake of a Chiniquy lecture. This is in contrast to the many properties and churches sheltering Chiniquy which were damaged and the many opponents who were arrested for violence or disturbing the peace. This indicates some restraint on Chiniquy's part.

We have already seen many instances of the stinging and memorable phrases Chiniquy employed. In her study of Quebec ultramontanism, Eid noted its proponents' use of a style of language that employed brutality and violence when speaking of government interference in education.[84] Chiniquy was deemed a master pupil in the rhetoric training of the period, which emphasized exaggeration, expansion and description.[85] The polemical approach of both anti-Catholicism and ultramontanism involved amplifying the polemic, repeating any assertions, adding details and often distorting the original stories.[86]

Social chaos was one image of ultramontanism that Chiniquy continued to exploit throughout his life. He often predicted a bloody cataclysm that would destroy his opponents. In general he described a revolution, patterned on that of France, which would destroy clerical power.[87] Sometimes he threatened to reveal dark secrets.[88]

Laverdure found Chiniquy's language to be typical of the excesses of 19th century oratory, in particular that of anti-clericalism. But "everyone agreed that Chiniquy's use of religious invective was unsurpassed."[89] He invented some new anti-clerical images but he used many more drawn from the long history of anti-Catholicism.

---

84. Eid, *Le clergé* (Montreal, 1976), pp. 155, 229.
85. Laverdure, "Charles Chiniquy: the Making" (*CCHA Historical Studies*, 1987), p. 53.
86. Ibid.
87. *50 Years*, p. 249 (back in the 1830s).
88. *Address delivered by Rev. C. Chiniquy on his Defence Before the Chicago Presbytery* (Sandwich, 1862), p. 8.
89. Laverdure, p. 51. Trudel, p. 257, singles out his unparalleled mocking of the Eucharist.

9. THE SOCIAL CONVERSION OF CHINIQUY

The caustic images that Chiniquy employed have not been typical of 19th or 20th century evangelical Protestants except for fringe fundamentalists. Evangelicals apparently enjoyed reading the Chiniquy assaults while conveniently blaming the excesses on his Catholic training. Only the *Montreal Witness* made repeated if limited attempts to tame the ex-priest's tongue.

The *Huntingdon Gleaner* summed up the non-evangelical Protestant critique of his language:

> Though we may accord to Mr. Chiniquy due credit for his evident sincerity and earnestness, it must be regretted by all whose fanaticism has not completely warped their better judgement that he has frequently seen fit to descend to a coarse, vituperative style of argument in his attacks on the Catholic clergy, which is to say the least, in very bad taste, and calculated to repel rather than attract all fair minded and tolerant persons ... Bigoted and abusive as his discourses may be, he has nevertheless a right to the free expression of his opinions.[90]

Chiniquy did not care about tolerant people. Most evangelicals must have agreed with much of the *Gleaner* critique but still supported Chiniquy in that zeal for truth and love for the lost should far outweigh concerns about good taste or 'political correctness'.

Chiniquy used mockery, humour, exaggerations, attacks on motives and many other means of shocking Catholics into rethinking their position. Most evangelicals allowed that Chiniquy's apparent success justified the means he utilized. "He may have been at times hasty in word and deed, but so were the reformers, and so were the apostles and the prophets."[91] Historian and church leader Duclos stated without disapproval that "Father Chiniquy ably handles the weapons of ridicule and sarcasm."[92] A few Protestants even denied that Chiniquy was too

---

90. Reprinted in *MW*, 27 April 1875, p. 1; also see Rev. Grant in *40 Years*, p. 301.
91. Dr. Burns eulogy in *40 Years*, p. 287.
92. Duclos (Montreal, 1913), vol. 1, p. 152.

harsh in his language. Rather, his great love for his people led him to express his strong emotions and state unpleasant but necessary facts.[93]

Along with most 19th century (and many 21st century) newspaper editors, Chiniquy was sceptical of the opposition's accounts. He maintained the licence to make his side sound better or his opponent's sound worse. Such a format tended to gladden one's followers while inflaming the opposition. Chiniquy aimed, though, to induce Catholic doubters by means of logic, and, even more, by their emotions, to consider another alternative.

HIS SOCIAL RELATIONS AND HIS LANGUAGE

Whatever Chiniquy's success in Illinois, back in French Canada he was shunned with horror as the great apostate.[94] He wrote:

> by giving up the Church of Rome, I had given up the church of my dear father and mother, of my brothers, my friends ... honor, country - everything! I did not regret the sacrifice, but I felt as if I could not survive it.[95]

Undoubtedly it was difficult for the excommunicated priest to create a completely new network of friends at the age of 50. Chiniquy's granddaughter read his "diaries" and commented on his solitary nature:

> We do not get any sense of the intimate hidden life. We are struck by the feverish activity, the need to go everywhere, I would even say to keep in the public eye, which consumed his noble soul. He lived alone in the midst of all, seemingly not needing exchange or communicating any intellectual or spiritual needs. A man who felt complete by himself.[96]

---

93. Bird, *A Few Reminiscences* (Leeds, 1878), p. 10; CC, 5 (1888), p. 143. *50 Years* (Wickliffe Press, London, n.d.), editor's preface on p. 12: "Father Chiniquy's story is written in a kindly Christian spirit. He speaks the truth in love and does not indulge in denunciation."

94. *50 Years*, p. 770.

95. *50 Years*, p. 791. This quote comes from the moments just after his final decision to refuse to submit.

96. Violet Lefebvre, p. 1 (**SL** c.2/103, mss. VDL, my translation).

9. THE SOCIAL CONVERSION OF CHINIQUY

So far the sources have not revealed any particular Protestant confidant who was as close as Brassard, Louis Cazeau or J.C. Chapais were during Chiniquy's Catholic years. Principal MacVicar and Chiniquy's son in law, Joseph Morin, came closest. All Chiniquy's new friends were English or Protestant and usually both. In fact two French Protestant pastors, whom Chiniquy helped, actually objected to his anglomania.[97]

Nevertheless, many people chose to associate themselves with him. Chiniquy cherished numerous English evangelicals and Orange Order members. He profusely thanked those who provided protection or financial aid.[98] Besides these English supporters, Chiniquy was on good terms with virtually all French Protestant co-workers. This most famous apostate was partial to other ex-priests, giving them second chances and supporting them in their precarious state. Of course those in St. Anne who had gone through the same conflict alongside Chiniquy and had honoured him as pastor for so long, had a special bond with him.

While marriage provided an intimate contact, so far, I have discovered only one letter to his wife.[99] Chiniquy carried on a voluminous worldwide correspondence with potential or actual converts from Catholicism, as well as with some Protestant admirers. This limited the time for any purely social correspondence. Alternatively, perhaps it was deemed too private to conserve.

As a workaholic, Chiniquy had little time for mere social contacts. How did he relax or replenish his energy, outside of his devotions? His

---

97. Serge Thériault, "La réforme catholique franco-américaine" (*Aujourd'hui credo*, 1983), p. 20. For an example see the introduction to Chiniquy's *The Perversion of Dr. Newman to the Church of Rome*, ³1896.

98. Chiniquy to *Presbyterian*, sent 29 September 1859 (**ASQ** 52:4 clipping).

99. Chiniquy to Euphémie (Allard), 31 July 1890 (Lois Meier collection, St. Anne IL). In part this absence stems from the nature of the sources, being mostly newspaper letters and church records. However the AP source contains many letters to other family members and his son-in-law. See Lois Meir, *The Apostate's Woman* (Bloomington, 2005) for an imaginative novel about Euphémie and the marriage.

favourite hobbies were hunting and fishing but he spent less time on these over the years. He had a massive library and subscribed to many periodicals to keep informed about Quebec, American and world events. In his recurring crises of burnout and physical exhaustion, travel became an energizer. Nothing much changed in the pattern of these activities after Chiniquy became a Protestant. When he retired Chiniquy did spend time each summer in the Lower Saint Lawrence around Tadoussac, and after 1896 at his rural retreat of Elgin Road (St. Damase).

For his English listeners part of the charm of Chiniquy's lectures came from his French accent, which never disappeared. Not surprisingly Chiniquy's English comprehension and expression became quite polished after years in the United States and in the Presbyterian denomination. In fact he wrote *40 Years* and other works in English without translation.[100]

This does not mean that the 'Luther of Canada' abandoned his French compatriots. He always gave a high priority to visits to French congregations. His tombstone was inscribed in French only. Still the major market for his writing was English, since his productions were prohibited by the Catholic Church and therefore to most of the French population of Canada. Chiniquy needed to perform well in English in order to raise funds for French mission. Fluency in French and English became indispensable for Chiniquy's role.

TRANSFORMATIONS AND CONTINUITY

As one who was banned as an apostate from the ranks of French-Canadian Catholics, Chiniquy was obliged to change his entire social life. This enforced change incited the anti-Catholicism that was characteristic of most French Protestants prior to Vatican II. Chiniquy adopted anti-clerical language and associated with the noted anti-cleric Joseph Doutre. However, after Pierre Blanchet's *Avenir* closed in 1858, the

---

100. *Times* of London, July 25, 1892, p. 4.

9. THE SOCIAL CONVERSION OF CHINIQUY

ex-priest had no hearing from any French non-Protestant paper or institution. It was too dangerous to be associated with him.

This disassociation left Chiniquy with contact and support only from English and French Protestants, Temperance groups, and the Orange Order. A huge following in the English-speaking world compensated for a narrowed social circle in Quebec. Inevitably, the ex-priest became more pro-English. Only the English could easily appreciate his view of the 1759 British conquest of Quebec: an entirely positive event except that it had failed to go far enough. Hence, there was a need for a new religious conquest funded by English Canadians.

The national identity of Chiniquy was quite flexible. He could draw on the potential anti-Catholic elements of any culture or nation, and identify himself with those. He stressed his American citizenship in Illinois, while he lauded Queen Victoria in England, Canadian freedoms in English Canada, liberty in Australia and anti-clerical rebels in French Canada. He was non-partisan in criticizing any party that conceded new rights to Catholics. As a Catholic he had not been aligned himself with a political party either, but he had supported the status quo. As a Protestant, Chiniquy was adamantly opposed to the status quo in Canada, where Catholic power was considerable.

Chiniquy's conversion resulted in a socialization, similar to the descriptions of Kilbourne and Richardson.[101] He learned the 'conversion script', and received a positive response from the new group. He also experienced the 'revitalization' mentioned by Wallace. He led his parish into a revitalization movement. Chiniquy's attempts to become the prophet for French Canada foundered because his compatriots did not face an acute crisis similar to his. Chiniquy's own experiences match the revitalization model better than do those of the St. Anne parish; that is to say that his personal crises were much more severe than those of the parish. Skonovd's study of apostates shows the power of a mass

---

101. See the beginning of this chapter.

conversion as happened in St. Anne where the parishioners supported each other in the momentous and perilous decisions.

Chiniquy always relished debate, polemics, and the process of inspiring a crowd. He even enjoyed being confronted, which enabled him to bring his points alive. From early in his Protestant career he expected martyrdom, although he took precautions to minimize the risk and demanded that civil authorities protect him. In his autobiography he recounts at length many incidents of assault, in order to show the "true face of Rome". Since he contended that the priests had inspired each act, he wrote and spoke out all the more forcefully against them.

The ex-priest's language was controlled enough to avoid inciting his audience to immediate violence. It was uncontrolled enough to allege many false motivations and plots, and to proclaim anti-Catholic legends as facts. Chiniquy's gift of oratory made his tendency to publicize rumours much more dangerous. Evangelicals were reluctant to criticize him since many of the legends were generally believed. They were especially careful to not give Catholic propaganda any more ammunition against this pivotal leader. In addition they insisted that the principle of freedom of speech should apply even to Chiniquy's occasional excesses. As a consequence he never changed his ways.

Charles Chiniquy travelled a long way from a poor family in rural Quebec to the heights of temperance fame, to the depths of infamy, and finally to worldwide fame as a debunker of Catholicism. Like his religious changes most of the social changes in his life had their foundations prepared ahead of time but they happened rapidly.

Unlike his religious conversion, the social conversion was a completely involuntary result of the excommunication. The lack of a family to pressure him and the support of most of his Illinois parish were key factors in making the process less painful. As social and financial support from Quebec was cut off, other avenues opened to supply the necessities. This Catholic rejection, matched with Protestant aid, reinforced Chiniquy's religious conversion.

10

THE LEGACY OF CHINIQUY

AMONG FRENCH PROTESTANTS

Every French Protestant pastor in Canada knows at least part of the Protestant myth of Chiniquy.[1] One would expect the memory of the best-known French Protestant leader in Quebec to be perpetuated. Through the years converts from Catholic backgrounds have been amazed to discover this inspiring character about whom they had heard nothing or had heard only abuse.

The Chiniquy name has been conserved with honour among the families who became French Protestants in the 19th century and who have stayed in Quebec. After all, many became Protestants through his ministry. While it would require much more research to estimate how many of his converts persevered,[2] there is no doubt that they were numerous and widespread. Minorities such as immigrants from France

---

1. See my Chapter 7.
2. Supporters mostly suggested tens of thousands of converts. McLoughlin, *Famous ex-Priests* (NY, 1968), p. 527, calculates their descendants in the millions. Chiniquy himself provided many estimates, as high as 25,000 in *Life and Work of Rev. Charles Chiniquy* (London, 1897), p. 18, which also links him with the total achieved by all denominations, of 45,000 French Protestant converts in Quebec.

to Montreal and Franco-Americans appear to have been most open to his message.[3] The parish of St. Anne constituted Chiniquy's major evangelistic success, and provided the largest number of his converts. Besides these there were at least hundreds of native francophone Quebecers. There are also reports of French converts from as far away as New Brunswick, Manitoba and Oregon.

Chiniquy's converts must have defied Catholic Church authorities initially by going to listen to the apostate. When they returned with news of their conversion due to Father Chiniquy, one can imagine how they were received. It is probable that Chiniquy's converts, experiencing greater rejection than other French Protestants, were more likely to emigrate from Quebec. This dispersion of Chiniquy's converts makes the legacy even more difficult to estimate.

The only prominent Quebecer to become a convert of Chiniquy was Louis Joseph Amadée Papineau, son of the rebel Louis Joseph. Despite Protestant claims, his conversion may have arisen more as the conclusion of a life-long anti-clerical process than as a truly spiritual transformation.[4] It appears that Chiniquy was more the symbol of his rebellion, rather than the cause of his conversion.[5]

Although Chiniquy's evangelism proved relatively fruitful, French Protestants regret that their only major impact in Quebec was limited to 1875-1877. Chiniquy's exhausting efforts in those years resulted in lists of thousands of ex-Catholics. The St. Jean Presbyterian Church and the new Église du Sauveur in Montreal were largely established by work done during those years. In terms of dynamism, the success of Chiniquy and of the French Protestant movement climaxed at that point.

When the ex-priest took several years off for health reasons, the tide swung back to a monolithic French Quebec. Even after he returned from

---

3. See *MW*, 25 March 1875, p. 2, for testimonies of such converts; and *MW*, 25 July 1876, p. 1, for a French-Canadian convert.

4. Trudel, pp. 267-70.

5. Papineau was not always a model Protestant. He wrote four years later to Chiniquy (12 January 1898), to complain that the Protestant church he had joined, Église St. Jean, was pressuring him to attend and to contribute financially (**SL** c.1/5).

10. THE LEGACY OF CHINIQUY

his Pacific voyage, Chiniquy became pastor in Illinois rather than in Montreal. From 1880 on Chiniquy rarely claimed more than several hundred converts in a year, as opposed to thousands in those three years of the mid 1870s. The brief heady optimism faded with the years.[6] The Église du Sauveur was eventually sold and the membership of the other congregations returned to previous low levels.

At Chiniquy's death many dreaded the consequences of losing the one who had chosen: "the maddest and foolhardiest thing a man of his ability ever set himself to do, to give the best forty years of his life to a thing so utterly hopeless as French evangelization."[7] Nevertheless, Chiniquy had shown that a breach could be made in the Catholic wall and provided some hope for a repeat of the same.[8]

Chiniquy was seen as "the great champion of liberty and the Gospel",[9] defending French Protestants against superior forces. Chiniquy's visits provided great encouragement and new vigour for the dispersed Protestant congregations and pastors. He was pictured as a stubborn Daniel willing to face lions,[10] a David against mighty Goliath,[11] a Joshua willing to enter the strange new land,[12] a Moses leading his people out of slavery,[13] a second apostle Paul rejected by his people,[14] and of course the new Luther.[15] The inspiration of such a leader was incalculable for

---

6. See *MW*, 1 May 1875, p. 1, for a prediction of a Protestant Montreal in one hundred years (1975).

7. *40 Years*, p. 495.

8. See Eugène Réveillaud (a Protestant from France), *Histoire du Canada et des canadiens-français de la découverte jusqu'à nos jours* (Paris, Grassart, 1884), p. 461. Also the *Presbyterian Record* (Montreal, Feb. 1899), p. 1.

9. John Herdt (Montreal) to Chiniquy, 17 September 1896 (**SL** c.1/5).

10. *A*, 5 May 1894, p. 6.

11. *MW*, 24 January 1870, p. 2; also, during his Catholic years, *Av*, 18 April 1849.

12. *40 Years*, pp. 129, 135.

13. A prophecy in *MW*, 4 March 1850, p. 68; then *MW*, 22 January 1870 and 20 January 1877, p. 1.

14. *CC*, 2 (1885), p. 50; *40 Years*, p. 494; *50 ans*, p. ii.

15. See p. 186 of this book

those who were a small, isolated and harassed minority, with no power and little future.

Chiniquy's single-handed combat inspired many but it left none able to take over after his death. The Catholic Church could henceforth ignore French Protestants or permit harassment of them, without fear of repercussions. Thus, even more than with his evangelism, the primary legacy was the eternal search for 'another Chiniquy'. The *Aurore* mourned, "will his spirit not be passed on to some friend at this time."[16] Prayers were frequently made for successors of their champion.[17]

In the 1850s Isaac Hellmuth had looked for an "Anglican Chiniquy". A century later Jacques Smith reports that Dr. Reid of the Presbyterian Church was still looking for "another Chiniquy".[18] Ever since the 1830s every evangelical group in Quebec has hoped for charismatic spiritual leaders to break through the wall. Confronting such a homogeneous anti-Protestant society, French Protestants often despaired of making any progress without an outstanding leader of proven public credentials. Chiniquy was the obvious model. While most pastors were cautious and unknown, he was widely known and dared to challenge fearlessly. "For many he will remain the ideal prototype for evangelical French-Canadian pastors: 'Golden-tongued' (Chrysostom), tremendous preacher, a man of action and destroyer of Catholics."[19]

Chiniquy was the last well-known French Protestant. Anglican pastor Victor Rahard provoked some controversy with his polemical style in the 1930s[20] but he lacked Chiniquy's impact and longevity. While the search for "another Chiniquy" proved fruitless, alternative models were very slow in developing. Chiniquy's granddaughter wished that his successors

---

16. *A*, 2 August 1900, p. 8 (my translation).
17. *A*, 11 February 1899, p. 6.
18. Interview with Jacques Smith, Montreal, 23 May 1992.
19. Goldberger, "La main tendue" (*Aujourd'hui credo*, April 1992), p. 15.
20. Although he produced many new members, according to Jacques Smith, he lacked the positive evangelical emphases of Bible study and prayer. His ministry was brief while his converts anglicized or joined other French denominations.

10. THE LEGACY OF CHINIQUY

had put more energy into the projects already in place[21] rather than waiting for another champion.

Father Chiniquy helped consolidate the natural cooperation of various Protestant groups that aimed to evangelize French Catholics. Although a few Baptists and Methodists found his methods not to be spiritual enough,[22] he maintained good relations with these denominations. He accepted all their offers to speak, even in isolated congregations, and regularly attended any interdenominational worship services, rallies or picnics. Chiniquy warned Protestants that they were less attractive as sectarian opponents of each other. He pressed constantly for visible evidence of unity to counteract Catholic prejudices.[23]

Despite his interdenominational stance, Chiniquy's very membership in the Presbyterian church assured that this group would dominate French Protestantism. He personally raised large sums of money for French Presbyterian mission, which financed by far the largest number of missionaries. Without doubt Chiniquy's presence made the Presbyterians **the** natural option for converts, as opposed to the Anglicans, Baptists or Methodists. Imagine the impact of the 14 future pastors for French churches, whom Chiniquy raised up from his own St. Anne congregation. This was more than any Canadian Presbyterian church in that period.[24] They never formed an organized block in French mission. However, these 14 constituted a very large percentage of pastors in French work, all loyal to their leader.

Ironically Chiniquy's legacy of endorsement of Presbyterian work became problematic when this denomination was one of the first to

---

21. Violet Lefebvre manuscript, "Réflexions faites après avoir parcouru 'diaries' 1891-92-95-96-97" (**SL** c.2/103 or **AP** 15-1-C2-F103).

22. "There is just now a larger, though more outward and more superficial agency at work in the presence and preaching here of Mr. Chiniquy" (*Grande Ligne Annual Report*, 1885, pp. 93-4).

23. Chiniquy to Rev. M. Smith, Editor of the "Standard", 16 April 1873, reprinted as a pamphlet of seven pages (**SL** c.1/12 or **AP** 15-1-C1-F012).

24. *A*, 16 July 1909, p. 5; *40 Years*, p. 147; Presbyterian Board of French Evangelization report, 1881 *General Assembly*, p. cxxii.

officially reject proselytism.[25] This effectively undermined French evangelism. The influence of the Chiniquy-MacVicar brand of polemical anti-Catholicism declined rapidly after their two deaths. First the liberal evangelical followers of George Grant and then the dominant social reform party[26] sought more positive relationships with Catholics. English Protestants outside of Quebec funded and also made the decisions for French mission. They lost interest in it.

While Chiniquy's memory was fresh, there still remained an alternative to anti-clericalism or ultramontanism in French Canada. Some predicted, "truth will triumph, justice will soon shine again, and the dawn of a new day will come in Canada where the School of Chiniquy will prosper."[27] He had demonstrated the intolerant aspects of ultramontanism and also opened a door for critics of Catholicism. This proved to be an ephemeral influence limited to those who were able to find and secretly read his banned writings.

"The book of the life of a man whom God designated to give a mortal blow to the giant of intemperance, and then to obscurantism and to moral and intellectual slavery ... can not be closed."[28] French Protestants prolonged the memory through literature. The 1913 history of French Protestantism by Duclos contained over one hundred pages on

---

25. Moir (Don Mills, 1987), p. 156; see the conclusions of Strout, "The Latter Years of the Board of French Evangelization of the Presbyterian Church in Canada" (Lennoxville, 1986), pp. 53-4, 60-76.

26. Barry Mack, "From Preaching to Propaganda: The Lost Centre of Twentieth-Century Presbyterianism" (Queen's University Conference on the Canadian Evangelical Experience, May 1995); Mack, "George Monro Grant: Evangelical Prophet" (Queen's U., 1992).

27. *A*, 30 December 1899, p. 8 (my translation).

28. Rev. Amaron in *A*, 3 March 1899, p. 9 (my translation). This was in response to *La Patrie*, 17 January, p. 8.

10. THE LEGACY OF CHINIQUY

the ex-priest. A condensed version of Chiniquy's autobiography was published in French in 1946[29] and it has remained in print since 1976.[30]

Prior to Vatican II, no Chiniquy book sold well in Quebec except the French version of *The Priest, the Woman and the Confessional*. Only a very few pamphlets were reprinted. Even Chiniquy's French version of *50 Years* was published, in its entirety, only in Europe. A few copies of Vol. 1 (the first half) of *Cinquante ans* constituted Chiniquy's only French publications in Quebec between 1876 and 1894. During that period Chiniquy produced more than 25 tracts, pamphlets or books in English. The Roman Catholic 'Index' of proscribed books must have been effective in limiting Chiniquy's Quebec readers to the small French Protestant community and to others who read English.

Chiniquy's involvement with the Orange Order opened the way for others. There is no evidence of sizeable membership gains but Jacques Smith established French branches in Quebec while Pastor Ludger Émard became Grand Master for Quebec.[31] The protection this group provided (e.g., for Rahard) provoked accusations of treason against French Protestants. Such a legacy faded with the Orange Order itself.

Even though Chiniquy facilitated freedom of speech about religion, this required frequent repetition. Again his legacy is found in his inspirational example rather than in any durable results. Nevertheless, Chiniquy's penchant for political comment was not emulated by his successors. This

---

29. *Mes Combats: Autobiographie de Charles Chiniquy* (Montreal, 1946). Jacques Smith and Plymouth Brethren worker John Spreeman organized this condensed version of *50 Years* and *40 Years*. See **AP** 15-C2-F110-16

30. *Chiniquy: l'homme qui osa défier le puissant empire de Rome* (Beauport, 1976), 508 p. This is the same book as *Mes combats* with minor changes. It has proved popular with frequent reprinting; for its origin see the letter from John Spreeman to Violet Lefebvre, Feb. 7, 1967 (**SL** c.2/105). See our Appendix 4 for a comparison of the contents of these.

31. *A*, October 1956, p. 4.

would have been an unnecessary provocation from the vulnerable French Protestant community.[32]

After Chiniquy's death, with the disappearance of their most notable fund-raiser, French Protestant schools and congregations eventually closed or became bilingual. Chiniquy had tried to persuade French Protestants to become self-financing. He provided an exemplary model by giving generously. Still, even his large Illinois congregation had trouble paying its expenses. Many Chiniquy speeches tended to stress the financial disadvantages experienced by converts and to appeal for English or American funds. Such an approach did not promote good stewardship locally. The French Protestant group he helped establish, which seemed so strong in 1899, was too dependent on Chiniquy both for fundraising, and for leadership in Presbyterian meetings, to carry on long after his death. Dependency on English money remains a major problem even now for French Protestants.

Chiniquy's converts and many other French Protestants had to survive the term *chiniquiste*[33]:

> The *Courrier [du Canada]* pretends to believe that Mr Chiniquy is the founder of a sect of which the francophone Protestants are all members. Surely it must know that this famous Canadian was Presbyterian and that French-speaking Protestants belong to many denominations which are as diverse as the waves but as united as the sea.[34]

Although one Franco-American convert was proud to be called a *Chiniquiste*,[35] in Quebec it was a destructive label. The church in St. Anne, Illinois and many others were called (by their enemies) the Church

---

32. The newspaper *Aurore* did make occasional comments, depending on the editors or correspondents, but outsiders took no notice.
33. Duclos, vol. 2, p. 211; Trudel, p. 276.
34. *A*, 21 February 1901, p. 4.
35. *CFA*, 18 May 1893, p. 3.

10. THE LEGACY OF CHINIQUY

of Chiniquy.[36] The *Aurore*,[37] the *Semeur canadien*[38] and the *Montreal Witness*[39] were each sullied by being called 'the Chiniquy newspaper'. This usage of Chiniquy's name for the purpose of discrediting French Protestants long outlived its reference.

It is surprising that French Protestants have named nothing after their great hero. No church, group, publication or foundation in Quebec or Illinois has borne his name. Probably the name became too controversial.[40] The French Protestant community could not afford to deter potential converts or to facilitate Catholic propaganda. It was only in the late 1990s that a historical conference about French Protestantism adopted the name 'Chiniquy Conference'. This was not repeated. All recent events relating to Chiniquy have been one time events.

Nevertheless when Chiniquy was maligned, French Protestants always jumped to his defence.[41] The epitaph from Heb. 11:4, "although dead, he still speaks" was applied to Chiniquy more than once, in hallowed tones.[42] It was said in 1924 that "for French Protestants, he remains a great figure with a halo."[43] The *Aurore* often reprinted his writings or stories thus keeping his memory alive. Even in 1993, when the French play "Chiniquy, God's Liar" was publicized in Quebec City, the local group of French Protestant pastors met to prepare a response.[44]

---

36. *40 Years*, p. 123; Trudel, p. 227; *A*, 13 August 1909, p. 7; even in the 1950s - Maurice Nerny, "A History of Franco- Canadian Protestantism" (McGill U., BD thesis, 1956), p. 47.

37. *A*, 28 December 1895, p. 4.

38. *Cour*, 27 July 1859, p. 2 and 19 December 1859.

39. *Le journal de Fraserville*, 31 July 1896, p. 22.

40. Meier, *The Saga* (St. Anne, 1976), pp. 6-7.

41. E.g., *A*, May 1865, p. 1.

42. Duclos, vol. 2, p. 102; *A*, 23 December 1899, p. 5.

43. Primeau-Robert, *La place des protestants dans la nationalité Canadienne-française* (Montreal, 1924), p. 37 (my translation).

44. "Chiniquy, menteur de Dieu". The play closed too quickly to afford them an opportunity.

In St. Anne, Illinois the ex-priest was honoured by French Protestants as founder and benefactor of the colony, besides being the liberator of his people.[45] A French pastor in Kansas came close to an un-Protestant prayer of intercession through the dead Chiniquy.[46] Chiniquy's American influence extended to a francophone Greek Orthodox priest in Florida, who urged Protestants to pride in their hero against Trudel's attacks.[47]

It is true that the memory of Chiniquy has faded with the years. His supporters possessed few means of reinforcing it. Still, a type of hero-worship for their champion remains very strong among many older Protestants and among those who have suffered marginalization in Quebec. Evangelical denominations in Quebec have spread Chiniquy writings and maintained his memory. However, the more ecumenically minded Protestant denominations have, at least until recently, been happy to forget the controversial ex-priest.[48] Until 1999 Chiniquy mementoes at Presbyterian College and the United Church Église St. Jean were confined to closets. Église St. Jean and the Presbyterian College's participation in a conference on Chiniquy on October 23, 1999, as well as the press coverage in *Aujourd'hui credo* marked a break with this tradition at least temporarily.[49]

AMONG CATHOLICS IN QUEBEC

It is ironic that the artist Pellan painted the Chiniquy black cross in 1941 and explained to the purchaser that it represented all that blocked

---

45. *A*, 17 February 1900, p. 10; 3 March 1900, p. 11; 3 September 1909, p. 5; *St. Anne Record*, 6 August 1909.
46. *A*, 6 September 1900, p. 6.
47. Father J.J. Laliberté in *A*, June 1966, p. 4.
48. Goldberger, "La main tendue" (*Aujourd'hui credo*, April 1992), provides a welcome insightful exception.
49. A groundbreaking conference on Chiniquy was co-sponsored by UQAM Department of Religious Studies, Presbyterian College, Église St. Jean, leaders of the 'Christian Catholic' movement and myself. In fact the first French edition of this book was launched there. See *Aujourd'hui credo*, November 1999.

10. THE LEGACY OF CHINIQUY

progress in Quebec.⁵⁰ Thus fifty years after his death, and almost a century after leaving the Catholic Church, his name was associated with spreading conservative ultramontanism.

On the other hand the horror, surrounding the apostasy of such an important figure, was memorialized by the construction of a Chapel of Reparation at Pointe aux Trembles in the east end of Montreal. This was built in 1896 specifically to counter Chiniquy's desacration.⁵¹ Although the horror wore off with the years, Chiniquy remained the archetypal apostate. "Chiniquy became the caricature of new converts: excessive, revengeful, lacking in elementary charity towards his former church, untrustworthy ... having denied the faith, and perhaps even, 'betrayed' his people."⁵²

THE SHRINE OF "LA RÉPARATION" TO THE SACRED HEART

Figure 49 *The Story of a Shrine* cover

Chiniquy's name continued to be used by Catholic authorities to denote an immoral, proud, rebellious man. During Chiniquy's life the images of wolf in sheep's clothing, Judas, Gavazzi,⁵³ and fallen angel continued to follow him. He was used as a bogeyman,⁵⁴ to warn others who were tempted to contact his followers or to take the first steps of rebellion. In a 1952 sermon Archbishop Paul Émile Léger of Montreal described Chiniquy as the epitome of hubris, a Prometheus who aspired

---

50. Charles Hill, description for National Gallery of "Nature morte Croix de Chiniqui", Ottawa, National Gallery, 1984.

51. Marie de la Roussellière, *The Story of a Shrine* (Pointe-aux-Trembles, L'Echo, 1981), p. 18, 24.

52. Goldberger, p. 15 (my translation).

53. Barrett, "Pastor Chiniquy" (Mundelein, 1958), p. 33.

54. In the St. Damase area according to pastor Guy Brouillet of the Baptist Union.

too high and thus was doomed.[55] This concept of a fatal flaw of pride continued to dominate as the primary clerical explanation of Chiniquy's apostasy.[56]

After his death most mention of the apostate priest came from clerical sources. A few remained concerned with the reasons for transformation, However, in the popular culture it was the results of the transformation that were commented. The *Événement* predicted correctly at his death:

> Chiniquy leaves to history a soiled name, which will be sadly remembered for a very long time. For the future generations as for us, this name will evoke the painful memory of a double apostasy: religious and national.[57]

Those who attended a Montreal play in 1971 were undoubtedly surprised that despite the title "Chiniquy", there was no mention of the 19th century ex-priest.[58] 'Chiniquy' had by then been a term of abuse for so long that it had entered the popular culture. It became a colloquial expression in Quebec to describe any rebel or accursed person.[59] Alphonse Villeneuve's approach and abusive language[60] in reference to the arch-apostate were maintained for 80 years or

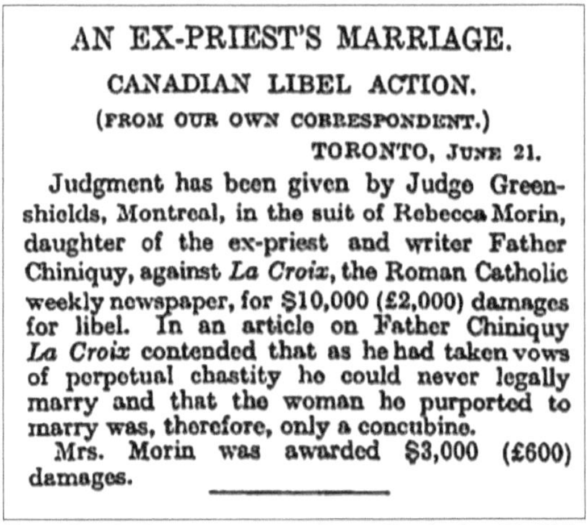

> **AN EX-PRIEST'S MARRIAGE.**
> **CANADIAN LIBEL ACTION.**
> (FROM OUR OWN CORRESPONDENT.)
> TORONTO, JUNE 21.
> Judgment has been given by Judge Greenshields, Montreal, in the suit of Rebecca Morin, daughter of the ex-priest and writer Father Chiniquy, against *La Croix*, the Roman Catholic weekly newspaper, for $10,000 (£2,000) damages for libel. In an article on Father Chiniquy *La Croix* contended that as he had taken vows of perpetual chastity he could never legally marry and that the woman he purported to marry was, therefore, only a concubine.
> Mrs. Morin was awarded $3,000 (£600) damages.

Figure 50 *La Croix* newspaper case (*Times* of London June 22, 1912)

---

55. Recounted by Paul Sylvestre OFM of Montreal in a personal conversation in August 1992.
56. See Maignage, *Le témoignage des apostats* (Paris, 1916).
57. *Événement* (Quebec), 17 January 1899, p. 2 (my translation).
58. *Montreal Star*, 26 December 1970; *Le Devoir*, 13 January 1971.
59. Jeanne Desrochers, *La Presse*, 29 April 1972, p. 8.
60. XYZ, *Honte et Mépris* (Montreal, 1875), 8 p.

10. THE LEGACY OF CHINIQUY

so. Chiniquy's daughter, Rebecca Morin, sued the newspaper *La Croix* for claiming that her mother was a concubine (since no priest could legally marry).[61] This case attained front-page coverage for the ex-priest long after his death.

A former nun reported that she was obliged to teach a sarcastic anti-Chiniquy song at her Joliette school in the 1930s.[62] Jacques Smith remembers villain[63] as the common reference for Chiniquy in the 1950s. Even in 1958 the Lemoyne Historical Society of Longueuil, uncharacteristically, wanted to demolish an old building because: "it does not remind us of any interesting person except for the apostate Chiniqui[sic]; it is a sacrilege existing beside the house which commemorates Sister Marie-Rose."[64]

In his lifetime, Chiniquy delighted in polarizing and focusing opposition on himself. "Chiniquy having frequently mixed contempt with his preaching of the Gospel, it is not surprising that this same contempt would be turned later on French Protestants."[65] Chiniquy's wicked reputation was applied to all French Protestants since he was the only one who was well known in Quebec history.[66] Somehow in Quebec whenever the name Chiniquy was mentioned, polemics resulted, either for or against him.

Somewhat in opposition to this vilification approach, certain Catholics encouraged avoidance or silencing of the Chiniquy name to avert the spread of scandal. "There is nothing to be gained, no religious or moral goal to be attained in evaluating, at this time, the career of Mr

---

61. She won in the case of Morin versus Bégin over an article in *La Croix* of 18 November 1911 (*La Patrie*, 11 and 20 June 1912 and *G*, 11 and 21 June 1912). The English judge was outraged.
62. Mennonite pastor Clyde Shannon in an interview in May 1993.
63. The French is *scélérat* or blackguard. See Resther, p. 3.
64. From a clipping in VDL mss. See the whole file in **SL** c.2/1 06 or **AP** 15-C2-F106.
65. Goldberger, "La main tendue", April 1992, p. 15 (my translation).
66. Similar stereotypes have accompanied followers of Ayatollah Khomeini, David Hubbard - the founder of Scientology, and even Ignatius of Loyola (for Chiniquy and other anti-Catholics).

Chiniquy. Let us close, with his death, the book of his life!"[67] This was an extension of the silencing policy of newspapers back in 1857.[68] The Quebec artist Pellan used the title 'Croix de Chiniqui' for his painting in an April 1942 New York exposition. However, in order to exhibit in Quebec City a month later, the title had to be changed to 'Nature morte à la croix'.[69]

It is not surprising that no street or place name in Quebec preserves the memory of the famous priest. Villains are not usually honoured publicly, even if they formerly made positive contributions. More proactive steps were taken by some persons, probably with some power, who destroyed a Plamondon painting of Chiniquy in St. Anne de Beaupré.[70] Possibly paintings by Krieghoff and Hamel were also intentionally destroyed. Of the four paintings only the one Plamondon portrait can be viewed at the moment; it was carefully hidden by the Chiniquy/Lefebvre family, then it was part of the AP Chiniquy collection until it came into the possession of the National Gallery recently. In the United States, there was an attempt to prevent Chiniquy books from being donated to the Boston Public Library.[71]

Chiniquy accused Catholic clergy of revisionist history to eliminate its opponents.[72] Quebec historians, trained in Catholic schools have tended to use this silencing approach more than vilification. Until the

---

67. *La Patrie* (Montreal), 17 January 1899, p. 8 (my translation).

68. Larocque pastoral letter of 15 February 1857, (*Mandements des évêques de St-Hyacinthe*, vol. 1, p. 300); *Av*, 1 June 1857 and 15 Sept. 1857; Bourget circular to clergy, 18 March 1875 (*MEM*, vol. 7, p. 103).

69. Charles Hill, description for National Gallery of "*Nature morte Croix de Chiniqui*" (Ottawa, National Gallery, 1984).

70. *50 Years*, p. 332; Resther, p. 2, for Catholic confirmation.

71. J. Moore, *Boston Public Library rejects Father Chiniquy's 'Forty Years in the Church of Christ'...* (Boston, c1900), 8 p.

72. *MW*, 18 August 1876, p. 1. This specifically refers to an alteration of the monument at Beauport. Probably the disappearance of the Hamel painting is also related.

10. THE LEGACY OF CHINIQUY

1950s, Quebec historians were silent (Groulx, Sulte, Bibaud)[73] or abusive and brief (Rumilly) about Chiniquy. Thomas Chapais combined the two approaches, criticizing Louis Fréchette for a more positive account of Chiniquy.[74] Later he refused to pronounce the name of the apostate priest since it was so dishonourable.[75] In 1939, the peace-seeking priest Arthur Maheux wrote on 'the Protestant problem' but: "there had been the possibility first of dealing with Chiniquy. I did not do it. ... because this person is well enough known; to say anything new it would be necessary to uncover degrading subjects."[76]

Commenting on books written in Chiniquy's lifetime, Illinois priest Barrett stated that "several have been printed with all references to his name blotted out, as if he had never existed, although, in one case, the original manuscript contains several citations."[77] Trudel probably is the most helpful describing how this silencing attempt related to his own book. He was pressured, denied documents and insulted just because he was studying Chiniquy.[78] Pre-Vatican II historians who mentioned Chiniquy felt obliged to apologize for writing anything about him.[79] The Apostle of Temperance's role in temperance has certainly been downplayed in history so that other priests received equal glory. The tenacious practice of the 'black cross' was attributed to others. Thus silencing helped to convey the impression that no one significant ever left the Roman Catholics for the Protestants.[80]

---

73. Noel, "The Errant Shepherd: Chiniquy and the Making of Ultramontane Quebec" (McMaster U. thesis, 1981), pp. 3, 29.
74. *Cour*, 14 August 1900, p. 2.
75. Chapais, *Discours et conférences* (Quebec City, Garneau, 1913), p. 303.
76. Maheux, "Le problème protestant" (*RSCHEC*, 1939), p. 43 (my translation).
77. Barrett, "Pastor Chiniquy" (Mundelein, 1958), p. 2.
78. Trudel, "Chiniquy, l'homme et sa légende" (Montreal, 2004), p. 131-133.
79. S. Smith, *Pastor Chiniquy* (London, 1908), p. 2; J.M. Lucey, *The Business of Vilification* (Brooklyn, n.d.), p. 1.
80. Albert Close, *Why 854 Priests Left* (London, ²1936), p. i.

THE CONTROVERSIAL CONVERSION OF CHARLES CHINIQUY

The counter forces of silencing and denigrating actually contributed to the creation of a durable Chiniquy myth. Although the Quiet Revolution in Quebec undermined this myth, the silence in sources remains. Most young Quebecers, including historians, have no more than a vague awareness of the name, or have read only Trudel's version.

Chiniquy's rebellion and anti-Catholicism actually seems to have encouraged the spread of ultramontanism in Quebec. Those aspects of traditional Catholicism that Chiniquy attacked most became the elements that were promoted most by clerics like Bishop Bourget:

> The more he insults the divine Eucharist, the more you ... will show zeal to make up for the terrible insults, by your constant respect in the presence of the very holy Sacrament ... The simplest means for you to refute the monstrous errors [about Mary] of this unworthy priest, is to be inspired more and more by devotion, faith and piety towards the most holy Mother of God, by showing yourselves more zealous than ever for her honour, through all the pious observances which you know that she finds pleasing.[81]

This is not to say that these practices were not well established already. However, due to Chiniquy's attacks, the Catholic Church in Quebec increased its teaching on those distinctive Roman Catholic practices.[82] Catholic faithful were henceforth better informed about Mary, the sacraments, the confessional and the Pope. Ceremonies became increasingly elaborate to focus even more on these aspects. Questioning of this process risked the charge of 'Chiniquism'.

Roman Catholic discipline was increased after the rebellion of the isolated priest. Chicago bishops now saw even more reason to centralize ownership of church property and oppose trusteeism. At the same time the church sought out more capable administrators who could deal with all dissidents diplomatically. The recent revision of Canon Law in the

---

81. Bourget pastoral letter, 19 March 1875 (*MEM*, vol. 7, p. 122-123; my translation).

82. It is no coincidence that Chiniquy's nemesis Alexis Mailloux wrote a Catholic manual to counter Protestants: *Le petit arsenal du catholique ou traité élémentaire de controverse* (Mile-End, Quebec, 1875), 422 p.

10. THE LEGACY OF CHINIQUY

Catholic church aims to protect accused clergy more until he is clearly found guilty by an impartial court.

Although Chiniquy received no credit, perhaps in the long-term he demonstrated enough problems with the confessional to be part of the movement that encouraged the Catholic Church to change its methods.[83] The ex-priest's Bible distribution certainly provoked the Catholic Church to increase the availability of Catholic translations. However, those who were too eager for Bible study and exhibited similarities to Chiniquy's positions were suspect.[84]

AMONG EVANGELICALS OUTSIDE QUEBEC

Due to his long life and many international tours, Chiniquy was well known in his lifetime. He profited from the distinction of having been first a celebrity in ultramontane Quebec, and then an ex-priest who took virtually his whole parish with him. Mary Bird of England called him "the most eminent convert from Popery, and the most successful missionary to Papists, since the days of the immortal Luther."[85] Chiniquy's fame has been durable in evangelical Protestant circles. From India to Haiti to Finland his admirers have publicized his feats and his writings.

Chiniquy formulated the standard evangelical Protestant interpretation of Roman Catholicism for years to come. He did this by renewing older anti-Catholic interpretation with fresh facts, critiques and examples. His unique combination of experiences entitled him to speak of the horrors of traditional Catholicism from the inside. Then he proceeded to suggest methods to counteract these. Chiniquy provided knowledge of Catholic theology and sources and maintained a barrage

---

83. The preface of *LQO* (Beauport, 1976), p. iii, exaggerates in suggesting that he was influential in changing Catholic attitudes towards the confessional, Bible distribution, reduction of statues and medals, as well as the questioning of clerical celibacy.

84. Mailloux, *Le petit arsenal* (Mile End, 1885), pp. xv-xvi, uses errors from St. Anne as examples of the result of reading the Bible without the Church as guide.

85. Bird, *A Few Reminiscences* (Leeds, 1878), p. 36.

of specific criticism of many Catholic practices. After he was asked by evangelicals in England to combat the confessional among Anglo-Catholics, he wrote what came to be a standard evangelical text on the 'evils of that practice'.[86]

Chiniquy made French Canada a *cause célèbre*. It came to be seen as a prime example of the Catholic aim for total socio-political control, that employed a modern bloodless form of the Inquisition. This particularly angered Protestants since it occured in a country with an English Protestant majority. Evangelical groups in Quebec who faced harassment immediately identified with the Chiniquy accounts. They then republished the accounts. Missionary John Spreeman had been forced out of the Lac St. Jean area[87] then felt motivated to print Chiniquy's *Mes Combats*.[88] Such 'persecution' was only to be expected when viewed from the Chiniquy perspective.

The ex-priest reinforced a strong religious reason for English Canadian Protestants to oppose separate schools and other Catholic rights. Those who resisted these schools in Manitoba or elsewhere now could claim francophone support. Chiniquy was of marginal political importance overall. However his standing in lay church circles outside Quebec was weighty when he pronounced on such political issues. In response this provoked French Catholic leaders to link language and religion even more closely.

The hundreds of thousands which Chiniquy raised for French mission constituted a major evangelical expenditure. Most of the money was spent on maintaining the private French Protestant schools and on staffing the many small congregations. After Chiniquy's death most donors switched their giving to overseas missions. Only a famous name and great oratory could maintain mission interest for Quebec where

---

86. *The Priest, the Woman and the Confessional*, 1875; see *American Advocate*, Feb. 1899, p. 83 and use by Loraine Boettner in his *Roman Catholicism* (Philadelphia, 1962).

87. Alayn Ouellet, "Le schisme religieux de Girardville" (MA thesis, Université Laval, 1984); Yves Petelle, *L'assemblée de Girardville* (Jonquière, 2008).

88. [John Spreeman] to Joseph Morin, 15 March 1946 (**SL** c.2/110).

10. THE LEGACY OF CHINIQUY

THE BRASS GUNS

Mystery surrounds the two brass guns which flank the flagpole outside the headquarters building at the barracks. No Royal Artillery unit ever served in Van Diemen's Land. British Army units there certainly were, but they were either foot regiments (infantry) or engineers.

The most likely origin of the guns is that they were landed from a ship of the Royal Navy, possibly without the permission of the captain.

It is believed they were cast before 1774, as the method used in forming the bore of the barrel was superseded in 1774. The earlier origin is suggested by the bright golden colour of the barrels, as naval guns were cast from an alloy of 88 per cent copper, 10 per cent tin and 2 per cent zinc. The short barrel length also supports the theory of naval origin because ship-borne guns had to have a shorter barrel to enable reloading in the cramped space of a ship a gun deck while they were 'run-in'. The loss of range caused by the shorter barrel was recovered by using stronger charges. The ring at the breech was another naval feature, to accept the 'breeching rope' to restrain the guns on recoil.

In 1879 these guns were deployed with the Southern Tasmania Volunteer Artillery in support of the civil power. In that year Hobart had a visit from a de-frocked Roman catholic priest who gave a series of fiery addresses under the auspices of the Methodist and Presbyterian parishes of Hobart. The Roman catholics and Anglicans were deeply offended, and Hobart's then large population of Northern Irish Orangemen also took a hand in the proceedings. The Governor, Sir Thomas Weld, was so concerned that he called out the military to assist the police in controlling the near riots which were a daily occurrence. In all, 500 militia troops were called to the Colours. The infantrymen were issued with five rounds of ball shot each and the artillery received three rounds of canister shot for each of the two brass guns. The guns were taken to the city but neither had to be loaded. In Napoleonic terms, the threat of a 'whiff of grapeshot' had a remarkable calming effect and the mobs dispersed at once. The danger was over. Soon after the old cannon were retired.

The magnificent brass guns outside the headquarters building.

Figure 51   Cannons in Hobart, Australia **AP** 15 (3) 001 GUNS

people already attended an apparently Christian Church, and where thousands of dollars had already been spent without any great religious or social transformations. The alternative of overseas missions had better conversion rates and less political and religious complications than Quebec.

With the wane of anti-Catholicism at the end of the 19th century, Chiniquy had no easy task of persuading people that Catholicism was still dangerous. Yet, he single-handedly energized anti-Catholic movements in England and Australia with his lecture tours. While these movements faded after his death, Chiniquy's writings still remained popular enough to perpetuate anti-Catholicism, even in areas with few Catholics.[89]

The courage of the ex-priest drew constant admiration from evangelicals.[90] His exemplary calm in the face of so much violence and persecution, at the frequent risk of death, made inspirational reading for subsequent generations. J.P.A. Muhr, a Swedish admirer, suggested

---

89. Mission historian Andrew Walls reported, in an April 1992 conversation, that he had been raised on Chiniquy material in a section of 1930s Glasgow where no Catholics lived.

90. E.g. Marsault, *De Rome à l'Évangile* (Paris, 1908), p. 124.

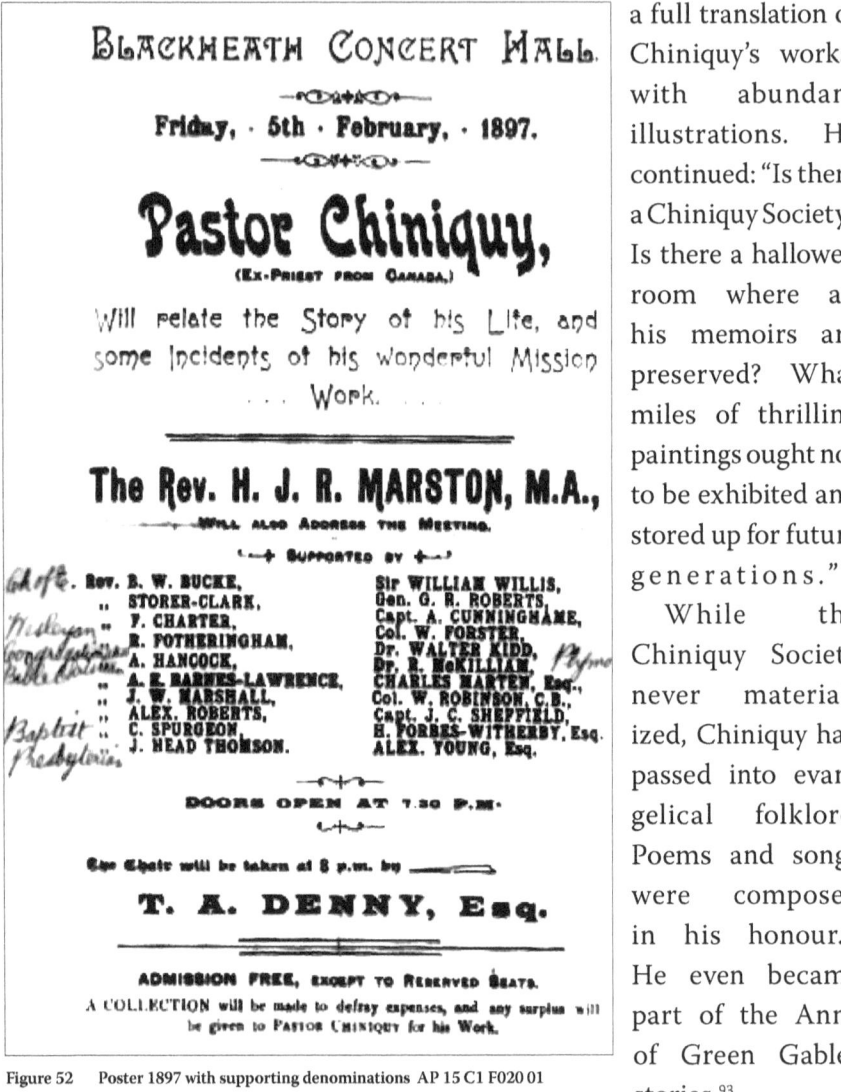

Figure 52   Poster 1897 with supporting denominations AP 15 C1 F020 01

a full translation of Chiniquy's works, with abundant illustrations. He continued: "Is there a Chiniquy Society? Is there a hallowed room where all his memoirs are preserved? What miles of thrilling paintings ought not to be exhibited and stored up for future generations."[91]

While the Chiniquy Society never materialized, Chiniquy had passed into evangelical folklore. Poems and songs were composed in his honour.[92] He even became part of the Anne of Green Gables stories.[93]

---

91. J.P.A. Muhr, from Stockholm, Sweden to Joseph Morin, 28 May 1908 **AP** 15-C2-F110-12. He had Chiniquy books published in Swedish in the 1890s. The Vicar Apostolate in Norway wrote pamphlets to refute Chiniquy in 1893 (**ACAM** 402.102, 893-1).

92. *MW*, 11 May 1875, p. 4; J. Moore, *Rev. Charles Chiniquy* (Boston, c1898), 2 p.

93. Lucy M. Montgomery, *Anne's House of Dreams* (NY, Bantam, 1981), pp. 142-3.

10. THE LEGACY OF CHINIQUY

Italian Protestants in Quebec still trace their origins to Chiniquy's evangelism among young Italian migrants.[94] Many missionaries involved in French work attributed their call to Chiniquy.[95] Ex-priests were often his chief publicists, after they found that he had passed through similar experiences to theirs.[96] An influential movement specializing in aid for ex-priests in Paris, New York, and Canada, was based on Chiniquy's work in Illinois.[97] Chiniquy claimed one notable convert outside Quebec: the secretary of Cardinal Manning in England, who had been sent to convince the ex-priest to return to the fold.[98]

The militancy of Chiniquy's writings and actions eventually provided ammunition for his critics to pass resolutions opposing proselytism. Non-evangelical Protestants had qualms about 'proselytizing' Catholics. While Chiniquy and MacVicar were still alive the opposition was weak. Though Chiniquy had striven powerfully for 40 years to stir up those at peace with Rome to join him in anti-Catholic battle,[99] peacemakers made great headway after his death. The English media and the moderates became more vocal. [100] In an era when home mission was declining, the absence of Chiniquy's motivating speeches accelerated the process to cease 'proselytism'. Today the Chiniquy writings continue to horrify people where the Catholic minority is respected as one of many branches of the Christian faith.

A narrowing of Chiniquy's influence did not prevent significant impact in other circles. H.M. Parsons warned just after Chiniquy's

---

94. *Christian Week* (Winnipeg), 13 December, 1994, p. 4.
95. See e.g. *CC*, 6 (1889), p. 234.
96. E.g. L.H. Lehmann in foreword to W. Anderson's *Father Chiniquy* (NY, 1946), pp. 3-6; Jacques Smith; J.L. Vinet, author of *I was a Priest* (Toronto, 1949), 143 p.
97. *A*, 24 November 1894, p. 5; *CC*, 13 (1896), pp. 4-5.
98. *A*, 24 December 1898, p. 7.
99. *Sydney Witness* (Australia), 19 April 1879, p. 1.
100. Warden to Amaron, 27 January 1899 (**UCM**, French Protestant collection, Amaron papers) expresses the kind of critique that was more rare when Chiniquy was alive.

death that Presbyterians with liberal theology would try to undo Chiniquy's evangelical work.[101] Such a conservative evangelical theology was increasingly sidelined in mainline Protestant churches. If he had still been alive, the ex-priest would probably have joined those who wrote *The Fundamentals*.[102] Today the evangelical denominations in Roman Catholic areas are those that still value Chiniquy. Those who have responded least to modern pressures, and are most sceptical of Vatican II, i.e. the fundamentalists, prize him most. Those crusaders who were most concerned about Catholic dominance, such as Protestant militants T.T. Shields in Ontario, Perry Rockwood in the Maritimes and Chick Publications in the United States, have all distributed Chiniquy material. One of the most belligerent and accessible versions of the Chiniquy story is a Chick comic, *The Great Betrayal*.[103] This condenses the Chiniquy story well and illustrates the incidents. However, it adds horrific malevolent priest images and assurance by the supposed ex-priest Rivera that nothing has changed since Chiniquy.

Evangelical missionaries around the world have often turned to Chiniquy's writings. I have found 28 translated documents in 15 languages, and reports of editions in four other languages.[104] Between them they include all major European languages, besides editions printed in native languages of Russia, India, Formosa, South America and Africa.[105] One wonders why these were needed in India, Russia, Sweden and Formosa, where Catholicism was weak. The lively accounts of the ex-priest's

---

101. Parsons to Amaron, 25 January 1899 (**UCM**, Amaron papers).

102. This was a series of books from 1910 to 1915 by an inter-denominational and international group designed to define evangelical doctrine. The word "fundamentalist" originally described supporters of this evangelical group (*DCA*, p. 463). It is true that Chiniquy supported to some extent Presbyterian pastor Macdonnell who had been accused of heresy. Chiniquy then had to defend himself (*MW*, 27 June 1876, p. 1).

103. *The Great Betrayal* (Chino, California, 1981), 64 p. This is still in print.

104. *40 Years*, p. 415; Trudel, pp. 262-3.

105. On Africa see Étienne Hermillon of La Vérité, Farges, France to *A*, sent on 26 May 1952 (**UCM**, French Protestant Collection).

10. THE LEGACY OF CHINIQUY

courage and evangelical doctrine were deemed worthy of translation. New converts in hostile areas often relate well to Chiniquy.

Chiniquy's major works, *50 Years* and *The Priest, the Woman and the Confessional*, have been continuously in print since the 1880s with well over 50 editions each in English.[106] The *American Advocate* brashly proclaimed Chiniquy's *50 Years* to be "a comprehensive and truthful picture of the designs and aims of the Roman Catholic Church upon the liberty of the people ... a complete library in itself ...the Book of the Century ... not a dull page in the volume."[107]

In his will, Chiniquy stipulated that part of his inheritance should go towards publication of popular editions of his works.[108] His writings, including tracts, have sold well over one million copies.[109] Even when his books are out of print, copies still circulate in church or public libraries, preserving his influence. Reprintings of his books have been the provocation for most Catholic critiques of Chiniquy.[110] By September 1999 there were already six internet sites on the subject of Chiniquy based in Quebec, English Canada, Australia and the United States. In October 2008 thousands of internet sites document Chiniquy. These are mostly split between anti-Catholic and Catholic defence sites but they also include Lincoln topics. Now many of Chiniquy's writings are on-line, and the **AP** collection provides much new material. One use of this new material is to revive old favourite topics like the Lincoln assassination.[111] Hopefully the present non-polemical portrait of his career

---

106. See Doran to Lighthall, 9 July 1894 (**SL** c. 1/3) for the terms of agreement for publishing between the Fleming Revell Co. and Chiniquy in 1894. His *40 Years* did not have the same success but has been reprinted.
107. *American Advocate*, Feb. 1899, p. 82 (SL c.1/23).
108. *A*, 4 February 1899, p. 8.
109. Axel Burman, *Bibeln Segrar* (Stockholm, 1958), back cover.
110. E.g., Barrett; S. Smith; Hull (Bombay, 1912); *Chronology of the Life of Pastor Chiniquy* (Huntingdon, n.d.).
111. C. Wilcox, *The Transformation of the Republic: the Origins of the Religious Hi-jacking of the American Government and the Truth Behind the Assassination of Abraham Lincoln* (Calgary, Veracity Press, 2005).

can defuse some of the continuing anti-Catholicism, which forms such a large part of Chiniquy's legacy.

A DIVERSE LEGACY

Chiniquy left no male heirs to continue his name. It would have been a difficult name to live up to, or to live down. Chiniquy's financial resources were not large, especially after the his Illinois home burned down. He left what resources there were to his daughters. His wife remained inconspicuous in a small apartment with her daughter Rebecca's family.

In the United States, Chiniquy's transformation of St. Anne likely expedited the assimilation of French language and culture despite his efforts to the contrary. Assimilation proved unavoidable as Quebec links were severed by the Catholic excommunication.

Chiniquy inspired artistic endeavours. A miraculous cure and his temperance exploits led to two paintings by Antoine Plamondon in 1837 and 1842,[112] one by Théophile Hamel in 1848[113] and another probably by Krieghoff.[114] Lithographs of Hamel's painting were widely sold and displayed on walls in French Canada. Another noted French Canadian artist, Alfred Pellan, painted "The Cross of Chiniquy".[115] Lesser Protestant artists often pictured Chiniquy's adventures[116] and illustrated one edition of *50 Years*.[117] The French Protestant *Aurore*, naturally, selected Chiniquy for its first published photo in 1895.[118]

---

112. Only the second survived, in the Chiniquy-Lefebvre family's possession. They had refused to put it on public display for fear it too would be destroyed. It was reproduced however as the cover of *LQO* and has recently been acquired by the National Gallery of Canada. See our p. 28.

113. Vézina, *Théophile Hamel*, 1975, pp. 92-96.

114. Dennis Read, *Krieghoff: Images of Canada* (Vancouver, Douglas & McIntyre, 1999), p. 151, 220. This portrait was also reported to have been destroyed.

115. "Nature morte : Croix de Chiniquy", 1941, National Gallery, Ottawa.

116. *Christian Herald* (London, England), 9 April 1897 **AP** C1-F022. See our p. 35 and 37.

117. The 832 p., 43rd ed. by Fleming Revell.

118. *A*, 12 October 1895, p. 6.

10. THE LEGACY OF CHINIQUY

On the anti-Chiniquy side, after reading the Lambert memoirs, Catholic journalist Auclair wrote in a private letter:

> certainly for villainy of every kind, Chiniquy is a genius inspired directly by Hell! He is infamous and will pass into history with the deserved appraisal of having eclipsed the great cloud of villains and bandits who have shone through the centuries but who remain mediocre when compared to Chiniquy.[119]

Chicago Diocese representative James McGovern maintained that there was no point mentioning the Chiniquy affair since virtually all his followers had deserted the apostate, leaving him a miserable outcast.[120] In a more sympathetic analysis Louis Fréchette still wrote:

> one wonders where is the work of this man of such talent, who if he had gone in another direction, could have accomplished so much good. I do not see any results... from my point of view his long life that could have been so productive was wasted - a failure.[121]

Certainly Chiniquy did not single-handedly defeat the Roman Catholic Church nor did he accomplish all of his many goals.[122] Even though Chiniquy was an apostate, in the sense of leaving his initial vows, his positive contributions deserve fair appraisal. Many gave up alcohol and strengthened their Christian faith and attachment to the Catholic Church as a result of his Catholic crusades. Many also came to value Christian faith and church commitment through his Protestant crusades, his books and his personal ministry.

---

119. Auclair letter to Mailloux, 5 August 1858 (**ASQ** 50:9b; my translation).
120. James McGovern to Richard Clarke, 6 May 1887 (**UND** I-2-N).
121. "Mémoires intimes", *Le monde illustré* (Montreal), 11 August 1900, reprinted in *Mémoires intimes* (Montreal, ²1977), p. 111.
122. Article in *A*, 6 September 1900, p. 6, refuting Fréchette's claim. The same writer would surely also refute the extravagance of McLoughlin, *Famous Ex-Priests* (NY, 1968), p. 127, who claims: "if it had not been for the dedication, energy and fearlessness of Charles Chiniquy, the United States would probably now be a Roman Catholic nation."

Figure 53   Tombstone on Mount Royal, Montreal. **AP** 15 C1F026 04

Overall, Chiniquy's legacy is diverse: a well-established but declining French Protestant church; a more traditional and intransigent Roman Catholic church; contrary mythical images and legends, used to further polarize both ultramontanism and Protestantism; a continuing world-wide influence in promoting anti-Catholicism among evangelical Protestants; and best-seller status. Above all Chiniquy left his many writings, many of which have been frequently republished.

Protestants should be more aware of the ex-priest's legacy of uncharitable language, exaggeration and polemics with their effects of polarization. If our portrait of Chiniquy helps diminish his anti-Catholic influence, then perhaps there can be greater appreciation of his many contributions. These include his courage in campaigns to protect the French language in Illinois and the right to free speech in Quebec.

Undoubtedly Chiniquy's French books have enjoyed better sales in Quebec since Vatican II. This is because of both the new freedom to choose literature, and the anti-clerical climate in which many are looking for such heroes. A few of my Catholic acquaintances have interpreted Chiniquy to be an early model advocating democratization of church structures. In a new age with new sources, at the close of the centenary of his death, the legacy of Charles Chiniquy is not yet complete. He deservedly remains a legend in Quebec.

CONCLUSION

The *Presbyterian* of Philadelphia understated the case when it commented, during one conflict, that "Father Chiniquy was certainly born to make a noise in the world."[1] His life-long involvement in controversy was climaxed by his stunning conversion. The standard historical interpretation of Charles Chiniquy has been that of a talented but selfish, rebellious, immoral fraud. Historiography has been clearly divided according to theological position until quite recently. The Catholic view of Chiniquy has predominated in historical circles, because of its better documentation. What this approach lacked, and did not search for, was an understanding of the Protestant appraisal of the ex-priest. Interpretations that research only one side of the theological polarity fail to do justice to all the evidence.

Diverse Protestant sources permit a more sympathetic reading of the situation. Early Protestant newspapers showed a gradual shift towards acceptance of the rebel priest. I found the contribution of Chiniquy family records and reminiscences indispensable to my search. Materials from the St. Anne area provided another invaluable perspective on their famous pastor. Finally, a review of the correspondence of and about Chiniquy has

---

1. *Presbyterian* (Philadelphia), 3 March 1860, p. 2.

permitted the discovery of new themes, and behind-the-scene elements. It has also contributed to a better assessment of the accuracy of statements. New discoveries have been constantly rechecked with the best Catholic sources, in particular, the Mailloux collection.

With such new material, there are new insights into Chiniquy's theology, his Protestant contacts, and his lecture themes. In addition different answers became apparent for old questions about his integrity, the nature of his conversion and his motives. Other researchers in the future can pursue new inquiries relating to Chiniquy using this clarification of the crucial events and the basic sources.

Chiniquy was at the heart of all the key socio-religious debates of mid-19th century French Canada. Through his leadership in combating alcoholism, French Protestant evangelism and anti-clericals, he embodied much of Bishop Bourget's ultramontanism. His focal position helps to explain the anguish, and then anger, that his later apostasy provoked.

It is crucial to understand the little-known French Protestant situation in order to comprehend Chiniquy. The ex-priest eventually suffered the same intense opposition and social isolation as other French Protestants. However, unlike them, his struggle occurred in a public setting. While other French Protestants were voiceless, he protested loudly and around the world.

On the Illinois frontier the picture develops of a troubled Catholic diocese in the context of a highly charged political debate between Democrats and Republicans over slavery and freedom. Chiniquy's rebellion and eventual conversion were at least sparked by an inflexible hierarchy that did not favour French Catholic parishes. In the wake of nation-wide battles over trusteeism, the conflicts over church property in St. Anne and in Chicago drew Protestant-oriented papers into the fray.

Chiniquy and the Chicago French Catholics effectively appropriated the evocative republican themes of opposition to slavery and tyranny for their disputes. This encouraged Protestant and republican media attention in Chicago and Quebec. The American Protestant society which was willing to fight to free black slaves and worried about unscrupulous city political organizations run by Irish Catholics (usually Democrats) was most welcoming

CONCLUSION

to Chiniquy. In Quebec, a weak French Protestant minority trumpeted the famous Chiniquy's critiques of Catholicism.

We also examined the worldwide ideological context of anti-Catholicism. In the context of great polemics by both Catholics and Protestants, conversions of clergy were very important. Chiniquy became a celebrity as a clergy convert with skills as a writer and as a polemical orator. Aside from the Orangemen, his many contacts came primarily from the circles that had adopted the particular evangelical version of anti-Catholicism. Adherents of this stance collaborated with others in political issues such as the countering of separate schools and Catholic political privileges (especially in Quebec). They opposed the intolerance and social control of ultramontanism.

Of great importance was the belief that Catholicism attacked the most precious elements of the evangelical faith: freedom of religion, the free use of the Bible, the need for evangelism and the doctrine of justification by faith alone. In their view, Catholicism was not only wrong but it prevented people from expressing or hearing the truth. It is important to bear in mind that the 19th century anti-Protestant propaganda in Quebec was as rabid as anti-Catholic propaganda elsewhere. Around the British Empire and in America, many both French and English, who were not enthusiastic about Chiniquy's message of evangelism, nevertheless supported his battle for freedom of speech.

Evangelical anti-Catholics, such as Chiniquy, often engaged in political activity. However, they all agreed that only by widespread evangelism of Catholics could society move past a state of constant battle. Chiniquy wrote: "Protestants! Remember the only way not to be slaves here, in your own country, is to convert the French-Canadian people."[2] Although this call was provocative, to say the least, it was not a call for forced or nominal conversion.

All evangelical anti-Catholics intensely hated the Catholic institutions and their effects. Still, they were not racist or violent in action and they did focus on the conversion of individuals. They would also not support

---

2. *MW*, 29 August 1870, p. 1.

speakers who were racist or violent, for any length of time. It was ideas and not origins that they opposed. This meant that any Catholic "seeing the light" was willingly helped.

Chiniquy appears to be a producer of hate literature. This neglects the context of anti-Protestantism, and also the positive evangelical elements in his lectures. Chiniquy had always been polemical. He had always polarized issues, demonizing his enemies. His opponents always condemned his tactics while his supporters (initially the Catholic Church) dismissed criticisms. Thus the first part of my hypothesis was demonstrated: that Chiniquy is best understood as a crusader who embraced evangelical anti-Catholicism in a polemical setting.

The biography of Chapters 1 to 6 and 8 enumerates Chiniquy's various crusades, successes, and provides a lengthy critical account of conflicts. I found many assumptions of previous biographers to be faulty, especially the one which presumed that Chiniquy habitually lied. After these chapters came a necessary exposition, as much as possible in their own words, of the two contending propagandist interpretations. These two versions eventually became so mythical that it was impossible to reconcile them in the hundred years after Chiniquy's death.

Chiniquy's conversion was the focal, and the most controversial, aspect of his life. I gathered elements of studies from many disciplines to consider the question of his conversion. The theological dogma of absolute submission to the Church hierarchy was central to Chiniquy's rebellion. After 50 years of being given the option of 'submit or you become a heretic', Chiniquy could not bring himself to give in, in this one instance. He did want to return to the only Church that he knew. He worked to produce two different submissions. Both times, however, he failed to admit guilt on the key point and thus qualified his submission. Chiniquy's temperamental aversion to total submission was supported by the theology of the evangelical Protestants whom he encountered.

I provided a detailed chronology of the events and interpretations of the prolonged conversion process. We saw that Chiniquy's transformation followed normal social and theological patterns for alleged conversions. Based on contemporary accounts and his subsequent consistency in theology and

CONCLUSION

action, the second part of this book's hypothesis was demonstrated: that what Chiniquy experienced corresponds to a genuine interior conversion following the evangelical model.

Trudel claimed that Chiniquy had no spiritual interest. In fact there is abundant evidence that in his conversion process the St. Anne priest struggled to understand both the theological ramifications and his interior relationship with God. Chiniquy's earliest accounts dwell on God's support of his struggle against the bishop. Gradually the convert mentioned more about the role in his conversion of the Bible, justification by faith, freedom of religion and the need for evangelism.

Chiniquy soon became a theologically consistent evangelical, remaining so until his death. He continued to promote the distinctive doctrines and practices of evangelicals. In turn, despite qualms about his methods, they never questioned Chiniquy's personal piety.

Sociological studies of apostasy and conversion illuminated the pressures that apostates face. These often produce harsh opposition to their former group. Other studies noted the varied motivations for conversion, and the crucial stage of the construction of a conversion story. Chiniquy was not exceptional either in the stages he proceeded through or in his motivations for conversion.

I contend that conflicting myths about Chiniquy have polarized relationships between Catholics and evangelicals in Quebec, ever since the 1850s. Otherwise all of the preceding conclusions and study would be primarily of academic interest. Given Chiniquy's life, the polarization was almost unavoidable before Vatican II and the Quiet Revolution. However, it is tragic and unnecessary that this has continued since. Defusing the propaganda is long overdue. Mainline Protestant Churches and Roman Catholics avoided talking about Chiniquy, hoping he would be forgotten. Perhaps this helped ecumenical dialogue but it tended to convince evangelical Protestants that there was a conspiracy against their Protestant hero.

It would help if Chiniquy's considerable accomplishments and contributions were recognized in Catholic or secular Quebec. It would also help if the harassment that he and other French Protestants years faced over the years were recognized. He should take his rightful place as an important

Quebec leader. New possibilities would open if there were an open evangelical admission that Chiniquy was, at times, an extremist who misjudged situations, exaggerated, used very violent language which provoked reaction, and quite possibly was involved in sexual harassment in his early years.

As for his legacy, Chiniquy's writings present a dilemma. They are fascinating to read and provide understanding of the atmosphere of his era. In addition they constitute an important part of the French Protestant heritage. However the anti-Catholic propaganda that they contain not only distorts. It also does not address the changed situation of a secular Catholic area such as present-day Quebec. The social control and the confessional, which Chiniquy attacked most, no longer exist. There are some new Protestants who had no problems with Catholicism previously; unfortunately however, when introduced to Chiniquy's writings they begin to view evangelicalism and anti-Catholicism as synonymous. Then past injustices and polemics justify present hostility. Perhaps the best solution would be to republish his works with a commentary included.

Few have faced so many serious crises and have survived for 90 years. Few have ever equalled Chiniquy's exceptional transformation in ideology and social context. No wonder some used the apostle Paul or the reformer Luther as bases of comparison. Yet Chiniquy was no pillar of virtue. He was a man with outstanding gifts and also outstanding faults. His future pastor Calvin Amaron stated that Chiniquy was "the chief leader of French Protestants, so far as the work of tearing down, exposing, dealing deadly blows to... Romanism [but] as a builder, as a pastor, [he] cannot be said to be a leader among us."[3]

Chiniquy was an inspirational general who never showed fear. He eschewed pacifism, assuming that all his opponents were plotting wars. He revelled most in the thick of combat. Feeling obliged to change sides in the war, he maintained his militancy and his leadership role.

---

3. *Cheering Words* (Boston, c1886), p. 3. **AP** 10-098

CONCLUSION

Charles Chiniquy is a man who was evaluated by Quebec notables such as Prime Minister Laurier,[4] Lafontaine,[5] Fréchette, Doutre, Joseph Papineau[6] and son Amadée, L. O. David, Thomas Chapais, Bishops Bourget, Baillargeon, Prince and Pinsoneault, as well as countless others whose opinions are not preserved. During his life, Chiniquy attracted almost continuous, front-page coverage in newspapers. At his death he was prominently featured in the *New York Times* and *The Times* of London. Plamondon, Hamel and Krieghoff painted him, while Pellan painted his cross. Vicar General Mailloux spent a lifetime collecting materials about him. He was a very significant Quebec historical personality. "We can not suppress [the remarkable personality of Chiniquy] from our accounts without leaving a gap in the history of French Canadian thought ... So many punches, gibes and stones were hurled at him during his life, that he well deserves the throwing of a few flowers on his grave."[7]

Both as a Catholic and as a Protestant, Chiniquy aimed to serve God by committing all his energy and talents to the most urgent practical and theological battles facing the Church. After playing a determinative role in the establishment of Catholic ultramontanism in Quebec, Chiniquy popularized a normative, evangelical, anti-Catholic approach that has outlived even Quebec ultramontanism. The ex-priest's victories in the fields of free speech and evangelism of Catholics were notable precedents, but they were more limited and short-lived. Only when the opposing myths are defused and religious motives are examined fairly can there be a truly historical appreciation of the personality and contributions of Charles Chiniquy.

---

4. Wilfrid Laurier to J.I. Tarte, 24 January 1899 (**LAC** Laurier vol. 96, 29904-5), in which he supports Catholic editor Tarte's unsympathetic obituary in the *La Patrie* of 17 January, p. 8 (suggesting that Chiniquy be mentioned no more).

5. Louis Lafontaine to Chiniquy, 5 April 1849 (**CBA**, Chiniquy letters file), in which the former praises the priest but refuses to cede on a temperance bill.

6. Letters of L.J. Papineau to his wife (24 June 1850), to the *Institut canadien* in late 1852, and to his son Amadée on 2 February 1859 (**LAC** MG 24 B2 vol.3, pp. 4537, 4786; vol.4, pp. 5825-5827).

7. Eve Circé-Côté, *Papineau* (Montreal, 1924), p. 171.

THE CONTROVERSIAL CONVERSION OF CHARLES CHINIQUY

FATHER CHINIQUY.

Our Ottawa Correspondent telegraphed last night :—
"Father Chiniquy, who occupied a prominent place in the religious life of Canada for many years, died at Montreal to-day. He was formerly a Roman Catholic priest, but in 1858 he seceded from the Church of Rome, taking a congregation, numbering over a thousand, with him. Subsequently he was ordained a minister of the Presbyterian Church of Canada."

Charles Chiniquy was born on July 30, 1809, at Kamouraska, in the Province of Quebec. He was educated for the priesthood, and ordained at Quebec in 1833. As parish priest of Beauport he became much concerned with the effects of drunkenness among his flock, and, joining the Oblate Fathers in 1846, he gave himself up to a crusade against the alcohol habit. A man of remarkable eloquence, his success was such that about 200,000 persons are said to have enrolled themselves as total abstainers at the missions conducted by him throughout Lower Canada. The unexpected strength of the temperance sentiment which is found in many purely French districts, leading in some cases so far as prohibition by municipal ordinance, is largely traceable to "the Father Mathew of Canada," as he has often been called, or "the apostle of temperance," as he was officially entitled by the Bishop of Montreal. In 1851 Father Chiniquy migrated at the head of about 10,000 of his fellow-countrymen to Illinois, where they established a settlement at Kankakee. In 1858, however, the priest left the Church of Rome, and a large number of his flock went with him. Thenceforward he devoted his powers of oratory and his extraordinary energy—he seemed to be always at white heat—to a campaign against the communion in which he had spent the first 50 years of his life. The opposition he now encountered matched his own militant fervour. The French-Canadians, friendly enough to English Protestants, have little patience with deserters from their own ranks ; and Mr. Chiniquy made patience doubly difficult by the injudiciousness and even bitterness of his attacks on the faith of his former friends. Intense admiration gave place to hatred equally intense. With characteristic recklessness Mr. Chiniquy carried his war into the heart of the enemy's country. Serious disorders occurred on his visiting Quebec in 1859, and Mr. Chiniquy was himself wounded. In the following year the ex-priest, now a Presbyterian Minister, spent six months in the United Kingdom, giving 182 addresses in the course of his tour—a record which he surpassed during subsequent visits in 1874 and 1882. In July, 1874, he was stoned after speaking against Roman Catholicism at Antigonish, Nova Scotia. Two years later he was struck down at Halifax, N.S., and the church in which he preached was injured. In 1879 he visited Australia, always on the same errand, and was roughly handled at Horsham, in Victoria. Relating this incident in public he said :— "They have so often attacked me with stones, sticks, daggers, and pistols ; I have been so often struck and bruised, that the idea of dying under their blows has become as my daily thought—I dare say, my daily bread. Besides that, at my age—70 years—death has absolutely lost all its terrors for me." He certainly defied it without a moment's flinching. A few months later Hobart Town, Tasmania, was thrown into an uproar by his activities, and the passion they evoked in the lower class of his opponents ; but the bodyguard of Orangemen who rallied round him here and elsewhere saved him from serious injury. In 1884 he was attacked on board a steamer at Montague, Prince Edward Island, and was rendered unconscious. A somewhat similar incident occurred at Escanaba, Michigan, in 1891 ; and stormy scenes marked his ministrations in many other towns.

Preserving his bodily vigour to a marvellous degree, Mr. Chiniquy was heard of climbing mountains in his native province at the age of 87, and soon after, in the autumn of 1896, he crossed the Atlantic again to obtain support for a Protestant school he was establishing among the French Canadians of L'Islet. After fulfilling many lecturing and preaching engagements in this country under the auspices of the Protestant Alliance, he returned to Canada, but not to rest. Writing in the autumn of 1898 to the leader of a remarkable Protestant movement among the priests of France, this *doyen des évadés* was able to say :—"I have entered my 90th year in perfect health. My hand does not yet tremble. My sight and hearing are as good as at the age of 20, and the last sermon I delivered gave me no more fatigue than the first, which I gave when I was scarcely 20."

Mr. Chiniquy wrote much, generally in a controversial strain, his principal work being "Fifty Years in the Church of Rome." Readers of *The Times* will remember a striking statement published in these columns a few years ago, in which he described the gradual displacement of the French language among his fellow-countrymen and attributed it to the intrinsic superiority of English. He himself made a practice of writing his books in English and then translating them into French.

It may be added that a Montreal newspaper, the *Daily Witness*, was laid under the episcopal ban for reporting Father Chiniquy's sermons in 1876 and has remained under it to this day.

Figure 54   Obituary in the *Times* of London, Jan. 17, 1899, p 10.

APPENDIX 1

Historiography of Chiniquy

WRITINGS BY CHINIQUY

Charles Chiniquy was probably the world's most published French Canadian author[1] as well as the most published anti-Catholic writer[2]. His writings addressed three major themes: temperance, Catholic errors, and his own life.

His first book became a best seller in French Quebec. The *Manual of Temperance*[3] was designed to persuade Roman Catholics of the need for total abstinence from alcohol. The original French version was

---

1. Léon Pouliot, analyzing the book of Trudel (below) (*RHAF*, 9,1 juin 1955), p. 31; Jeanne Desrochers, "Le Diable et le Bon Dieu", *La Presse* (Montreal, 29 avril 1972), p. 9. Although its impossible to prove these hypotheses others who concur are Marcel Trudel, *Chiniquy*, pp. 78, 263, 298 and Jacques Cotnam, "Biography and Memoirs in French" in William Toye, ed., *The Oxford Companion to Canadian Literature* (Toronto, 1983), p. 68.

2. Donald Kinzer, *An Episode in Anti-Catholicism* (Seattle, 1964), p. 31, and G.H. Smith, "A French-Canadian Missionary - Rev. 'Father' Chiniquy" (Toronto, 1907), p. 143.

3. In French, *Manuel ou règlement de la Société de Tempérance* (Quebec, 1844), 158 p. Also 1847, 1849 and in English.

translated into English and reedited twice, but the subject assumed secondary importance for Chiniquy after 1850. After his conversion to Protestantism Chiniquy published numerous writings on controversial religious subjects. These were often responses to personal attacks. They were primarily critiques of Catholic dogma and practice but the danger of Catholic political involvement was also addressed.

Later in his life Chiniquy was persuaded to publish his autobiography in two lengthy volumes. Numerous shorter editions of Chiniquy's life story also appeared, sometimes as autobiographical introductions to his writings. His books of religious controversy and his autobiographies were read by evangelicals, nativists, French anti-clericalists and other anti-Catholics. In addition many secular 19th century readers who were simply looking for a lively story or polemics were attracted by Chiniquy's impassioned writings.

Chiniquy's most voluminous written contribution was his public letters. He was a constant reader of and writer to newspaper editors. Then there was his extensive private correspondence. Chiniquy's autobiographies are remarkable for the percentage of quotations or references to his correspondence that they contain. Many of his other publications are simply reprints of his letters. As someone who revelled in controversy, Chiniquy repeatedly employed letters to the newspapers to keep his causes before the public. He even attacked editors of Protestant papers who dared to limit his access to their columns.[4]

Chiniquy's gift in writing and speaking was not so much in original thought as in popularizing causes and energizing people for them. Although one could analyze Chiniquy's sources[5] and his exact theological views,[6] this book simply situates him in the general Protestant evangelical field. Since my focus is primarily historical I have only briefly

---

4. *MW*, 15 November 1877, p. 2; 16 November 1877, p. 4.

5. Paul Laverdure, "The Religious Invective of Charles Chiniquy" (McGill University thesis, 1984), pp. 40-1, 45, 55-6.

6. Ibid., pp. 86-7 for an incomplete introduction. See the upcoming article by Jason Zuidema on his Presbyterianism.

APPENDIX 1

examined Chiniquy's major doctrinal work, *The Priest, the Woman and the Confessional*,[7] and his many pamphlets on doctrinal subjects.[8]

However, we are left with no shortage of sources. Above all, there are Chiniquy's two extensive autobiographical volumes. *Fifty Years in the Church of Rome* was published first in 1885 while *Forty Years in the Church of Christ* was published posthumously in 1900. Since Chiniquy specified so many dates, names, and quotations from letters his autobiographies are at the centre of our historical debate. The autobiographies were so substantial that they seemed to preclude sympathizers from writing anything besides brief biographies of the ex-priest. These condensed biographies simply repeated stories from Chiniquy's own writings.[9]

The stated intention of these two volumes was not to produce a complete autobiography nor to reveal Chiniquy's inner personality. They were, rather, to provide

> facts which suggest and teach lessons, and stir up greater activity on the part of Protestants to resist the aggressions of Romanism, and to spread the truth among the benighted dupes and slaves of the Pope.[10]

> Besides the most interesting biographical incidents, they contain incisive refutations of the most plausible assumptions and deadly errors of the Romish Church.[11]

---

7. London, W.T. Gibson, 1874, 192 p.; Montreal, F.E. Grafton, 1875, 184 p.

8. See Steve Cyr, "Charles Chiniquy et le confessionnal: la clef du Catholicisme Québécois" (Montreal, Acadia University, 2009); Laverdure, "The Religious Invective", for an analysis of the content of this book and the two autobiographies.

9. See Duclos, *Histoire du protestantisme français au Canada* (Montreal, 1913); Villard, *Up to the Light* (Toronto, 1928); George H. Smith, "A French-Canadian Missionary" (Toronto, 1907), pp. 133-43; Anderson, *Father Chiniquy: His Life and Services* (NY, ²1946); Lindsey, "Evangelization of the French Canadians" (Victoria University, 1956); Fines, ed., *Album du Protestantisme français* (Montreal, 1972), pp. 10-31.

10. *40 Years*, p. 18.

11. *50 Years*, p. 5.

This polemical aim must be taken into account whenever the autobiographies are used.

Most of Chiniquy's correspondence with Montreal and Quebec Roman Catholic dioceses has been catalogued and evaluated. Yet previous studies have paid no attention to his forty years of Protestant correspondence.

WRITING ABOUT CHINIQUY

There has been no end to pamphlets, articles and books about Chiniquy. Every decade from his temperance triumphs in the 1840s to the 2000s has witnessed some theological or historical treatment of Charles Chiniquy. Right up until Vatican II these works were, predictably, either Roman Catholic condemnations or Protestant hagiographies.

There was more variety in the genre within Catholic ranks from Villeneuve's vulgar prophecy about the dying Chiniquy[12] to Marcel Trudel's scholarly history.[13] Catholic interpretation started late. The first was by an English Jesuit, Sydney Smith. In 1908 he produced an admirable compilation of the evidence.[14] He had an apologetic aim: to convince Protestants in England of Chiniquy's basic untrustworthiness. This required that Smith avoid propaganda, treating Chiniquy and Protestantism with equity.

André Saveate provided an account of Chiniquy[15] based on private memoirs related to Bishop Bourget. This follows Chiniquy up to the 1860s but Trudel and other authors missed it. Most earlier Catholic writings were summarized and assessed by Trudel in his 1955 biography of Chiniquy. However, mitigating details were brought forward about

---

12. Villeneuve (under the pseudonym XYZ), *Honte et Mépris du renégat. La vie et la mort de l'apostat Chiniquy* (Montreal, 1875), 8 p.

13. Trudel, *Chiniquy* (Trois Rivières, 1955), 339 p.

14. Sydney Smith, *Pastor Chiniquy: An Examination of His 'Fifty Years in the Church of Rome'* (London, 1908).

15. Saveate, *Mgr Bourget* (Paris, 1916), v. 9 of *Vers l'abime* series, ch. 11.

APPENDIX 1

Chiniquy's Illinois years in two articles by Price.[16] Carrière,[17] a contemporary of Price, contributed additional details to clarify the Oblate Order's involvement with Chiniquy.

Trudel, Price and Carrière shared a common concern for historical accuracy and documentation. They also shared a common reverence for Catholic authorities. This made Chiniquy's rebellion too horrible to treat objectively. While Trudel was a layman in a Catholic university, Price and Carrière were clerics. It would be hard to imagine any Catholic historian who would publicly express positive comments about Chiniquy in pre-Vatican II times. The fact remains that the trio severely undermined the credibility of the Chiniquy autobiographies.

These extensive French publications about Chiniquy during the 1950s[18] effectively ended French Catholic treatment of him. Trudel's volume has now become the standard biography of Chiniquy. Most historians have assumed his conclusions, at least on non-theological matters, to be accurate.

Several Protestant summaries of the Chiniquy autobiography have been published in the 20th century. While these add very little to the facts, their selection of material does show which aspects of Chiniquy continued to interest the authors. There were various Protestant publications prior to Chiniquy's major autobiographies. These either draw from Chiniquy's accounts or from independent sources.[19] In addition,

---

16. Price, "Aux origines d'un schisme - le centenaire d'une réconciliation avortée" (*RHAF*, 1959). Unfortunately the third section which was to be the conclusion was never written.

17. Carrière, "Une mission tragique aux Illinois: Chiniquy et les Oblats" (*RHAF*, 1955), pp. 518-555. A slightly different version with more complete quotations can be found in his *Histoire documentaire de la Congrégation des Missionnaires Oblats* (Ottawa, 1975), Vol. IV, pp. 247-286. I employed the more accessible article.

18. Maybe this followed the appearance of the condensed autobiography, *Mes Combats* in 1946 or else (according to Barrett, "Pastor Chiniquy, Illinois Apostate", Mundelein, 1958, p. 1) because of the republishing of Chiniquy books by the journal *Converted Catholic*.

19. Baird, *The French Canadian Mission in Illinois* [Yonkers, 1860]; Bird, *A Few Reminiscences of the Life and Labours of Pastor Chiniquy* (Leeds, 1878); Butler, *Abbé*

THE CONTROVERSIAL CONVERSION OF CHARLES CHINIQUY

several unpublished accounts of Chiniquy have recently been uncovered that bring novel perspectives of events.[20]

A mixture of French and English, Catholic and Protestant publications appeared until 1946. Since Trudel's book, French articles have been sparse except for Chiniquy's condensed autobiography and one thesis.[21] Recently Hudon[22] and Rannou[23] discussed the 1851 Chiniquy\Roussy debate and Levasseur commented on the Catholic crackdown on the ex-priest.[24]

Protestant accounts of Chiniquy can be found from every decade between 1858 and 2008. Despite this, nothing of any length has ever been written on Chiniquy from a Protestant perspective, except long ago by Marsault[25] and Duclos[26] and more recently in a Swedish book.[27] These tend to be pale imitations of the autobiographies. The absence, prior to our book, of a Protestant biography in English is particularly surprising.

Chiniquy. A Brief Sketch of his Life and Labours (London, c1879) and *The Reformation in Canada* (London, c1877); Kemp, *The Rev. C. Chiniquy, the Presbytery of Chicago* (Montreal, 1863); L. Roussy, *Récit de la discussion entre M. Chiniquy et M. Roussy* (Napierville, 1851); and *Father Chiniquy, the Reformer of the Far West* (London, 1860).

20. J. Provost, "Chiniquy: Sa vie, son temps et son œuvre" (this stops with the year 1851), 1899 republished with his *Maison de Coteau*, ed. Levasseur (Sillery, 2001); I. P. Bruneau, "Le père Chiniquy comme je l'ai connu", c1915 **AP** 15-C2-F102-01 ; Morin, "Apologie. Chiniquy devant l'histoire tel qu'il est et Chiniquy caricature", n.d. **AP** 15-C2-F111; and Violet Lefebvre, various manuscript notes, [1960s] **AP** 15-C2-F103-9.

21. J-P. Ares, "Les campagnes de tempérance de Charles Chiniquy: Un des principaux moteurs du réveil religieux montréalais de 1840" (UQAM thesis, 1990).

22. Christine Hudon, "Le prêtre, le ministre et l'apostat. Les stratégies pastorales face au protestantisme canadien-français au XIXe siècle" (*SCHEC, Études d'histoire religieuse*, 1995), pp. 81-99.

23. Pierre Rannou, *Confrontation entre Chiniquy et Roussy à Sainte-Marie-de-Monnoir le 7 janvier 1851* (Longueuil, 2001), 36 p.

24. Jean Levasseur, "La censure du protestantisme dans le Québec et la Franco-Américanie de la seconde moitié du XIXe siècle: les cas de Joseph Provost et de Charles Chiniquy" (*Francophonies d'Amérique*, 2003).

25. F. Marsault, *De Rome à l'Évangile* (Paris, 1908), 100 pages on Chiniquy besides 3 chapters on other converts.

26. Duclos, *Histoire du protestantisme français au Canada...* (Montreal, 1913).

27. Axel Burman, *Bibeln Segrar* (Stockholm, 1958), 84 p.

APPENDIX 1

Instead there have been lectures, notes, introductions to his autobiographies, and several projects that were never pursued.[28]

Since Vatican II and the Quiet Revolution in Quebec a new wave of historical interest in Chiniquy has surfaced. Perhaps the republication of an abridged version of his two autobiographical volumes in 1976[29] helped spark some of this interest. Since the Trudel account there have been a popularizing chapter by Pierre Berton,[30] the *DCB* article of Roby[31] and the series *Nos Racines*.[32]

Before my writings Paul Laverdure had been the most voluminous analyst of Chiniquy. First his thesis considered Chiniquy as a writer in the genre of anti-Catholic literature.[33] Later Laverdure wrote several articles that attempted to explain Chiniquy's conversion.[34] In his view Chiniquy was primarily a virulent anti-Catholic with paranoid tendencies, rather than Trudel's immoral apostate. His research has advanced understanding of Chiniquy and stimulated interest. However, he follows Trudel on most points. These modern biographers lack any positive appreciation for Chiniquy.

---

28. Jacques Beaudon and Joseph Boucher of the United Church apparently had intentions to work on biographies to counter Trudel. More recently Jacques Smith, Nelson Thomson and Wesley Peach, representing three other denominations mentioned the need and their interest in writing on the subject. For each of them the time or materials were lacking.

29. *L'homme qui osa* (Beauport, 1976), 508 p. (never out of print) is a revised version of the 1946 *Mes Combats* (edited by John Spreeman with the advice of Joseph Morin). Violet Lefebvre, another Chiniquy family member, produced the 1976 version to defend his name.

30. Berton, "Zeal of Charles Chiniquy" (Toronto, 1976), pp. 142-160.

31. Roby, "Charles Chiniquy", *Dictionary of Canadian Biography* (Toronto, 1990), v. 12, pp. 205-209. Also online.

32. Luc Lacoursière ed., "Chiniquy apôtre, Chiniquy apostat", *Nos racines : l'histoire vivante des Québécois* (St. Laurent, 1982), ch. 116, pp. 2319-20.

33. Laverdure, "The Religious Invective", 107 p.

34. The various articles are summed up in "Charles Chiniquy: The Making of an anti-Catholic crusader" (*CCHA Hist. Studies*, 1987), pp. 39-56.

THE CONTROVERSIAL CONVERSION OF CHARLES CHINIQUY

Since 1968, several articles have appeared that contribute substantial new insights. The scene of Chiniquy's ministry in Illinois is the focus of several researchers: Houde,[35] George,[36] Kantowicz,[37] Meier,[38] Needham[39] and Brettell.[40]

The most revisionist historical production on Chiniquy has been that of Jan Noel, a specialist in the history of the temperance movement in Canada. She found Chiniquy to be the key figure in popularizing nationalist ultramontanism in Quebec.[41] After Chiniquy became very popular as a nationalist reformer and temperance speaker, even among the anti-clericals, he was able to introduce ultramontane themes effectively. Although Noel never contradicted Trudel, her work brings an atypical positive slant to the history of Chiniquy.

In the same vein, though independently, Jean Patrice Ares[42] participated in UQAM research on Catholic revival in Montreal in the 1840s. He examined the influence of Chiniquy's temperance campaigns without delving into biographical details. Most strikingly, he skimmed over Chiniquy's apostasy, although surely this must have affected his longterm influence. Since Ares sidestepped the apostasy and the sexual allegations of Trudel, one is left with an entirely favourable impression of Chiniquy.

---

35. Houde and Klasey, "Chiniquy's Revolt" (Chicago, 1968), pp. 101-116.
36. George, "The Lincoln Writings of Chiniquy" (*Journal of Illinois State Historical Society*, 1976), pp. 17-34.
37. Kantowicz, "A Fragment of French Canada" (*Journal of Illinois State Historical Society*, 1982), pp. 263-76.
38. Meier, ed., *The Saga of St. Anne* (St. Anne, 1976).
39. Needham, "The Stormy Petrel" (*Christian Heritage*, 1976).
40. Brettell, "From Catholics to Presbyterians: French-Canadian Immigrants in Central Illinois" (*Journal of Presbyterian History*, 1985), pp. 285-298.
41. Noel, "Dry Patriotism: The Chiniquy Crusade" (*CHR*, 1990), pp. 189-207 and *Canada Dry: Temperance Crusades before Confederation* (Toronto, 1994), ch. 11-12.
42. Ares, "Les campagnes de tempérance" (UQAM thesis, 1990), 347 p. and IN Rousseau and Rimiggi, *Atlas historique des pratiques religieuses: le Sud-Ouest du Quéebec au XIXe siècle* (Ottawa, 1998), pp. 71-72.

APPENDIX 1

Ares advanced Chiniquy research through his evaluation of the *Manuel de tempérance* (first edition) and his geographical mapping of the Chiniquy temperance campaigns between 1846 and 1851. He drew both geographical and statistical conclusions. Bishop Bourget and the Oblates provided the base for temperance. Then Chiniquy brought the necessary charisma, spatial organization through his tours, momentum through his tireless schedule, and structure through his *Manuel*. Without Chiniquy's charisma and creativity the temperance campaign would have been weak.

Ares and Noel thus provide strong evidence for the centrality of Chiniquy at this pivotal point of 19th century Quebec history. In the 21st century popular historian Jacques Lacoursière[43] and recent plays and television documentaries have continued the trend of giving Chiniquy more balanced coverage. The novelist and intellectual Victor Levy Beaulieu even chose Chiniquy along with Papineau as the two rebel prophets in Quebec.[44] Unfortunately the two recent Trudel publications provide no new research. They provide no corrections except for dropping the anti-Protestant elements. They now add scepticism of all religious elements. Slipping as easily into the modern sceptical worldview as Trudel's original book did into the ultramontanist worldview of the 1950s, they offer new insight into Trudel and the 1950s but not into Chiniquy.

Meanwhile, on the Internet, the countless sites are very polarized maintaining the traditional conflict. On the one hand, the Catholic[45] and Lincoln[46] sites discount anything that the propagandist Chiniquy

---

43. Romain Dubé, Jacques Lacoursière and André Ségal, "La mémoire amnésique: le cas de Charles Chiniquy" IN *Le patrimoine des minorités religieuses du Québec* (Lévis, 2006), pp. 3-11.

44. Victor-Lévy Beaulieu, *La grande tribu, c'est la faute à Papineau* (Notre-Dame des Neiges, 2008), 874 p. This still follows the Trudel line but with awe for Chiniquy's daring.

45. Eg. http://www.catholicity.elcore.net/PastorChiniquyTheSeducer.html and http://www.geocities.com/chiniquy

46. Eg. http://home.att.net/~rjnorton/Lincoln74.html

writes. On the other hand there are fundamentalist sites[47] which repeat all Chiniquy's stories as if they were contemporary accounts. With the AP collection now available there is abundant material for new research.

THIS BOOK'S HISTORICAL APPROACH

Objective and primary sources

This book aims to discern the truth between the two propagandas and to explore the Protestant sources more fully. The two propagandas each presumed that the other side was lying. I presume that the two sides generally told the truth as they saw it. An interpretation that explains both sides is sought. Of course in each polarity there is considerable exaggeration, much misunderstanding, plentiful gossip and repetition of legends. There are also divergent interpretations of the Christian faith. However I found no evidence of pure invention. This conclusion certainly diverges from Chiniquy's own version, which found widespread Catholic conspiracy. It also diverges from Trudel's version which considered Chiniquy an habitual liar[48] (followed by Roby in *DCB*, Berton, Keating and al). For more details that counter Trudel's version see Chapters 1 to 4 of this book.

In brief, Trudel's apparently comprehensive history neglected the Protestant information. No Protestant historian gathered and documented the sources about French Canadian Protestantism's leading figure. On the other hand, Catholic archives, which are well organized and accessible, often possess Chiniquy files.[49] Much Chiniquy and French Protestant material has been conserved **only** in Catholic archives.

---

47. Eg. http://www.jesus-is-savior.com/ or http://www.chick.com

48. Trudel, *Chiniquy* (Trois Rivières, 1955), p. 300. In his new version (Montreal, 2004) without reading any new information, his anticlerical stance makes him suspect that Chiniquy's accounts of Catholic scandals may be the only trustworthy parts (p. 150).

49. Of most note are the voluminous collection in the archives of the Séminaire de Québec (ASQ), as well as less imposing collections in the archives of the Archdiocese of Quebec (AAQ) and the Archdiocese of Montreal (ACAM). The Chiniquy file of the Centre d'histoire de St. Hyacinthe should also be consulted for its Desaulniers papers.

APPENDIX 1

Oral history constituted a second vital source. Two elderly people who are now dead aided me enormously: Jacques Smith and descendant Samuel Lefebvre.[50] Both knew Chiniquy's daughter, Rebecca, and his son-in-law Joseph Morin, who preserved much of the family history. Smith, as a former monk in the Capuchin Catholic religious order, shared some of the same experiences of social isolation and Catholic antagonism as Chiniquy. As a critical admirer of Chiniquy, Smith was also able to indicate numerous traces of the French Protestant hero's influence in the 20th century. Others shared old and recent stories about how the Chiniquy myth lived on in Catholic and Protestant circles long after his death. Lois Meier and Minnie Bedard brought an Illinois Protestant perspective about Chiniquy's value to their community.

I compiled a list of Chiniquy's available correspondence[51] as an important part of this study. There is little personal correspondence from the 1850s (after numerous fires) so I drew from newspapers of the period. The Protestant and secular press complete the context and show how prominent Chiniquy was. Most importantly, they reported contemporary interpretations of Chiniquy, before and after his excommunication.

Protestant newpapers in Quebec were of most interest since they regularly commented on and interpreted Chiniquy. The muffling of Catholic presses after 1858, except for 'approved' stories, makes them a less interesting source, although I consulted them for critical periods. The *Avenir* and other anti-clerical sources were also helpful ressources.

Chiniquy's personal archives lay hidden for a century. Part was finally donated to the McGill University Rare Book Department in 1992 as the Lefebvre collection.[52] The other much larger part of this priceless collection,

---

50. See Desrochers, "Le Diable et le Bon Dieu" (*La Presse*, Apr. 29, 1972), pp. 8-11. Lefebvre died in April 1994. Smith died in 2001.

51. See appendix 2 for a complete list.

52. Henceforth **SL**. Its value, for the most part lies in the information it provides on the last decade of Chiniquy's life. It includes an excellent collection of Chiniquy brochures and clippings and an invaluable summary of Chiniquy's Illinois legal battles along with several unpublished short biographies. Most of this is now available in **AP 15-01**.

at least the elements that survived a flood in the Lefebvre basement, were recuperated in 1998 and form the Allan Pequegnat "Chiniquy collection". The AP collection has been further expanded to include scans of the McGill documents and many other related books, pamphlets, photos and newspapers. I have examined most parts thoroughly and skimmed through it all. This still leaves much room for further study. For example one could now analyze Chiniquy's own editing of his drafts of *40 Years*. Other unexamined material remains in Presbyterian archives in Chicago and Philadelphia.

Important secondary material was found in the United Church Conference Archives in Montreal, at the Canadian Baptist Archives at McMaster University, McGill University Rare Books, the Chiniquy collection at the Kankakee Historical Society, certain documents of the University of Notre Dame Archives and Lois Meier's private collection. Most of these include material favourable to Chiniquy.

Methodology

An understanding of Chiniquy must include his two almost separate lives. Of particular interest is the 1850 to 1862 span. In this period his transformation from ardent ultramontanist to fervent anti-Catholic became complete. At the centre of this transformation emerged the whole question of conversion. What is it according to the various theologies? What evidence is there?

First a reliable, more objective account of key biographical details was essential. Then the complex matter of conversion was addressed using a separate treatment of first the religious or interior conversion and then the social or exterior conversion. No restricted meaning of conversion has been adopted. I did not wish to convey either, at one extreme, simply an unverifiable internal crisis experience, or, at the other extreme, simply an observable change in actions. The term "conversion" has been used here without value judgement. It is as equally applicable to Catholicism as to Buddhism or secularism. Chiniquy was evaluated in this book both from a faith-centred or religious approach and also from a sociological approach. The two provide complimentary understandings.

APPENDIX 1

The basic materials for this study have been the corpus of available accounts of Chiniquy's "conversion" (Protestant) or "apostasy" (Catholic), whatever their source. These were weighted both for their chronological proximity to the events, and also for their presuppositions and biases. Interpretations of the conversion developed over time. The earliest accounts were crucial for establishing the facts and interpretations at the time. Later accounts were invaluable for tracing development of interpretation and introduction of mythical elements.

Chiniquy's own early and late conversion versions were evaluated with particular attention to how he varied these according to the audience, and how they developed over time. Because the other Protestant accounts follow Chiniquy's autobiographies[53] very closely they were the least useful, except as a means of tracing the development of themes and the selection of material. Fortunately, a significant body of independent Protestant accounts of the change is now available.[54]

Trudel summarized the traditional Catholic accounts and manuscripts except Savaete. These provide a well-documented check on the Protestant accounts. I did examine the limited evidence of a few Roman Catholics who supported Chiniquy despite official decrees. Finally, there are modern accounts that aspire to objectivity.[55] In each of these categories the alleged motives, whether theological, social, political, psychological or moral, were assessed: which events were highlighted or ignored, and what images were used?

Additional insights about conversion were sought using a few concepts from sociology, anthropology, psychoanalysis, psychology, theories of personality type, and theology. This secondary literature on conversion helped show that Chiniquy's was not such a unique case.

---

53. For example, Provost, Duclos, Villard and Boucher. See the first section of this appendix.
54. Early newspapers, accounts of various citizens of Illinois, and the manuscript of Bruneau.
55. For example, Neeser, Laverdure and Roby (*DCB*).

Trudel did not provide a Protestant context for Chiniquy. In 1955 this young historian was apparently baffled that responsible Protestants would welcome such an unsavoury character.[56] This lack of a Protestant context required various methods to fill out. Tracing Chiniquy's friends and acquaintances was crucial. Where did he lecture? Who published his works? What were the views and the influence of his close friends? An analysis of Chiniquy's lecture topics over many years, and their relationship with his publications was also revealing. The Protestant context only became clear after perusing many French Protestant and English Protestant newspapers over a long period of time.

An important part of the Protestant context was strong anti-Catholicism among evangelicals world-wide. We described the key figures, the types of literature and the social-economic plight of "apostates". The little-studied phenomenon of ex-priests is elucidated. Then there is a discussion of the reasons why Chiniquy was invited to England and Australia.

Any desire to understand French Protestantism and its historiography revolves around the subject of Chiniquy. It is evident that Chiniquy held a central role among French Protestants both in his day and also long after. His influence continued through the myths of both Protestants and Catholics. Examination of these illuminates Chiniquy's legacy as well as his historiography.

In summary, the methodology of this study has been diverse. It stressed content-analysis of conversion accounts. Patterns of ideology, behaviour and propaganda appeared from the issues that Chiniquy and his commentators raised. Finally the clustering of ideological and social themes permitted the start of a demystification of the enigma of Charles Chiniquy.

---

56. Trudel, 1955, pp. 302-3, 306. Even the mature Trudel (Montreal, 2004) remains totally sceptical.

APPENDIX 2

Correspondence of Chiniquy

(a partial list of available correspondence by, to, and about Chiniquy)

f = (when after the number) letter available only in French (at least this copy).
Bold in the middle of a line = the publication or archives where the original or a copy is accessible, according to the abbreviations below.
*= related letter but not to or from CC (mostly in French)

A=*Aurore*   **AP**=Allan Pequegnat Chiniquy Archives   **AS**=Archives of St. Anne-de la Pocatière   **Av**=*Avenir*   **B**=Bourget usually or someone mentioned just before   **C**=Carrière   **Ca**=*Canadien*   **CBA**=Canadian Baptist Archives   **CC**=Chiniquy   **Conv C**=Converted Catholic   **CT**=*Chicago Tribune*   **Ch**=Mémoires Chapais   **Co**=*Courier du Canada*   **Dio**=Diocese   **É**=*Église de Rome*   **F**=*50 Years*   **FC**=*Father Chiniquy the RFW*   **FCA**=*From Chicago to Australia*   **G**=Duclos   **H**=Houde   **J or Jl**=*Journal d'Illinois*   **K**=Kelly   **KH**=Kankakee Historical Society   **L**=LQO   **M**=AAM   **Mac**= MacVicar letters   **MC**=*Mes Combats*   **MR**=*Mélanges religieux*   Mtl=Montreal   **N**=UND   **NAC**=National Archives, Ottawa   **O**=OMI provincial archives   **P**=Price   **PCL**=Presbyterian College Library   **Pr**=Presbyterian   **Presby**=*Presbyterian* newspaper   **Q**=AAQ   **QC**=Quebec City   **R**=McGill Rare Books   **S**=Smith   **SC**=*SC*   **SL**=SL papers   **SQ**=ASQ   **T**=Trudel   **Temp**= temperance   **U**=UCT   **V**=Persécutions   **W**=*MW*   **Y**=*40 Years*

* (Leprohon (Nicolet) to QC Diocese about CC and Dionne .... **AAQ** .... 13 Oct **1825**
* (Crevier (Sandwich) to QC Dio wants CC as teacher .... **AAQ** .... 17 Nov **1825**)
1f. CC (Nicolet) to Dio .... **AAQ** .... 9 Nov **1828**
2f. Dio to CC: initial vows .... **AAQ** .... 27 Sept **1829**
3f. Dio to CC: ordained to minor orders (Nicolet) .... **AAQ** .... 4 May **1831**
4f. Dio to CC: ordained deacon (Nicolet) .... **AAQ** .... 13 May **1832**
5f. Quebec Dio to CC: ordained priest .... **AAQ** .... 21 Sept **1833**
6. Dio to CC: appointed curate of St. Charles, River Boyer .... **F mention** .... 24 Sept **1833**
7. Antoine Bedard to CC at St. Gervais: please replace him in Charlesbourg .... **F** .... 25 May **1834**
* (Bishop Provencher to Bishop Signay: CC is selfish .... **AAQ 1s**
* (Leprohon to S. asking for CC as assistant director .... **Douville p.248** .... **1835**)
8f. CC to Dio: 17 abjurations .... **AAQ** **1835-7**

THE CONTROVERSIAL CONVERSION OF CHARLES CHINIQUY

9. CC and 3 curates to Signay: resignation from the 3 Mass Society .... F mention .... Feb **1836**
10. Charles Cazeault (Dio) to CC: summons by the bishop .... F .... Feb 1836
11. CC and others to all the priests: the 3 Mass Society .... F mention .... Feb 1836
* (Signay to Bishop Lartigue: 3 Mass Society .... AAQ Reg 17 .... 8 Feb 1836)
12f. CC to Provencher: apology (mention in **letter of Aug 23**) .... ca 21 Aug 1836
13f. Provencher to CC .... AAQ .... 23 Aug 1836
* (Provencher to S: describes the preceding letter .... AAQ & T 29 .... 26 Aug 1836)
* (Provencher to Dio: wants CC as missionary .... AAQ:1:80 .... 23 Nov 1836)
14f. CC and 5 priests to *Canadien*: thanks .... Ca .... 6 Feb **1837**
15. Chambers (a thief from prison) to CC .... F extract .... Spring 1837
16f. Signay to CC: sending him to Beauport .... AAQ .... 21 Sept **1838**
17f. CC (Beauport) to Quebec Diocese: administration .... AAQ .... 8 Oct 1838
18f. CC to Dio: about a suicide .... AAQ .... 28 Oct 1838
19. CC (Beauport) to Father Mathew of Ireland: .... F mention
20. Father Mathew to CC .... F extract
21. CC to 4 neighbouring priests: come and see temperance fruits .... F mention .... Feb **1839**
22. Father Pierre Roy (Charlesbourg) to CC: mocking response .... F .... 5 Mar 1839
* (*Le Canadien*, p. I. 1st media publicity for CC .... Ca .... 8 May **1840**)
* (also 27 May & 12 Aug, & in 1841 the 7 Apr, 6 and 10 Sept)
23f. CC to superior of the Seminary .... SQ Letters, S,9 .... 27 Jan **1841**
24f. Jérôme Demers to CC: critique .... SQ
25f. CC to Bishop Bourget: experiences in Beauport .... extract *MR*, II, 342 .... 19 Nov 1841
26f. CC & 100 priests to Signay: we want Bibles .... extract MC 1841
27f. Bishop Signay to CC: prefers sobriety of Mailloux to abstinence .... AAQ .... 5 Dec 1841
28f. CC to Bourget: Dr. Douglas will come .... M .... mid Dec 1841
29f. CC to Bourget: retreat for Hurons of Lorette (17 pp) .... M .... 13 Dec 1841
30f. CC to Bourget: .... 18 pp ....M .... 15 Dec 1841
31f. CC to *Canadien*: temperance .... Ca .... 18 Mar **1842**
32f. Tribute to CC: also portrait & response of CC .... LAC, *MR* 1er Apr ....29 Mar 1842
33f. Grand Vicar Turgeon to CC: come to QC .... L .... Sept 1842
* (Father Varin of Kamouraska to Signay: opposed to CC .... L extract .... ca 15 Sept 1842)
34f. CC (Beauport) to Cazeault: learning of the move .... T extract AAQ:Beauport:I,37 ....24 Sept 1842
35. Signay to CC: sent to Kamouraska .... AAQ, F .... 28 Sept 1842
36f. CC (Kamouraska) to Dio: his reception by Varin .... AAQ .... 2 Oct 1842
37f. CC to Dio (K) .... AAQ .... 5 Oct 1842
38. Mailloux and priests around Kamouraska to CC: don't want temperance here .... F mention .... ca Oct 1842
39f. Parish of Beauport to CC: regret at his departure .... Ca .... 21 Oct 1842
40f. CC to Dio: better relations with Varin .... AAQ .... 23 Oct 1842
41f. CC to Dio: sickness, Jubilee success .... AAQ .... 24 Oct 1842
42f. CC to Dio: alcohol, a trial .... AAQ .... 25 Nov 1842
43f. Signay to CC: trustees lost the trial but don't appeal .... AAQ .... Dec 1842
44f. CC to Dio: religious state of the parish is positive .... AAQ .... 24 Jan **1843**
45f. Signay to CC .... AAQ Reg .... 26 Jan 1843
* (St. A College to Dio: CC working out well .... AAQ .... 1 Feb 1843)
* (Quertier to Dio: visited an exhausted CC .... Ch .... Mar 1843)
46f. CC to Turgeon: doesn't want to become priest in charge .... AAQ .... 4 Apr 1843
47f. Signay to CC: don't work too hard .... AAQ Reg 20:319 ....14 Apr 1843
48f. CC to Dio : accepts charge of Kamouraska, his sickness .... AAQ .... 21 Apr 1843
49f. Signay to CC: take 2 weeks holiday .... AAQ Reg .... 24 Apr 1843
50f. CC to Father Mathew: .... *MR* July 21 ......ca Apr- May 1843
51. Mathew to CC: response .... 2 June 1843
52f. CC to Dio: hesitant to become priest in charge .... AAQ .... 4 Aug 1843
53f. CC to Dio: vs moderate temperance of Quertier .... AAQ .... 18 Sept 1843
54f. CC to Dio: vigils and Lent .... AAQ .... 2 Oct 1843
55f. JB Meilleur to CC: Education bill .... *Cahiers des Dix* 1973 .14 Oct 1843
56f. CC to Abbé Benjamin Desrochers .... SQ .... 28 Oct 1843
57f. CC to Dio: temperance in Madawaska NB .... AAQ .... 9 July **1844**
58f. CC to Dio: too many requests for temp retreats .... AAQ .... 29 July 1844
59f. CC to Dio: critique of miserly Catholics in Quebec City .... AAQ .... 11 Sept 1844
60f. CC to Dio: conflict in St. Anne College .... AAQ .... 20 Dec 1844
* (Someone (St. Anne) to Dio: false accusations by Dionne .... AAQ .... Jan, Mar **1845**)
* (Mailloux to Turgeon: Dionne is persecuting CC .... AAQ .... 30 Jan 1845)
61f. CC to Dio: favourable to the division of the parish .... AAQ .... 9 Feb 1845
* (M to Turgeon: trouble with Dionne. CC in court .... AAQ .... 14 Mar 1845)
62f. CC to *MR* 6 **March**: any suggestions for the *Manuel* 2nd edition .... 28 Feb **1846**
63f. Signay to CC: he had examined the *Manuel* .... AAQ Reg 21:411 ....13 Mar 1846
64f. Signay to CC: CC lost his voice .... AAQ .... 6-17 Apr 1846
65. Poor man (QC) to CC: profits of the *Manuel* could support his family .... Y extract 1846
66. Father Baillargeon QC to CC: praise of *Manuel* .... Y extract 1846
67f. CC to Father Guigues .... the original in Rome, O .... 13 Aug 1846
68f. Guigues to CC .... C .... 22 Aug 1846
69f. CC to Guigues .... O .... 25 Aug 1846
70f. CC to Guigues .... C .... 28 Aug 1846
71f. CC to Bourget .... M Chiniquy file, folder 1 also C ....28 Aug 1846
72f. Kamouraska parish to CC: praise .... T extract....*MR* 20 Oct, ... 27 Sept 1846

APPENDIX 2

73f. CC to the parish: response .... *MR* 20 Oct .... 27 Sept 1846
* (Someone (Trois Rivières) to QC Dio .... AAQ .... 6 Oct 1846
74f. CC to QC Dio(Cazeau): long résumé of Kamouraska & Oblates .... AAQ (C) .... 9 Dec 1846
75f. CC to J. C. Chapais .... AAQ 52: 112 1846
76f. CC to J. C. Chapais .... AAQ 52: 19 1847
77f. B (Rome) to Paré: praise for CC and his *Manuel* .... M .... 16 Feb 1847
78f. CC to Guigues: toward the end of the year .... C .... ca Oct 1847
79f. CC to Guigues .... C .... 27 Oct 1847
80. T.F. Allard (Oblate superior): recommendation of CC .... F .... 1 Nov 1847
81f. G to CC: another year of noviciate is required .... C .... ca Nov 1847
82f. CC to Cazeau .... AS (C) .... 14 Nov 1847
83f. CC to QC Dio: still likes the solitude .... AAQ .... 24 Nov 1847
84f. CC to Bourget: asks to join Dio of Mtl .... M, C .... 24 Nov 1847
85f. CC to Guigues: suggestion of reforms for Oblates .... OMI Rome, C .... 27 Nov 1847
* (Allard to Bourget: about CC .... M .... 27 Nov 1847
86f. Bourget to CC: needs recommendation of Dio QC .... C .... 27 Nov 1847
87f. CC to QC Dio(Cazeau): explains departure from Oblates .... AAQ, C .... 6 Dec 1847
88f. CC to Guigues: explains departure .... O, C .... 7 Dec 1847
89f. CC to QC Dio: explains departure from Oblates .... AAQ but missing .... 27 Dec 1847
90f. CC to E. L. Boucher de Montizambert: translation .... private archives 1847
91. CC to Nielson .... AAQ 1847
92f. CC to QC Dio: asks for transfer .... C 1848
93f. CC to Sir Hector Langevin .... AAQ 1848
* (QC Dio to Guigues .... C .... ca Feb **1848**)
94f. CC to QC Dio: asks to return to Quebec Dio .... AS .... 7 Feb 1848
*Someone to QC Dio: about CC .... AAQ .... 7 Feb 1848
95f. QC Dio to CC: response (presumed existence but not found in AAQ) .... ca Feb 1848
* (Bourget to Tellemont (Bytown): Guigues' bishopric blocked .... M .... 4 Mar 1848)
* (Bourget to Brassard: I understand the anger .... M .... 29 Mar 1848)
* (Bourget to Brassard: you & CC have gone to far .... M .... 6 Apr 1848)
* (Bourget to Champeaux: permits retreat for CC .... M .... 10 Apr 1848)
* (Bourget to Bishop of Marseilles: critical of CC vs. Oblates .... M .... 10 Apr 1848)
* (Brassard to Bourget: false accusations by Barthe vs. CC .... AAQ extract .... 11 Apr 1848)
* (Brassard to Bourget: CC exonerated about Kamouraska .... AAQ extract .... 28 May 1848)
96f. CC to Bourget .... M .... 3 Sept 1848
* (Laity of Mtl to Bourget: proposed construction of statue of CC .... M .... 5 Oct 1848
* (Bourget to Labelle: preaching of CC is positive in general .... M .... 18 Oct 1848
97f. Bourget to CC: 12 criticisms of CC .... M, AAQ .... 26 Oct 1848
98f. CC to QC Dio: success of temperance retreats .... AAQ .... 6 Nov 1848
99f. ?? to CC: temperance .... LAC .... 1848 or 49
100f. CC to Sulpicians: temperance .... LAC 1849
101f. Dedication to Bishop Bourget .... *Manuel de temperance* 1849
102f. CC to the youth of Canada .... *Manuel de tempérance* 1849
103f. Bourget to CC: about an anonymous letter .... M .... 6 Feb 1849
104f. Bourget to CC: critique of his methods .... M .... 3 Mar 1849
105f. CC to Col de Salaberry: support for temperance .... LAC .... 3 Apr 1849
106f. CC to Dio: success of temperance .... AAQ .... 3 Apr 1849
107f. Louis Hippolyte Lafontaine to CC: praise but no agreement .... CBA .... 5 Apr 1849
108f. P. Blanchet to CC: Invitation to the *Institut Canadien* .... U .... 6 Apr 1849
109f. CC to *Av* **18 Apr**: critique & retraction .... 16 Apr 1849
* (Bourget to Quintal: defence of CC vs. accusations .... M .... 20 Apr 1849)
110f. Bourget to CC: too bold in your temperance preaching .... AAQ extract .... 3 May 1849
111f. CC to *Av* **26 Apr** .... M .... 21 May 1849
* (Someone to QC Dio: success of temp in St. David .... AAQ .... 31 May 1849)
112f. CC to *Av* **16 June** .... M .... 9 June 1849
113f. CC to La *Minerve* **21 June** .... AP 08-9-10 .... June 1849
114f. CC to *Av* **28 June**: his last letter .... 23 June 1849
115f. 'Un citadin' to CC: thanks in .... *Minerve* 27 June ..... AP 08-11 .... 2? June 1849
116f. CC to *Minerve*: temperance success .... handwritten AP 08-12 .... 11 July 1849
* (Turgeon to Bourget: info about CC .... Aug 1849)
* (Bourget to Turgeon(QC): answer to T .... M .... 21 Aug 1849
117f. CC to *Canadien* **1 Sept**: temperance (9 pp) .... SL AP 15-C1-F006-01 .... 12 Aug 1849
118. Bourget to whomever: testimonial letters in Latin .... M, LAC .... 25 Sept 1849
* (Bourget to Marechal (St. Jean): CC retreat in Troy .... M .... 2 Oct 1849)
119f. Achille Chiniquy (Panama) to CC .... *Ca* 26 Dec SL .... Dec 1849
120f. CC to Cazeault .... AAQ 1850
* (Hector Langevin justifies his praise of CC in the *Manuel* .... AAQ .... 19 Jan 1850)
* (Bourget to Manseau (Industrie): CC very sick .... M .... 28 Feb 1850)
* (Bishop Olivier to Bourget.: asks for French-Canadian priests .... AAQ .... 4 Mar 1850)
* (Bourget to Gov. General Elgin: thanks for gift of £10 for CC .... M .... 11 May 1850)
* (Someone to QC Dio: scandal of CC .... AAQ .... 19 May 1850)
121. Bishop Bourget to CC: becomes the Apostle of Temperance .... F .... 6 June 1850
* (L.J. Papineau to his wife: CC and temperance .... LAC .... 24 June 1850)
122f. CC to Bourget. .... M .... 26 July 1850
123. CC (Longueuil) to Pope: letter accompanying the *Manuel* delivered by Charles Baillargeon . F mention .... July 1850

323

THE CONTROVERSIAL CONVERSION OF CHARLES CHINIQUY

```
* (Someone (Toronto) to QC Dio: CC successful for the law and given money ............... AAQ ..................... 12 Aug 1850)
124f. Charles Baillargeon (Rome) to CC: papal benediction transmitted ................. AP-07 ..................... 18 Aug 1850
125f. CC to QC Dio: congratulations to Signay ............................................ AAQ ..................... 16 Oct 1850
126f. CC to La Minerve: Please leave this anonymous; incident in St. Hyacinthe ......... LAC ..................... 11 Nov 1850
127f. CC to Bourget ................................................................................... M ..................... 17 Nov 1850
* (Bourget to Joseph Marcoux: CC will preach to the Iroquois  ........................... M ..................... 28 Nov 1850)
128. Bishop. Van De Velde = Olivier (Chicago) to CC: invitation to IL ................... F ...................... 1 Dec 1850
129. CC to VV ..........................................................................paraphrase in F, Y ..................... 20 Dec 1850
130. D'Arcy McGee (NY) to CC: wants to follow CC example of rural Catholic colonization but with Irish. . F mention ..................... 1851
131f. CC to QC Dio: payment to Caisse St. Michel ........................................... AAQ .................. 1851, 53, 1856
* (Brassard to B: keep CC despite problems in Kamouraska  ............................... AAQ copy .................. 26 Jan 1851)
* (Parent to Cazeault  ................................................................................ M ..................... 27 Jan 1851)
132f. Bourget to CC: authorization to be Brassard's assistant ............................. M .................... 3 Feb 1851
133. CC to MW 10 Feb: answer to critiques about his financing  ........................................................ 4 Feb 1851
134f. Bourget to CC: critiques of political remarks ........................................ M, AAQ ................. 31 Mar 1851
135f. CC to Bourget ................................................................................... M ..................... 3 Apr 1851
136f. CC to Bishop Pinsoneault  ................................................................. M ..................... 5 Apr 1851
* (Olivier to B: priests to come  ............................................................. M ..................... 15 Apr 1851)
* (Morrier to L. Duvernay (La Minerve): CC\Dorion, Barthe debate in St. Édouard .......... LAC .................. 14 Apr 1851
137. Bishop Lefebvre (Detroit) to CC: invitation ............................................ F mention ........... early May 1851
* (Bourget to Van de V: sending of CC. Answer to 15 Apr  ................................. M 442, AAQ copy ... 7 May 1851)
138f. Bourget to CC: precautions for trip to Chicago ....................................... M, AAQ transcription ..... 7 May 1851
139f. CC to B: response to 7 May calumny  ................................................... AAQ ..................... 13 May 1851
* (Bourget to priest of Chambly: error of CC  ................................................ AAQ ..................... 14 July 1851)
140. CC (Mtl) to newspapers: emigrate to Illinois ........................................... AAQ, F ................... 13 Aug 1851
141f. Jos. Paré to CC: convocation to see Bishop Bourget  ................................. L ..................... 25 Aug 1851
142. Bourget to CC: interdict received the 23 Sept 1851 .................................... F ..................... Sept 1851
    or Bourget to CC: interdict .................................................................. P ..................... 28 Sept 1851
* (Retraction by the woman reported by ....................................................... F ..................... ca 28 Sept 1851)
143f. Bourget to CC:..................... (in Bourget letter of 6 May 1857) ................ S ..................... 29 Sept 1851
144f. CC (Collège St. Marie) to B:  confession (extract in letter B of 18 Mar 1857) ...P but original has disappeared ...4 Oct 1851
145f. Bourget to CC: you must repent .......................................................... M, AAQ typed copy ... 6 Oct 1851
146f. Bourget to CC: transfer letter to Chicago ............................................. M, L ..................... 13 Oct 1851
* (Bourget to Brassard: don't need exceat of QC  ............................................ M ..................... 13 Oct 1851)
* (Olivier to B: I will give CC a chance  .................................................... M, AAQ .................. 15 Oct 1851)
* (Van de V to B: arrival of CC  .............................................................. P extract ............... ca Oct 1851)
* (Bourget to Turgeon: send excorporation for CC to Chicago ................................ AAQ ..................... 15 Oct 1851)
* (Bourget to Van de Velde: CC will save souls in Illinois ................................. M ..................... 18 Oct 1851)
147f. Longueuil to CC: farewell address ....................................................... MR, L ................... 20 Oct 1851
148. CC to Longueuil: response ................................................................. MR 31 Oct F .......... Oct 1851
* (Lebel to Bourget  .................................................................................. M ..................... 5 Nov 1851)
* (Van de Velde to B: CC established, Chicago French church in debt  ..................... M, AAQ ................. 27 Nov 1851)
* (Bourget to Olivier: I hope CC will succeed  ............................................... M, AAQ .................. 9 Dec 1851)
* (Olivier to B: letter of CC about immigration  ............................................. M, AAQ ................. 28 Dec 1851)
149f. CC to anonymous  .............................................................................. P mention .............. 1851-1852
150. D'Arcy McGee to CC: wants to start a temperance group  ............................... Y, FCA .................. 1852
151. John Henderson to CC: sends his book on Sabbath observance  ......................... FTÉ ..................... 1 Jan 1852
* (Bourget to Van de Velde: greetings to CC  .................................................. M ..................... 20 Mar 1852)
152. CC to Van de V: title for the property  ................................................. SQ polyg ............... 25 Mar 1852
* (Van de V to Moniteur Canadien  ............................................................... M ..................... 27 Mar 1852)
* (Van de V to Bourget  .......................................................................... M ..................... 27 Mar 1852)
* (Bourget to Van de Velde: letter of CC may empty Quebec  ................................. M ..................... 14 Apr 1852)
* (Van de V to Bourget  .......................................................................... M ..................... 23 Apr 1852)
* (Lebel to Bourget  ............................................................................. M ..................... 4 May 1852)
153. CC to merchant of Montreal: order for Catholic Bibles  ................................ F mention ............... May 1852
154. V to CC: CC will cover Bourbonnais also  ................................................ F ..................... 20 May 1852
155. Father Lebel (Chicago) to CC: threats vs. CC & church  ................................ F mention ............... 23 May 1852
156f. CC to Chapais: pro emigration ........................................................... Ch ..................... Autumn 1852
* (L.J. Papineau to Institut Canadien: visit of CC  .......................................... LAC ..................... 25 Nov 1852)
157. CC to R. Mason(Illinois Central RR): asks for land  ................................... KH ...................... 8 Jan 1853
158f. CC to Morin ................................................................................. M ..................... ca Jan-Feb 1853
159f. CC to Abbé Thomas Aubert de Gaspé ....................................................... SQ ..................... 8 Feb 1853
160f. CC to Bishop Turgeon: health insurance  ................................................ AAQ ..................... Oct-1853
161f. CC to Bishop Turgeon: health insurance  ................................................ AAQ ..................... 8 Nov 1853
* Spink to CC: property deed  .................................................................. U ..................... 7 Nov 1853
* (De Maistre (Bourbonnais) to Bourget  ....................................................... M ..................... 8 Nov 1853)
162f. CC to Bourget ................................................................................. M ..................... 12 Nov 1853
163f. Bourget to CC: illness; accusation of having pocketed money raised ................. M, AAQ .................. 21 Nov 1853
164f. Bishop Turgeon to CC  ....................................................................... LAC, É..... AP 15-01-C1-F001-06 ....  1 Dec 1853
165f. CC to QC Dio:  recovered from illness  ................................................. AAQ .................. 16 Dec 1853
166f. CC to QC Dio .................................................................................. AAQ: I, 167 ............... 1854
167f. G. Lambert to CC (mention in 24\7\57) .................................................. .......................... Jan 1854
* (Mailloux to QC Dio: asks about CC  ......................................................... AAQ ..................... 14 Apr 1854)
168f. CC to QC Dio: wants to start a college  ................................................ AAQ .................. 10 May 1854
169f. CC to Dio: Canada must prevent emigration ............................................... AAQ .................. 15 Dec 1854
```

APPENDIX 2

170f. Cazeault to CC	M, LAC	AP 15-C1-F001-2	30 Jan **1855**
171. Dillon (sec of Chicago Dio) to CC: spiritual retreat	F		24 July 1855
172f. CC to QC Dio: progress of his colony		AAQ	16 Aug 1855
173-4f. CC to Cazeault		AAQ 263 & 270	**1856**
* (Bishop Baillargeon to Caroline Desorniers: chalice for CC		AP 15-C1-F001-3	9 Mar 1956)
175f. CC to Bishop Larocque: need of nuns		M	14 Mar 1856
176f. CC to Father Brisard		SQ	16 Mar 1856
177f. CC to Chapais		Ch	29 Mar 1856
178f. Bourget to CC: good work; will look for nuns		M	2 Apr 1856
179. CC to D'Arcy McGee	*American Celt* 19 April	K p.194	Apr 1856
180. CC to Abraham Lincoln: telegraph asking him to become his lawyer		F mention	May 1856
181. Lincoln to CC: answer Yes		F	May 1856
182f. Baillargeon to Miss Descorniers: gift of a chalice for CC		M	9 May 1856
183f. CC to Soc for the Propagation of the Faith: urgent financial needs		AP 01-85	14 June 1856
184f. CC to Sister Fréchette: help me to stop the Spink trial		M	24 June 1856
185. CC to Bishop O'Regan: about consecrated oil		F mention	
186. O'Regan to CC: abusive answer requesting $5		F	
187f. CC to Bourget: wants to return to Quebec. Irish persecution		M, P	9 Aug 1856
188. CC to O'Regan		F	19 Aug 1856
* (O'R to Brisard: on the subject of CC		SQ	21 Aug 1856)
189f. CC to O'R		*Av* 1er **March V**	24 Aug 1856
* (O'R to Father Cartuyvels: excommunication of CC		SQ	25 Aug 1856)
* (4 witnesses of St. Anne: meeting with O'Regan		F	ca 27 Aug 1856)
* (M. Fréchette (l'Érable) to Sister Fréchette		M	28 Aug 1856)
* (O'Regan to Cartuyvels: public announcement		SQ	30 Aug 1856)
* (O'Regan Pastoral Letter: excommunication of CC		SQ, F	3 Sept 1856)
* (Lebel to QC Dio: apostasy of CC		AAQ	13 Sept 1856)
* (O'Regan to Brother Facile: you are collaborating with CC		M	17 Sept 1856)
190. CC to the American public: announcement of need for funds		H p.131	18 Sept 1856
* People of St. Anne to O'Regan		F, *Av* 30 Oct	21 Sept 1856)
* (Besse (St. Anne) to Bourget		M	25 Sept 1856)
191f. St. Roch to CC	*National*	Feb 1857 mention	Oct 1856
* (Larocque to Bourbonnais: you must submit		*Av* 30 Oct	4 Oct 1856)
* (O'Regan to *CT* **6 Oct**: explains excommunication			ca 5 Oct 1856)
* (Lemoine and al to *CT*: answer to preceding		*Av* 30 Oct	10 Oct 1856)
* ('Faithful Catholic' to QC Dio: **mention** in answer by Dio of **31 Oct**			20 Oct 1856)
192. CC to O'Regan: refusal to submit; he stands on his American citizenship		AP 15-C1-F010-01	25 Oct 1856
CT 29 Oct, *Av* **18 Dec**, V p.4<u>: wrong date of 25 Sept in F, P</u>			
* (O'Regan to Bourget		M	27 Oct 1856)
* (O'Regan to Facile		N	27 Oct 1856)
* (O'R to Bishop Lefebvre		N	27 Oct 1856)
* (O'Regan to Bourget		M	29 Oct 1856)
* (O'R to Lefebvre		N	29 Oct 1856)
* (QC Dio (Langevin) to St. Anne		SQ	31 Oct 1856)
193. Theodore Lafleur to CC		Y early on in the conflict	n.d. 1856
* (O'Regan to Bourget		M	4 Nov 1856)
* (Bishop of London to Bourget		M	4 Nov 1856)
* (Desaulniers to Bourget		M	4 Nov 1856)
* (Des to Bourget		M	7 Nov 1856)
* (Des to Bourget		M	13 Nov 1856)
* (Facile to B: O'R and CC		M	n.d. 1856)
* (Bourget to O'R		M	17 Nov 1856)
194f. O'R to C and openly to *Av* **4 Dec**		P É mention	20 Nov 1856
* (Des to Bourget		M	23 Nov 1856)
* (Des to Bourget		M	24 Nov 1856)
* (M to Abbé Moreau: Desaulniers & CC		SQ, S	24 Nov 1856)
195. CC to O'Regan: submission as proposed by Brassard		M, F, S	25 Nov 1856
* (Des to Bourget		M	25 Nov 1856)
* (Desaulniers to Bourget: very long		M	26-7 Nov 1856)
* (Des to Bourget		M	28 Nov 1856)
196. O'Regan to CC: unconditional submission required		M	ca 28 Nov 1856
* (Des to B: 2 letters to report on St. A)		M	28 Nov 1856)
* (Desaulniers to Bourget		M	30 Nov 1856)
* (Des to Bourget		M	4 Dec 1856)
* (O'Regan to Bourget		M	4 Dec 1856)
197f. Troy to CC: praise		*Av* **15 Jan**	6 Dec 1856
* (O'R to Bourget		M	9 Dec 1856)
198f. CC to P. Moreau	published extract	SQ	9 Dec 1856
* (Mailloux (Caraquet) to Dio: sadness because of CC		AAQ	9 Dec 1856)
* (Desaulniers to Bourget		M	10 Dec 1856)
* (O'Regan to Bourget		M	14 Dec 1856)
* (Desaulniers to Bourget		M	15 Dec 1856)
* (O'R to Des: rejection of the CC submission		M, AAQ	15 Dec 1856)
* (Desaulniers to Bourget		M	17 Dec 1856)
199f. CC to Troy		*Av* **Jan 15**	17 Dec 1856

THE CONTROVERSIAL CONVERSION OF CHARLES CHINIQUY

* (Desaulniers to St. Hyacinthe Dio: report about CC .... AAQ .... 17 Dec 1856)
* (Des to Bourget .... M .... 18 Dec 1856)
* (Bourget to O'Regan: explains the mission and defends Brassard; can't send more .... AAQ .... 20 Dec 1856)
* (Desaulniers to Bourget .... M .... 22 Dec 1856)
* (Des to Bourget .... M .... 26 Dec 1856)
200. Brassard to CC: pressure to lie .... F extract .... Dec 1856
201f. CC to Brassard .... SQ extract .... 27 Dec 1856
* (Bourget to Des: don't favour CC but pray for him .... AAQ .... 31 Dec 1856)
* (Desaulniers to St. Hyacinthe Dio: reports about CC .... AAQ .... 31 Dec 1856)
* (A Catholic (Bourbonnais) to Bourget .... M .... 1 Jan **1857**)
* (Desaulniers to Bourget: list of faithful Catholics in St. Anne .... M .... 3 Jan 1857)
* (Bourget to Des: shock at the excesses and accusations by CC .... AAQ .... 4 Jan 1857)
* (Raymond to Bourget .... M .... 10 Jan 1857)
* (Desaulniers to Bourget .... M .... 12 Jan 1857)
* (Des to Bourget .... M .... 14 Jan 1857)
* (Catholics of Chicago to Bourget .... M .... 28 Jan 1857)
202f. Manteno syndic to CC .... V pp 21-2 .... 1 Feb 1857
* (Desaulniers to Bourget .... M .... 2 Feb 1857)
203f. CC to *Journal de Québec*: 50 points in 24 p. .... V, SQ .... 2 Feb 1857
204f. Moreau to CC .... SQ .... 2 Feb 1857
205f. CC to *Minerve* .... SQ .... around beginning 1857
(French speakers of Chicago to *CT*: vs. O'Regan; support for CC .... F
* (Desaulniers to Bourget .... M .... 3 Feb 1857)
* (Bourget to QC Dio: need for concerted action vs. CC .... AAQ .... 4 Feb 1857)
* Desaulniers to St. Hyacinthe Dio: need of declaration vs. CC .... SQ .... ca Feb 1857)
* (Bourget to QC Dio: tell newspapers not to mention CC .... AAQ .... 4 Feb 1857)
* (Desaulniers to Bourget .... M .... 6 Feb 1857)
* (O'Regan to Bourget: need of priests to combat CC .... M, AAQ .... 10 Feb 1857)
* (Baillargeon to M: Mailloux sent to Illinois .... SQ .... 11 Feb 1857)
* (Bourget to Des: help is coming; don't mention CC in newspapers .... AAQ .... 14 Feb 1857)
* (Bourget to Bishop. Baillargeon: some success in Illinois .... AAQ .... 14 Feb 1857)
* (Des to Bourget .... M .... 18 Feb 1857)
* (St. Anne + 'CT' of St. Pie to *Av* .... M .... 18 Feb 1857)
* (Facile to O'Regan .... M .... 19 Feb 1857)
* (Des to Bourget .... M .... 20 Feb 1857)
* (Bourget to O'R: sympathy; 3 priests coming .... AAQ .... 22 Feb 1857)
* (Someone (Kamouraska) to QC Dio: fight vs. CC .... AAQ .... 23 Feb 1857)
* (Desaulniers to Bourget .... M .... 23 Feb 1857)
206f. CC to Moreau .... SQ .... 24 Feb 1857
* (Desaulniers to Raymond (St. Anne) .... M .... 25 Feb 1857)
207f. CC to Moreau .... SQ .... 26 Feb 1857
* (Cartuyvels to Bourget .... M .... 26 Feb 1857)
* (Hébert to Moreau .... SQ .... 1 Mar 1857)
* (O'Regan to Bourget .... M .... 2 Mar 1857)
* (Desaulniers to Bourget .... M .... 2 Mar 1857)
208f. French Catholics (Chicago) + CC to Pinsoneault: long letter .... *Av* 15 Apr, M, V .... 5 Mar 1857
* (Lebeau (St. Anne) to Bourget .... M .... 6 Mar 1857)
* (Raymond(Grand Vicar) to Bourget .... M .... 7 Mar 1857)
* (Bourget to Raymond (St. Hyacinthe): how long will Mailloux be there .... AAQ .... 9 Mar 1857)
* (Bourget to Champeaux (Priest of St. Julienne): go to Illinois .... AAQ .... 9 Mar 1857)
* (Facile to Bishop Larocque: O'Regan is impossible to deal with .... M .... 15 Mar 1857)
* (Desaulniers to Bourget .... M .... 16 Mar 1857)
* (Bourget to Des: Mailloux & Champeaux are on the way .... AAQ .... 19 Mar 1857)
* (Bourget to Bourbonnais: about the suspension of CC in 1851 .... F, S, *Cour* 7 Apr, *Av* 1ᵉʳ Apr .... 19 Mar 1857)
* (Bourget to Champeaux: 16 rules to follow in Illinois vs. CC .... AAQ .... 21 Mar 1857)
* (Bourget to Jean Lebeau (St. Anne): rules for Catholics in St. Anne .... AAQ .... 21 Mar 1857)
* (Mtl to QC Dio: CC losing ground .... AAQ .... 23 Mar 1857)
* (Brassard to Mailloux: Desaulniers has destroyed the mission .... SQ .... 24 Mar 1857)
* (O'R to Mailloux: rules for him on arrival .... SQ .... 25 Mar 1857)
* (Someone (Bourbonnais) to QC Dio: Bourbonnais is opposed to CC .... AAQ .... 27 Mar 1857)
* (Lapointe to Mailloux .... SQ .... 1 Apr 1857)
* (Bourget to Brassard: you must confront CC publicly .... AAQ .... 1 Apr 1857)
* (Desaulniers to Bourget .... M .... 1 Apr 1857)
209f. CC to Mailloux: invitation to St. Anne .... SQ .... 2 Apr 1857
210. CC to Dillon .... *CT* April 13 .... 6 Apr 1857
211. Brassard to CC: dissociates himself from CC .... *Cour, Jl*, F .... 9 Apr 1857
* (Bourget to Desaulniers: be gentle with those who leave CC .... AAQ .... 10 Apr 1857)
* (Baillargeon to M Mailloux .... SQ .... 11 Apr 1857)
* (Des to Bourget .... M .... 13 Apr 1857)
* (Grand Vicar Gauvreau to Mailloux .... SQ .... 17 Apr 1857)
212. CC to B: Bourget is a liar about suspension .... *Av* 1ˢᵗ May,É, F .... 18 Apr 1857
* (Des to Bourget .... M .... 19 Apr 1857)
213. Brassard to CC: accusing Bourget [major chronological problem] .... received 1 Apr (sic)
214f. CC to Brassard: speak the truth in public .... Lettre du PC à Brassard, *Av* .... 22(3) Apr 1857
* (Citizens of Kankakee to Desaulniers .... *Jl* .... 27 Apr 1857)

APPENDIX 2

* (Sanschagrin to Mailloux) ... SQ ... May 1857
* (Des to Bourget) ... M ... 4 May 1857
* (Bourget Pastoral Letter to Montreal Diocese: answer to lies of CC) ... MEM ... 6 May 1857
* (Someone (Bourbonnais) to QC Dio: CC is losing ground) ... AAQ ... 6 May 1857
* (Champeaux to Bourget) ... P ... 8 May 1857
* (Father Labelle to parishioners of Chicago: about O'R) ... JI ... 8 May 1857
* (Champeaux to Bourget) ... P ... 10 May 1857
215f. CC to B: wants reconciliation ... M ... 10 May 1857
* (Champeaux to Bourget) ... P ... 12 May 1857
* (Desaulniers to Bourget) ... P ... 13 May 1857
* (Bourget to Desaulniers: heresy evident in CC) ... M, AAQ typed ... 15 May 1857
* (Hellmuth to *Record*: about CC) ... F p.10 extract ... 16 May 1857
216f. Bourget to CC: happy about attempt for reconciliation ... M ... 19 May 1857
217. Lincoln to CC: bill ... LAP 11-9 ... 23 May 1857
* (Bourget to Brassard: hope in reconciliation) ... AAQ ... 23 May 1857
* (Baillargeon to Mailloux) ... SQ ... 25 May 1857
* (Bourget to Champeaux: hopes for submission of CC) ... AAQ ... 26 May 1857
* (Bourget to Champeaux: be careful but seek peace) ... M ... 28 May 1857
218. Brassard to CC: obliged to write vs. CC ... F ... 29 May 1857
* (Bourget to Dio: no Catholic is permitted to read the writings of CC) ... AAQ ... 29 May 1857
* (Bourget to Baillargeon: explains his Pastoral Letter) ... M ... 29 May 1857
* (St. Germain to Mailloux) ... SQ ... end May 1857
* (Desaulniers to Bourget) ... M ... 31 May 1857
* (O'Regan to Mailloux) ... SQ ... 1 June 1857
* (Mailloux to Bourget) ... M ... 1 June 1857
* (Champeaux to Bourget) ... M ... 2 June 1857
* (Mailloux to QC Dio: poor strategy of O'Regan) ... AAQ ... 9 June 1857
* (French Canadian Association of Chicago to *CT* & *KD*) ... SQ ... 9 June 1857
* (O'Regan to Mailloux) ... SQ ... 15 June 1857
* (Mailloux to Dillon: don't abandon us) ... SQ ... 15 June 1857
* (Champeaux to Bourget) ... M ... 18 June 1857
* (L'Espérance to Mailloux) ... SQ ... 21 June 1857
* (Catholics of Quebec to Mailloux) ... SQ ... 23 June 1857
* (O'Regan to Mailloux 1st) ... SQ ... 26 June 1857
* (O'R to Mailloux 2nd) ... SQ ... 26 June 1857
* (Mailloux to QC Dio: met CC who faked repentance) ... AAQ ... 27 June 1857
219f. Mailloux letter to CC ... SQ ... 28 June 1857
* (Mrs Lambert to M: voluminous attack vs. CC) ... SQ ... 29 June 1857
* (Mailloux notes about interview of CC) ... SQ ... end June 1857
* (O'Regan to Mailloux) ... SQ ... 1 July 1857
220f. Mailloux to CC: your submission was insufficient ... SQ ... 2 July 1857
* (Champeaux to Pilon) ... M ... 3 July 1857
* (Chicago French Canadians to *Av* 1st Sept) ... 10 July 1857
221f. CC to J. C. Taché: I am not betraying my nationality *Av* 1st Sept   *Réponse du Rév M. Chiniqui* ... 20 July 1857
222f. Lambert to CC: threat to sue him over Mrs. Lambert ... M mention ... ca 22 July 1857
223f. CC to G. Lambert: denies all ... SQ Mailloux notes ... 24 July 1857
* (Mailloux to Dio: court case vs. Mailloux and news of CC) ... AAQ ... 27 July 1857
224f. CC to Mailloux: accusations of Lambert ... SQ ... 29 July 1857
225f. Lambert to CC: answer ... SQ ... ca Aug 1857
* (Baillargeon to Mailloux) ... SQ ... 7 Aug 1857
* (People of St. Anne to *JI* (long)) ... M ... 14 Aug 1857
* (O'Regan declaration about the original suspension of CC) ... JI 16 April 1858 ... 14 Aug 1857
* (Mailloux to QC Dio (B): Protestants encourage CC) ... AAQ ... 19 Aug 1857
* (O'Regan to Bourget: I am going to resign) ... M ... 19 Aug 1857
* (Baillargeon to Mailloux) ... SQ ... 3 Sept 1857
* (O'R to M: about resignation) ... SQ ... 4 Sept 1857
* (O'Regan to Mailloux) ... SQ ... 17 Sept 1857
* (Baillargeon to Mailloux) ... SQ ... 28 Sept 1857
226f. Sacerdos (?CC) to *Av* 15 Oct ... 6 Oct 1857
* (Mailloux & L. to Dillon) ... SQ ... 27 Oct 1857
* (St. Anne to *Av*) ... M ... 2 Nov 1857
* (Mailloux notes: the *Tondeurs*) ... SQ ... 3 Nov 1857
* (Desrochers to Mailloux) ... M ... 6 Nov 1857
* (Desrochers to Mailloux: lies about CC) ... JI ... 11 Nov 1857
* (St. Anne to Mailloux & Lapointe: accusations) ... JI ... 13 Nov 1857
* (Mailloux & Lapointe to *JI*) ... SQ ... 23 Nov 1857
* (Sacerdos to *Av* Dec 22) ... 7 Dec 1857
* (Mailloux to Dio (B): CC will become Protestant soon) ... AAQ ... 16 Dec 1857
227. CC to the Pope: (200 pp) accusations vs. O'Regan ... Y, F extract
* (Bishop Prince to Mailloux) ... SQ ... 19 Jan **1858**
* (CC? of St. Michel d'Archange) ... SQ ... 27 Jan 1858
* (O. Huot (Bourbonnais) to Mailloux: very angry) ... JI ... 5 Feb 1858
* (Assembly of French-Canadians to the bishops: anti-O'Regan about Chicago & CC) ... JI ... 12 Feb 1858
* (Mailloux to QC Dio: internal conflict among the Chiniquy group) ... AAQ ... 10,26 Feb 1858
* (Dillon to Mailloux: Dunn, CC & Smyth) ... SQ ... 3 Mar 1858

327

* (Mailloux to Dio (Bourbonnais): many abandon CC	AAQ	16 Mar 1858
228. CC + 4 to Bishop Smyth: desire for submission	Jl, Pays, MW, SQ, Y...	20 Mar 1858
229f. CC to Bourget: finally peace	M	25 Mar 1858
230. Bishop Smyth attestation of the acceptance of CC	Y mention	25 Mar 1858
231. CC to Bishop Smyth: thanks	F	
* (Mailloux to QC Dio (B): CC is saying that the bishop accepted him	AAQ	27 Mar 1858
* (Mailloux to Dio (Bourb): CC submits to Bishop Smyth	AAQ	27 Mar 1858
* (Mailloux to QC Dio: Mailloux questions the decision	AAQ	28 Mar 1858
* (Mailloux to Smyth	SQ	28 Mar 1858
* (Dillon to Mailloux	SQ	30 Mar 1858
* (Mailloux to QC Dio: confusion again about disciplinary action	AAQ	30 Mar 1858
* (Smyth Pastoral Letter to Kankakee County	Jl, SQ	31 Mar 1858
232. Dunn to CC (at St. Joseph retreat): be careful of the Jesuits	L mention ... received	5 Apr 1858
233f. CC (South Bend) to M: stop the persecution	AAQ	1 Apr 1858
234f. CC (Kankakee) to Mailloux	SQ	2 Apr 1858
* (Kenrick to St. Anne: I never supported CC	Jl	2 Apr 1858
* (Desaulniers to Mailloux	SQ	ca 2-3 Apr 1858)
* (Mailloux to Dio: conditions for a reconciliation of CC	AAQ	3 Apr 1858
235. Bishop Smyth to CC: summons to Dubuque	F mention ... received	6 Apr 1858
* (Mailloux to QC Dio: info about CC in Illinois	AAQ	5 Apr 1858)
* (Smyth to Mailloux: critiques of M, D + gives conditions for the acceptance of CC	SQ	7 Apr 1858)
* (Mailloux to Kenrick	SQ	8 Apr 1858)
* (Mailloux to Dio: info about CC in Illinois	AAQ	8 Apr 1858)
236f. CC (South Bend) to Cazeault: his difficulties with O'Regan & Smyth	AAQ	8-22 Apr 1858
* (Mailloux to Dio: the CC cause is dying	AAQ	9 Apr 1858)
* (Someone (Petites Îles) to QC Dio: letter from Canadian bishops	AAQ	10 Apr 1858)
* (Dillon to Mailloux: visit of bishop	SQ	12 Apr 1858)
* (Mailloux to Dio(B): disciples of CC abandoning him	AAQ	13 Apr 1858)
* (Bishop Prince to Mailloux	SQ	15 Apr 1858)
* (O'Regan to Damon	Cour 2 June SQ	18 Apr 1858)
237f. CC to Av **25 May:** failure of his submission		18 Apr 1858
* (Bishop Larocque to Mailloux	SQ	19 Apr 1858)
* (Smyth to Mailloux: unconditional submission required	SQ	23 Apr 1858)
* (Mailloux to Dio: success of CC in holding his people	AAQ	28 Apr 1858)
* (Baillargeon to Mailloux: resignation of O'Regan accepted	SQ	6 May 1858)
* (JB Lemoine JP to Mailloux: visit of Smyth to St. Anne	SQ	12 May 1858)
* (Lambert to Mailloux: accusations vs. CC (50 pp.)	SQ	22 May 1858)
* (Dubord to Mailloux: government about Paré	SQ	26 May 1858)
238. CC to Mailloux	Têtu, S extract	27 May 1858
* (Cartuyvels to Mailloux: CC and Smyth	SQ	28 May 1858)
* (Étienne Parent to Mailloux	SQ	30 May 1858)
* (Brassard to Bourget: denies part of the account in Av	AAQ	8 June 1858)
* (Mailloux to QC Dio	AAQ	13 June 1858)
* (Father Lapointe (Illinois) to Bourget	M	14 June 1858)
239. CC to Archbishop Kenrick (**mention** by Smyth in his 15 June letter)		
* (Mailloux to Dillon	SQ	15 June 1858)
* (Smyth to Mailloux	SQ	15 June 1858)
* (Mailloux to Auclair: vow of the bishop	SQ	ca June 1858)
* (Mailloux to Abbé Auclair: his own trials	SQ	19 June 1858)
* (Mailloux to Auclair: Dunn and CC	SQ	21,27 June 1858)
* (Mailloux to Baillargeon: Brassard and Paré	SQ	24 June 1858)
* (A Faithful Catholic (Bourbonnais) to Co	SQ	26 June 1858)
* (Cazeau to Mailloux	SQ	27 June 1858)
* (Mailloux to Auclair: errors of the extract in Av	SQ	27 June 1858)
* (Smyth to Mailloux: it is better not to react to Chiniquy	SQ	28 June 1858)
* (Mailloux notes: evidence that the excommunication was valid from the beginning	SQ	30 June 1858)
* (Bourget to Brassard: you must write a formal disavowal	AAQ	2 July 1858)
* (Mailloux (Illinois) to Bourget	M	4 July 1858)
* (Dillon to Mailloux	SQ	5 July 1858)
* (Brassard to B: Mailloux and the others are too aggressive against CC	AAQ	6 July 1858)
* (Brassard to B: CC has lost me as a friend	AAQ	10 July 1858)
* (Bourget to Mailloux (Bourb): no replacements coming	M	12 July 1858)
* (Bourget to Brassard: model for repudiation	AAQ	13 July 1858)
* (Mailloux to Duggan: visit planned	SQ	17 July 1858)
* (Dug to M: the visit	SQ	20 July 1858)
* (Dug to others bishops: CC and his own visit to St. A	L extract	ca July 1858)
* (Mailloux to Dio: CC relations with Lafleur	AAQ	27 July 1858)
* (Dug to Mailloux: visit of bishop	SQ	27 July 1858)
* (Cazeau to Mailloux: approves mission vs. CC	SQ	3 Aug 1858)
240. CC to CT: **mention** by Duggan on 20 Aug		mid Aug 1858
* (Auclair to Mailloux	SQ	5 Aug 1858)
* (Dunn to (Bishop?) Lefevre: CC	SQ	10 Aug 1858)
* (Mailloux to Dio: reception of Duggan in St. A	AAQ	11 Aug 1858)
* (Dillon to Mailloux	SQ	11 Aug 1858)
* (Smyth to Mailloux: excommunication of CC by O'Regan and Kenrick	SQ	15 Aug 1858)

APPENDIX 2

* (Prince(St. Hyacinthe) to Mailloux: defeat of the 'Calvin of Canada' .... SQ .... 15 Aug 1858)
* (Dug to Mailloux: results of his visit .... SQ .... 20 Aug 1858)
* (Baillargeon to Mailloux .... SQ .... 24 Aug 1858)
* (O'R to Cartuyvels: notice of suspension of CC .... SQ .... 30 Aug 1858)
* (Mailloux to Dio: CC is eternally lost .... AAQ .... ca June- Aug 1858)
* (Mailloux to Dio: loss of disciples of CC .... AAQ .... Sept 1858)
* (Bishop Larocque to Mailloux: CC lowered to the level of the 'Swiss' .... SQ .... 6 Sept 1858)
* (St. Louis Council of Bishops: Pastoral Letter .... SQ .... 12 Sept 1858)
* (Daoust to Bourget .... M .... Oct 1858)
* (Dug to Mailloux: visit of CC to QC planned .... AAQ .... 1 Oct 1858)
* (Kenrick to Mailloux: CC .... SQ .... 1 Oct 1858)
* (Kenrick to Mailloux: visit to Kankakee .... SQ .... 5 Oct 1858)
* (Lemoine to Mailloux .... SQ .... 15 Oct 1858)
* (Mailloux to QC Dio: CC declaration of 22 Aug, abandoning Rome .... AAQ .... Nov 1858)
* (O'R to *CT* or <u>faked letter by</u> CC (according to **S**) .... pre 20 Nov 1858)
* (Mailloux to Dio: the real CC has been revealed .... AAQ .... 15 Nov 1858)
* (Nelson Parent (St. Anne) to Bourget .... M .... 16 Nov 1858)
* (Pat O'... to Bourget .... M .... 16 Nov 1858)
* (Mailloux to Duggan: summary document of his files on CC (9pp) .... SQ .... 19 Nov 1858)
* (Duggan: interdict of CC for insubordination & violent language .... Y .... 20 Nov 1858)
* (Duggan to Bourget .... M .... 26 Nov 1858)
* (Auclair to Mailloux .... SQ .... 30 Nov 1858)
241. CC to *CT* **3 Dec**: I am not a Democrat and I am against slavery .... 2 Dec 1858
* (Duggan to Mailloux: CC lecture .... SQ .... 8 Dec 1858)
* (F. Lapointe (QC) to Baillargeon .... SQ .... Dec 1858)
* (Lottinville to Mailloux .... SQ .... 20 Dec 1858)
* (Mailloux to Dio: CC work exploding. Money extorted .... AAQ .... 27 Dec 1858)
* (Brassard to Mailloux .... SQ .... 27 Dec 1858)
242. Catholics of Quebec to CC: please explain why you left .... Y .... Jan 1859
* (Converts (St. Anne) to Montreal newspapers: inviting CC .... *MW* 4 Feb M, AAQ .... 23 Jan 1859
243. Étienne Parent to CC: govt. tries to dissuade him from returning .... Y .... end Jan 1859
244. CC to Parent: ready to shed his blood .... Y .... end Jan 1859
* (Langevin to J-O Paré: CC left Toronto for Montreal .... M .... 31 Jan 1859)
* (Pinsoneault to Bourget .... M .... 1 Feb 1859)
* (Pinsoneault to Bourget .... M .... 2 Feb 1859)
* (LJ Papineau to son Amadée: evaluation of CC .... LAC .... 2 Feb 1859)
* (Pinsoneault to Bourget .... M .... 3 Feb 1859)
* (Bishop Prince to M: CC to St. Hyacinthe .... SQ .... 3 Feb 1859)
* (Someone (Mtl) to QC Dio: CC to Montreal .... AAQ .... 3-4 Feb 1859)
* (Bourget Pastoral Letter: avoid contact with the apostate CC .... M .... 4 Feb 1859)
* (Bourget circular letter to clergy: the former pastor has become a wolf ..... M .... 5 Feb 1859)
* (Bishop Larocque to Mailloux: CC to Montreal .... SQ .... 7 Feb 1859)
* (Bishop Prince to Mailloux: CC to St. Hyacinthe .... SQ .... 8 Feb 1859)
* (Abbé Morrison to Mailloux: CC to St. Cyprien .... SQ .... 10 Feb 1859)
* (Abbé Langevin to Mailloux: CC to Quebec City .... SQ .... 11 Feb 1859)
* (Ed Fabre to M: CC to Mtl .... SQ .... 11 Feb 1859)
* (Baillargeon to M: CC to QC .... SQ .... 14 Feb 1859)
* (Abbé Auclair to M: CC to St. Roch .... SQ .... 15 Feb 1859)
245. CC to Hellmuth: evangelization .... *MW* **25 May**, *Presby* **21 May** .... 18 Feb 1859
* (Hellmuth to *Record* .... *Presby* 21May............. 19 Feb 1859)
* (Mailloux to QC Dio(B): doctrine and tour of CC .... AAQ .... 24 Feb 1859)
* (Duggan to Mailloux .... SQ .... 24 Feb 1859)
246. CC (Longueuil) to all newspapers: .... *KD* 2 March, *Cour*? **16 March**, SQ extract .... ca Feb 1859
* an admirer of Abbé CC to *Quebec Mercury*: .... AP 08-47 .... Mar 1859)
247. CC open letter to QC .... *SC*, shortened in *MW* **30 March**, M ... AP 08-50 .... 5 Mar 1859
* (Hellmuth to *Record*: about CC .... FC extract .... 5 Mar 1859)
* (Baillargeon to M: CC is diabolical .... SQ .... 6 Mar 1859)
* (Someone (Kankakee) to QC Dio: report on CC .... AAQ .... 7 Mar 1859)
* (Father Laviolette (Napierville) to Mailloux .... SQ .... 14 Mar 1859)
* (Bourget to Bishop Dumas (Vancouver): failure of the tour .... M .... 16 Mar 1859)
.... Only mention of CC in the Bourget Register between May 1857 and 1863!!!
* (Hellmuth to *Record*: CC .... FC extract .... 19 Mar 1859)
* (Brassard to Mailloux: critique of Mailloux and CC .... SQ .... 4 Apr 1859)
248. CC to *CT*: he calls himself a Protestant. Reported in .... SQ .... beginning Apr 1859
* (Lottinville to Mailloux: Brunet trial .... SQ .... 16 Apr 1859)
* (Someone (Bourbonnais) to QC Dio: Brunet trial .... AAQ .... 27 Apr 1859)
* (Someone (Kankakee) to QC Dio: Duggan plans a coup .... AAQ .... 6 May 1859)
* (Abbé Brouillette to M: CC visit to Baltimore .... SQ .... 6 June 1859)
* (Staples to *Presby* **13 Aug**: stories about changes in St. A. and appeal for funds .... 25 July 1859)
249. CC to *Presby* **6 Aug**: story about changes and financial needs .... 26 July 1859
* (Duggan to M: visit to St. A .... SQ .... ca 2 Aug 1859)
* (Mailloux to *Courr du Can*: lies of CC .... SQ .... 2 Aug 1859)
* (G.D.(St. Anne) to *SC* **19 Aug**: defeat of Grand Vicar Brouillette in debate .... SQ .... 5 Aug 1859)
* (Someone (Kankakee) to QC Dio: CC boasts about his excommunication .... AAQ .... 6 Aug 1859)
250. CC to *Presby* **27 Aug**: thanks for gift .... 18 Aug 1859

THE CONTROVERSIAL CONVERSION OF CHARLES CHINIQUY

* (Duggan to B: new bishop, Brunet, success of CC .... M .... 27 Aug 1859)
* (Paillard to *Journal of Commerce*, ... *KD* 7 Sept SQ .... Aug 1859)
* (T.N. Haskill (Chicago) to his congregation: praise of the CC reform .... *MW* 10 Sept.................. Aug 1859)
* (Catholic Christians resolutions .... *KD* 7 Sept SQ .... 3 Sept 1859)
251. CC to *Presby* 17 Sept.. 7 Sept 1859
252. CC to *NY Observer*: blessings and financial needs .... AP 08-83......................27 Sep 1859
253. CC to Hellmuth: needs money .... FC, S., *Times* of London......... 28 Sept 1859
* (Father Brisard (IL) to Bishop Lefevre (Detroit) N..28 Sept 1859
254. CC to *Presby* 15 Oct: difficult choice of a denomination .... 29 Sept 1859
255. CC to *Churchman*: not becoming Anglican .... *MW* 22 Oct AP 08-54 .... 29 Sep 1859
* (Louis Auger (St. Anne) to *SC* 7 Oct: the visit of dignitaries and the progress... 29 Sept 1859)
* (T. Lafleur to *MW* 5 Oct: the reform of CC commended.. start Oct 1859)
* (Lebel to CC: avoid the fate of Judas and return .... SQ ....Oct 1859)
* (Duggan to Mailloux: The others bishops about CC .... SQ ....11 Oct 1859)
* (Hellmuth to *Record*: about CC .... FC............................ 17 Oct 1859)
* (Louis Auger (St. Anne) to *SC* 28 Oct: details of the region..18 Oct 1859)
* ("Calvin" to *Presby* 5 Nov: praise and needs... 19 Oct 1859)
* (Hellmuth to *London Record* 9 Nov: testimonial for CC .... FC extract .... 28 Oct 1859)
* (Mesac Thomas to *Record*: about CC .... FC............................ 17 Nov 1859)
* ("Anti-Begging Committee" vs. the begging to *KD* 7 Dec .... SQ ....26 Nov 1859)
* (Rev Beaubien to *KG* 8 Dec: positive report of the state of St. A .... SQ .... 7 Dec 1859)
* (Achille Chiniquy to *KD* 7 Dec: vs. errors of *Press & Tribune* (Chicago) .... SQ .... ca 6 Dec 1859)
* (Pastor Staples to *Presby* 10 Dec: defence of CC.. 7 Dec 1859)
256. CC to *Presby* 24 Dec.: back from Europe vs. article of *P&T* .... 13 Dec 1859
257. CC to *CT* .... *KD* 5 Jan , SQ .... 21 Dec 1859
* (Someone (Bourb) to QC Dio: internal conflicts for CC .... AAQ........................ 26 Dec 1859)
258. Dr. Guthrie, Cunningham & Begg to CC: invitation to Edinburgh .... L, F mention 1860
259. Frédéric Monod to CC: invitation to meetings of the Free Church in France .... L.................................. 1860
* (Lemoine to *KG* 5 Jan: favourable to CC *P&T* .... SQ .... Jan 1860)
* (P. Worcester to *KG* 5 Jan .... SQ .... ca 4 Jan 1860)
* (Ned to *KG* 8 Jan: counters CC version of how he chose the Presbyterians .... SQ .... Jan 1860)
260. CC to *Presby* 21 Jan: spiritual progress but still physical needs... 9 Jan 1860
* (Baillargeon to Mailloux: criticizes Mailloux letter to the bishop of Chicago .... SQ .... 12 Jan 1860)
* (Mailloux (Bourb) to QC Dio: CC more daring and lying than ever .... AAQ...................... 14 Jan 1860)
* (Duggan to Mailloux: a loan to aid vs. CC .... SQ .... 16 Jan 1860)
* (Baillargeon to Mailloux: trial vs. Brunet .... SQ .... 18 Jan 1860)
* (English from Rockville to *KD* 1 Feb .... SQ .... 18 Jan 1860)
* (46 Kankakee English to *KD* 25 Jan: pro CC .... SQ .... 21 Jan 1860)
* (Mailloux (St. Anne) to *Cour*? 14 March: choice of Presbyterians .... SQ Poly 52, 4 .... 7 Feb 1860)
261. CC to *Presby*: choice of Presbyterians but will co-operate with all .... *MW* 18 Feb .... 9 Feb 1860
* (Pastor AH to *Presby* 7 Apr... 20 Mar 1860)
* (Mailloux (Kank) to QC Dio: disciples of CC abandon him .... AAQ..................... 25 Mar 1860)
262. CC to Rebecca Snowdon? (Philadelphia) ....extract *Presby* 7 Apr............. end Mar 1860
* ("Calvin to *Presby* 28 Apr: visit of Presbytery to St. Anne..11 Apr 1860)
* (Pastor AH to *Presby* 21 Apr... 17 Apr 1860)
* (Baird to *Presby* 5 May ....extract in *The French Canadian Mission in Illinois* (Baird)........26 Apr 1860)
* (Someone (St. Marie) to QC Dio: CC detested by his former disciples .... AAQ........................ 1 May 1860)
* (Someone (Bourb) to QC Dio: failures of CC .... AAQ..................... 20 May 1860)
* (Lebel to Lefevre: French Church of Chicago .... N............................. 5 June 1860)
* (Mailloux notes: CC a failure in Kankakee and elsewhere .... SQ 50,12N .... 14 June 1860)
* (Someone (Bourb) to QC Dio: CC losing ground .... SQ .... 16 June 1860)
* (Someone (Kank) to Dio: CC only survives because of money .... AAQ................... 25 June 1860)
* (Dunn (VG) to Mailloux: Duggan does appreciate you .... SQ .... 1 July 1860)
* (Staples and others to *Presby* 21 July: physical needs have been met .... July 1860)
263. CC to *Presby* 11 Aug : goodbye to US and financial needs .... 25 July 1860
264. CC to *MW* : thanks for Canadian givers; St. Anne missionaries to QC .... AP 08-61 .... 25 July 1860
   CC to *NY Observer*: same as above before leaving for Europe .... AP 08-83-56f.............. 25 July 1860
* (Someone (Kankankee) to Dio: CC leaves for England .... AAQ...................... 6 Aug 1860)
* (Father Gingras (Bourb) to Mailloux (QC): Protestant schisms in St. A .... SQ .... 20 Aug 1860)
* (Staples to *Presby* 29 Sept : financial report of the Committee .... 15 Sept 1860)
265. CC (Glasgow) to IL: he revokes power of attorney for Staples .... AP 06-56 .... 1 Oct 1860
* (Staples to *Presby* 10 Nov : attacks the divisions of Anglicans and Baptists.. 27 Oct 1860)
266. CC (Boston) to a pastor *KG* 17 Jan 1861: success in GB and funds .... SQ .... 26 Dec 1860
267. CC to a friend in Mtl.: send me a liberal Montreal newspaper *MW* 27 Feb .... AP 08-63................. 21 Jan **1861**
* (Someone of Bourb to QC Dio: CC shameful .... AAQ..................... 18 Feb 1861)
* (Biggs to *KG*: lies of Hellmuth about Kankakee .... SQ .... 27 Feb 1861)
268. CC group to *KG*: help needed for Kansas .... SQ .... ca 1 Mar 1861
* (L. Fluet to *KG*: very positive about CC .... AAQ...................... 11 Mar 1861)
* (Williamson to *KG* ca 11 March: Biggs & CC .... SQ .... 11 Mar 1861)
* (Mailloux to Biggs: very long résumé of the CC situation .... SQ .... 11 Mar 1861)
269. CC to *KG* ca 21 March: justification of his brother Achille's accounting .... SQ .... 12 Mar 1861
270. CC to *MW* (6 Apr): refuting accusation vs. his brother .... AP 08-65 .... 13 Mar 1861
* (Staples to Williamson: *KG* ca 21 March .... SQ .... 18 Mar 1861)
271.'Public' (CC?) to Biggs *KG* ca 21 March .... SQ .... 20 Mar 1861
* (Staples to Biggs: vs. CC ....extract *Cour* 28 Aug............ 20 Mar 1861)

APPENDIX 2

* (Williamson to *KG*: Biggs & CC ....SQ ....25 Mar 1861)
* (Rev Spring to *KG*: the facts will come out, preparation to accuse CC ....SQ ....25 Mar 1861)
* (Alfred Hamilton to *Presby* **6 Apr**: pro CC and anti-Biggs...26 Mar 1861)
272. CC to Father Brunet in prison: mocks him ....Y......................end Apr 1861
* (Someone (Kank) to Dio: CC in conflict with the Presbyterians ....AAQ ....2 May 1861)
* (Alfred Hamilton to *Presby* **8 June**..14 May 1861)
* (Someone (Bourbonnais) to Dio: CC is even less popular with the Protestants ....AAQ ....16 May 1861)
273. CC to *Presby* **15 June**: difficulties are necessary...21 May 1861
* (Alfred Hamilton to *Presby* **20 July**..ca 1 July 1861)
* (Staples to Biggs: *Cour* **28 Aug** ....SQ ....July 1861)
* (Biggs to *Cork Examiner* ....*Cour* **28 Aug SQ**...ca 9 July 1861)
* (Alfred Hamilton to *Presby* **31 Aug**: almost everyone in St. A supports CC........................12 Aug 1861)
274. CC to MW **Sept 18**: need for theological college ....AP 08-68...................22 Aug 1861
275f. Antoine Allaire to CC: finances ....AP 06-88...................30 Aug 1861
276. CC to *Presby* **5 Oct**: progress continues ....13 Sept 1861
277. CC to *MW*: Father Brunet escapes from prison ....AP 06-68...................21 Sept 1861
* (Alfred Hamilton to *Presby* **16 Nov**: CC acquitted again..Nov 1861)
* (Someone (Bourbonnais) to Dio: CC is never mentioned here ....AAQ ....2 Jan **1862**)
* (Cyrille Migneron & others Protestants to *KG* **ca 6 March**: CC not popular ....SQ ....15 Feb 1862)
278. CC to *KG* **13 March** : polemics vs. the critics ....SQ ....10 Mar 1862
* (Presbytery of Chicago to *Presby* **10 May**: no true college exists in St. Anne ....23 Apr 1862)
* (Pro CC group (St. Anne) to *KD* **21 May** ....SQ ....13 May 1862)
* (Alfred Hamilton to *Presby* **17 May**: refutation of letter of 23 April................................May 1862)
* (Pro CC group (St. Anne) to *KG* **29 May** ....SQ ....ca21 May 1862)
279. '*Verita alias*' CC to *KG* **29 May** ....SQ ....mid May 1862
* (Morel to *KG* **26 June**: vs. CC and his defenders ....SQ ....10 June 1862)
* (Staples to *KG* **26 June**: vs. CC and his defenders ....SQ ....ca25 June 1862)
* (L'Hôte (Philadelphia) to *KG* **29 May**: vs. CC ....SQ ....25 June 1862)
* (Demars to *KG* **3 July**: answer to Staples and Morel ....SQ ....27 June 1862)
280. CC (St. Anne) to Abraham Lincoln: thanks and praise ....George....AP 03................29 Sept 1862
281. Baillargeon (Muskegon) to CC: invitation ....Y.......................end Sept 1862
282. CC to editor in Britain (*KG* **12 March**): intro of documents to justify himself............................8 Mar **1863**
*...included in *Prospectus* of Stevens, Faris and Monod of May 1863
283. Angus Cameron gift of an Anti-Catholic book ....PCL..........................14 Sept 1863
284. CC (Washington) to Abraham Lincoln: needs funds for college ....George....AP 03.......10 June **1864**
* (A. Chester (IL) to Abraham Lincoln: recommendation of college CC ....**George mention**....10 June 1864)
* (L.G. Chiniquy to Dio: wants to become priest in spite of his uncle CC ....AS........................4 Sept 1864)
* (Father Maréchal (Kank) to Bourget ....M ....18 Aug **1865**)
285f. CC to Joseph-W. Montour ....*Confession générale* ....12 Dec **1866**
286. CC to *MW* **2 Jan, 1867**+ reprinted in ....*MWW* **6 Jan**..........16 Dec 1866
* (Kemp to *MW* **8 Jan**: needs for trial vs. CC, financial committee established..........................3 Jan **1867**)
* (Lemoine (Catholic) to *MW* **16 Jan**: concert in Kankakee to counter CC.................................Jan 1867)
* (Kemp to *MW* **21 Jan**: CC always keeps very detailed accounts ....16 Jan 1867)
287f. CC to *Moniteur* **24 Jan**...Jan 1867
288. CC to W.F. Lighthall (Montreal) Thanks for help ....AP 03...................29 Jan 1867
289. CC to Duke St., Montreal Sunday School: students are transformed at St. Anne ..*MW* **12 Feb** ....1 Feb 1867
* (Kemp to *MW* **16 Feb**: long account of statistics and details about St. A ....Feb 1867)
290. CC to *Northwest Presbyterian*: Immaculate conception ....*MW* **9 March** ....cFeb 1867
291. CC to Mackey (Treasurer for CC Funds in Montreal): sued in court by bishop ......*MW* **15 Apr**................9 Apr 1867
292f. CC to Gavazzi...(original in Vaud) **Sylvain** p.75 ....5 Mar **1868**
293. CC to *Christian Times* **30 Apr**: sound the alarm for Vatican I ....AP 01-28 ....4 Mar **1869**
* (Kemp to the public: published report on St. Anne....................................AP 15-C1-F011-01...16 Apr 1869
294f. Bruyères to CC ....É............................12 Nov 1869
295f. CC to Bruyères: long answer ....É............................21 Dec 1869
* (Bishop of London to Bourget ....M............................13 Jan **1870**)
296. CC to *MW* **4 Feb**: persecution by Rome..ca 3 Feb 1870
* (Vicar General Truteau to Bourget (Rome): CC coming to Montreal and is dangerous....M....................11 Feb 1870)
* (Gavazzi to his friend: mentions CC as friend ....*MW* **4 Apr**...................Mar 1870)
* (Vernon to *MW* **17 May**: about CC ....May 1870)
297. CC to *MW* **27 Aug** with list of 116 abjurations ....ca 26 Aug 1870
298. CC to pastors of QC: win by conversions...*MW* **29 Aug**...........ca 28 Aug 1870
* (Father Beaudin in Illinois to B: need of a priest, CC is less influential ....M....................17 Oct **1871**)
299. Charles Hodge to CC ....Y...**1872**
* (Mailloux (St. Henri) notes about CC ....AAQ ....13 June 1872)
* (Priest (St. Anne) to Beaudry: CC is very dangerous ....M.......................28 Oct 1872)
300. CC to Hodge: answer ....A **Nov 1872**...............Nov 1872
301. Catholics (Antigonish NS) to CC: threatening him ....Y extract **1873**
302. CC to Lt. F. W. Haultain (FCMS): competition ruins French mission ....AP 03..................10 Mar 1873
303. CC to *Standard*: denies a Baptist leaning and criticizes Auger ....SL....................16 Apr 1873
304. MacVicar to Chiniquy..Mac 83..........................7 May 1873
305. CC for publication: explains rebaptism *Why Father Chiniquy was Re-baptised* AP 01-27..............20 Nov 1873
306. MacVicar to Chiniquy..Mac 110....................15 Feb **1874**
307. MacVicar to Chiniquy..Mac 111....................23 Feb 1874
308f. Doutre to CC (England): fund raising for the Guibord case ....U..............................8 May 1874
* (Hugh McNeile (Ripon GB) to Christopher: should publish CC on confessional ....AP 07..............20 May 1874)

309. MacVicar to Chiniquy..Mac 113-4.................19 Oct 1874
310. MacVicar to Chiniquy..Mac 114 ....19 Oct 1874
311. MacVicar to Chiniquy..Mac 119 ....28 Oct 1874
312f. Louis Fluet to his friend CC: note accompanying the book *Old Rome* ....PCL..1874
* ("Free Speech" to MW **25 Feb**: riots vs. CC...Feb **1875**)
313. CC to *MW* **20 March**: auricular confession...Mar 1875
* ("A Catholic wife" to *MW* **15 March**: must punish Chiniquy about the confessional..............................Mar 1875)
* (Bourget Pastoral Letter vs. CC and *MW*: apostate and impostor ....MEM ....18 Mar 1875)
* (Bourget circular letter to clergy vs. CC and *MW* ....MEM.....................19 Mar 1875)
* (A.A. Parent(Mtl) to *MW* **23 March** (not printed): accuses CC of immorality...Mar 1875)
* (48 wives to B: in agreement with CC on the confessional ....*MW* **29 March** .... Mar 1875)
* (Bishop Taschereau (QC) circular letter to clergy: condemning the apostate and ....*MW*.......................10 Apr 1875)
314. CC to A. Mackey (Montreal): his conflicts and the Orange Order ....*MW* **18 Apr**   12 Apr 1875
315f. CC to Bourget ....*Le vrai contre-poison*, *MW* **20 May**.......May 1875
316. Douglas to CC ....**Douglas biog**.....................May 1875
317. CC (Montreal) to Douglas ....**Douglas p.244** ......22 May 1875
318. CC to *MW* **31May**..'May 1875
319. CC to *MW* **9 Sept**..Sept 1875
320. CC to Protestants of Canada: beware of Catholics..*MW* **10 Nov**   ....Nov 1875
321f. CC to Bourget: list of 160 abjurations..*MW* **20 Nov**   .....15 Nov 1875
322f. CC to *MW* **20 Dec**: Indians at Oka..15 Dec 1875
323. CC to B: 150 abjurations..*MW* **28 Dec mention**..ca21 Dec 1875
324. CC to *MW* **1er Jan**: list of 296 abjurations ....Dec 1875
325. CC to *MW* **21 Jan**: list of 450 abjurations ....18 Jan **1876**
326f. CC to *MW* **29 Jan**: list of 500 abjurations..21 Jan 1876
* (Bourget Pastoral Letter vs. liberalism and CC ....MEM ....1 Feb 1876)
327. MacVicar to Chiniquy..Mac 119 ....14 Feb 1876
328. CC to all the Press *MW* 17 **Feb**: about converts...15 Feb 1876
329f. CC to *MW* (Fr) **17 Feb**: list of 400 abjurations..15 Feb 1876
* ("Just weights and measures" to *MW* **18 March**: vs. Anglican critique of CC ....19 Feb 1876)
330. CC (Halifax) to *MW* **29 March**: gift and praise of *MW*..7 Mar 1876
331. CC(Putnam CT) to *MW* **28 March(Fr), 15 Apr(Eng)**: progress here + list of 23 abjurations.................20 Mar 1876
* (LeMettayeur to *MW* **3 Apr**: accusing CC... ca 2 Apr 1876)
* (Campbell to *MW* **5 Apr**: defending CC..4 Apr 1876)
* (Z. Lefebvre to *MW* **6 Apr**: defending CC..4 Apr 1876)
* (LeMettayeur to *MW* **13 Apr**: will sue Lefebvre ....6 Apr 1876)
332. MacVicar to Chiniquy..Mac 205 ....13 April 1876
333. MacVicar to Chiniquy..Mac 208 ....13 April 1876
334. Claude Poncet (Montreal convert) to CC ....*MW* **18 Apr**   16 Apr 1876
335. Marie Ste-Marie(Manitoba) to CC: her conversion and CC's help ....*MW* **18 Apr mention** 1876
336. Mrs Goyette (Oregon) to CC: recounting the conversion of her husband and requesting a visit ......**Y extract**.................1876
* (Court to Presbyterian Assembly ....**Court** pamphlet p.9........start of June 1876)
337. CC to *MW* **12 June**: arrests and converts..ca 11 June 1876
338. CC (St. A) to *CT*: his moderate position in a heresy trial ....*MW* **27 June**   18 June 1876
339. CC (Mtl) to *MW* **25 July**: a convert due to the spectacle of the wafer..24 July 1876
340. CC (on the boat) to *MW* **18 Aug**: QC, Beauport, the boat ....11 Aug 1876
341. CC(PEI) to *MW* **2 Sept** need a mission to Gaspé..15 Aug 1876
342. CC (PEI)au *MW* **20 Sept** about politics in PEI...30 Aug 1876
343. MacVicar to Chiniquy..Mac 224........................18 Oct. 1876
344. CC (PEI) to *Presbyterian* (PEI) Dec. 7 about Catholic persecution.. ca 6 Dec. 1876
345. CC (St. Anne) to Bishop Bourget "Why I will never return" on return from Maritimes, ...*Papal Idolatry*......pre 1877
* (Cazeau to Burke; notes about CC ....AAQ ....Jan 1877)
346. CC to *MW* **20 Jan**: accounts of conversion ; he is impoverished...20 Jan 1877
347. Stephen Moore (CC lawyer) to CC: a summary of his court proceedings ....SL.................................1 Mar 1877
348. MacVicar to Chiniquy: objections to CC's financial statements ....Mac 235 .... 16 Mar 1877
* (**Court pamphlet**: disputes the statistics of abjurations and integrity of Chiniquy ....**Court pamphlet**......ca Aug 1877)
349. CC(Mtl) to Bishop Fabre: 7 reasons for remaining Protestant ....*MW***17 Sept SL**.........3 Sept 1877
* (Presbyterian Board of French Evangelization to *MW* **17 Sept**: vs. the accusations of Court ....14 Sept 1877)
* (Court to *MW* **18 Sept**: accusations maintained vs. the Presbyterian BFE..17 Sept 1877)
350. CC to M. Butler ....**Reformation in Canada, p.11-2**...........17 Sept 1877
351. CC to *MW* **20 Sept**: foolish of *MW* to expect justice from Catholics...18 Sept 1877
R.H. Warden to *Globe*: the final word vs. W.B. Court ....*MW* **1 Oct**..............Sept 1877)
352. CC to *MW* (**mention** but not printed **1 Oct**): long refutation of Court ....Sept 1877
353. MacVicar to Chiniquy..Mac 249.....................27 Sept 1877
354. Sicard to CC *MW* **15 Nov**: gift ....7 Oct 1877
355. CC to *MW* **15 Nov**: need of jobs for converts; some people are undeserving..7 Oct 1877
356. CC to *MW* **16 Nov (mention** but not printed because too political and extremist) ....Nov 1877
357. CC to *MW* **16 Nov**: attack by Irishmen vs. one of his evangelists ....Nov 1877
* (*TW* to *MW* **26 Nov**: CC liar about the creation of the *True Witness* ....Nov 1877)
358. CC to *MW* **28 Nov**: list of 109 abjurations..27 Nov 1877
359. CC to *MW* **29 Nov**: his involvement in the creation of the *True Witness*..27 Nov 1877
360. CC to *MW* **5 Dec**: answer to *TW*..Dec 1877
361. CC to *MW* **5 Jan**: refutation of Bishop Lynch ....15 Dec 1877
362f. CC to A-L Therrien : about a visit to Burlington ....**CBA, Ruddel** .... 3 May **1878**
363. George Sutherland to CC: invitation ....**L mention**...........................1878

APPENDIX 2

364. CC (Washington) to *Sentinel*: French-Canadian immigrants in the region .... **FCA** ...**AP 01** .... 23 Aug 1878
365. CC (San Francisco) to *Sentinel*: the Rockies .... **FCA** .... 26 Aug 1878
366. CC (San Fran) to *Sentinel*: Oregon .... **FCA** .... 2 Sept 1878
367. CC (San Fran) to *Sentinel*: D'Arcy McGee and San Francisco .... **FCA** .... 3 Sept 1878
368. CC (on the boat) to *Sentinel*: the sea .... **FCA** .... 3 Sept 1878
369. CC (on the boat) to *Sentinel*: the evangelization of Hawaii .... **FCA** .... 20 Sept 1878
370. CC (on the boat) to *Sentinel*: the volcanoes of Hawaii .... **FCA** .... 20 Sept 1878
371. CC (on the boat) to *Sentinel*: the beauties of the sea .... **FCA** .... 28 Sept 1878
372. CC (on the boat) to *Sentinel*: tornado while at sea .... **FCA** .... 30 Sept 1878
373. CC (Sydney) to *Sentinel*: the city of Sydney .... **FCA** .... 31 Dec 1878
374. CC (Sydney) to *Sentinel*: about Canadian friends .... **FCA** .... 21 Jan **1879**
375. CC(Sydney) to *Sentinel*: conversion of a Catholic .... **FCA** .... 25 Jan **1879**
376. CC (Ballarat) to *Witness* (Australia) **19 Apr**: attacks in Horsham vs. CC .... **SL** .... 3 Apr 1879
377. CC(Australia) to *Witness*: attacks in Horsham Australia .... **SL** .... 17 Apr 1879
378. CC to *Church of England Messenger* .... **AP 15** .... 13 May 1879
379. CC to James Douglas .... **Douglas** .... 15 Oct **1880**
380. MacVicar to Chiniquy: stop saying that I demand pay for talks .... **Mac** 311 .... 31 Mar **1881**
381. Mary Williams (Sandwich ON) to CC.. **Y** .... 10 July **1881**
382f. CC to *A* **12 Jan** about the *Priest, Woman and the Confessional*.. 2 Jan **1882**
383. Badenoch to CC: invitation to England .... ca Oct 1882
384f. CC to Badenoch: answer .... **A 15 Feb** .... 15 Nov 1882
* (Bishop of Seychelles to Bishop Fabre .... **M** .... 24 July **1883**
385. Stephen Moore to CC: report on trip to Minnesota for Lincoln info .... **AP 11-4** .... 30 Oct 1883
386. Edwin A. Sherman (Oakland CA) to CC .... **AP 07** .... 28 Nov 1883
387. CC will handwritten .... **AP 06** .... 5 Nov 1883
388. Edwin A. Sherman (Oakland) to CC .... **AP 07** .... 29 Dec 1883
389. Edwin A. Sherman (California) to CC .... **AP 07** .... 3 Feb **1884**
* (Resther (SJ) to someone in England .... **M**................................. 25 Feb 1884
390. CC (St. A) to Mrs W.F. Lighthall .... **AP 03**........................... 19 June 1884
391. CC (St. A) to Bishop Lynch (Toronto) .... *Papal Idolatry* .... **AP 01-32** .... 22 June 1884
* (Mayor Beaudry (Mtl) to Cruchet: promise to protect CC .... **AP 15-01-C1-F003-03** .... 8 Nov 1884)
392. CC (St. A) to Mrs W.F. Lighthall .... **AP 03**............................ 13 Jan **1885**
393. CC + St. Anne to Father Gibaud (Mtl) *A* Apr 9, ... **AP 09** .... 26 Mar 1885
394. CC to newspapers "Mr. Editor": announcement *50 Years* .... **IL State Historical Lib** .... 13 July 1885
395. CC to Robert Lincoln: note with gift of *50 Years* .... **AP 03-17**..................... 7 Sept 1885
396. Robert Lincoln to CC: thanks, plainly a great friend of his father .... **AP 07** .... 10 Sept 1885
397. CC(Lowell MA) to Miss K.M. Lighthall .... **AP 03** .... 10 Nov 1885
398f. Jos. Provost (MA) to CC: triumphal visit so poem .... **A**24 Dec 1885 .... **AP 09** .... Dec. 1885
399. CC to Miss K.L.: editions & finances .... **AP 03** .... 20 Feb **1886**
400. CC (St. A) to Miss K.L. .... **AP 03** .... 18 May 1886
401. Craig & Barlow to CC: receipt for *50 Years* sales .... **AP 06** .... 27 July 1886
402. CC (St. A) to *Converted Catholic* **4, p. 35**: praise .... 11 Jan **1887**
403f. CC (St. A) to *A* **24 Feb**: conversion of Father Leclerc .... 15 Feb 1887
404. CC to *Providence Telegraph*: his accusations proven in .... **F**, *Conv C* .... 7 Apr 1887
405 CC to T. Fenwick: thanks for book on Waldensians .... **AP 03** .... 21 Apr 1887
* (Catholic archivist McGovern (IL) to Richard Clarke: documentation on O'R and CC.... **N** .... 6 May 1887)
406. CC (St. A) to Cardinal Gibbons: Dedication to your future conversion .... *Papal Idolatry* **AP 01** ...... Jan **1888**
407. CC (St. A) to *Conv C* **5, p. 67**: praise .... 10 Feb 1888
* (Catholic newspapers (Germany) about CC .... **M** ....19 Nov 1888)
* (A Catholic (Cologne) to Bishop Corrigan (NY) .... **M** .... 6 Dec 1888)
* (German newspapers with the letter above .... **M** .... 6 Dec 1888)
408. CC (Mtl) to *Converted Catholic* **6, p. 128**: annual report .... 7 Mar **1889**
409f. CC to TGA Côté: Louis Martin .... **CBA** .... 23 Apr 1889
410f. CC (Niagara Falls) to Joseph Allard: going to Presbyterian meeting .... **AP 03** ....11 June 1889
* (Bishop of Strasbourg to Bishop Fabre .... **M** .... 14 June 1889)
411f. Cruchet and Presbyterians of Mtl. to CC. .... In *MW*? **AP 09**.......................... 4 Aug 1889
412. CC to *American Citizen*, Boston: to refute 'Justice' about Lincoln assassination **SL AP 15-C1-F003-02** .... ca Sep 1889
413f. CC to TGA Côté: ex-priest Louis Martin .... **CBA** .... 13 Dec 1889
414f. CC to TGA Côté: ex- priest Louis Martin .... **CBA** .... 27 Dec 1889
415f. CC to Bourgoin: his daughter is at the Pointe-aux-Trembles school .... **UCM** .... 28 Dec 1889
416. CC (Mtl) to T.A. Crawford (Toronto): thanks for gift .... **Rev. J. Ernest Nix** .... 29 Jan **1890**
417f. CC to Morin: welcome Louis Martin as prodigal son .... *Mon voyage à Tracadie* end May1890
418f. CC (Worcester MA) to his wife: success and health. Nautical image. .... **AP 03** .... 31 July 1890
419. CC (St. A) to T.A. Crawford: thanks for gift .... **Rev. J. Ernest Nix** .... 1? Aug 1890
420f. CC (Mtl) to Joseph Allard: you libelled me .... **AP 03** .... 12 Feb **1891**
421f. CC to *A*: destruction of temperance societies after his conversion .... *CFA* ..... **AP 09-113** .... Mar 1891?
422. CC (14 Park Ave., Mtl) to Hardie: proposes a lecture .... **Presby Archives Toronto** ..... 20 Apr 1891
423. CC to Mederic Drolet: CC's debt .... **AP 06-96** .... 10 Jul 1891
424. Calvin Amaron to CC: sorry I forgot to mention your role in New England .... **AP** .... 21 Oct 1891
425. Côté (Mass.) to CC: Allard misusing his name vs CC .... **AP 10-80** .... 22 Oct 1891
426f. H.J. Schouten (Ommeren Holland) to CC: proposes Dutch translation .... **AP 07** .... 15 Nov 1891
427. CC to General Harris: The two agree about Lincoln .... **F** p.213
428. Harris (Harrisville) to CC: *50Y* persuaded me of Catholic plot vs Lincoln............... **AP 07** .... 21 Nov 1891
429f. J.E. Paradis (Lowell MA) to CC: Allard used my name to abuse you .... **AP 07** .... 21 Nov 1891
430. CC (Mtl) to *CFA*: résumé of persecutions, conversions .... **SL AP 15-C1-F014-05** ....Jan **1892**

THE CONTROVERSIAL CONVERSION OF CHARLES CHINIQUY

431f. J.E. Paradis (Lawrence MA) to CC: ignore the Allard controversy .... AP 07 .... 4 Jan 1892
432. Edith Huie to CC: a French card representing Ps 121 .... AP 05 .... 31 Jan 1892
* (A Catholic (Iowa) to Bishop Fabre .... M .... 7 Feb 1892)
433. Hubert Taylor (IL) to CC: .... AP 07 .... 19 Feb 1892
434. CC to *MW*: refutation of 'Kentucky Ben' *Father C. to Kentucky Ben, L* .... AP 01 .... 10 Mar 1892
435. CC to general public: will remain Prot. .... AP 01-26 .... 23 Mar 1892
436. Harris (Harrisville) to CC: will send my book proofs for comment .... AP 07 .... 24 Mar 1892
437. CC to [H.]C. Taylor: documents re Lincoln; please write vs. Catholics .... AP 15-C1-F003 .... 25 Mar 1892
438. Andrew O. Nash? (Washington) to CC .... AP 07 .... 29 Mar 1892
439. Hubert Taylor (IL) to CC .... AP 07 .... Mar 1892
440. CC to court: revokes power of attorney for Simon Allard .... AP 06 .... 27 Apr 1892
441. CC Declaration (St. A) before his surgery in case of his death CC in *CFA*, *Conv C* 9, p.174
    and: in *Primitive Catholic* **11 June** .... SL AP 15-C1-F014-03 .... June 1892
442. Harris (Harrisville) to CC: the reasons for his own book .... AP 07 .... 18 June 1892
443. Harris (Harrisville) to CC: will read *50Y* & change my proofs if convinced ..... AP 07 .... 20 June 1892
444. CC to *Witness*: crusades in Wisconsin & Minnesota .... *CFA* **7 July** .... June 1892
445f. CC (St. A) to Amaron: gift for college .... *CFA* **29 Sept** .... Sept 1892
446f. CC to Paul Cayer (New England): French Protestant financial self-sufficiency is essential .. *CFA* **6 Oct** .... Sept 1892
447f. CC (St. A) to Rev. & Mrs. Morin: 4 pages .... AP 03 .... 17 Nov 1892
448. Harris (Harrisville) to CC: await your bk. I had to concentrate on political ..... AP 07 .... 19 Nov 1892
449. Stephen Moore to CC: report on trip to Minnesota to investigate .... AP 11-3 .... 29 Dec 1892
   Pamphlet *Two Chiniquys* .... AP 10 1893
450f. CC (14 Park Ave Mtl) to Amaron: big success in Montreal .... *CFA* **2 Feb** .... Jan 1893
451. CC to Frank White: British aid in mission *The Christian* .... AP 09-105 .... Jan 1893
452f. CC to *A*: maybe CC should move to Montreal .... AP 09-103 .... 24 Jan 1893
* (Boudreau to Amaron: the burning of CC's home .... *CFA* **16 Feb** .... Feb 1893)
453f. CC to parishioners of St. Anne: newspaper of **17 Feb** .... AP 09 .... Feb 1893
454. T.Y. Cusack? (Folkstone Kent) to CC: Nun of Kenmore sends her books, support ..... AP 07 .... 15 Feb 1893
455f. J.A. Derome (Cottage Grove MN) to CC: remembers library before the fire ..... AP 07 .... 18 Feb 1893
456. *The Citizen* (Boston) to CC .... AP 07 .... 20 Feb 1893
457f. CC (St. Anne) to Joseph Morin and Emma Chiniquy .... AP 03 .... 22 Feb 1893
458f. CC (St. A) to Joseph Morin .... AP 03 .... 23 Feb 1893
459f. CC (St. A) to Joseph Morin .... AP 03 .... 27 Feb 1893
460. H.W. Duncan (Kendal, GB) to CC .... AP 07 .... 16 Mar 1893
461. CC to NY Witness **29 March** .... AP 09 .... Mar 1893
462. Adam Craig (Craig Press, Chicago) to CC: clipping re fire; send manuscript ..... AP 07 .... 3 Apr 1893
463. CC (Mtl) to *Chicago Tribune*: 5 pages .... AP 03 .... 5 Apr 1893
464. A. Bassett (Ware MA) gift of *Theol.Germanica* .... PCL .... 18 Apr 1893
465. Hubert Taylor (Lake Forest IL) to CC .... AP 07 .... 21 Apr 1893?
466. Hubert Taylor (Lake Forest IL) to CC .... AP 07 .... 1 May 1893?
* ('Chiniquiste' to *CFA*: evaluation of CC **18 May** .... May 1893)
467. CC to C.W. Sherman .... AP 09 .... 5 June 1893
468. CC to NY *Weekly Witness* **14 June**: accomplishments but Catholic fires .... AP 15-C1-F015-1 .... June 1893
469. Hubert Taylor (IL) to CC .... AP 07 .... 13 June 1893
470. CC to *Christian Leader* **Sept 21**: appeal .... 21 June 1893
471f. CC to *CFA*: praise of Amaron and Collège Franco-américain .... UCM .... 22 June 1893
472. Hubert Taylor (IL) to CC .... AP 07 .... 3 July 1893
473f. L.J.A. Papineau (Montebello) to CC: thanks for support; his father on Luther ...... AP 07 .... 24 Sept 1893
474f. L.J.A. Papineau (Montebello) to CC: both are committed to truth .... AP 07 .... 29 Sept 1893
475. CC to MacVicar: fires so asks for info for new biog **SL** .... AP 15-C1-F003-04 .... 4 Oct 1893
476. CC (Beau Séjour) to Rev Bennett: burning of his house .... U 1893
477. CC to *Chicago Interior*: in *Prot Standard* .... SL .... 26 Oct 1893
478. CC to Bosworth: no Catholic wafers available .... CBA .... 10 Nov 1893
479. Moore to CC: résumé of all his legal trials .... SL. AP 15-C1-F003-05 .... 26 Nov 1893
* (Bishop in Norway to Bishop Fabre .... M .... 9 Dec 1893)
480f. LJA Papineau to CC: to the 'Luther of Canada': .... **Douville p117** .... 11 Jan 1894
481f. LJA Papineau to CC: thanks for having me at your 30th anniversary & at night
    joined church; only regret was publicity; don't use me as a model .... AP 07 .... 11 Jan 1894
482f. Église St. Jean to CC: no controversial publicity permitted .... **Église St. Jean elders' minutes** .... 11 Jan 1894
483. CC to Hardesty: the Catholics of Kankakee .... *MW* **3 Feb** .AP 15-C1-F016-06 .... Jan 1894
484-5. CC to Tassé(*Minerve*): *Dr. Chiniquy to Senator Tassé and Mgr. Lynch* .... AP 01 .... ca 1894
486. CC to St. Anne Church at dedication of new bldg. .... *MW*?**22 Feb.**.AP 09 .... Feb 1894
487. CC to *Toronto Mail*: his suspension as a Catholic and *La Minerve* .... SL .... 24 Feb 1894
* (AJ Lebeau to the *A* **21 April**: CC visit to St. Marie... 21 Mar 1894)
488f. CC to Amaron: mission in Lowell. .... *A* **14 Apr extract** .... Apr 1894
489f. L.J.A. Papineau (Montebello) to CC: can't attend for cornerstone, money sent .... AP 07 .... 15 Apr 1894
490. Miss Inger Hoel (Che Ju, W. China) to CC: 2nd Luther, enthralled .... AP 07 .... May 1894
491. Publisher Revell to CC: terms of publication of his books .... AP 15-C1-F003-02 ... 9 July 1894
* (Lighthall to his lawyer in Chicago : stop all publication by Skidmore **SL** ..... AP 15-F003-6 .... 10 July 1894)
492f. CC (Montreal) to the Countess of Beaujeu ?: 9 pages .... AP 03 .... 18 July 1894
493. Warrens to CC: birthday greetings .... AP 10 .... 30 July 1894
* (notes of Mrs Trudel - a Catholic woman trying to set up a CC\Fabre meeting ..... M .... 29 Oct 1894)
494f. Father G-J. Hamon (Collège St. Marie Mtl) to CC: visit to CC **Y**, *A* **17 Nov** .... AP 07 .... 2 Nov 1894
495f. CC by Morin: answer .... *A* **17 Nov, L** .... 5 Nov 1894
496f. Presbyterian pastors of Mtl to CC: praise and best wishes .... *A* **1 Dec** .... 19 Nov 1894

APPENDIX 2

497ef. CC (8 Hutchinson St). to Fabre after his illness..AP 01-25,38+ ....8 Dec 1894
498ef. Mr & Mrs. von Hanstein (Berlin) to CC: German translation, come to Germ ....AP 07 ....16 Dec 1894
499f. L.J.A. Papineau (Montebello) to CC: good letter to Fabre; most religious letter ....AP 07 .... 10 Jan **1895**
500. CC (65 Hutchinson St.) to *Converted Catholic* **12, p. 63**: praise ....14 Jan 1895
501. John Darby (Deanery, Chester) forwarded to CC ....AP 07 .... 14 Jan 1895
502. CC to Gov. General Aberdeen: his conversion + request for aid for St. Jean Church AP 03.......................... c Jan 1895
503. G.G. Aberdeen (Govt. House, Montreal) to CC: thanks for book but respects Catholics .. AP 07 .... 26 Jan 1895
* (LJA Papineau to Amaron: Yes to a Prot picnic at Montebello and bring CC ....UCM ....25 Feb 1895)
504. Harris (Harrisville) to CC: writing new book all about assassination ....AP 07 ....16 Mar 1895
505. Harris (Harrisville) to CC: give your documents to archives; eyesight failing ....AP 07 ....23 Mar 1895
506. Mary Pavitt (Brighton GB) to CC ....AP 07 ....17 Apr 1895
507 Isaac Pool (APA) to CC: welcome Published ....AP 10-55 ....17 Apr 1895
508f. L.J.A. Papineau (Montebello) to CC: confidential; rescued daughter from RC teacher .. AP 07 .... May 1895
509. Rev. John Moore of Boston to CC: schedule for lectures here in June ....AP 07 ....17 May 1895
510f. L.J.A. Papineau (Montebello) to CC: money for church ....AP 07 ....10 July 1895
511. Wm Kitching (Clevdon GB) to CC ....AP 07 .... 3 Jan **1896**
512. CC (65 Hutchinson St.) to *Converted Catholic* **13, p. 4**: ex-priests ....6 Jan 1896
513. ER Parker (Australia) gift of book ....PCL................................ ca Jan 1896
514. Canadian Dept of Agriculture to CC: deposit books for copyright ....AP 15-C1-F004-01. 20 Feb 1896
515. Mrs. Julie McIntyre (Toowoomba, Aust.) to CC: appeal for money ....AP 07 .... 5 May 1896
516. Mary Fluet Williams (Sandwich ON) to CC ....AP 07 ....22 June 1896
517. A.H. Guinness (Prot. Alliance London GB) to CC ....AP 07 .... June 1896
518f. CC (Waterville ME) to Rebecca Chiniquy..AP 03-8.........................11 July 1896
* (Someone (St. Aubert) to QC Dio: efforts of CC to return to Catholics ....AAQ ....13 July 1896
519. George Cruickshank (Bath GB) to CC ....AP 07 ....20 July 1896
520. Emily Gardner (Kineton? Warwickshire GB) to CC ....AP 07 ....22 July 1896
521. M.A. Koch (Johannesburg SA) to CC ....AP 07 .... 5 Aug 1896
522f. 'Jn Charbonneau' (Central Falls RI) to CC: incriminating letters ....AP 07 ....13 Aug 1896
523. A.J. Marshall (Halifax) to CC: note kept in CC's Bible ....AP 05 ....17 Aug 1896
524. CC (Mtl) to Muller ....AP 03 ....17 Aug 1896
525. Église St. Jean to CC and all: commending him to raise money ....AP 15-C1-F004-02 .... 7 Sep 1896
526. S.G. Thomas MD (Fall River MA) to CC: about incriminating letters ....AP 07 .... 9 Sept 1896
527. CC to Franco-Protestants: vs. Catholic schools ....Y.....................................10 Sept 1896
528. CC will: English translation ....AP 06 -097 ....10 Sept 1896
* (Father Hamilton (Fall River MA) to Fabre ....M....................................12 Sept 1896
529. Wm. C. Porter (Natal, Brazil) to CC ....AP 07 ....14 Sept 1896
530ef. Herdt to CC (GB): praise , St. Jn Church is poor..SL AP 15-C1-F004-03-4 .....17 Sept 1896
531. Charles Thynne (editor in London GB) to CC: offers deal for book or pamphlet ....AP 07 ....18 Sept 1896
532. Alfred Brandon (Chelsea GB) to CC ....AP 07 ....23 Sept 1896
533f. Amaron to CC: Amaron will be in GB for finances...SL AP 15-C1-F004-06.....24 Sept 1896
534. Mrs. Spence (Kettering, GB) to CC ....AP 07 ....25 Sept 1896
535f. Jos. Duparquier (Liverpool GB) to CC: confidential reference needed ....AP 07 ....26 Sept 1896
536. Arthur Morris (Lewes (Prot. Alliance) GB) to CC ....AP 07 ....26 Sept 1896
537. Mrs. Spence (Kettering GB) to CC ....AP 07 .... Sept 1896
538. "A Catholic" (Bedford Row WC, GB) to CC: return to Catholics.....................................AP 07 ....1 Oct 1896
539. Father Begue (Oban Scotland) to CC: challenge...Y.....................................2 Oct 1896
540. Charles Thynne (London) to CC: publisher ....AP 07 ....3 Oct 1896
541. Alfred Millard (Prot. Union Gloucester GB) ....AP 07 ....5 Oct 1896
542. Guinness (Prot. Alliance London GB) to CC ....AP 07 ....5 Oct 1896
543. Henrietta Sharp (Camden Rd, NW, GB) to CC ....AP 07 ....12 Oct 1896
544. Editor Thynne (London) to CC: concerning an edition..SL AP 15-C1-F004-07 ..... 13 Oct 1896
545. John I. Packwood (St. Leonard, GB) to CC ....AP 07 ....25 Oct 1896
546. CC (London) to Begue: the challenge accepted (newspapers) ....AP 03 + 09...................3 Nov 1896
547. Mr. Lucas (Dowanhill, Scotland) to CC ....AP 07 ....17 Nov 1896
548. Wm Dougall (Coatbridge Scotland) to CC ....AP 07 ....17 Nov 1896
549f. Amaron (Glasgow) to CC: needs money...SL AP 15-C1-F004-08 ....23 Nov 1896
550f Amaron (Glasgow) to CC: news..SL AP 15-C1-F004-10.....25 Nov 1896
551. CC (Charlottetown) to *Presby*: voyage to Maritimes..AP 09-6.........................7 Dec 1896
552. Clarence Fry (S. Kensington, London) to CC ....AP 07 ....Dec 1896
553. Mrs. Phelps (Hyde Park, London) to CC ....AP 07 .... 11 Dec 1896
554. M.L. Hutchins (Melbourne Aust) to CC ....AP 07 ....21 Dec 1896
555. Mrs. I.C. Bruce (Wellington, NZ) to CC ....AP 07 ....21 Dec 1896
556. Mr. Lavington (Devizes GB) ....AP 07 ....23 Dec 1896
557. W.H. Bagshawe (Chapel en le Frith GB) to CC ....AP 07 ....28 Dec 1896
558. Sgt. G.H. Lifton (Wythe, GB) to CC: willing to finance pamphlet vs Catholics ....AP 07 ....1897?
559. Fleming Revell (Chicago) to CC: royalties ....AP 06 .... 2 Jan **1897**
560. Mrs. Edith Auffray (W. Dulwich, GB) to CC ....AP 07 .... 17 Jan 1897
561. S.D. Maddock via Opie Rodway (Bristol GB) to CC...AP 07 ....18 Jan 1897
562. Mrs. W. Bryden (Wimbledon GB) to CC ....AP 07 ....18 Jan 1897
563. Col. J. Robinson (Whitehall London GB) to CC ....AP 07 ....19 Jan 1897
564. Mrs. K. Graham (Barnstaple GB) to CC ....AP 07 ....20 Jan 1897
565. Mrs. Brown (Oban Scotland) to CC ....AP 07 ....20 Jan 1897
566. Alice Jane Wright (Chorley GB) to CC ....AP 07 ....23 Jan 1897
567. J. Keer (North Malvern GB) to CC ....AP 07 ....23 Jan 1897
568. Michael Honeyman (Glasgow Scotland) to CC ....AP 07 ....25 Jan 1897

THE CONTROVERSIAL CONVERSION OF CHARLES CHINIQUY

569. E. Manico? (Buckingham, GB) to CC .... AP 07 .... 26 Jan 1897
570. W. H. Bagshawe (Chapel en le Frith GB) to CC .... AP 07 .... 26 Jan 1897
571. Frank White (Bournemouth GB) to CC: sends money............................ AP 07 .... 28 Jan 1897
* (Monthly letter of Protestant Alliance: CC's tour schedule in England. ......AP 15-C1-F019-04 ..... Feb 1897)
572. Otto J. Baertich (Troy Indiana) to CC: 50Y best book after the Bible, RC fiancé .... AP 07 .... 11 Feb 1897
573. John Nesbitt (Belfast IR) to CC: cheque & regrets CC missed Belfast .... AP 07 .... 12 Feb 1897
574f. Herdt (St. Jn Ch. Montreal) to CC: thanks for gift of $1500 ....SL AP 15-C1-F019-11.... 12 Feb 1897
575. Clement Wittherby & Col Robinson (Lewisham GB) to CC...................... AP 07 .... 13,15 Feb 1897
576. Alex Belanger? (W. Dulwich S.E. GB) to CC: working in London mission......... AP 07 .... 14 Feb 1897
577. J. Berger (Cannes FR) to CC: money, come visit us .... AP 07 .... 16 Feb 1897
578f. L.N. Leichan (Sark, Channel Islands GB) to CC: come & stay here.......... AP 07 .... 17 Feb 1897
579. Charles Stirling (Whi... GB) to CC: huge crowd though CC missed meeting .... AP 07 .... 17 Feb 1897
580. Col. J. Robinson (Blackheath GB) to CC.. AP 07 .... 17 Feb 1897
581. W.H. Bagshawe (Chapel en le Frith GB) to CC .... AP 07 .... 20 Feb 1897
582. Philip H. Lord (Southsea GB) to CC .... AP 07 .... 22 Feb 1897
583. W.H. Bagshawe (Chapel en le Frith GB) to CC .... AP 07 .... 25 Feb 1897
584. Fleming Revell (F. Revell Co. Chicago) to CC .... AP 07 .... 25 Feb 1897
585. Frank Carey (Orange House, Guernsey GB) to CC .... AP 07 .... 28 Feb 1897
586. Peter Atherton to CC: gift of book and tracts .... PCL .... Feb 1897
587. Jas V. Scott (Belfast IR) to CC .... AP 07 .... 2 Mar 1897
588. Henry Guerrier (Chichester GB) to CC: watch out for Jesuits in Jersey .... AP 07 .... 8 Mar 1897
589. Col. J.S. Elliot (Toronto) to CC .... AP 07 .... 15 Mar 1897
590. Clara B. Mitchell (Leeds GB) to CC .... AP 07 .... 28 Mar 1897
591. de Carteret (Le Village GB? to CC: lecture here tomorrow on plots to kill you ...... AP 07 .... 1 Apr 1897?
592f. L.N. Leichan (Sark, Channel Islands GB) to CC: come visit next month .... AP 07 .... 7 Apr 1897
593. E. Schneider (Magdeburg, Germany) to CC: German .... AP 07 .... 7 Apr 1897
594. A.H. Guinness (Prot. Alliance London GB) to CC .... AP 07 .... 7 Apr 1897
* (Dr. Thomas (Montreal hotel) to Morin: full explanation of Allard affair, warns of others .... AP 07 .... 13 Apr 1897)
595f. Calvin E. Amaron (Montreal) to CC: hope you bring back $2000 .... AP 07 .... 19 Apr 1897
596. Henry Egby (Reading GB) to CC .... AP 07 .... 25 Apr 1897
597f. L.J. Bertrand (Russell Square) to CC: Duparquier will be helped .... AP 07 .... 27 Apr 1897
598. L. von Hanstein (Berlin, Germany) to CC: can't go to England .... AP 07 ...... **Good Friday** Apr 1897
* (Emma Chiniquy (Mtl) to Rebecca (GB) .... AP 03 .... 4 May 1897
599. CC to AH Guinness: thanks to Protestant Alliance ....SL AP 15-C1-F005-01 ..5 May 1897
600. W. Johnston Hewson (Barrow in Furness GB) to CC .... AP 07 .... 5 May 1897
601f. H.J. Schouten (Ommeren Holland) to CC: proposed tour, publishing remarks .... AP 07 .... 5 May 1897
602. Alf Fowler (Prot. Alliance London GB) to CC .... AP 07 .... 6 May 1897
603. Rev. W. Standen (Bolton, Lancashire GB) to CC .... AP 07 .... 7 May 1897
604f. Jos. Duparquier (St. Louis MO) to CC: would like job in US or France .... AP 07 .... 9 May 1897
605. L. Thomson (Eng. Ch., Amsterdam) to CC: please preach here .... AP 07 .... 10 May 1897
606. Mrs. John Norets? (S.W. London) to CC .... AP 07 .... 11 May 1897
607. Rev. A.W. Frater (Middelburg, Holland) to CC .... AP 07 .... 12 May 1897
608. A.H. Guinness (Prot. Alliance London GB) to CC .... AP 07 .... 12 May 1897
609. George Higgins Cleland (Glasgow Scotland) to CC via Guinness: clipping .... AP 07 .... 13 May 1897
610f. Joseph Morin (Brussels) to CC (Amsterdam): post card .... AP 03 .... 13 May 1897
611f. H.J. Schouten (Utrecht Holland) to CC: schedules, mention crucifix stolen........ AP 07 .... 13 May 1897
612f. A.E. Schouten (The Hague, Holland) to CC: meetings set up, money sent .... AP 07 .... 14 May 1897
613. von Hanstein (Badgastein, Austria) to CC: here for spas, will write Schneider, Weimann ..... AP 07 .... 15 May 1897
614. A.E. Schouten (Gravenhage Holland) to CC: in Dutch .... AP 07 .... 15 May 1897
615. Bas Barker (Apeldoorn, Holland) to CC: meetings arranged & stay here .... AP 07 .... 15 May 1897
616. H.A. Fowler (Prot. Alliance London GB) to CC .... AP 07 .... 18 May 1897
617f. H.J. Schouten (Ommeren by Tiel Holland) to CC: schedules, good crowds ..... AP 07 .... 22 May 1897
618f. H.J. Schouten (Ommeren Holland) to CC: more schedules, meet Morin .... AP 07 .... 22 May 1897
619. Schneider (Magdeburg, Germany) to CC .... AP 07 .... 22 May 1897
620. Gertrude de Lynden (Utrecht Holland) to CC: glad to have hosted CC ...... AP 07 .... 23 May 1897
621. J.E. Snelgrove (Northampton GB) to CC: wants info on Lincoln faith... AP 03 .... 24 May 1897
622f. CC (la Haye, Holland) to Mr. Editor : praises Holland .... AP 03 .... 25 May 1897
623f. Gertrude de Lynden (Wiesbaden, Germany) to CC: good hosting you... AP 07 .... 25 May 1897?
624f. Bas Barker (Apeldoorn, Holland) to CC: invitation to Baronness Ittersum .... AP 07 .... 28 May 1897
625. J. von Hanstein (Berlin, Germany) to CC .... AP 07 .... 29 May 1897
626f. H.J. Schouten (Ommeren, Holland) to CC: notarized act; 2 ex-priests... AP 07 .... c1 June 1897
627f. Baronne W.A. d'Albaing (Kensington GB) to CC: missing CC in Holland........ AP 07 ....May-June 1897
628. Schneider (Magdeburg, Germany) to CC: stay with me & preach at service .... AP 07 .... 3 June 1897
629f. H.J. Schouten (Ommeren Holland) to CC: need notarized act vs calumny .... AP 07 .... 5 June 1897
630f. Mrs. Bas Basker (Ommeren? Holland) to CC: CC like Peter with Cornelius ..... AP 07 .... 7 June 1897
631f. A.E. Schouten (The Hague, Holland) to CC: want to translate 50Y in Dutch ..... AP 07 .... 8 June 1897
632. Edith F. Huie (Toronto) to CC .... AP 07 .... 10 June 1897
633f. CC (Magdeburg, Germ) to Joseph Morin (Paris) .... AP 03 .... 13 June 1897
634f. CC (Magdeburg, Germ) to Morin (Paris) .... AP 03 .... 14 June 1897
635. CC (Berlin) to *MW* **8 July** .... AP 09 .... 20 June 1897
636f. CC (Berlin) to the *Aurore* **10 July**: lectures in GB, Holland, France and Germany............ AP 07 .... 20 June 1897
637. Mrs. Spence (Kettering GB) to CC .... AP 07 .... 20 June 1897
638f. Rebecca (Paris) to Papa (CC in Germany) .... AP 03 .... 21 June 1897
639f. CC (London) to Rebecca Chiniquy.. AP 03 .... 25 June 1897
640. Margaret Scott (*The Christian*, London GB) to CC .... AP 07 .... June 1897.

APPENDIX 2

641. Mary Stirling (Bayswater W., GB) to CC .... AP 07 .... 30 June 1897
642f. Ablaing de Gessenburg (Matlock Br. GB) to CC: money, regrets to miss CC .... AP 07 .... pre July 1897
643f. Baronne W.A. d'Ablaing (Kensington GB) to CC: have good return .... AP 07 .... pre July 1897
644. Robert Bank & Son (London) to CC .... AP 07 .... 7 July 1897
645. CC (Mtl) to *MW* **20 July:** trip in Europe .... AP-09 .... July 1897
646f. A.E. Schouten (Birkhaven Holland) to CC: election of Kuyper with RC help .... AP 07 .... 22 July 1897
647. J.W. Cook (Detroit MI) to CC .... AP 07 .... 23 July 1897
648e,f. S.G. Thomas (Richelieu Hotel, Mtl) to CC: repentant for Allard plot .... AP 07 .... 25 July 1897
649. Guinness (Prot. Alliance London GB) to CC .... AP 07 .... 5 Aug 1897
650 Henry Klopper (San Francisco) to CC: thanks for letter used to combat Catholics .... AP 07 .... 9 Aug 1897
651f. Léon Colomb (Nomingue) to CC: advice about move to California .... AP 15-C1-F005-02 .... 9 Aug 1897
652. John Moore (Boston) to CC: proposed lecture in Boston on Oct 18 .... AP 07 .... 14 Sept 1897
653. Harris (Harrisville, W Va) to CC: sends copy of new book, you're ready to die .... AP 07 .... 28 Sept 1897
654f. V. Aubert (Canterbury GB) to CC: ex-Jesuit working interim in Cant. .... AP 07 .... 30 Sept 1897
655. Sarah Small (London GB) to CC .... AP 07 .... 2 Oct 1897
656e,f. Hanstein (Berlin, Germany) to CC: sick again, blessings .... AP 07 .... 16 Dec 1897
657. T.M. Harris (Harrisville W Va) to CC: glad you like my book .... AP 07-186 .... cDec 1897
658. C. McCormick (GB) to CC .... AP 07 .... Dec 1897
659. Carl Busch?(Montgomery US) to CC: write about Europe trip .... AP 07 1898
660f. Betsy Pape (La Haye Holland) to CC: thanks for *50Y*, sends money .... AP 07 .... Jan **1898**
661f. Louis Amadée Papineau (Montebello QC) to CC: complaint about Amaron .... SL AP 15-C1-F005-03 ... 12 Jan 1898
662. Primmer (Dunfermline GB) to CC: gift of book *JP in Rome* .... PCL .... 10 Mar 1898
663. CC to *Sentinel* **17 March**: esteem for Orange Order .... AP 09 .... 11 Mar 1898
664. Finlayson to CC: thanks for visit; poem .... CBA .... 16 Mar 1898
665. CC to *Mtl Herald*: vs. his editor Banks **SL** .... AP 09 .... 5 Apr 1898
666f. C.E. Amaron (Mtl) to CC: news from Mtl ch; sending via KS missionary .... AP 07 .... 29 Apr 1898
667f. J.L. Loiselle (Marlboro MA) to CC: thanks for concern but leaving pastorate .... AP 07 .... 30 Apr 1898
668f. CC to Amaron: no money .... UCM .... 9 May 1898
669. Mary Williams (Sandwich ON) to CC: sends info on her father Fluet .... AP 07 .... 14 May 1898
670f. Mrs. Bas Basker (Apeldoorn, Holland) to CC: still no Dutch translation .... AP 07 .... 3 June 1898
671. McLean (Glasgow) to CC .... AP 07 .... 1 July 1898
672. M. Mead (Mechanicsville IO) to CC Published .... AP 07 AP 10 .... 6 July 1898
673. Ambrose G. Townshend (Glasgow GB) to CC .... AP 07 .... 7 July 1898
674. L. J. Weichmann to CC: testimony re Lincoln for your book .... AP 11-8 .... 8 July 1898
675. B.F. Bradbury (Boston MA) to CC .... AP 07 .... 11 July 1898
676. Wm Bennett (Peterborough ON) to CC .... AP 07 .... 12 July 1898
677f. Immigrants from FR (St. Ignace-de-Nomingue QC) to CC: need cheap land .... AP 07 .... 18 July 1898
678f. A.F. Rivard (Montreal) to CC: resolution from St. John Church for your health .... AP 07 .... 2 Aug 1898
679. Mrs. Mary Kent (Los Angeles CA) to CC: need cheap edition of excellent *50Y* .... AP 07 .... 5 Aug 1898
680f. Calvin Amaron (Strabane ON) to CC: raising money in Ontario tour .... AP 07 .... 13 Aug 1898
681f. J. Bourgoin (Pte aux Trembles QC) to CC: glad you recommended student .... AP 07 .... 16 Aug 1898
682. Frank White (Notting Hill GB) to CC .... AP 07 .... 26 Sept 1898
683. MacLean (Glasgow GB) to CC .... AP 07 .... Oct? 1898
684f. L.J.A. Papineau (Montebello QC) to CC: $15 for church .... AP 07 .... 19 Oct 1898
685. E. Schneider (Magdeburg Germany) to CC: money sent, send new book .... AP 07 .... 24 Nov 1898
686. Mrs. E.S. Alexander (Rochester NY) to CC: avoid ice, enjoyed visit with you .... AP 07 .... 28 Nov 1898
687. E. Schneider (Magdeburg Germany) to CC: more money from Germany .... AP 07 .... 14 Dec 1898
688f. Archbishop Bruchési (Montreal) to CC: willing to visit CC if desired .... AP 07 .... 10 Jan **1899**

689. CC (Montreal) to Frank Holtz (US) .... AP 03-22 .... 24 Aug ??
690. CC (Montreal) to *Star*: defence vs Charles Herbert .... AP 09-100 .... 14 Jun ??
691. James Rawlinson (Atherton GB) to CC: would like to meet CC or receive letter .... AP 07-105 .... ??
692f. CC to *A*: Catholics want to kill all Protestants .... AP 09-100 .... May ??
693. CC to the *Witness*: on the confessional vs. "Truth" Published .... AP 01-41 .... ??

* (L.J.A. Papineau (Montebello QC) to Morin: very important homage .... AP 07 .... 17 Jan 1899)
* (Murray (Halifax) to Morin: corrections for *40Y* on 1876 CC visit to Halifax .... AP 07 .... 3-18 Mar 1899)

Image 6   Wife and Daughters, Kankakee   **AP** 04-051

APPENDIX 3

Equivalencies among Chiniquy autobiographies

TOPIC	50 YEARS	50 ANS	40 YEARS	MES COMBATS	LQO
Introduction by	self	Reveillaud	MacVicar	Langevin + Reveillaud	Langevin
Childhood; Priest + Bible	ch.1	ch.1	--	pp.17-22	ch.1
St. Thomas school	2a	--	pp. 27-28	--	2
Monk and celibacy	2b	2	--	22-29	--
Children at confession	3	3	--	30-41	--
A priest disciplined	4	4	--	--	4
Purgatory, Widow's cow	5	5	--	42-50	5
Drunks in manse	6	6	pp. 27-28	51-59	6
Worshipping Mary	7	pp. 69-74	--	60-63	7
First communion	8	--	--	--	--
Call to priesthood	--	--	p.29	--	--
Intellectual submission	9	pp. 74-87	--	64-74	8
Pagan education (Greeks)	10	87-101	--	75-86	9
Protestants in RC schools	11	101-112	--	--	--
Separate schools	12	--	--	--	--
Immoral RC theology	13	112-123	--	86-95	--
Celibacy	14	124-137	--	96-107	10
Immoral confessional	15	138-156	--	108-116	11
Church Fathers vs. Bible	16	--	--	--	--
Idolatrous priesthood	17	156-169	--	116-127	12
Transubstantiation	18	170-183	--	128-139	13
St. Charles, Boyer River	19	183-202	--	139-154	14
Papineau; Papers burned	20	203-214	--	155-156	--
Banquet; Crazy woman	21	214-230	--	167-180	15
Charlesbourg; Good priests	22	231-244	--	181-191	16
Cholera; Brave priests	23	244-255	pp. 29-30	--	--
1837 Rebellion	--	--	pp. 31-32	--	--
St. Roch Quebec City	24	255-261	--	192-196	17
Simony + 1 Mass Society	25	261-273	--	197-206	18
Simony stopped	26	273-281	--	207-211	--
Wafer God in pocket	27	--	--	--	--
Temperance conviction	28	282-299	pp. 30,34-5	211-226	19
Conversion of Protestants	29	299-307	--	226-233	--
Chambers gang thefts	30	--	--	--	--
Prison chaplain	31	308-316	--	233-240	20
'Miraculous' cure	32	316-338	--	240-257	21
Alcohol in Beauport	33	338-347	pp. 33-34	258-265	22
1st Temperance Society	34	348-356	--	266-273	23
Bp Forbin-Janson aid	35	356-368	--	273-282	24
Wafer eaten by rats	36	--	--	293-301	--
John Dougall visit	37	369-374	--	--	--
Beauport success	38	374-387	p. 36	282-292	25
Bible publication	--	--	Ch. 3	302-312	--
Kamouraska arrival	39	387-400	pp. 36-37	313-323	26
Confession to priest	(54)	408-438	(Ch. 5)	--	--
RC scandals; leaving	40	438-440	p. 37	324-333	27
Newman to Catholics	41	--	--	--	--
Miracle with Temp. Manual	--	--	pp. 38-41	333-336	--
Oblate novice	42	440-464	--	336-353	28
Priest's distillery	--	--	pp. 41-42	--	--

THE CONTROVERSIAL CONVERSION OF CHARLES CHINIQUY

TOPIC	50 YEARS	50 ANS	40 YEARS	MES COMBATS	LQO
Leaving Oblates; temperance	43	460-464	--	364-367	262-5
Temperance triumphs	44	464-480	--	367-380	265-75
Sermon on Virgin Mary	45	481-494	--	381-391	Ch. 31
Church Fathers # 2	46a	494-501	--	391-396	32
Purgatory, Sucking pig	46b	501-507	--	396-401	33
Darkest hour before	--	--	Ch. 4	353-364	29
Invited to IL; Detroit	47	507-510	p. 43	402-404	293-295
IL trip; Plot vs. CC	48	511-527	--	404-414	295-306
Interdict; To Illinois	49	527-537	--	414-424	307-317
Early success in IL	50	537-545	--	424-430	318-323
Clergy scandals	51	545-547	--	430-431	324-325
Fire; Bishop O'Regan	52	--	--	--	--
Immaculate conception	53	--	--	--	--
Confession to a priest #2	54	(408-438)	(Ch. 5)	--	--
Celibacy #2	--	--	--	629-633	--
Drunk priests; Bible	55	547-549	--	432-434	326-328
O'Regan vs. CC, Lincoln	56	549-550	--	434-435	328
Excommunication	57	551	--	435	328
Popular support	58a	551-553	--	435-437	329-332
Triumph in court	58b	--	p. 43	438-451	Ch. 38
RC political aims	59	617-635	--	--	--
CC warns Lincoln	60	635-653	--	573-586	446-455
Lincoln assassination	61	653-682	--	586-588	456-457
Reconciliation fails	62	553-555	--	451-452	345-346
Brassard conclusion	63	--	--	--	--
Appeal; Peace again	64	555-561	pp. 43-44	452-456	346-350
Submission vs. gospel	65	561-578	pp. 44-5;Ch.2	456-470	350-365
Evangelical transformations	66	578-597	--	470-485	Ch. 41
Confessional in Chicago	(54)	(408-438)	Ch. 5	512-521	--
Temptation	--	--	6	485-493	42
Father Brunet in jail	p. 828	--	7	493-499	43
Famine	--	--	8	--	--
Angel - Snowdon	--	--	9	--	--
Subsequent events	67	597-616	--	499-511	44
Mercies disguised	--	--	10	554-560	--
Debts paid	--	--	11	--	--
New missionaries	--	--	12	--	--
Invitation to Quebec	--	--	13	522-527	45
To Montreal, Napierville	--	--	14	528-537	46
Quebec visit; riots	p. 824	--	15	537-547	47
Liberty of conscience	--	--	16	--	--
Death attempt; Grande Ligne	--	--	17	548-554	48
Becomes Presbyterian	--	--	18	--	--
Muskegon visit	--	--	19	560-566	49
Muskegon death threat	--	--	20	567-573	50
Lincoln assassination	--	--	21	--	--
Presbyterian College (Mtl)	--	--	22	--	--
Antigonish riot	--	--	23	--	--
His Re-baptism	--	--	24	--	--
Stratagem-riot	--	--	25	--	--
vs. Charles Hodge	--	--	26	--	--
Rev. Robert F. Burns	--	--	27	--	--
vs. Rev. George Grant	--	--	28	--	--
Australian trip	--	--	29-33	--	--
Hobart town	p. 827	--	34	--	--
Australian riots	p. 825	--	35	--	--
Conversion of Fluet	--	--	36	--	--
Riot in Montague PEI	--	--	37	--	--
Protestant testimonials	--	--	38	616-628	52
Papineau Jr. converted	--	--	39	--	--
RC proselytism vs. CC	--	--	40	634-645	53
Britain; debate in Oban	--	--	41	646-660	54
Europe; conclusion	--	--	42	660-667	--
CC declaration; funeral	--	--	43	672-8,685-8	55
More on funeral	--	--	--	678-684	--

APPENDIX 4

Chronologies

For a more detailed chronology of Chiniquy see the Articles section at: http://www.shpfq.org/

1809-13?	Kamouraska	(Eastern Quebec =	13 years)
1813?-18	Malbaie		
1818-21	St. Thomas (school)		
1821-22	Kamouraska (school)		
1822-33	Nicolet	(Nicolet =	11 years)
1833	St. Charles	(Quebec City =	9 years)
1834-38	St. Roch de Québec	area	
1838-42	Beauport		
1842-46	Kamouraska	(Eastern Quebec =	4 years)
1846-51	Montreal: Oblates + Diocese	(Montreal =	5 years)
1851-56	St. Anne's curate	(Illinois =	24 years)
1855-58	Conflicts in St. Anne's		
1859-74	St. Anne's Protestant pastor	Retirement age	
1875-78	Montreal	(Montreal =	3 years)
1878-80	World tour especially Australia + NZ	(world =	2 years)
1880-92	St. Anne's	(Illinois =	12 years)
1893-99	Montreal	(Montreal =	6 last years)

So   36 years in Illinois   (mostly Protestant)
     18 years in Eastern Quebec   (Catholic in youth)
       (10 in Kamouraska)
     14 years in Montreal   (mostly Protestant)
     11 years in Nicolet   (Catholic education)
     9 years in Quebec City area   (Catholic priest)
     2 years travelling   (Protestant)

Montreal Bishops		Quebec Bishops	
Jean-Jacques Lartigue	1836-1840	Joseph-Octave Plessis	1806-1825
Ignace Bourget	1840-1876	Bernard-Claude Panet	1825-1833
Edouard-Charles Fabre	1876-1896	Joseph Signay	1833-1850
Paul Bruchési	1897-1939	Pierre-Flavien Turgeon	1850-1867
		Chas-François Baillargeon	1867-1870
Trois-Rivières Bishops		Elzéar-Alex Taschereau	1870-1898
Thomas Cooke	1852-1870	Louis-Nazaire Bégin	1898-1925
L.-F. Laflèche	1870-1898		
F.X. Cloutier	1899-1934		
		Ottawa Bishops	
St. Hyacinthe Bishops		Jos-Eugène Bruno Guigues	1848-1874
Jean-Charles Prince	1852-1860	Joseph-Thos Duhamel	1874-1909
Joseph Larocque	1860-1865		
Charles Larocque	1866-1875	London Bishop	
Louis-Zépherin Moreau	1875-1901	Pierre-Adolphe Pinsoneault	1856-1867

THE CONTROVERSIAL CONVERSION OF CHARLES CHINIQUY

Chicago Bishops

James O. Van de Velde (Jacques Olivier)	Feb 1849- Oct 1853	Resigned after many problems; became Missis Bishop. Died 1855 at age 60
Anthony O'Regan	Aut+ 1854-8 Jun 1858	Absent from Oct 1857; resigned unable to cope; ret. to England Died 1866 aged 55
Clement Smyth(interim)	Nov 1857-pre 15 Jun 1858	Bishop of Dubuque. Died 1865 aged 55.
James Duggan	June 1858-1870	Mentally ill at age 44 till death (1869-99)
Thomas Foley	1870-1879	Died aged 57

Bourbonnais priests

Crevier		1st to visit Bourbonnais
Badin, Étienne		Pioneer & visitor to Bourbonnais
Pontavisse, Hypollite de	1839	Visits and built chapel
Courjault, René	Sept(Nov) 1847-Apr 52	1st resident priest (suspension for immorality)
Huicq (Hoey,Wieg), L.	Apr 1852-Nov 1852(interim)	(Hincq in Trudel)
Chiniquy, C.	28 Nov 1852-13 Sept 1853	Replaced by full time priest
Maistre, J.	Sept 1853-Nov 1854	(Lemaitre in Trudel)
Lebel, Isidor (J-A)	Nov 1854-Jul 1855	Obliged to leave the diocese
Chiniquy, C.	9-18 Sept 1855	
Cartuyvels, Louis	16 Dec 1855-27 Dec 1856	
Desaulniers, I.L.	4 Dec 1856- 4 Jun 1857	From St. Hyacinthe Diocese
Mailloux, Alexis	26 Mar 1857- Autumn 1862	From Quebec Diocese
Champeaux, J. Baptiste	26 Mar 1857- 20 Jul 1857	
Gingras, Nérée (Jos)	Oct 1859-30 Aug 1863(2)	
Côté, Jacob	Spring 1860-1863	
Paradis, Pierre	Feb 1861-	

<u>St. Marie (Beaverville) and area</u>

Lapointe, Épiphane	16 Oct 1857-Jun 60+	<u>L'Érable</u>		
Côté, Jacob	Spring 1860-1862(3)	Huicq(Hoey)	Jan-May? 1853 Left IL missions	
Ducroux, C.	1862-1863	C. Brisard	Spring 1856-Aut 1859 (request to go to Detroit)
Gauthier, T	1863	Vandepoole	Jun 1860+ Critic of Lebel & other priests
Marchal, Auguste	1863-1866		
Boisvert, Léon (CSV)	1866-1867		
Kerston, Georges	1867-1869		
Demers, Louis B.	1869-1871		

<u>St. Anne</u>

mission of St. Marie	1858-1871	(old frame church)
Letellier, Michel	23 Feb 1871-1883	(1873 new church built)

<u>Chicago French parish priest</u>

Lebel, Isidor-A.	Oct 1850-1854? (then Bourbonnais, Sandwich Diocese, Kalamazoo-1871)

APPENDIX 5

Supporters of Chiniquy by country

(a preliminary list with places of origin and dates of known involvement with Chiniquy or his writings)

The dates following the names refer to the period when there was proven contact with Chiniquy or his books. All those mentioned here co-operated with Chiniquy except those classified as "critics". Look at his writings in foreign languages for some other publishers.

GREAT BRITAIN
Intimate friends: G.R. Badenoch (LLD invited Chiniquy in 1859, 1885 and 1889, Secretary of the Scottish Reformation Society; author); Mesac Thomas (Secretary of the Colonial Church and School Society 1860+ and later Bishop of Goulburn, Australia 1876+); Montagu Russell Butler (Fund organizer, author 1876-9+); Mrs. Mary Faulkner Bird (Leeds 1878+); A.H. Guinness (Secretary of Protestant Alliance 1896-7+); Rev. Stirling (arranged his tour in 1897)
Correspondents: Kendall (1893), Alfred Millard (Protestant Union 1896)
Critics: Thomas Biggs (1861), Sydney Smith (1897-1900)
Associations: Colonial Church and School Soc.(1858?-60), Evangelical Alliance, Religious Tract and Book Soc. of Scotland (1861+), Protestant Institute of Scotland (1862), Père Chiniquy Aid Fund (1876-9+), John Kensit and the Protestant Truth Society (1883+), British and Foreign Bible Society (1883+), Protestant Alliance (1896-7), Scottish Protestant Alliance (1896), Calvinistic Protestant Union (1897)
Newspapers: *Record* (Anglican evangelical 1862), *British Ensign* (1862), *British Standard* (1864+) *The Rock* (1876+), *The Christian* (London 1876-99), *Protestant Times* (London 1887), *Protestant Alliance Monthly Newsletter* (London 1896-9), *The Bulwark* (monthly 1896-9), *Christian Herald* (London 1897-9), *Christian Commonwealth* (London 1897+), *Christian Leader* (Glasgow 1899), *Christian Church* (1899)
Publishers: The Record (London 1860), Religious Tract and Book Society of Scotland (Glasgow 1861), W.T. Gibson (London 1874), Operative Jewish Converts' Institution (London 1877), J.W. Bean and Sons (Leeds 1878), A.S. Mallett (London 1879), Thomas Gee (Dinbych, Wales 1880), Marshall Press (London 1883), Protestant Literature Depository (London 1886), R. Banks (London 1886-1901), John Kensit (London 1887), Protestant Truth Society (London ca1887, 1948), Allan Printers (Barnstaple 1897), Charles Thynne (London 1897), A. Holness (London ca1900), Hodder and Stoughton (London 1900)

IRELAND
Correspondents: John Nesbitt (Belfast 1897), James V. Scott (Belfast 1897)
Critics: Thomas Biggs (1861)
Newspaper: *Presbyterian* (Belfast 1899)

UNITED STATES
Intimate friends: Stephen Moore (lawyer, Kankakee 1857-83+), Miss Rebecca Snowdon and George Stuart (philanthropists from Philadelphia 1859 who continued to fund him after), Rev. Alfred Hamilton (Presbyterian 1859-62), Dr. Thomas (1889-93+), Dr. Warren MD (homeopath 1879 in Australia and in Boston 1894+), James

THE CONTROVERSIAL CONVERSION OF CHARLES CHINIQUY

O'Connor (1880-99+), John Moore (Boston 1897-9+)
Correspondents: General Harris (1891-7), Hubert Taylor (1892-3), Edwin Sherman (1883)
Critics: Matthew Dillon, Rev. L'Hote, Moses Staples, Chicago Presbytery, *Kankakee Gazette* (Philip Worcester and the editor, Mr. Parker), "Kentucky Ben"
Associations: La Société des Tondeurs (1857-8?), AFCU (1859+), American Tract Society (1860+), Loyal Women of American Liberty (1878?), Pauline Propaganda, Collège Protestant Français (Springfield MA -1899)
Newspapers: *Journal d'Illinois* (1857-9), *Kankakee Democrat* (1857-60+), *Journal of Commerce* (NY 1858-9), *Chicago Tribune* (1858-60), *NY Observer* (1862), *Presbyterian* (Phila. 1859-99), *Primitive Catholic* (Brooklyn 1892-7), *Converted Catholic* (NY 1883-1899+), *Christian Register* (Boston, 1887), *Christian Guide* (1887?), *Semeur franco-américain* (MA 1887-90), *American Citizen* (Boston 1889?), *CFA* (MA 1890-5), *St. Anne Record* (1893+), *Protestant Standard* (Phila. 1873, 1893+), NY *Christian Advocate* (1892), *NY Weekly Witness* (1893+), *Messiah's Herald* (Boston 1894+, American Millennial Assoc), *Daily Mirror and American* (Manchester NH 1895), *APA Magazine* (1895), *American Advocate* (Iowa 1899-9), *Interior* (Chicago 1899), *Citizen* (Boston 1899), *The American* (Omaha 1899), *Observer* (NY 1899), *Sunday School Times* (1953), *Christian Heritage* (1976)
Publishers: anonymous but in French (Chicago 1863), J.C.W. Bailey (Chicago 1867), anonymous (Kankakee IL 1867), Loyal Women of American Liberty (1878?), Revell (NY 1880-1900), *Fidèle Messager* (Manchester NH 1881), *Protestant Standard* (Philadelphia 1882), Craig and Barlow (Chicago 1882-89), R.W. Mercer (Cincinnati 1884-94), anonymous (St. Anne 1884), *Converted Catholic* (NY 1885), Curtis and Jennings (Cincinnati 1889 in German), Allied Publishing (Cleveland c1890), Adam Craig (Chicago 1891), anonymous (Minneapolis 1892), Ironclad Press (Minneapolis 1893), American Baptist Publication Society (Philadelphia 1899), Menace Publishing (Aurora MO 1914), A Geringera (Chicago 1921), Rail Splitter Press (Milan IL c1925), Agora Publishing Co.(New York 1933-46), Christ's Mission (NY 1948), Continental Press (Philadelphia 1953), Baker Book House (Grand Rapids 1958-1970), Carol Publishing Group (USA 1968), Chick (Chino CA 1979-93+), E. Wingren (Chicago, in Swedish, n.d.), Life Messengers (Seattle n.d.), Assurance in Life (Tulsa 1998+), Hard Press (2008)

QUEBEC
Intimate friends: while a Catholic - Moïse Brassard, I. Leprohon, Judge Mondelet, Louis Cazeau, Dr Douglas
 - **while a Protestant** - Pierre Blanchet, Théodore Lafleur, Narcisse Cyr, Alex Kemp, John Dougall, Principal MacVicar, John Campbell, R.P. Duclos, Calvin Amaron, Joseph Provost, Placide Boudreau, I.P. Bruneau, Joseph Morin, Laurent Rivard, Charles Coussirat, Charles Doudiet, L.J.A. Papineau, William Grant Stewart (his doctor), the Lighthall family, A. Mackey, Narcisse McLaren
Critics: Bishop Prince, Isaac Desaulniers, Alexis Mailloux, *Courrier du Canada*, Alphonse Villeneuve, W.B. Court
Associations: Jeune Canada (1857), the *Francs frères* (1859), the *Institut Canadien*, FCMS (1869-70+), Ladies French Evangelization Society of Presbyterian Church of Canada (1875-), Protestant Defence Association (or Alliance) (1875-80), *Société de bienfaisance des protestants de langue française de Montréal* (1876), *Jeunes gens protestants* (1876+), Montreal Religious Tract Society (1876), International Protestant League (1877+), Orange Order (c1876+), Independent Order of Rechabites (1899)
Newspapers: *Semeur canadien* (1856-61), *l'Avenir* (1857-8), *Montreal Witness*, *l'Aurore, La Liberté* (1876), *Montreal Herald* (occasionally)
Publishers: *l'Avenir* (Mtl 1857-8) *Canada Observer* (Mtl 1863), *Witness* (Mtl 1870+,1896-9), *l'Aurore* (Mtl 1870-1962), Mitchell (Mtl 1872), Mitchell and Wilson (Mtl 1874),

APPENDIX 5

Grafton (Mtl 1870-86), Librairie évangélique (Mtl 1875), Wm. Drysdale and Rivard (Mtl 1885), Musson Book Co. (Toronto 1907), Éditions Beauport (Quebec 1976-95+)

ENGLISH CANADA
Intimate friends: Rev. George Sutherland (Presbyterian, Charlottetown PEI 1857+), Bishop I. Hellmuth (Anglican 1858-60), Dr. R.F. Burns (Presbyterian)
Associations: Presbyterian Committee on French Evangelization (1867-1875), Board of French Evangelization (1875-99)
Newspapers: *Ecclesiastical and Missionary Record* (PCC 1859+), *Home and Foreign Record of CPC* (1862-), *Canada Presbyterian* (1875+), *Presbyterian Witness* (NS 1876+), *The Sentinel* (Toronto), *Presbyterian Review* (Toronto)
Publishers: Essex Journal (Sandwich ON 1862), Canada Observer (Montreal 1863), Sentinel (Toronto c1864,1878), Thomas Maddocks (Stratford 1866), London Free Press (1870), NS Print Co. (Halifax 1873,76), Lovell (Toronto 1875), Willard Tract Depot (Toronto 1888+), Wm. Briggs (Toronto 1892,1914), Gospel Witness (Toronto 1940), Wittenburg Press (Toronto 1987), Christ is the Answer (Toronto 1991+)

AUSTRALIA
Intimate friends: Rev. George Sutherland DD (editor *Presbyterian*, Sydney NSW 1878+), Dr Warren MD (involved in Anti-Catholic and other political movements pre 1894)
Newspapers: *Witness* (Sydney 1878-9); *Victorian Standard* (1887), *Protestant Standard* (Sydney 1887), *Southern Cross* (Melbourne 1899), *The Protestant* (Sydney 1899), *Presbyterian Press or Witness* (Tasmania 1899), *Evangelical Press* (Brisbane 1899)
Publishers: Lee and Pon (Sydney 1878), Lee and Ross (Sydney 1879), Hutchinson (Melbourne 1879)

NEW ZEALAND
Newspaper: *Protestant Ensign* (1887)
Publisher: Otago Bible Tracts (Otago, 1880), John Browne (Auckland 1880)

INDIA
Newspapers: *India Watchman* (Bombay 1897)
Critic: Examiner Press (Bombay 1912)

FRANCE
Intimate friend: Eugène Réveillaud (editor *Le Signal,* evangelical activist and member of the government 1880-1900)
Critic: Rev. Théodore Monod (1860-2 during his stay in Illinois)
Associations: Église évangélique libre(1860), Société Coligny (a Protestant society to promote colonization, 1897)
Newspapers: *Bulletin du monde Chrétien* (1860), *Chrétien évangélique* (1860+), *Le chrétien français* (Paris 1898)
Publishers: Desrues (Melun 1860), Grassart (Paris 1880), Librairie Fischbacher (Paris 1908)

SWITZERLAND
Publisher: J.H. Jeheber (Geneva 1902)

BELGIUM
Publishers: A.N. Lebegue (Brussels 1877), La Prévoyance évangélique (n.d.), Éditeurs de Littérature Biblique (Braine l'Alleud 1962-78)

GERMANY
Correspondents: Hanstein (Berlin 1894-98), Gertrude de Lyden (Berlin)
Publisher: Weimann (Barmen 1890)

NETHERLANDS
Correspondents: H.J. Schouten (1891-97), A.E. Schouten (Gravenhage 1897), E. Schneider (1897-98)
Publisher: A.J. Kropholler (Amsterdam, Hoveker)

ITALY
Intimate friend: Alessandro Gavazzi (1868-70+)
Publishers: A. Ettore (Rome 1898), Émilio Comba (Florence 1917)

SWEDEN
Publisher: Forlaget Filadelfia (Stockholm 1958)

HUNGARY
Publisher: Mezo Tur (1890)

RUSSIA
Publisher: Petrograd (1901-02)

SOUTH AFRICA
Correspondent: M.A. Koch (Johannesburg 1886)
Publisher: Nelspruit (1947)

CHILE
Publisher: Helfmann (Valparaiso 1886)

ARGENTINA
Publisher: Libreria La Aurora (Buenos Aires 1936)

URUGUAY
Publisher: El Siglo Illustrado (Montivideo 1886)

BIBLIOGRAPHY

Primary Sources

Manuscripts:
    Allan Pequegnat archives (Elliot Lake ON): many Lefebvre documents not sent to McGill Rare Books plus copies of those sent to McGill.   http://www.chiniquy.ca/
    Archives de l'Archevêché de Québec (Quebec City): États Unis VII
    Archives de l'Archevêché de Montréal: Chiniquy File, Bourget registers
    Archives du Séminaire de Québec (Quebec City): "Polygraphies", Cartons 50-52
    Archives nationales du Québec (Montreal).
    Archives of the University of Notre Dame (South Bend IL): misc. Letters, brochures and copies of Séminaire de Québec material.
    Canadian Baptist Archives (McMaster Divinity School, Hamilton ON): Chiniquy file
    Kankakee Historical Society (Kankakee IL): Chiniquy files
    McGill Rare Books (McGill University Library, Montreal): Samuel Lefebvre collection, Lighthall collection.
    Meier, Lois (St. Anne IL): small private Chiniquy collection
    Presbyterian Church Archives (Toronto): a few letters, Presbyterian records
    Presbyterian Historical Society (Philadelphia): Chiniquy clippings
    United Church Archives (Toronto): C. Chiniquy personal papers
    United Church Archives Montreal-Ottawa Conference (Montreal): Église St. Jean records, Amaron papers, Biéler papers, Société d'histoire papers, Franco-American papers

Secondary sources

Chiniquy works (books and printed brochures). These are just a fraction of all his pamphlets and editions:

1. *Manuel ou règlement de la Société de Tempérance*, Quebec, Stanislas Drapeau, 1844, v + 158 p.
2. *Manual of the Temperance Society*, Montreal, Lovell and Gibson, 1847, 113 p. [Translation of #1] AP 01
3. *Manuel des sociétés de tempérance*, Montreal, Lovell and Gibson, ²1847, 149 p. [New edition of #1]
4. *Manuel des sociétés de tempérance*, Montreal, J. Bte. Rolland, ²1849, 173 p.
5. *Manuel des sociétés de tempérance*, Montreal, J. Bte. Rolland, ³1849, 192 p.   AP 01
6. *Le suisse méthodiste confondu et convaincu d'ignorance et de mensonge*, Montreal, n.p., 1851, ix + 40 p.   AP 01
7. *Persécutions de l'Abbé Chiniquy, l'Apôtre de la Tempérance. Les Français catholiques de Chicago et l'évêque O'Regan* [Montreal, l'Avenir, 1857], 6 p.
8. *Les Français catholiques de Chicago et l'évêque Oregan*, Montreal, l'Avenir, [1857], 6 p.
9. *French Catholics and Bishop O'Regan*, n.l., n.p., [c1857], 8 p. [Translation of #8]
10. *Persécutions aux Illinois, de l'abbé Chiniquy, l'apôtre de la tempérance au Canada*, Montreal [l'Avenir, Mar. 1857], 36 p.
11. *Lettre du Père Chiniquy à M. Brassard*, Montreal, l'Avenir, 1857, 23 p.
12. *Father Chiniquy's Letter to Mr. Brassard, Curate of St. Roch L'Achignan*, Montreal, n.p., 1857, 24 p. [Translation of #11]
13. *Réponse du Révérend Messire Chiniquy aux calomnies de Mr. J.C. Taché, Rédacteur du Courrier du Canada*, 1857, 2 p.
14. *The Life and Labours of the Rev. Father Chiniquy*, with introduction by Rev. Wm. Arnot, Glasgow, Religious Tract and Book Society of Scotland, 1861, 33 p.
15. *Address Delivered by Rev. C. Chiniquy on his Defence Before the Chicago Presbytery*, Sandwich ON, Essex *Journal*, 1862, 11 p.   AP 01

16. *L'Ennemie de la Sainte Vierge et de Jésus-Christ est l'Église de Rome*, Chicago, n.p., 1863, 42 p.
17. *Rome est l'ennemi de la Ste Vierge et de Jésus-Christ*, n.l., n.p., ²1863. [New edition of #16]
18. *The God of Rome eaten by a rat*, Toronto, Sentinel, [c1863], 16 p.
19. *Jésus crucifié et le bon larron*, n.l., n.p., [c1864].
20. *The Church of Rome is the Enemy of the Holy Virgin and of Jesus Christ*, Stratford ON, Thomas Maddocks, 1866, 59 p. [Translation by Fanny MacPherson of #17]   AP 01
21. *Confession générale; Lettres du Père Chiniquy dans lesquelles il semble faire une confession générale de tous ses crimes pendant 25 ans de Prêtrise*, Montreal, n.p., [1867], 2 p. [edition by his opponents]
22. *L'Immaculée Conception de la Sainte Vierge*; par le Père C. Chiniquy, [c1867].
23. *The Immaculate Conception of the Virgin Mary*, Chicago, J.C.W. Bailey, 1867, 8 p.   AP 01
24. *The Church of Rome as it is*, [Kankakee IL, 1867], 4 p.   AP 01
25. *The Church of Rome: Reply of Rev. Father Chiniquy to Vicar-General Bruyère*, n.l., n.p., 1869, 16 p.; London, London Free Press, 1870, 23 p.
26. *Sound an Alarm!*, pamphlet of letter to *Christian Times*, St. Anne Illinois, 1869, 4 p.   AP 01
27. [A pamphlet in French on the Catholic Ecumenical Council], Montreal, Grafton, "proceeds for the Illinois mission", cJan 1870.
28. *L'Église de Rome; Réponse du Révérend Charles Chiniquy au Rév. J.M. Bruyère, Grand-Vicaire de London, Ontario. Contenant six lettres autographes de la plus haute importance écrites par les évêques du Canada*, Montreal, l'Aurore, 1870, 16 p.; Montreal, Witness, 1870, 20 p. AP 01
29. *Discours du Père Chiniquy prononcé à l'Église Évangélique de la rue Craig*, Montreal, l'Aurore, 1870, 8 p.   AP 10-103
30. *Discours du Père Chiniquy contre l'infaillibilité papale*, Montreal, l'Aurore, 1870, in two parts of 8 p.   AP 01
31. *The Church of Rome. Reply of Rev. Mr. Chiniquy to Vicar-Gen. Bruyère*, Montreal, l'Aurore, ²1871, 16 p.   AP 01
32. *The Church of Rome. Replies of Chiniquy to Mgr. Bruyère and Mr. Kilroy*, Montreal, Mitchell & Wilson, ³1872, 31 p.   AP 01
33. *Father Chiniquy's Exposure of the Confessional*, n.l., n.p., [c1873], 4 p.
34. *Why Father Chiniquy was Re-baptised*, St. Anne Illinois, n.p., 1873, 8 p.   AP 01
35. *A Solemn Question. Can the Protestants conscientiously build up the churches of the Pope?*, by Rev. Chas. Hodge and Chiniquy, Halifax, Nova Scotia Print Co., 1873; Chicago, Craig and Barlow, 1884, 16 p.   AP 01
36. *L'Immaculée Conception de la Sainte-Vierge*; par le Père C. Chiniquy, Montreal, Mitchell and Wilson, 1874, 16 p. [New edition of #16; included in *50 Ans*]
37. *The Priest, the Woman and the Confessional*, London, W.T. Gibson, 1874, 192 p.; Montreal, F.E. Grafton, 1875, 184 p.; Grafton, ²1876, 184 p.; Grafton, ³1876, 184 p.; Grafton, ⁵1878, 184 p.; Brisbane, J. U. M'Naught, 1879, 189 p., Chicago, Craig, ²⁹1886.   AP 01
38. *Le vrai contre-poison pour faire disparaître la confession auriculaire; respectueusement présenté à Monseigneur l'Évêque Bourget, par son ancien prêtre et ami Chiniquy*, Montreal, l'Aurore, 1875, 22 p.; Montreal, l'Aurore, ²1878, 22 p.; Montreal, l'Aurore, ³1884 [including 2 letters by Pierre Boisvert], 27 p.   AP 01 AP 10
39. *Le Chiniquy d'autrefois: Le suisse méthodiste confondu et convaincu d'ignorance et de mensonge*, Montreal, n.l., 1875, 29 p. [hostile reprinting of #6]   AP 15
40. *Father Chiniquy's Three Lectures in Toronto: under the auspices of the "Prentice boys" together with the remarks of each chairman and others*, Toronto, Lovell, 1875, 23 p.   AP 01
41. *Le prêtre, la femme et le confessionnal*, Montreal, Librairie évangélique, 1875, 337 p.; ²1877, Montreal, l'Aurore, 337 p.; Brussels, A.N. Lebegue, ³1877, 364 p.; Paris, Grassart, ⁴1880, 368 p.; "nouvelle édition", Montreal, l'Aurore, 1925, 253 p.
42. *A True narrative of a real penitent: a warning to parents and guardian of youth, and all who advocate the introduction of the confessional into our reformed church*, Oxford, Alden's Printing, 1875, 31 p. [from PWC]
43. *Le Bon Dieu de Rome mangé par les rats*, n.l., n.p, 1876, 8 p.   AP 01
44. *Letter from Rev. C. Chiniquy to the Bishop of Montreal*, Toronto, Orange Sentinel Printers, 1877, 14 p.
45. *Chiniquy Lectures as delivered in the Protestant Hall Sydney and Temperance Hall, Melbourne*, Melbourne, M.L. Hutchinson, 1879 (45th thousand), 48 p.; *A Series of Lectures delivered by the Rev. Charles Chiniquy in the Protestant Hall, Sydney*, Sydney, Lee and Pon, ³1878, 48 p. AP 01
46. *Mr. Chiniquy in California*, [San Francisco], Loyal Women of American Liberty, 1878, 4 p.   AP 01
47. *Romish Idolatry: Rev. C. Chiniquy versus Bishop Lynch*, Toronto, Sentinel Printing, 1878, 16 p.
48. *Papal Idolatry: an exposure of the mariolatry of Mons. Lynch and Archbishop Vaughan of Sydney. With "The God of R..." and "Reasons why I will never return..."*, Sydney, Lee and Ross, 1879, 23 p.
49. *Auricular Confession in Australia + Chiniquy Vindicated* (From the "Protestant Standard"), Melbourne, M.L. Hutchinson, 1879, 16 p.   AP 01
50. *Pastor Chiniquy and the Roman Catholic Riots in Hobart Town with Account of Disturbances and Closing Lecture on Dangers Ahead*, Revised and enlarged by the Pastor, Hobart Town Tasmania, Mercury, 1879, 29 p.   AP 01 AP 10
51. *Papal Idolatry: An Exposure of the Dogmas of Transubstantiation and Mariolatry*, Melbourne, Australia, Hutchinson, 1879, 48 p.; edition with "The reasons why ...", London, Robert Banks & Son, 1887, 54 p.   AP 01
52. *Purgatory – a lecture*, Dunedin, New Zealand, Otago Bible Tracts, 1880, 8 p.   AP 01
53. *The Priest, the Woman and the Confessional*, N.Y., Revell, ²³1880, 296 p.; Chicago, A. Craig

BIBLIOGRAPHY

and Co., 1880; Chicago, Craig and Barlow, ²⁹1886; Chicago, Craig, ³²1888; San Francisco, Brier & Dobbins, 1888; NY, Christ's Mission, 1950; N.Y., Revell, ⁴³1967. AP 01
54. *My First Years: the Bible and the Priest of Rome*, n.l., n.p., [pre 1885], 4 p [Ch 1 of *50 Y* and in Bird].
55. *Rome and Education*, Auckland, Free Press, 1880, 15 p.; lecture given at Manchester NH, n.l., n.p., 1881, 16 p. AP 01
56. *From Chicago to Australia*, Philadelphia, Protestant Standard, 1882, 55 p.; Chicago, Craig, [1879], 58 p. [Consists of 12 letters by Chiniquy mostly from *50 Y*] AP 01
57. *Papal Idolatry: An Exposure of the Dogma of Transubstantiation and Mariolatry*, Philadelphia, Protestant Standard, 1882, 58 p.; Chicago, A. Craig, 1888. [includes "The God of Rome eaten by a Rat, Reasons why I will never return, Mariolatry, Crucified Jesus and the penitent thief" plus Chiniquy letters] AP 01
58. *The Priest, the Woman and the Confessional*, London, Marshall Press, 1883, 161 p.; London, London Protestant Truth Society, 161 p.
59. *President Lincoln's Assassination traced directly to the doors of Rome*, Cincinnati, R.W. Mercer, 1884, 46 p.
60. *Father Chiniquy's Defence Against the Chicago Presbytery*, [St. Anne], n.p., [1884], 2 p.
61. *Father Chiniquy to Mgr. Lynch, Archbishop of Toronto*, Chicago, Craig and Barlow, 1884, 4 p. AP 01
62. *The Crucified Jesus and the Penitent Thief*, published in *Converted Catholic*, vol. II, 110-116 and then in 1885 by them as pamphlet 22 p.; London, John Kensit, 1887, 11 p. AP 01
63. "The Prodigal Son and His Father", published in *Converted Catholic*, vol.2, 202-6.
64. *Fifty Years in the Church of Rome*, Chicago, Craig and Barlow, 1885, xvi + 832 p.; NY, Revell, ²1886; Chicago, Craig, ¹²1888; (new illustrated), Toronto, Willard Tract Depository, ¹⁶¹1888 + ³¹1890; Chicago, Craig, 1892; Montreal, Drysdale, [1900?].
65. *Cinquante ans dans l'Église de Rome*, Montreal, Librairie de Wm. Drysdale et Cie. et de L.E. Rivard, 1885, Vol. I, 540 p. [no vol. II]. AP 01
66. *Pastor's Register 1881-1887*, 64 p. AP 10
67. *Fifty Years in the Church of Rome*, London, Protestant Literature Depository, 1886, 597 p. [with intro. by Badenoch, 5th thousand, corrected and rev; same material as #64]; reprinting in Grand Rapids, Baker Book House, 1958 and 1970, 597 p.; Chino CA, Chick, 1981, 597 p.
68. *Fifty Years in the Church of Rome*, London, R. Banks, 1886, 678 p.
69. *The Priest, the Woman and the Confessional*, London, R. Banks and Son, new ed., c1886, 232 p.
70. *Why I left the Church of Rome*, London, Protestant Educational Institute, c1883, 24 p.; Protestant Truth Society, [c1887], 30 p.; London, Protestant Truth Society, 1958, 24 p.AP 01 AP 12
71. *Fifty Years in the Church of Rome*, rev. ed., London, R. Banks, 1888, 580 p.; Toronto, William Briggs, 1914, 580 p.
72. *Dr. Chiniquy to 'Truth': some severe reflections upon the latter's statements*, n.l., n.p., n.d., 2 p. AP 01
73. *The Assassination of Lincoln*, n.l., n.p., 1890, 23 p.; Cleveland, Allied Pub. Co., [1890?], 38 p.; Milan IL., Rail Splitter Press, [c1925], 32 p. [from *50 Years*] AP 02
74. *L'Église de Rome est l'ennemie de la Sainte Vierge et de Jésus-Christ*, Montreal, n.p., 1891, 48 p. [2nd ed, of #17] AP 01
75. *Papal idolatry: An Exposure of the Dogma of Transubstantiation and Mariolatry*, Chicago, Adam Craig, 1891, 58 p. AP 01
76. *Father Chiniquy to Kentucky Ben*, Minneapolis, Penny Printer, 1892, 19 p. AP 01
77. *The Two Chiniquys: Father Chiniquy vs Minister Chiniquy*, Montreal, The True Witness, 1893, 24 p. [Translation of #39] AP 10
78. *The Murder of Abraham Lincoln planned and executed by Jesuit priests*, Indianapolis, The Ironclad Age, 1893, 11 p.
79. *Lettre du Dr Chiniquy à l'archevêque Fabre*, Montreal, n.p., 1894, 16 p. AP 01
80. *Chiniquy to Fabre: "your besieging me with your priests"...*, Montreal, n.p., printed letter, 1895, 7 p. AP 01
81. *Dr. Chiniquy to Senator Tassé and Mgr. Lynch, Archbishop of Toronto*, n.l., n.p., 1894, 36 p. [Expansion of #61] AP 01
82. *President Lincoln's assassination traced directly to the doors of Rome*, Cincinnati, R.W. Mercer, 1894, 46 p. [compiled from *50 Y*]
83. "President Lincoln's assassination traced directly to the doors of Rome", *APA Magazine*, 1, 6 (Nov. 1895), 547-561. [compiled from *50 Y*]
84. *Papal Idolatry.... dedicated to Cardinal Gibbons of Baltimore MD...*, Montreal, n.p., 1895, 51 p.
85. *Le sacerdoce de Rome*, [Montreal, l'Aurore, 1895], 16 p. AP 01
86. *The Perversion of Dr. Newman to the Church of Rome*, Montreal, Witness Print House, ³1896, 39 p.; London,W.T. Gibson, n.d., 36 p. [Expansion of ch. 41 of *50 Y*]. AP 01
87. *Why I left the Church of Rome*, Barnstaple, England, Allan Printers, 1897, 4 p.
88. *Father Chiniquy D.D. A Reply to Accusations circulated by Roman Catholics*, England, n.p., [1896-7], 1 p. AP 01
89. *Father Chiniquy's Dying Confession*, London, A. Holness, ³1899, 16 p.; Aurora MO, Menace Pub. Co., 1914, 28 p. AP 01
90. *La confession de foi du Père Chiniquy six jours avant sa mort*, Philadelphia, American Baptist Publication Society, no. 3215, n.d., 8 p. AP 12
91. *Fifty Years in the Church of Rome*, London, Robert Banks and Son, rev. ed. 1899, 590 p.; London, Banks, 1901; London, Banks, 1906; London, Banks, 1911; London, Banks, 1919; London, Marshall Press, 1978 [same as #71 except added appendix with his 1893 statement around death, notarized statement 6 days before death, letter from Bourget 1899 and Coussirat's reply, funeral description and eulogy + extract from his will].

THE CONTROVERSIAL CONVERSION OF CHARLES CHINIQUY

92. *Fifty Years in the Church of Rome*, London, Protestant Truth Society, 1900, 472 p.; New York, Agora Publishing Co., n.d.; London, Protestant Truth Society, 1948; NY, Christ's Mission, 1948; Grand Rapids, Baker, 1953; NY, Christ's Mission, 1953.
93. *Forty Years in the Church of Christ*, Toronto (Chicago, NY), Fleming Revell, 1900, 498 p.; Chicago, Revell, ³1901; Chino CA, Chick, [198?]; Toronto, Wittenburg Press, 1987. AP 01
94. *Cinquante ans dans l'Église Romaine*, Geneva, Librairie J.-H. Jeheber, 2 vol. 1902-1903, 682 p. AP 01
95. *Le prêtre, la femme et le confessionnal*, Montreal, l'Aurore, 1931, 259 p.; l'Aurore, 1962, 317 p.
96. *The Priest, the Woman and the Confessional*, Toronto, Gospel Witness, ⁴⁴1939, 144 p.; Toronto, Gospel Witness, ⁴⁵1940; Chino, Chick, 1979.
97. *Mes Combats: Autobiographie de Charles Chiniquy*, Montreal, l'Aurore Publishing, 1946, 691 p. [condensation of *Cinquante ans* and *Forty Years* by John Spreeman]
98. *Fifty Years in the Church of Rome*, New South Wales, Australia, Protestant Publications, 1952, 495 p. AP 01
99. *The Gift of Salvation: A Holy Year Message*, Philadelphia, Continental Press, 1953, 16 p. [a condensation of part of *50Y*]; NY, Agora, [1946], 27 p. AP 12
100. *The Finished Wonder*, Seattle, Life Messengers, n.d., 31 p. AP 12
101. *Merveilleux mystère*, Braine l'Alleud, Belgium, Éditions de Littérature biblique, 1962-78, 29 p. AP 12
102. *Chiniquy: l'homme qui osa défier le puissant empire de Rome*, Trois-Rivières, Éditions Beauport, 1976, 508 p.; also 1978 and 1986. [a revised edition of #97]
103. *Le don*, Philadelphia, n.p., 16 p.; also Brussels, La Prévoyance évangélique, 16 p.
104. *The Big Betrayal*, Chino, Chick, 1981, 64 p. [comic book format]
105. *Fifty Years in the Church of Rome*, condensed edition, Chino, Chick, 1985, 366 p.
106. *Le miracle parfait*, Canada, Christ is the Answer, c1991, 38 p: Montreal, La Croisade du Livre Chrétien, n.d. AP 12

Foreign language translations of Chiniquy writings (these are just a known fraction of the total):

I *A pap, a no és a gyotatoszék...Forditotta Révész Mihaly*, Mezo Tur, Hungary, 1890, 197 p.
II *Davushki i ikh prosvietiteli* [transliteration of the Russian title], Petrograd, 1902, 178 p.
III *Ispovied' zhenshchtay-katolichki* (Russian transliteration) Petrograd, 1901, 166 p.
IV *Die Ermordung des Präsidenten Abraham Lincon eine That der Jesuiten*, Barmen, Wiemann, 32p (FreunschaftlicheStreitschriften; Nr.26).
V *Der priester, die frau und die ehrenbeichte...deutsch ubersetzung nach der 29 englischen zu fl...hrag from Friedrich von Schwarzbach*, Barmen, Weimann, n.d., 268 p.
VI *Der priester, das weib und die ohren-beichte, Nach der 41 englischen auflage hergestellt*, Cincinatti, Curtis and Jennings, 1889, 240 p. [transl by F. v. Schwarzbach]
VII *Die Ermondung des Präsidenten Abraham Lincoln eine That der Jesuiten*, Barmen, Weimann, 1890, 32 p.
VIII *Pater Chiniquys Erlebnisse oder 50 Jahre in der romischen Kirche*, ed. F. Schlachter, Elberfeld, Evangelischer Gesellschaft fur Deutschland, 1910, 359 p. cover AP 01
IX *Vierig jahre in der kirche Christi*, Barmen, Wiemann, n.d., 303 p. AP 01
X *40 jahre in der kirche Christi*, Baden, Verlag Christeche Buchhandlung, E. Jucker, n.d., 104 p. AP 01
X *Der biecht stuhl*, Baden, Verlag Christeche Buchhandlung E.Jucker, 1961, 112 p. AP 01
XI *De Werken van Vader Chiniquy: vijftig jaren in de kerk van Rome, en de priester, de vrouw en de biecht*, ed., A.J. Kropholler, Amsterdam, Hoveker, 502 p.; Rotterdam, Geloof in Vrijheid, n.d. 320 p.
XII *De afgoderij van het pausdom en de redenen waarom ik nooitzal terugkeeren tot do kerk van Rome*, Rotterdam, Geloof in Vrijheid, n.d. 64 p. AP 01
XIII *El cura, la mujer y el confesonario*, Buenos Aeres, Libreria "La Aurora", Nueva ed. 1936, 188 p.; Barcelona, Editorial Atlante Continuadora de Las Publicaciones, n.d., 192 p. cover AP 01
XIV *El sacerdote, la mujer y el confessonario* [sic] *o, Cosas de suma importancia para el pueblo*, trans. and notes by Guillermo Young, Montivedeo, "El siglo Illustrado", 1886, 164 p.
XV *Gissah al-ab Shinikuy: al-kahin al-Kathuliki sabiqa*, s.l., s.n., 1890, 61 p. [Arabic]
XVI *Il prete, la donna ed il confessionale*, Roma, A Ettore, ³1898.
XVII "Il prete, la donna ed il confessionale", part of *Claudio de Torino, ossia, la Protesta di un vescovo*, Emilio Comba, ed., Firenze, Tipografia Claudiana, ⁷1917, 730 p.
XVIII *50 Years*, Chinese edition, Voice Books, 1998. cover AP 01
XIX *Knez, zena a zpoved*, Chicago, A Geringera, 1921, 114 p. [Serbian?]
XX *Okwangenza (ukuba) ngishiye iBandla lase-Roma* (translated by V.T.E. Ngwenya), Nelspruit, South Africa, 1947, 27 p.
XXI *Okwangenza (ukuba) ngishiye iBandla lase-Roma*, (Ihunyushwe ngu V.T.E. Ngwenya), Nelspruit, South Africa,²1947, 33 p.
XXII *O Padre,a Mulher, e o Confessionario...Traducçao da vigesmima-quarta ediçao ingleza*, Porto, Portugal, 1887, 188 p.
XXIII *Otets Chynykii. Opratsiuvav na ukrainsku movu I. Shkula*, Saskatoon, Vyd-vo Bo[f]zhoho slova, 1957,112 p. [Ukranian]
XXIV *Pabyddiaeth, a'r Jesuitiaid. saith o ddarlithiau... Gyda Hanes plaid y Jesuitiaid*, Dinbych, Thomas Gee, 1878, 1890, 64 p. [Welsh] cover AP 01
XXV *Prasten, kvinnan, och bikten*, Chicago, E. Wingren, 1900, 251 p. [Swedish] cover AP 01
XXVI *Femti aar i romerkirken*, Kirkegatten Oslo, Norsk Bok Duplicering, 1932, 264 p. cover AP 01
XXVII *Pięćdziesiąt Lat w Kościele Rzymskim*, Warsaw, M. Wierszyłowski, reprint 2006, 527 p. cover AP 01
XXVIII *Ang Kura, ang Babai at ang Pakumpisalan*, Manila, 1914; Hard Press, reprint 2008, 202 p. [Tagalog] AP 01

BIBLIOGRAPHY

+ mention of Japanese, Danish and Czech editions

The Priest, The Woman and the Confessional = #V, VI, XIII-XIV, XVI-XVII, XIX, XXII, XXV, XXVIII above (at least).
50 Years = VIII-IX, XI, XVIII, XXVI-XXVII (at least)

Publications directly concerning Chiniquy:

Adresse des Associés de la tempérance de Longueuil au Rév. Père Chiniquy, Montreal, Bureau des Mélanges Religieux, 1848, 6 p. AP 10
"Charles Chiniquy 1809-1899", *Aujourd'hui credo*, novembre 1999, 3-14.
"Chiniquy pour rire, par 'Bossu'", 1857 [see the *Avenir* May 15, 1857].
Chronology of the Life of 'Pastor' Chiniquy, Author of "Fifty Years in the Church of Rome", Huntingdon IN, National Catholic Bureau of Information, n.d. [post 1906 and pre 1955], 11 p.
Cheering Words, [Boston], n.p., [1886?]. AP 10
Father Chiniquy in the Presence of Death, St. Anne, Illinois, March 23, 1892, Broadsheet. AP 01
Father Chiniquy, the Reformer of the Far West, London, The Record, [1860], 12 p. AP 10
In Memoriam: Charles Paschal Télesphore Chiniquy 1809-1899, Montreal, Witness Publishing House, 1899, 71 p. AP 13
Life and Work of Rev. Charles Chiniquy DD, London, Chas. Thynne, 1897, 20 p. AP 10
"Maria Monk and 'Pastor' Chiniquy", New Zealand Tablet, February 25, 1909, p. 301.
Pastor Chiniquy at Bible House, [London], n.p., [1883], 4 p.
Le Père Chiniquy, le réformateur canadien. Récit de la conversion de près de 4,000 catholiques français, passés au protestantisme, Melun FR, Desrues, 1860, 11 p.
Statement and Correspondence of the Pictou Presbytery, P.L.C.P. respecting the Antigonish Riot, Pictou, William Harris, 1874, 76 p.
Subjects of Lectures by Pastor Chiniquy, n.l., n.d., 1 p. AP 10
ANDERSON, Whitaker, *Father Chiniquy; His Life and Services in Canada and the United States*, New York, Agora Publishing Co., 1933, 24 p.; ²1946, 40 p. AP 12
ARES, Jean-Patrice, "Les campagnes de tempérance de Charles Chiniquy: un des principaux moteurs du réveil religieux montréalais de 1840", M.S.Rel. thesis, Université de Québec à Montréal, 1990, 347 p.
BAIRD, D., *The French Canadian Mission in Illinois*, [Yonkers, NY], n.p., [1860], 16 p.
BARRETT, John F., "Pastor Chiniquy, Illinois Apostate", MA thesis, St. Mary of the Lake Seminary, Mundelein IL, 1958, 151 p.
BERTON, Pierre, "The Zeal of Charles Chiniquy" IN *My Country; The Remarkable Past*, Toronto, McLelland and Stewart, 1976, 142-160.
BIRD, Mrs. Mary, ed., *A Few Reminiscences of the Life and Labours of that Eminent Servant of Christ, Pastor Chiniquy*, Leeds, J.W. Bean and Sons, 1878, 46 p.; 1878, 38 p. AP 15
BOISSONAULT, Charles-Marie, "Le Chiniquy de M. Marcel Trudel", *La Revue de l'Université Laval*, 9, 10 (June 1955), 900-5.
BOONE, Ardis, *Fr. Chas Chiniquy's Ledger* Ardymae@comcast.net
BRETTELL, Caroline B., "From Catholics to Presbyterians: French-Canadian Immigrants in Central Illinois", *American Presbyterian*, 63, 3 (Fall 1985), 285-298.
BRUNEAU, I-P., "Le père Chiniquy comme je l'ai connu", unpublished ms. of a lecture, [Montreal, c1915] 13 p. AP 15-C2-F102
BURMAN, Axel, *Bibeln Segrar*, Stockholm, Forlaget Filadelfia, 1958, 83 p.
BURNS, Robert Ferrier, *Our Modern Babylon: a discourse delivered in Ft. Massey Church, Halifax on ... the Sabbath succeeding the 'Chiniquy riot'*, Halifax, Nova Scotia Print Co., 1876, 22 p. AP 10
BUTLER, Montagu R., *Abbe Chiniquy. A Brief Sketch of his Life and Labours*, London, A.S. Mallett, [1879], 20 p.
- *The Reformation in Canada. A Report of the 'Père Chiniquy Aid Fund 1876-1877'*, London, Operative Jewish Converts' Institution, [1877], 16 p.
CARRIERE, Gaston, "Une mission tragique aux Illinois: Chiniquy et les Oblats", *RHAF*, 8,4 (Mar. 1955), 518-555.
- "Chiniquy, Charles Paschal", *New Catholic Encyclopedia*, vol. 3, Toronto, 1967, p. 617.
THE CHRISTIAN, London, July 29, 1886, Morgan and Scott, 549-550.
COURT, William B., *The Story of my Connection with the Chiniquy Movement in Montreal of 1874-77 or A Presbyterian Church Assembly Report Criticized*, Montreal, n.p., 1877, 18 p. AP 15
CYR, Steve, "Charles Chiniquy et le confessionnal: la clef du Catholicisme Québécois", ThM thesis, Montreal, Acadia University, 2009.
DAVID, Laurent-Olivier, "Chiniquy" IN *L'Établissement d'un état français*, Montreal, Librairie Beauchemin, 1926, 71-5. AP 15
DEBANNÉ, Marc, "Le cas Chiniquy: Quelle attitude prendre ?", *Ensemble: Revue chrétienne française au Canada*, 12, 4 (Oct.-Nov. 1990), 20, 26.
DESJARDINS, Georges-S., "Le mythe Chiniquy tué en 400 pages!", *Photo-Journal* (Feb. 19, 1955), p. 3.
DESROCHERS, Jeanne, "Le Diable et le Bon Dieu", Perspectives (*La Presse*) 14,18 (April 29, 1972), 8-11.
DODGE, William E., *Sea la luz: la historia de un avida religiosa por ed Pere Chiniquy*, traducido del Ingles al Castekkabi yarreglade con permiso del autor venerable, Valparaiso, Helfmann, 1886, 50 p.

THE CONTROVERSIAL CONVERSION OF CHARLES CHINIQUY

DUBÉ, Romain, Jacques Lacoursière and André Segal, "La mémoire amnésique: le cas de Charles Chiniquy" IN *Le patrimoine des minorités religieuses du Québec : Richesse et vulnerabilité*, Marie-Claude Rocher and Marc Pelchat eds., Quebec, Les Presses de l'Université Laval, 2006, 3-11.
GAGNON, Philéas, "Chiniquy (Le Père)", *Essai de bibliographie canadienne*, Québec, private printing, 1895, 114-6.
GEORGE, Joseph, "The Lincoln Writings of C.P.T. Chiniquy", *Journal of Illinois State Historical Society*, 69 (Feb. 1976), 17-34.
HOUDE, Mary Jean and John Klasey, "Chiniquy's Revolt" IN *Of the People*, Chicago, General Printing Co., 1968, 101-116.
HULL, Ernest R., *Maria Monk, Chiniquy and Jovinian*, Bombay India, Examiner Press, 1912, 39 p.
KEMP, Alexander F., *The Rev. C. Chiniquy, the Presbytery of Chicago and the Canada Presbyterian Church*, Montreal, reprinted from *Canada Observer*, 1863, 21 p.   AP 10
LANGLOIS, Conrad, "Chiniquy: ange ou démon", *La Patrie*, 4 avril 1966, 10-11.
LAVERDURE, J.F. Paul, "Religious Invective of Charles Chiniquy, anti-Catholic crusader 1875-1900", M.A. thesis, McGill University, 1984, 107 p.
- "Charles Chiniquy's The Priest, the Woman and the Confessional: Protestant Pornography?", *Canadian Society of Presbyterian History Papers*, 1984-85, 59-71.
- "Charles Chiniquy: The Making of an Anti-Catholic Crusader", *CCHA Historical Studies*, 54 (1987), 39-56.
- "Creating an anti-Catholic crusader: Charles Chiniquy", *J. of Rel. Hist*, 15 (June 1988), 94-108.
LEVASSEUR, Jean, "La censure du protestantisme dans le Québec et la Franco-Américanie de la seconde moitié du XIXe siècle: les cas de Joseph Provost et de Charles Chiniquy", *Francophonies d'Amérique*, 15 (Spring) 2003, 175-184.
LOUGHEED, R., "The Controversial Conversion of Charles Chiniquy", PhD thesis (theol), U. de Montréal, 1994, 435 p.
- "A Major Stimulant for both Quebec Ultramontanism and World-wide Anti-Catholicism: the Legacy of Chiniquy", *Canadian Society of Presbyterian History Papers*, 1994, 36-55.
- "Anti-Catholicism among French Protestants", *Canadian Society of Church History, 1995 Papers*, 1996, 161-180.
- *La conversion controversée de Charles Chiniquy*, Québec, La Clairère, 1999, 322 p.
- "Le Luther du Canada: la conversion de Charles Chiniquy comme modèle évangélique", *La Revue Farel*, 3, 2008, 23-37.
MARSAULT, F., *De Rome à l'Évangile*, Paris, Librairie Fischbacher, 1908, 303 p.
McLOUGHLIN, Emmett, "Charles Chiniquy: 1809-1899" IN *Famous Ex-Priests*, New York, L. Stuart, 1968, 109-127.
MEIER, Lois, ed., *The Saga of St. Anne*, St. Anne IL, Bicentennial Ctee, 1976, 198 p. Also online.
- *The Apostate's Woman* [novel about Euphémie Chiniquy)], Bloomington IN, Lightning Source/ Author House/Kindle Press, 2005, 276 p.
MOORE, John, *Rev. Charles Chiniquy's recent tour abroad*, n.l., n.p., 1897, 4 p.   AP 10-100
- *Rev. Charles Chiniquy D.D.*, n.l., n.p.,[c1898], 2 p. [poem]   AP 10-099
- *Boston Public Library rejects Father Chiniquy's 'Forty Years in the Church of Christ'...*, [Boston, 1900], n.p., 8 p.   AP 12
MOORE, Stephen [pseud Vox populi], "The R.C. Bishop vs. Father Chiniquy", *Kankakee Times*, 1869, 1 p.   AP 10-101
MORIN, Joseph, "Apologie devant l'histoire: Ce qu'il est et Chiniquy caricature", unfinished ms.   AP 15-C2-F111
NEEDHAM, Helen I., "The Stormy Petrel", *Christian Heritage*, Apr, May, June, September 1976, total of 20 p.   AP 12-92
NOEL, Jan "The Errant Shepherd: Chiniquy and the Making of Ultramontane Quebec", unpublished ms., Hamilton, McMaster University, 1981, 39 p.
- "Dry Patriotism: The Chiniquy Crusade", *CHR*, 71,2 (June 1990), 189-207.
- *Canada Dry*, Toronto, U. of Toronto Press, 1994, 310 p.
PAILLARD, M. J., "Life and History of Father Chiniquy", from *The Journal of Commerce*, NY, 1859; found in Staples, *Report*.
PERRY, Charles E., *Lectures on Orangeism and other subjects*, Toronto, William Briggs, 1892, 131 p.
PRICE, W.J., "Aux origines d'un schisme - le centenaire d'une réconciliation arrêtée", *RHAF* 12,4 (Mar 1959), 517-534; 13,1 (Jun. 1959), 45-78 [the intended conclusion was never written].
PROVOST, Joseph, "Chiniquy, sa vie, son temps et son œuvre", [up to 1851], 1899, ms., 47 p. [**UCM**, French Protestant collection, Côté mss. now available in the commented edition of his novel by Levasseur; see above].
RANNOU, Pierre, *Confrontation entre Chiniquy et Roussy à Sainte-Marie-de-Monnoir, le 7 Janvier 1851*, Longueuil, Chantal Deragon, 2001, 36 p.
RESTHER, P., [Manuscript letter to England], 1884, 7 p.
ROBY, Yves, "Charles Chiniquy", *Canadian Dictionary of Biography*, Toronto, 1990, v. 12, 189-93. Also online.
ROUSSY, Louis, *Récit de la discussion entre M. Chiniquy et M. Roussy au village de Ste-Marie-de-Monnoir le mardi 7 janvier, 1851*, Napierville, Le Semeur Canadien, 1851, 30 p.
SABBATH, Lawrence, "Playing with Quebec's Past", *Montreal Star*, Dec. 26, 1970.
SANDHAM, W.H., "Data on the Life and Work of Rev. Chiniquy", unpublished ms., 4 p.
SANSOUCY, Thérèse, "Chiniquy et Lincoln", *Le Phare, revue Franco-Américaine*, 1,2 (Mar. 1948), pp. 17, 40-1.
SCHLACHTER, F., *Pater Chiniquy's Erlebnisse*, Biel, Expedition der Brofamen, 1899, 359 p.; 1901, 159 p.

BIBLIOGRAPHY

SEVILLE, George Hugh, "Charles Chiniquy", *Sunday School Times*, 3 (Sept, Oct 1953), 815-6, 839-40, 870-1, 909-10, 928-9.
SIROIS, Georges, "La venue de Chiniquy au Madawaska, 1844", *La Société historique acadienne -Les Cahiers*, 6,2 (June 1975), 101-3.
SMITH, George H., "A French-Canadian Missionary, Rev.`Father' Chiniquy" IN *Missionary Pathfinders*, Toronto, Musson Bk. Co., 1907, 133-43.   AP 15-36
SMITH, Rev. Sidney F., *Chiniquy*, Catholic Truth Society (#23), 1897.
-*Pastor Chiniquy: An Examination of His "Fifty Years in the Church of Rome"*, London, Catholic Truth Society, 1908, 64 p.   AP 15
STAPLES, Moses, *Report of the committee at Kankakee ILL on the French colony at St. Anne under the ministry of Rev. C. Chiniquy made to the [AFCU] committee at NY in December 1859*, [N.Y., AFCU, 1860], 8 p.
STEVENS, L.M., John Faris and Theodore Monod, [Prospectus of a book defending Chicago Presbytery against Chiniquy], Chicago, Kennedy and Campbell Printers, 1863, 8 p.
SUTHERLAND, David, "'Father' Chiniquy Comes To Halifax: Sectarian Conflict in 1870s Nova Scotia", *NSHS, Journal* 10 (2007), 15-26.
SUTHERLAND, George, *Who is Chiniquy? Important Original Documents Establishing the High Character and Standing of Pastor Chiniquy...*, Auckland, John Browne, 1880, 19 p.
TETU, Horace, *Notes biographiques sur l'apostat Chiniquy*, Quebec, n.p., 1900, 6 p.
THÉRIAULT, Serge-André, "Charles Chiniquy et les Églises catholiques-chrétiennes", *Aujourd'hui credo*, novembre 1999, 3-10.
TRUDEL, Marcel, *Chiniquy*, Trois Rivières, Éditions du Bien Public, ²1955, 339 p.
- *Chiniquy: prêtre catholique, ministre presbytérien*, Montreal, Lidec, 2001, 62 p.
-"Chiniquy, l'homme et sa légende" IN *Mythes et réalités dans l'histoire du Québec*, tome 2, Montreal, HMH, 2004, 129-154.
VILLENEUVE, Alphonse, *Contre-poison; faussetés, erreurs, impostures, blasphèmes de l'apostat Chiniquy*:
- *1.Dialogue sur la confession*, Montreal, Typ. Le Franc-Parleur, 1875, 38 p.   AP 15-20
- *2. Dialogue sur l'eucharistie*, Montreal, Typ. Le Franc-Parleur, ² 1875, 81 p.
- [XYZ] *Honte et Mépris du renégat. La vie et la mort de l'apostat Chiniquy*, Montreal, n.p., 1875, 8 p.

Brief biographies:

ALLAIRE, J-B-A, *Dictionnaire biographique du clergé canadien-français*, Montreal, Imprimerie des Sourds-muets, 1910, vol.1, p. 121.
BALMER, Randall, *Encyclopedia of Evangelicalism*, Waco, Baylor University Press, 2004, 153-4.
BIBAUD, Maximilien, *Dictionnaire historique des hommes illustres du Canada et de l'Amérique*, Montreal, Cérat, 1857, p. 83.
BOASE, Frederic, *Modern English Biography*, London, Frank Cass, 1965, vol. 4, col. 656-7.
BRAUER, J.C., ed., *The Westminster Dictionary of Church History*, Philadelphia, Westminster, 1971, p. 185.
COTNAM, Jacques, "Biography and Memoirs in French" IN *The Oxford Companion to Canadian Literature*, William Toye ed., Toronto, Oxford Press, 1983, 63-70.
DE GUBERNATIS, Angelo, *Dictionnaire international des écrivains du jour*, Florence, 1888, vol.1.
HAMEL, Reginald et al., *Dictionnaire des auteurs de langue française en Amérique du Nord*, Montreal, Fides, 1989, 303-4.
KIRK, John F., *A Supplement to Allibone's Critical Dictionary of English Literature and British and American Authors*, Philadelphia, J.P. Lippincott, 1891, vol.1, p. 325.
LACOURSIÈRE, Jacques, "Chiniquy apôtre" + "Chiniquy apostat" IN *Nos Racines*, St. Laurent, Éditions Transmo, ch. 116 (1982), 2319-21.
LAGUE-HOBLER, Margaret, "Felaway with Chiniquy", *The French Canadian/Acadian Genealogists of Wisconsin Quarterly*, 189, 3 (Spring 2004).
LE JEUNE, Louis, *Dictionnaire général de biographie, histoire,...*, Ottawa, l'U. d'Ottawa, 1931, vol. 1, 385-6.
LOUGHEED, Richard, "Charles Chiniquy", IN *The Blackwell Dictionary of Evangelical Biography 1730-1860*, Donald Lewis ed., Oxford, Blackwell, 1995, p. 218.
MORGAN, Henry - *Bibliotheca Canadensis or a Manual of Canadian Literature*, Ottawa, Desbarats, 1867, p. 74.
- *Canadian Men and Women of the Time*, Toronto, Briggs, 1898, p. 184.
MOYER, Elgin and Earl Cairns, eds., *Wycliffe Biographical Dictionary of the Church*, Chicago, Moody, 1982, p. 90.
PRATT, Michel, *Dictionnaire historique de Longueuil, de Jacques Cartier et de Montréal-Sud*, Longueuil, Société historique de Marigot Inc., 1995, 102-3.
SIMPSON, Donald, *Biography Catalogue of the Library of the Royal Commonwealth Society*, London, R.C.S., 1961, p. 68.
VOISINE, Nive, "Cinquante Ans" and "Manuel de la Tempérance" IN *Dictionnaire des oeuvres littéraires du Québec*, Maurice Lemire ed., Montreal, Fides, 1978, 1, 127, 469.
WALLACE, William S., ed., *The Macmillan Dictionary of Canadian Biography*, Toronto, Macmillan, ⁴1978, p. 153.
WIKIPEDIA contributors, "Charles Chiniquy", *Wikipedia, The Free Encyclopedia*, 20 July 2008, 20:55 UTC.

THE CONTROVERSIAL CONVERSION OF CHARLES CHINIQUY

Newspapers and Official Reports (with the years consulted):

Roman Catholic:

    Courrier du Canada: 1864, 1900
    Mélanges religieux: 1899
    La semaine religieuse de Québec: 1899
    True Witness: 1850-1852, 1875-1876

Protestant:

English:
    Acts and Proceedings of Synod of the Presbyterian Church of Canada: 1848-1861
    Acts and Proceedings of General Assembly of the Canada Presbyterian Church: 1861-1875
    Acts and Proceedings of General Synod of Presbyterian Church in Canada: 1876-1900 [especially annual reports from the Board of French Evangelization]
    Canadian Congregationalist: January 1899
    Canadian Independent (Congregational): 1859, 1888
    Converted Catholic, James A. O'Connor (ed.) NY: 1884-1897,1944
    Ecclesiastical and Missionary Record of the Presbyterian Church of Canada: 1845, 1850-61
    Grande Ligne Mission Annual Reports: 1886-1935
    Home and Foreign Record of the Canadian Presbyterian Church: 1862-1865
    Montreal Daily Witness: 1849-1851, 1855-1860, 1862, 1864, 1866-70, 1874-78, 1880
    Presbyterian, Montreal: 1859-63, 1871-75
    Presbyterian Record: 1876-91
    Presbyterian, Philadelphia: 1860-1862
    Presbyterian College Journal: 1881-1908
French:
    L'Aurore: BNQ and FTÉ collections (1882-83, 88, 94-1901, 1908-09)
    Le Citoyen Franco-américain: FTÉ collection (1892-1893)
    Semeur canadien: BNQ and FTÉ collections (1851-3, fragments 1856-61)

Secular:

English:
    Chicago Tribune: 1857-8
    Kankakee Gazette: scattered ASQ clippings
    Montreal Daily Star: 1869, 1970
    Montreal Gazette: 1855, 1877, 1899
    New York Times: Jan. 17, 1899
    Quebec Mercury: 1859
    The Times, London: Jan.-Feb. 1899
French:
    La Presse: 1863-4, 1884
    La Patrie: January 1899

Anti-clerical:

    L'Avenir: 1847-1857
    Le Pays: 1852-1854, 1856-1859
    Journal d'Illinois: 1857-1859

General bibliography:

    Les Conversions: Compte-rendu de la huitième semaine de missiologie de Louvain, Louvain, Museum Lessianum, 1930, 272 p.
    -*Mandements, lettres pastorales, circulaires et autres documents publiés dans le diocèse de Montréal depuis son érection jusqu'à l'année 1869*, Tome 1, Montreal, Typographie Le Nouveau Monde, 1869.
    -*Mandements, lettres pastorales et circulaires des évêques de Québec*, Tomes 2 and 3, Quebec, A. Coté et Cie., 1888.
    -*Portrait and Biographical Record of Kankakee County, Illinois*, Chicago, Lake City Pub. Co., 1893, 736 p.
ALLEN, James Paul, *We the People: An Atlas of America's Ethnic Diversity*, New York, Macmillan, 1988, 315 p.
ALLIER, Raoul, *La psychologie de la conversion chez les peuples non-civilisés*, Paris, Payot, 1925, 2 tomes.
AMARON, Calvin, *The Evangelization of the French Canadians*, Lowell, S.E., 1885, 15 p.
    - *Your Heritage: New England Threatened*, Springfield, French Protestant College, 1891, 203 p.AP 10
    - *The Future of Canada: The Extraordinary Privileges of the Roman Catholic church in Quebec*, Ville St. Paul, N. Gelinas, c1899, 16 p.   AP 10
BADENOCH, G.R., ed., *Ultramontanism. England's Sympathy with Germany as Expressed by the Public Meetings held in London on Jan. 27, 1874*, London, Hatchards, 1874, 629 p.

BIBLIOGRAPHY

BAKER, Derek, ed., *Religious Motivation, Biographical and Sociological Problems for the Church Historian*, Oxford, Blackwell, 1978, 516 p.
BARNARD, Julienne, *Mémoires Chapais*, Montreal, Fides, 1961, 2 vols.
BEAULIEU, Victor-Levy, *La grande tribu: c'est la faute à Papineau*, Notre Dame des Neiges, Éditions Trois-Pistoles, 2008, 876 p.
BEBBINGTON, David W., *Evangelicalism in Modern Britain. A History from the 1730s to the 1980s*, London, Unwin Hyman, 1989, 364 p.
BERNARD, Jean-Paul, *Les Rouges; Libéralisme, nationalisme et anticléricalisme au milieu du XIXe siècle*, Montreal, Les Presses de l'Université du Québec, 1971, 395 p.
BILLINGTON, R. Allan, *The Protestant Crusade, 1800-1860: A Study of the Origins of American Nativism*, Chicago, Quadrangle, 1964 (1938 orig.), 514 p.
BLACK, Robert Merrill, "Different visions: The Multiplication of Protestant Missions to French Canadian Roman Catholics, 1834-1855", IN *Canadian Protestant and Catholic Missions, 1820s-1960s*, J.S. Moir and C.T. McIntire eds., New York, Peter Lang, 1988, 49-73.
- "A Crippled Crusade: Anglican Missions to French Canadian Roman Catholics in Lower Canada, 1835 to 1868", ThD thesis, University of Toronto, 1989, 452 p.
BORRAS, Alphonse, *L'excommunication dans le nouveau code de droit canonique: Essai de définition*, Paris, Desclée, 1987, 350 p.
BRETTELL, Caroline, *French Canadian Immigrants in Central Illinois: Marriages, Fertility and Household Structure*, Chicago, Newbury Library, 1984, 38 p.
- "From Catholics to Presbyterians: French Canadian Immigrants in Central Illinois," *Journal of Presbyterian History*, 63 (1985), 285-298.
- "From Time to the Other: An Alternative to the Assimilation Model of Immigration History", unpublished manuscript, ca1990, p. 18.
- "French Canadians in the Kankakee Valley", *Illinois History Teacher*, 12 (2005), 28-39.
BRISTOL, A.M., ed., *Atlas of Kankakee County Illinois*, Chicago, J.H. Beers and Co., 188[3], 169 p.
BROMLEY, David G., ed., *Falling from the Faith: Causes and Consequences of Religious Apostasy*, Newbury Park, Sage, 1988, 266 p.
CAMPBELL, John, *A Concise History of French Protestantism*, Montreal, Presbyterian Board of French Evangelization, 1898, 32 p. AP 12-120
CAREY, Patrick W., *People, Priests and Prelates: Ecclesiastical Democracy and the Tensions of Trusteeism*, South Bend, Notre Dame Press, 1987, 362 p.
CIRCÉ-COTÉ, Eve, *Papineau. Son influence sur la Pensée Canadienne*, Montreal, R.A. Regnault, 1924, 247 p.
CLOSE, Albert, *Why 854 Priests Left the Church of Rome*, London, Protestant Truth Society, ²1936, 317 p.
COTE, F.-X., "Mgr Forbin-Janson et le mouvement religieux du Québec vers 1840", *SHEC*, 1941-2, 95-118.
DARTEVELLE, Patrice et al., *Blasphèmes et libertés*, Paris, Cerf, 1993, 144 p.
DENNIS, Lane T., "Conversion in an Evangelical context: A Study in the Micro-Sociology of Religion", PhD thesis (Religion), Northwestern University, Evanston, 1980, 222 p.
DOUGLAS, James, *Journal and Reminiscences of James Douglas, M.D.*, N.Y., n.p., 1910, 254 p.
DOUMERGUE, E., *L'Attrait catholique et l'attrait protestant*, Paris, Fischbacher, 1927, 93 p.
DOUTRE, Joseph, *Ruines cléricales*, Montreal, A. Filiatreault, 1893, 182 p.
DUCLOS, Rieul-P., *Histoire du protestantisme français au Canada et aux États Unis*, 2 vols. Montreal, Librairie évangélique, 1912-1913. AP 12-123
DUMONT, Fernand, Jean-Paul Montminy, and, Jean Hamelin, *Idéologies au Canada français, 1850-1900*, Quebec, Les Presses de l'Université Laval, 1971, 327 p.
EID, Nadia F., *Le clergé et le pouvoir politique au Québec: Une analyse de l'idéologie ultramontaine au milieu du XIXe siècle*, Montreal, Éditions Hurtubuise HMH, 1976, 318 p.
FATH, Sébastien, *Du ghetto au réseau: Le protestantisme évangélique en France, 1800-2005*, Geneva, Labor et Fides, 2005, 426 p.
FERM, Robert O., *The Psychology of Christian Conversion*, Westwood, Fleming Revell, 1959, 255 p.
FINES, Hervé, ed.; *Album du protestantisme*, vol. 1, Montreal, l'Aurore, 1972, 128 p.
FRASER, Brian John, "The Christianization of Our Civilization: Presbyterian Reformers and Their Defence of a Protestant Canada 1875-1914", PhD thesis, York University, Toronto, 1983.
FRÉCHETTE, Louis, *Mémoires intimes*, Montreal, Fides, ²1977, 104-114.
GAFFEY, James, P., "Patterns of Ecclesiastical Authority: The Problem of Chicago Succession, 1865-1881", *Church History*, 42, 2 (June 1973), 257-70.
GARRAGHAN, Gilbert J., *The Catholic Church in Chicago, 1673-1871*, Chicago, Loyola U. Press, 1921, 236 p.
GILBERT, Claude, "Une communauté protestante de langue française dans l'Outaouais au XIXe siècle : le cas de Namur", *Cultures du Canada français*, 7 (automne 1990), 79-87.
GOLDBERGER, Pierre, "Comme un grain de sénevé. Éléments d'histoire des Protestants de langue française au Canada", *Aujourd'hui Credo*, 39, 3-6 (Mar.-Nov. 1992).
GORDON, Albert I., *The Nature of Conversion. A Study of 45 Men and Women who Changed their Religion*, Boston, Beacon Press, 1967, 333 p.
GORDON, Charles, "The Presbyterian Church and Its Missions" IN *Canada and Its Provinces*, vol. 11, Adam Short ed., Toronto, Glasgow Brook and Co., 1914, 278-9.
GRANT, John, *The Church in the Canadian Era*, Burlington, Welch, ²1988, 258 p.
GREEN, Thomas J., "Sanctions in the Church" IN *The Code of Canon Law. A Text and Commentary*, Jas. Coriden, Thomas Green and Donald Heintschel eds., London, Geoffrey Chapman, 1184 p.
HALL, Basil, "Alessandro Gavazzi: A Barnabite Friar and the Rissorgimento" IN *Church, Society and Politics*, Derek Baker ed., (Studies in Church History, 12), Oxford, Blackwell, 1975, 303-356.

THE CONTROVERSIAL CONVERSION OF CHARLES CHINIQUY

HAMELIN, Jean and Nive Voisine, eds., *Les ultramontains canadiens-français*, Montreal, Boréal, 1985, 347 p.
HARDY, René, "La rébellion de 1837-38 et l'essor du protestantisme canadien-français", *RHAF*, 29, 2 (Sept. 1975), 163-189.
HIGHAM, John, *Strangers in the Land: Patterns of American Nativism, 1860-1925*, New York, Atheneum, 1968, 259 p.
HUDON, Christine, "Le prêtre, le ministre et l'apostat: les stratégies pastorales face au protestantisme canadien-français au XIXe siècle", *SCHEC, Études d'histoire religieuse*, 61 (1995), 81-99.
JOHNSON, Cedric B. and H. Newton Malony, *Christian Conversion: Biblical and Psychological Perspectives*, Grand Rapids, Zondervan, 1982, 190 p.
JOMBART, E., "Des délits et des peines" IN *Traité de Droit canonique*, Raoul Naz ed., Paris, Letouzey et Ané, 1954, 583-799.
JOYAUX, Georges J., "French Language Press in the Upper Mississippi and Great Lakes area", *Mid-America*, 43, 4 (Oct. 1961), 242-259.
KANTOWICZ, Edward R., "A Fragment of French Canada on the Illinois Prairies", *Journal of Illinois State Historical Society*, 75, 4 (Winter 1982), 263-76.
KEATING, Karl, *Catholicism and Fundamentalism: the Attack on "Romanism" by "Bible Christians"*, San Francisco, Ignatius, 1988, 360 p.
KEEFE, Thomas M., "The Catholic Issue in the Chicago Tribune before the Civil War", *Mid-America*, 57, 4 (Oct. 1975), 227-245.
KELLY, Mary Gilbert, *Catholic Immigrant Colonization Projects in the United States 1815-1860*, New York, U.S. Catholic Historical Society, 1939, 290 p.
KENAGA, William F. and George R. Letourneau, eds., *History of Kankakee County*, Chicago, Middle West Publishing Co., 1906, 617-1235.   AP 15
KILBOURNE, Brock and James Richardson, "Paradigm Conflict, Types of Conversion and Conversion Theories", *Sociological Analysis*, 50, 1 (1989), 1-21.
KINZER, Donald K., *An Episode in Anti-Catholicism: The American Protective Association*, Seattle, U. of Washington Press, 1964, 342 p.
KLAUS, Robert, *The Pope, the Protestants and the Irish*, New York, Garland Publishing, 1987, 365 p.
LAFLEUR, Théodore, *A Semi-Centennial Historical Sketch of the Grande Ligne Mission*, Montreal, D. Bentley, 1885, 60 p.
LALONDE, Jean-Louis, *Des loups dans la bergerie: Les protestants de langue française au Québec 1534-2000*, Montreal, Fides, 2002, 451 p.
- *L'Église de Pinguet*, Montreal, by the author, 2005, 138 p.
- *Belle-Rivière : 1840-2006*, Montreal, Société d'histoire du protestantisme franco-québécois, 2007, 2 v., 703 p.
LEHMANN, L.H., *Ex-Priest and the Riddle of Religion*, n.l., n.p, 1932, 9 p.
- *The Soul of a Priest: My Conversion to the Pauline Succession*, New York, Loizeaux Brothers, 1933, 163 p.
LEMIEUX, Lucien, *Les années difficiles: 1760-1839* (Histoire du catholicisme québécois, vol. 2, T. 1), Montreal, Boréal, 1989, 438 p.
LEWIS, James R., "Apostates and Legitimation of Repression: Some Historical and Empirical Perspectives on the Cult Controversy", *Sociological Analysis*, 1989, 4, 386-96.
LOUGHEED, Richard, "Les traditions protestantes" IN *L'étude de la religion au Québec: Bilan et prospective*, Jean-Marc Larouche and Guy Ménard eds., Quebec, Corporation canadienne des sciences religieuses, Les Presses de l'Université Laval (PUL), 2001, 63-75; also found online.
- "Cooperative religion in Quebec", *Journal of Ecumenical Studies*, 41, 2 (Spring 2004), 174-204.
- "La marginalisation des franco-protestants" IN *Le patrimoine des minorités religieuses du Québec: richesse et vulnérabilité*, Marie-Claude Rocher ed., Québec, PUL, 2006, 25-36.
LUCEY, J. M., *The Business of Vilification Practised by 'Ex-Priests' and Others*, Brooklyn, International Catholic Truth Society, [2] n.d., 43 p.
MacBETH, Roderick G., *Our Task in Canada*, Toronto, The Westminster Co., 1912, 146 p.
McCAFFREY, Lawrence et al., *The Irish in Chicago*, Chicago, U. of Illinois Press, 1987, 171 p.
MacVICAR, John, *Life and Work of Principal MacVicar*, Toronto, Westminster, 1904, 351 p.   AP 15
MAHEUX, Arthur, "Le problème protestant", *RSCHEC*, 1939, 43-50.
MAIGNAGE, Th., *Le témoignage des apostats*, Paris, Beauchesne, 1916, 439 p.
MARTIN, Louis, *Mon voyage à Tracadie*, Montreal, Librairie L.E. Rivard, 1891, 76 p.
MARX, Jacques, ed., *Problèmes d'histoire du Christianisme. Propagandes et contra-propagandes religieuses*, Brussels, U. de Bruxelles, 1987, 237 p.
MEILLON, Félix, *L'Ancien prêtre et le ministère évangélique*, Cahors FR, n.p., 1901, 101 p.
MELLOR, Alec, *Histoire de l'anticléricalisme français*, Paris, Veyrier, [2]1978, 462 p.
MILLER, J.R., "Anti-Catholic Thought in Victorian Canada", *CHR*, 66, 4 (1985), 474-494.
- "Bigotry in the North Atlantic triangle: Irish, British and American influences on Canadian anti-Catholicism", *Studies in Religion*, 16, 3 (Summer 1987), 289-301.
MOIR, John, *Enduring Witness: A History of the Presbyterian Church in Canada*, Don Mills, Presbyterian Church, [2]1987, 327 p.
MONET, Jacques, *The Last Cannon Shot*, Toronto, U. of Toronto Press, 1969, 422 p.
MYERS, Gustavus, *History of Bigotry in the United States*, New York, Capricorn, [2]1960, 474 p.
NAZ, Raoul, *Dictionnaire de droit canonique*, Paris, Letouzey et Ané, 1935-65.
NEESER, Marcel, *Du Protestantisme au Catholicisme, du Catholicisme au Protestantisme: Essai de psychologie des conversions confessionnelles*, Neuchâtel, Éditions Victor Attinger, 1926, 238 p.

BIBLIOGRAPHY

NOLL, Mark, *A History of Christianity in the United States and Canada*, Grand Rapids, Eerdmans, 1992, 576 p.
"An Orange Order member", *Orangeism in Ireland and Throughout the Empire*, vol. II (1828-1938), London, Thynne and Co., 1939, 693 p.
PAGNUELO, Siméon, *Études historiques et légales sur la liberté religieuse en Canada*, Montreal, Beauchemin et Valois, 1872, 409 p.
PASCAL, Roy, *Design and Truth in Autobiography*, Cambridge, Harvard U. Press, 1960, 202 p.
PAZ, D.G., *The Priesthoods and Apostasies of Pierce Connelly. A Study of Conversion and Anti-Catholicism*, (Studies in American Religion, 18), Queenston, Edwin Mellen Press, 1986, 422 p.
PETERSON, Linda, *Victorian Autobiography. The Tradition of Self-Interpretation*, New Haven, Yale University Press, 1986, 228 p.
POULIOT, Léon, *La réaction catholique de Montréal 1840-1841*, Montreal, Imprimerie du Messager, 1942, 119 p.
 -"Impulsion donnée par Mgr Bourget à la pratique religieuse", *RHAF*, Sept. 1962, 66-80.
PRIMEAU-ROBERT, Alphonse, *La place des protestants dans la nationalité Canadienne-française*, Montreal, n.p., 1924, 47 p.
PROVOST, Joseph, *La maison du coteau : nouvelle canadienne*, critical edition with biography by Jean Levasseur, Sillery QC, Éditions de la huit, 2001, 299 p.
RAMBO, Lewis, *Understanding Religious Conversion*, New Haven, Yale University Press, 1995, 260 p.
 - "Bibliography: Current Research in Religious Conversion", *Religious Studies Review*, 8, 2 (1982), 146-159.
RICHARD, Adrien M., *The Village. A Story of Bourbonnais*, Bourbonnais, Centennial Ctee., 1975, 138 p.
RIDDELL, Walter A., *The Rise of Ecclesiastical Control in Quebec*, New York, AMS Press, ²1968, 195 p.
ROCHER, Marie-Claude and Catherine Drouin, *Un autre son de cloche: Les protestants francophones au Québec*, Quebec, Musée du Séminaire de Québec, 1993, 46 p.
ROUSSELLIÈRE, Marie de la, *The Story of a Shrine*, Pointe aux Trembles, l'Echo, 1981, 64 p.
ROUSSEAU, Louis and Frank W. REMIGGI, eds., *Atlas historique des pratiques religieuses: le Sud-Ouest du Quebec au XIXe siècle*, Ottawa, Presses de l'Universite d'Ottawa, 1998, 235 p.
ROUSSY, Louis, *Appel à la raison et à la conscience des habitants des paroisses de Ste-Marie et de St-Grégoire*, Napierville, Imprimerie du Semeur canadien, 1851, 84 p.
ROY, Pierre-Georges, "Les traitres de 1759", *Cahier des Dix*, 1 (1936), 37-58.
RUDDEL, David Thierry, *Le protestantisme français au Québec 1840-1919* (Dossier-Musée national de l'homme - Histoire, 36), Ottawa, National Museums of Canada, 1983, 76 p.
RUMILLY, Robert, *Histoire de Longueuil*, Longueuil, Société d'histoire de Longueuil, 1974, 472 p.
RUNYAN, William M., ed. *Psychology and Historical Interpretation*, Oxford, Oxford University Press, 1988, 306 p.
RUTTER, Peter, *Sex in the Forbidden Zone. When Men in Power - Therapists, Doctors, Clergy, Teachers and Others- Betray Women's Trust*, New York, Fawcett Crest, 1989, 288 p.
SAIT, Edward McChesney, *Clerical control in Quebec*, Toronto, The Sentinel, 1911, 158 p.
SAVAETE, Arthur, *Mgr Ignace Bourget: sa vie, ses oeuvres, ses œuvres*, 'Vers l'abime' series, v. 9, Paris, Librairie Générale Catholique, 1916, 462 p.
SHANABRUCH, Charles, *Chicago's Catholics: The Evolution of an American Identity*, South Bend, Notre Dame Press, 1981, 296 p.
SHUTE, Daniel, "An Inquiry into the Presbyterian Work of French-Canadian Evangelization: Crucial Factors in its Foundation which were Simultaneously the Seed of its Ruin", unpublished ms., Montreal, Presbyterian College Library, 1981, 30 p.
SKONOVD, L.N., "Apostasy: The Process of Defection from Religious Totalism", PhD thesis, Ann Arbor, 1981, 230 p.
STROUT, Richard, "The Latter Years of the Board of French Evangelization of the Presbyterian Church in Canada 1895-1912", MA thesis, Bishop's University, Lennoxville QC, 1986, 98 p.
SYLVAIN, Philippe (Robert), "Aperçu sur le prosélytisme protestant au Canada français de 1760 à 1860", *Mémoires de la Société royale du Canada*, 3, 55 (1961), 65-76.
 - *Alessandro Gavazzi 1809-1899*, 2 vol., Quebec, Le centre pédagogique, 1962, 572 p.
SYLVAIN, Philippe and Nive VOISINE, *Réveil et consolidation 1840-1898* (Histoire du Catholicisme Québécois, vol. 2, T. 2), Montreal, Boréal, 1991, 507 p.
THÉRIAULT, Serge André, *Msgr. René Vilatte: Community Organizer of Religion (1854-1929)*, Berkeley, Apocryphile Press, 2006, 308 p.
THOMSON, W. Nelson, "Two French-Canadian Baptist Pastors 1821-1920" IN *Celebrating the Canadian Baptist Heritage*, Paul Dekar and Murray Ford eds., Hamilton, McMaster University Divinity College, 1985, 75-96.
 - "The Socio-Religious Context of Quebec: French-Canadian Baptist Perceptions, 1868-1914" IN *Costly Vision*, Jarold Zeman ed., Burlington, Welch, 1988, 167-180.
TRUDEL, Marcel, *Mémoires d'un autre siècle*, Montreal, Boréal, 1987, 313 p.
UNDERWOOD, Kenneth W., *Protestants and Catholic Religious and Social Interaction in an Industrial Community*, Boston, Beacon Press, 1957, 484 p.
VAUDRY, Richard W., *The Free Church in Victorian Canada 1844-1861*, Waterloo, Wilfrid Laurier University Press, 1989, 183 p.
VILLARD, Paul, *Up to the Light*, Toronto, Ryerson Press, 1928, 237 p.   AP 12-124
VOGT-RAGUY, Dominique, "Les communautés protestantes francophones au Québec: 1834-1925", PhD thesis, Bordeaux, U. de Bordeaux III, 1996, 938 p (1024 p. with annexes).
VOISINE, Nive, *Histoire de l'Église catholique au Québec 1608-1970*, Montreal, Fides, 1971, 112 p.

- "Les croisades de tempérance" IN *Un patrimoine méprisé: La religion populaire des Québécois*, Jean Simard ed., Montreal, Hurtubise, 1979, 129-156.
- *Les Frères des Écoles Chrétiennes au Canada*, vol.1, Quebec, Éditions Anne Sigier, 1987, 443 p.

WHITNEY, Henry C., *Life on the Circuit with Lincoln*, Caldwell, Caxton Printers Ltd., 1940, p. 74.

WOLFFE, John, *The Protestant Crusade in Great Britain 1829-1860*, Oxford, Clarendon Press, 1991, 366 p.
- "Anti-Catholicism and Evangelical Identity in Britain and the United States, 1830-1860 IN *Evangelicalism: Comparative Studies of Popular Protestantism in North America, the British Isles, and Beyond 1700-1900*, Mark Noll, David Bebbington and George Rawlyk eds., Oxford, Oxford University Press, 1994, 179-197.

WOODS, Shirley, *The Molson Saga*, Toronto, Doubleday, 1983, 370 p.

WYETH, Walter, *Henrietta Feller and the Grande Ligne Mission: A Memorial*, Philadelphia, W.N. Wyeth, 1898, 234 p.

Theatre Plays

"Chiniqui', Pierre Collin co-author, Montreal, Centre du Théâtre d'Aujourd'hui, December 1970-January 1971.

"Chiniquy, le menteur de Dieu", Jean Guy director, Quebec City, Palais Montcalm, March 1993.

"Chiniquy", Romain Dubé author, Pierre Lévesque director, Kamouraska, Ancien Palais de Justice, Summers 2003-2004.

"L'abbé Charles Chiniquy méritait-il la hargne dont il a été l'objet?", Cyrille-Gauvin Francoeur director, Quebec City, Musée de l'Amérique française, April 2006.

Online Sites (a few among many)

Allan Pequegnat collection – www.Chiniquy.ca
Catholic Christian site - http://netministries.org/see/churches/ch02186
Kankakee Valley Genealogical Society – www.kvgs.ordstanne/saga
Wikipedia - http://en.wikipedia.org/w/index.php?title=Charles_Chiniquy&oldid=226868711
Catholic critiques of Chiniquy - http://www.geocities.com/chiniquy/

INDEX

A

Aberdeen, Governor General 335

Abjurations 3, 18, 24, 157-159, 161, 321, 331-332

Admirers of Chiniquy xiii, 184ff, 269, 289, 291, 317, 329, 343-346

Amaron, Calvin 152, 165, 194, 234, 278, 293, 304, 333-337, 344, 347

American Protective Association (APA) 139, 144, 148-150, 168, 169, 335, 344, 349

Anglicans 12-13, 117-118, 133, 165, 170, 184, 277, 330

Anti-Catholicism xv, 3, 13, 15, 17-19, 25, 70, 88, 90, 128, ch. 5, 160, 165ff, 176, 182, 197, 238, 248ff, 266, 270-272, 278, 288, 291, 293, 295, 298, 301, 304-305, 307-308, 313, 320, 331, 345, 352, 356-357

Anti-Chiniquy activity 100ff, 285

Anti-clericalism 9-12, 20, 24, 26-27, 32, 50, 60, 77. 91, 149ff, 161, 196, 213, 217-218, 223, 228, 241, 259, 266, 274, 298, 300, 308, 314, 316-317, 354-356

Antigonish, Nova Scotia 164, 253, 331, 351

Anti-Protestantism 51-52, 68, 102, 135ff, 139, 154, 241, 265, 276, 301-302, 315

Apostle of Temperance 2-3, 5, 43, 45, 47-50, 55, 65, 180, 189-190, 226, 236, 259, 287, 323

Archival materials ix, 7, 65, 316, 318, 321, 335, 347

Ares, Jean-Patrice 21, 41, 44-46, 233, 246, 312, 314-315

Aurore 18, 33, 143, 152, 165, 173, 212, 280-281, 296, 321, 336, 345, 348-350, 354-355

Australia 3, 133, 164, 169, 253, 265, 291, 293, 295, 320, 333, 335, 343-344, 348-350

Avenir 17, 21, 27, 45, 49-51, 53, 67, 78, 92-93, 151-152, 218, 222, 257, 260, 270, 317, 321, 345, 347, 351, 354

B

Baillargeon, Bp. Charles 25, 38, 42, 47, 86, 92, 101, 103, 115, 208-209, 305, 322-331, 341

Baillargeon, Étienne 34

Baird, Charles 124, 311, 330, 351

Baptism 31, 118, 125, 180, 195-196, 224, 240, 331, 340

Baptists xiii, 13, 15, 17, 22, 109, 117-118, 124, 162, 165, 223-224, 243, 277, 330-331, 344

Barrett, John 181, 186, 283, 287, 295, 311

359

Barthe, Joseph Guillaume 33, 49-50, 323-324

Beauport, Quebec 1, 5, 37-40, 47, 279, 286, 289, 313, 322, 332, 345, 350

Bebbington, David 131, 357

Begue, Father F. 335

Berton, Pierre 31, 42, 180, 233, 313, 316

Biggs, Thomas 100, 104, 115-116, 124, 247, 330-331, 343, 344

Bird, Mary 79, 170, 186, 230, 268, 289, 311, 343

Black, Robert 13, 18, 166-167

Blanchet, Pierre 49, 92-93, 151, 152, 270, 323, 344

Blasphemy 4, 115, 157, 182, 261

Bourbonnais, Illinois 53, 57, 59-60, 65-68, 74, 91, 98, 101, 104, 117, 124, 209, 220, 324-329, 331, 357

Bourget, Bp. Ignace 2, 9, 12-13, 16, 20, 24, 26, 33, 39, 41, 44-45, 47-49, 51, 53-55, 64-68, 70, 78, 80, 83, 92, 95, 97-99, 101, 114, 157-158, 174, 180-182, 209, 217, 220, 227, 233, 243, 251, 255, 261, 286, 288, 300, 305, 310, 315, 321-329, 331-332, 347-349, 356

Brassard, Moise 33, 43-44, 53-54, 64-65, 94, 95, 97-98, 100-101, 103, 218, 220, 222, 269, 323-329, 344, 347

Brettell, Caroline 42, 61, 116, 123, 314

Bruchési, Bp. Paul 178, 337

Bruneau, Ismael 124, 127, 188, 265, 312, 319, 344

Brunet, Auguste 11, 116-117, 241, 329-331

Burns, Robert Ferrier 121, 159, 166, 267, 345

C

Calvin, Jean 112, 118, 146, 183, 329

Campbell, John 160, 166, 344, 353

Campbell, Robert 332

Carey, Patrick 66, 79

Carrière, Gaston 44-45, 117, 311, 321

Caven, William 121

Cazeau, Charles Felix 34

Cazeau, Louis 42-45, 100, 222-223, 225, 268, 321, 323-325, 328, 332, 344

Champeaux, Jean-Baptiste 96, 101, 323, 326-327

Chapais, Jean-Charles 30, 34, 41, 55, 68-70, 102, 216, 257, 268, 323-325, 355

Chapais, Thomas 181, 287, 305

Chicago 2-3, 5, 52-53, 57, 59-68, 71, 74-79, 82, 85-91, 93-96, 99, 101-105, 118-125, 127, 130, 182, 185, 188, 210-211, 216-217, 220-221, 223, 226, 234, 237-238, 247, 257-258, 266, 288, 297, 300, 312, 314, 318, 321, 324-327, 330-331, 334-336, 344, 347-350, 352-357

Chicago Tribune 61, 76, 87-90, 93, 226, 258, 321, 334, 344, 354, 356

Chiniquy, Emma
(Delagneau) 30, 126, 334, 336, 338

Euphémie (Allard) 8, 30, 122, 126, 254, 262, 269, 333, 338, 352

Rebecca (Morin) 30, 126, 167, 285, 296, 317, 330, 335-336, 338, 344

Mina (Morais) 30

Church property issues 61,- 63, 66-67, 75-80, 82, 85, 89, 92, 118, 121, 123, 185, 216, 219, 227-228, 232, 238, 288, 300, 324,

Cinquante ans book 127, 171, 190, 279, 339-340, 349, 350

Confessional 42, 132, 144, 149, 187, 213, 236, 256, 261-262, 288-290, 304, 331-332, 337, 339-340

Conspiracy ideas 55, 68, 74, 103, 105, 120, 127, 135, 138, 149, 154, 161, 216, 221, 237, 249, 303, 316

INDEX

Conversion 107, 109, 141ff, Chapters 7-9, pp. 191, 205, 241

Converted Catholic 134, 169, 172, 190, 255, 311, 333, 335, 344, 349, 354

Converts of Chiniquy 16, 112, 114, 118, 122-123, 157-158, 161, 183, 189, 229, 235, 250, 255, 269, 273-275, 280, 293, 332, 340, 351

Correspondence of Chiniquy 7, 43, 50, 54, 67, 89-90, 123, 165, 269, 308, 310, 317, 321-337, 343-346

Courjault, Father Rene 67-68, 85

Courrier du Canada 92, 102, 139, 152, 184, 280, 344, 347, 353

Court, James 14, 161, 166

Court, William B. 152, 161-162, 166, 332, 344, 351

Crusades of Chiniquy 13, 18, 52, 129, 187, 215, 240, 249, 260, 294, 297, 302, 306, 313-314, 334

Cyr, Narcisse 17, 109, 151, 165, 223, 226, 344

D

Dawson, William 166

Delagneau, Samuel 30, 224

Denominational attachment of Chiniquy 14, 108, 110, 113, 117, 122, 125, 162, 164-165, 196-197, 224, 229, 233, 277, 292, 330,

Desaulniers, Isaac 34, 78, 95-98, 100-103, 316, 325-328, 344

Dillon, Matthew 77, 80, 96, 103, 112, 325-328, 344

Dionne, Amable 30, 32, 41, 55, 321-322

Doudiet, Charles 165, 252, 344

Dougall, John 14, 21, 148, 215, 335, 344

Douglas, Dr. James 35, 38-39, 215, 322, 332-333, 344

Doutre, Joseph 27, 152, 210, 270, 305, 331

Duclos, Rieul-P. 17, 160, 165, 174, 231, 267, 278, 280-281, 309, 312, 319, 344

Duggan, Bp. James 62-63, 80, 96, 102, 104-105, 107, 112, 210, 223, 225, 328-330

Dunn, Dennis 95-96, 99, 103, 105, 221, 241, 327-328, 330

E

Elgin, Lord 49, 323

Elgin Road, Quebec 31, 175, 177, 270

England 3, 10, 12, 22, 60, 62, 104, 127, 130, 132-133, 136, 141, 144, 158, 163-164, 176-177, 181, 190, 192, 254, 271, 289,

291, 293, 296, 310, 320, 330-331, 333-334, 336

English Language xvi, 2, 16, 18, 25, 32, 60, 118, 127, 154, 227, 259, 269-270, 279, 295, 308, 311, 335, 345

Evangelism 2-4, 12-19, 24-25, 108, 113, 118, 132, 135, 149, 154-155, 166, 190, 195-197, 235, 239-240, 243, 254, 274-275, 277-278, 292, 301, 303, 305, 329

Excommunication 2, 8, 15, 24, 50, 70, 75, 79-87, 92, 94-97, 100-102, 105, 107-109, 120, 157,180, 185, 212, 216, 218, 222, 225, 235, 237, 243, 249, 251, 256, 268, 296, 317, 325, 328, 329

Exhaustion 49, 69, 162, 175-176, 188, 270, 274, 322

Ex-priests 3, 7, 33, 122-123, 141-147, 149, 154, 167, 178, 180, 185, 187-188, 197-198, 235, 237,251, 256, 261-262, 269, 271,284-285,289, 293, 295, 300, 320, 335-337

F

Fabre, Bp. Edouard-Charles 173, 210, 329, 332-335, 349

Facile, Brother 78, 82, 95, 260, 325, 326

Fifty Years book 5, 8, 31, 44, 69, 95, 127, 142, 149, 152, 164, 204, 222,

361

225, 231-232, 252, 279, 294-296, 309-310, 333, 339-340

Financial aspects 4, 32, 84, 116-118, 145, 162, 173, 178, 181-183, 193, 214, 234, 254, 259, 277, 280, 290, 324, 329-330, 334-337

Foley, Bp. Thomas 62

Forbin-Janson, Bp. Charles de 20, 26, 38, 339, 355

Forty Years book 5, 69, 109, 113, 125, 164, 168, 173, 176, 182, 185, 232, 253-254, 262, 270, 279, 295, 309, 318, 339-340

France 10, 15-16, 20, 22-23, 26, 29, 38, 60, 83, 91, 109, 119, 133, 136, 142, 144, 149-151, 157, 171, 176, 186, 201-202, 216, 266, 273, 275, 294, 330, 336, 355

Fréchette, Louis 36, 41, 50, 181, 183, 232-233, 287, 297, 305, 325

Freedom of religion/ conscience 4, 16-19, 24, 27, 67, 88-92, 114, 132, 136, 138, 152, 154-155, 176, 185, 189-190, 199, 203-204, 211, 221, 230, 250, 254, 256, 275, 301, 303, 340

Freedom of speech 4, 15, 17, 23, 115, 145, 160, 162, 174, 182, 189, 262, 267, 272, 279, 298, 301, 305, 332,

French Canadian Missionary Society (FCMS) 14, 17, 25, 51, 160-161, 166, 227, 254, 331

French language 4, 7, 14-17, 19, 22-23, 25, 52, 60-61, 91, 100, 103, 117-118, 121, 125, 154, 178, 245, 248, 257, 260, 269-270, 277, 279-280, 296, 298, 300, 307

G

Gaffey, James P. 62-63, 66, 83, 96, 105

Gavazzi, Alessandro 115, 136, 142, 145, 151, 171, 182, 259, 262, 283, 331, 346

George, Joseph 73-74, 125, 149, 168, 278, 314, 331

Germany 163, 176, 201, 260, 333, 336-337, 354

Goldberger, Pierre 276, 282-283, 285

Grande Ligne Mission 13-15, 51, 223, 277, 354, 356-357

Grant, George M. 167, 254, 267, 278, 344

Gregg, William 14, 122

Guibord, Joseph 12, 27, 151-152, 210, 259, 331

Guigues, Bp. Joseph 43-44, 322-323

Guinness, A. H. 170, 335-337, 343

H

Hamel, Theophile 47, 286, 296, 305

Hamilton, Alfred 120, 331, 335, 344, 347, 352, 357

Hanstein, J. von 335-337, 346

Harris, General Thomas Maley 333-337, 344

Hellmuth, Bp. Isaac 114, 167, 185-186, 227-228, 230, 254, 276, 327, 329-330, 345

Higham, John 70, 130, 134-135, 140

Hobart Town, Tasmania, Australia 164, 170, 348

Hodge, Charles 251, 331, 348

Hoel, Inger 334

Holland 176, 333, 336-337, 346

I

Institut canadien 11-12, 17-18, 27, 49, 67, 151, 259, 305

International reputation 3, 144, 163-165, 137, 171-172, 176-177, 187, 259, 289-291, 345-346, 350, 353

Ireland 20, 45, 75, 79, 119, 151, 164, 170, 252, 322

INDEX

J

Journal d'Illinois 91, 101, 223, 344, 354

K

Kamouraska, Quebec 1, 30-32, 40-42, 53, 68, 70, 73, 322-324, 326, 358

Kankakee, Illinois 57, 59, 60, 69, 71, 73, 78, 86, 90-91, 101, 104, 110, 116-118, 122-124, 126, 188, 221, 318, 321, 326, 328-331, 334, 344

Kankakee Gazette 90, 344, 354

Kemp, Alexander 120, 122, 188, 312, 331, 344

Kenaga, William 60, 90

Kenrick, Archbp. Peter 62, 83, 105, 210, 328-329

Kilbourne, Brock 198, 246, 271

L

Lafleur, Theodore 15, 109, 151, 162, 165, 223-224, 232, 241, 243, 325, 328, 330, 344

Lafontaine, Louis H. 11, 305, 323

Lambert, Godefroi and Mrs. 74, 84, 103, 215, 221, 235, 260, 296, 324, 327-328

Langevin, Edouard 33, 46, 109, 323, 325, 329

Larocque, Bp. J. 86, 100-101, 110, 286, 325-326, 328-329, 341

Laurier, Prime Minister Wilfrid 12, 305

Laverdure, Paul 6, 33, 42, 127, 129, 213, 266, 308-309, 313, 319

Lebel, Father Isidore 67, 324-325, 330, 342

Lefebvre, Bp. 324-325

Lefebvre, Samuel xv-xvi, 7, 127, 178, 286, 296, 316-317, 324-325, 347

Lefebvre, Violette xiii, 268, 277, 279, 312-313

Lefebvre, Zotique 332

Legal conflicts 2, 15, 24, 62, 73-74, 79-80, 82, 85-86, 103, 115, 117, 120, 123, 161, 187, 216, 241, 249, 252, 285, 322, 327, 331-332, 334, 340

LeMettayeur Masselin 161, 332

Leprohon, Father Joseph Onesime 32, 35, 214, 321, 344

Lighthall, W. F. and daughter Kate 178, 295, 331, 333-334, 344, 347

Lincoln, President Abraham 2, 64, 73, 88, 125-127, 149, 155, 169, 258, 295, 314-315, 325, 327, 331, 333-334, 336-337, 349-350, 352, 357

Longueuil, Quebec 34,

44, 51, 65, 94, 285, 312, 323-324, 329

LQO= L'homme qui osa defier book 5, 279, 313, 339-340

Lucey, John M. 142, 144-145, 168, 180, 287

Luther, Martin 146, 176, 183, 186, 192-193, 201-202, 229-230, 270, 275, 289, 304, 334, 352

M

MacVicar, Donald 157, 166, 173, 269, 278, 293, 334, 344, 356

Maignage, Theodore 201-202, 236, 238, 284

Mailloux, Father Alexis 39, 65, 74, 78, 80-81, 84, 94-96, 98-104, 106, 109-113, 115-116, 124, 180, 183, 186, 209, 218-223, 225, 227, 229, 247, 257, 260, 262-263, 288-289, 297, 300, 305, 322, 324-331, 344

Malbaie=Murray Bay 31, 341

Manning, Cardinal Henry 293

Manual of Temperance book 1, 8, 21, 33, 43-47, 257, 307, 315, 322-323, 339, 347, 353

Maps 31, 46, 56, 58, 156

Marsault, F. 112, 143, 291, 312

363

Martin, Louis 333

Mathew, Father Theobald 20, 38, 41, 45, 47, 52, 322

McGee, D'Arcy 69, 324-325, 333

McLoughlin, Emmett 142, 192, 197, 273, 297

Meier, Lois xiii, xvi, 97, 110, 121-122, 124, 178, 269, 281, 314, 317-318, 347

Meilleur, J. B. 41-42, 322

Meillon, Felix 142, 144

Mes Combats book 5, 279, 290, 311, 313, 339-340, 350

Miller, J. R. 130

Mondelet, Charles 21, 256-257, 344

Monod, Frédéric 330

Monod, Théodore 119-120, 331, 345

Montreal 2-5, 7, 9-11, 13-15, 19-26, 31, 34, 36-37, 39, 42-45, 47-48, 50-52, 54-55, 60, 65, 69, 80, 82, 90-91, 93-94, 97, 109, 114, 120-121, 123-124, 127, 130, 133, 137, 139, 142, 148, 151-152, 155, 157-162, 164-167, 173-174, 177-178, 181, 183, 188, 189, 190, 193, 194, 196, 200, 209-210, 217-220, 223, 225-227, 231, 233, 251-253, 255-257, 262, 265-267, 274-276, 279, 281, 283-284, 286-287, 297, 305, 307, 309-310, 312, 314, 316, 318, 320-321, 324, 327, 329-332, 334-337, 345, 347-357

Montreal Gazette 166, 190, 354

Montreal Witness 148, 151-152, 157, 161, 165, 173, 182-183, 217, 219-220, 225-226, 255, 262, 265, 267, 281, 333-334, 337, 345, 348-349, 351, 353-354

Moody, Dwight L. 165

Moore, John 158, 168, 187, 286, 292, 335, 337

Moore, Stephen 80, 117, 123, 167, 188, 332-4, 344

Morin, Joseph 30, 126-127, 160, 173, 178, 192, 269, 285, 290, 292, 312-313, 317, 324, 333-334, 336-337, 344

Myths concerning Chiniquy 5, 179ff, 191-193, 235-237, 273, 287, 297, 302-303, 305, 317, 319-320

N

Nationalism 10-12, 16-17, 21-22, 25-26, 46-47, 78, 92, 134, 136, 138, 151, 256-260, 271, 284, 314, 327

Neeser, Marcel 202, 203, 204, 222, 237, 238, 239, 319

Newman, Cardinal John Henry 141, 142, 149, 188, 209, 269, 349

Newspapers ix-x, 2, 7, 12, 18, 49, 52, 64, 68, 71, 78, 91-94, 96, 104, 110, 137, 139-141, 147-148, 152, 159, 161, 165-167, 210, 217, 225, 286, 299, 305, 308, 317, 319-320, 324, 326, 329, 333, 343-346, 353-354

New Zealand 3, 8, 133, 139, 164, 170, 348, 351

Nicolet, Quebec 1, 31-35, 37, 97, 214, 240, 321

Noel, Jan 13, 19, 21, 42, 47, 259, 286, 314, 315

Normandeau, Louis Leon 13, 33

O

Oblate Order 2, 42-45, 55, 1, 200, 311, 315, 323, 339-341

O'Connor, James 134, 142, 167, 344, 354

Orange Order 115, 160, 164, 167, 169, 248, 252-253, 259, 269, 271, 279, 332, 336-337, 345, 348, 356

O'Regan, Bp. Anthony 61-64, 74-75, 81-89, 91-103, 121, 216-217, 220, 238-241, 249-250, 260, 325-328, 340, 342, 347

P

Papineau, Amadee (son) 173-174, 274, 305, 329, 334-335, 337, 340, 344

INDEX

Papineau, Louis Joseph 10, 26, 50, 68, 274, 305, 315, 323-324, 329, 339, 354-355

Pellan, Alfred 282, 286, 296, 305

Pequegnat, Allan xv, xviii, 7, 318, 321, 358

Piety of Chiniquy 33, 188, 215, 224, 229, 234-235, 303

Pinsoneault, Bp. Adolphe 98, 219-220, 305, 324, 326, 329

Plamondon, Antoine 28, 36, 286, 296, 305

Polemics 5-7, 48, 93, 129-130, 138-143, 147, 154-155, 168, 173, 186, 188, 190, 219, 236, 239-240, 251, 254, 264-266, 272, 276, 278, 285, 298, 301-302, 304, 306, 308, 310, 331,

Price, W. J. 20, 32-33, 42, 67, 76, 79, 311, 352

The Priest, The Woman and the Confessional book 8, 33, 127, 236, 279, 290, 294, 309, 333, 351

Primeau-Robert, Alphonse 189, 281

Prince, Bp. Jean Charles 22, 33, 85, 101, 164, 183, 305, 327-329, 344

Propaganda 147, 168, 278, 344

Provencher, Bp. Joseph 36, 321, 322

Provost, Joseph xiii, 40, 165, 186, 312, 319, 333, 344, 352

Publicity 12-13, 36, 45, 47, 49, 52, 60, 67, 77, 87-93, 98, 136, 144, 148, 151-152, 158-159, 165-167, 169-170, 173, 183, 218, 239, 289, 322, 334

Publishers 4-6, 93, 120, 125, 127, 157, 173, 218, 279, 290, 292, 294-295, 331, 334-335, 343-346

Q

Quebec City 1, 20, 22, 29, 34-36, 40-41, 51, 84, 164, 281, 286, 322, 329

R

Recreation for Chiniquy 269-270

Redpath, John 14, 166

Resther, Father P. 42, 74, 181, 183, 285-286, 333

Réveillaud, Eugene 275, 339, 345

Riots 4, 48, 115, 159-161, 164, 182, 189, 201, 252-253, 265, 332, 340, 348, 351

Rivard, Laurent 344-345, 349, 356

Roden, Lord 170

Rousseau, Louis 26, 44, 314

Roussy, Louis 51, 162, 312, 352

S

St. Anne, Illinois 2-3, 8, 59-61, 63-64, 67-71, 73-75, 77-80, 82-83, 87, 89-92, 95-101, 103, 105, 107, 109-114, 116-125, 127, 144, 155, 162, 172-173, 178, 180, 183, 205, 209, 216, 218-221, 223-225, 230, 237-238, 246-248, 269, 271, 274, 277, 280-282, 286, 289, 292, 296, 299-300, 303, 314, 321-322, 325-334, 344, 347-349, 351-353, 357

St. Hyacinthe, Quebec 22, 34, 48, 60, 66, 92, 97, 100-101, 286, 316, 324, 326, 329, 341-342

St. Roch, Quebec 34, 36-37, 40, 94, 325, 329, 339, 341

Schouten, A. E. 333, 336-337, 346

Scorgie, Glen 14

Scotland 119, 170, 176, 192, 335-336, 343

Semeur Canadien 18, 68, 90, 151, 165, 223, 225-226, 229, 281, 344-345, 352, 354, 357

Sexual allegations 2, 4, 40, 42-43, 53-55, 65, 81-85, 103, 119, 143, 146, 149, 188, 215, 220, 235, 239, 243, 304, 314

Shaftesbury, Earl of 164, 170

Sherman, Edwin 333-334, 344

365

Signay, Bp. Joseph 34-39, 41, 186, 214, 321-322, 324

Skonovd, Norman 206-208, 222, 237-239, 248, 271

Smith, George H. 307, 309

Smith, Jacques xiii, xvi, 252, 276, 279, 285, 293, 313, 316-317

Smith, Sydney 32, 42, 94, 144, 147, 181, 225, 287, 295, 310, 321

Smyth, Bp. Clement 99-100, 102-103, 210, 221-223, 230, 327-328

Snowdon, Rebecca 167, 330, 344

Spink, Peter 66, 69, 71, 73-74, 79-80, 85-87, 97, 216, 237, 324-325

Spreeman, John xiii, 279, 290, 313, 350

Spurgeon, Charles (Jr.) 170, 292

Staples, Moses 104, 120, 260, 329-331, 344, 352

Starr, Judge Charles R. 126

Strout, Richard xvi, 14, 278, 290

Submission 4, 80, 82-3, 90-91, 97-100, 107, 208, 210, 212, 214, 216-218, 220, 237-238, 243, 268, 302

Suspension 53, 55, 75, 80-1, 85, 104-105, 119, 121, 216

Sutherland, George 166, 169, 332, 345, 353

T

Taché, J. C. 327, 347

Taylor, Hubert C. 254, 334, 344

Temperance 1-5, 8, 19-21, 31, 35, 37-43, 45-52, 55, 65, 72, 89, 94-95, 102, 132, 167, 181, 184, 189-191, 214-215, 226, 246, 249-250, 257, 259, 271-272, 278, 287, 296, 305, 307, 314-315, 322-324, 333, 339-340

Tétreau, Hubert 33

Têtu, Father Henri 32, 183, 328, 353

Thériault, Bp. Serge xv, 110, 143, 269

Thomas, Bp. Mesac 170, 330, 343

Thomson, Nelson xiii, xvi, 313, 357

Thynne, Charles 335, 343, 351, 356

Totalism (religious) 206ff, 212, 237, 357

Translations of Chiniquy writings 125, 270, 335

Trudel, Marcel 4-6, 10, 21, 29, 31-32, 34, 36-38, 40-42, 44-45, 47, 53, 64, 73, 76, 79, 95, 99, 103, 113-115, 121, 172-174, 180, 182-184, 193, 202, 233, 240, 258, 260, 263, 266, 274, 280-282, 287-288, 294, 303, 307, 310-316, 319-320, 334, 351

True Witness 139, 158, 160, 182, 262, 332, 349, 354

Turgeon, Bp. Pierre Flavien 42, 53, 322-324

V

van de Velde, Bp. Jacques (Olivier) 61, 63-67, 71, 74-75, 82, 96, 105, 324

Villard, Paul 15, 160, 165, 185, 309, 319

Villeneuve, Alphonse 121, 157, 184, 187, 233, 284, 310, 344

Violence, physical 3, 24, 51, 64, 110, 115, 137, 145, 154, 159-161, 182-183, 216, 228-229, 235, 248, 251, 261-262, 264-266, 272, 291, 301-302

Violence, verbal 8, 85, 215, 263, 267, 272, 304, 329

W

Wilkes, Henry 14, 166

Wolffe, John 131, 133-134, 136, 138, 140-141, 147-149, 151, 170, 357

Z

Zuidema, Jason xiii, xvi, 125, 308

www.ingramcontent.com/pod-product-compliance
Lightning Source LLC
Chambersburg PA
CBHW021051080526
44587CB00010B/213